# GLOBAL CHANGE, ECOSYSTEMS, SUSTAINABILITY

# GLOBAL CHANGE, ECOSYSTEMS, SUSTAINABILITY

## Theory, Methods, Practice

**EDITED BY**
**Pranab Mukhopadhyay**
**Nandan Nawn**
**Kalyan Das**

**⑤SAGE**

Los Angeles | London | New Delhi
Singapore | Washington DC | Melbourne

*First published in 2017 by*

**SAGE Publications India Pvt Ltd**
B1/I-1 Mohan Cooperative Industrial Area
Mathura Road, New Delhi 110 044, India
*www.sagepub.in*

**SAGE Publications Inc**
2455 Teller Road
Thousand Oaks, California 91320, USA

**SAGE Publications Ltd**
1 Oliver's Yard, 55 City Road
London EC1Y 1SP, United Kingdom

**SAGE Publications Asia-Pacific Pte Ltd**
3 Church Street
#10-04 Samsung Hub
Singapore 049483

Published by Vivek Mehra for SAGE Publications India Pvt Ltd, typeset in Adobe Garamond 10/12 pts by Zaza Eunice, Hosur, Tamil Nadu and printed at Chaman Enterprises, New Delhi.

**Library of Congress Cataloging-in-Publication Data Available**

**ISBN:** 978-93-864-4646-6 (HB)

**SAGE Team:** Rajesh Dey, Sandhya Gola, Megha Dabral, and Ritu Chopra

*To students and teachers of Ecological Economics*

Thank you for choosing a SAGE product!
If you have any comment, observation or feedback,
I would like to personally hear from you.
*Please write to me at* **contactceo@sagepub.in**

**Vivek Mehra,** Managing Director and CEO, SAGE India.

## Bulk Sales

SAGE India offers special discounts
for purchase of books in bulk.
We also make available special imprints
and excerpts from our books on demand.

*For orders and enquiries, write to us at*

Marketing Department
SAGE Publications India Pvt Ltd
B1/I-1, Mohan Cooperative Industrial Area
Mathura Road, Post Bag 7
New Delhi 110044, India

*E-mail us at* **marketing@sagepub.in**

## Get to know more about SAGE

Be invited to SAGE events, get on our mailing list.
*Write today to* **marketing@sagepub.in**

This book is also available as an e-book.

# Contents

# List of Tables

# List of Figures

# Acknowledgements

This book would not have been possible without the cooperation of the authors who have contributed to this book and kept to their deadlines and their patience in seeing this book come together. We are deeply honoured by INSEE's (Indian Society for Ecological Economics) invitation to edit this book. We would like to thank the staff at SAGE—Commissioning Editor, for his interest and efforts in publishing this work, Production Editor, for efficiently handling the production of this book, the copyeditor, and the cover designer.

# 1

# Introduction

## Pranab Mukhopadhyay, Nandan Nawn, and Kalyan Das

## Introduction

The world around us is changing—partly through its own natural interactions and cycles and also owing to intense anthropogenic pressures. Global changes are "planetary level changes in the Earth system" which refer to the "interacting physical, chemical, and biological processes" and include the *effect of* and *impact on* human society (International Geosphere-Biosphere Programme [IGBP]). Human interaction with natural systems assumes an important dimension especially since unabated human pressures could threaten the very sustenance of human life and well-being on Earth. This realization has led to a surge in research that is broadly classified as sustainability research (Kates et al. 2001).

The global economy has grown at an unprecedented rate in the last millennium or so if we look at the long history of economic growth from around 0 AD from when some estimates have been prepared (Maddison 2001). For the first thousand years (0–1000 AD), the world economy grew at 0.01 per cent per year. By this standard, it gathered incredible momentum between 1000 and 1820 (the eve of the Industrial Revolution) growing at 0.22 per cent per annum. This was of course dwarfed by the growth of the world economy in the post-industrialization (1820–1998) phase when it achieved an unprecedented rate of 2.21 per cent per annum. Though this may seem trivially small, in view of the double-digit growth of Southeast Asia, China, and now South Asia, even this was unprecedented in human history.

The rapid economic growth has, however, caused much to worry about, especially in the area of environment. The scientific evidence is overwhelming that anthropogenic pressures are pushing global life on earth to a finite end and there is an urgent need for a corrective action. One of the most talked about manifestations of global change has been on the climate. This has most elaborately been collated in the various scientific assessments such as in the Intergovernmental Panel on Climate Change (IPCC) reports (the most recent being the fifth report). What has engaged researchers is the identification of its drivers, its *dimensions*, and its impact on the ecosystems from which human beings draw their direct sustenance.

What makes the understanding of these complex systems difficult is the inherent non-convexities and uncertainties, and the need for a corrective action is critical as these processes are often irreversible. There have been numerous international efforts such as the DIVERSITAS, the IGBP, the International Human Dimensions Programme (IHDP), and the World Climate Research Programme (WCRP), some of which have now merged into the Future Earth programme, IPCC, and the Millennium Ecosystem Assessment. Similar to the IPCC, the Intergovernmental Science-Policy Platform on Biodiversity and Ecosystem Services (IPBES) coordinates its global assessment efforts on biodiversity and the ecosystem services it provides to society. These efforts have improved our knowledge of global change and emphasized the need for an urgent global coordinated action. Some of the outcomes of these efforts are heartening—2015 Paris Universal Climate Agreement and the subsequent Marrakesh Proclamation on Climate and Sustainable Development signed by 196 countries and the EU bloc provide hope towards some political action at least.

There is a wide recognition that notwithstanding the limitations on the knowledge of ecosystems' functions and functionalities, the management of ecosystems is crucial. Lack of effective management of ecosystems has been recognized as one of the major challenges to sustainable development.

The question of sustainability is also connected with the trajectories of development, which is of particular importance to those interested in the ecology–economy–society interface. The research on sustainability accelerated after the United Nations' Conference on Environment and Development (UNCED) popularly known as the Earth Summit held at Rio de Janeiro in 1992.

One of the important missing dimensions in the traditional economic development debate was the issue of environment and ecology (Dasgupta and Mäler 1995; Dasgupta 2010). The other important bridge that needed to be built was the linking of social and economic processes with natural system dynamics. One does not work in isolation from the other and the quicker the two are studied together, the better would be our understanding of the nature and dimension of crises, which would allow us to find solutions. One of the most significant contributions from the trans-discipline of ecological economics is to connect global changes with the broader question of development (Brandt et al. 2013). The moment one connects these two phenomena, we are then in the realm of the discussion on vulnerability, adaptation, and mitigation.

Adaptation has been variously defined in the literature, but there are a few common elements that have emerged as universal components: (a) it involves behavioural response on the part of the natural or human systems, (b) such response or adjustment is in response to a stimulus or its effects, and (c) the objective of this response is to minimize or moderate harm, or to maximize the benefits from an opportunity (McCarthy et al. 2001, 982 as cited in Füssel 2007, 265). Diversity in the adaptation activities cuts across multiple dimensions: domains (agriculture and forests to coastal protection and health), type of stimulus (current or future, observed or expected), predictability (degree of uncertainty/confidence), conditions (climatic as well as non-climatic including political and economic), degree of purposefulness (autonomous or planned), nature of response (reactive/proactive, top-down/deliberative), time duration (few months to multiple decades), scale (global, regional, local), form (technical, financial, managerial, institutional, legal, behavioural), type of system (household, community, group, sector, region, country), and agents/participants (governments, industries, farmers, consumers) (Smit and Skinner 2002, 86; Smit and Wandel 2006, 282; Füssel 2007, 266; Nelson, Adger, and Brown 2007, 396).

Understandably, just like any other behavioural responses, there exist limits to adaptation, both exogenous and endogenous. Former involves ecological, physical, economic, and technological, and the latter includes "ethics (how and what we value), knowledge (how and what we know), risk (how and what we perceive), and culture (how and why we live)" (Adger et al. 2009, 337–38). It follows that the identification and recognition of "diverse and contested values" is essential for making meaningful adaptation strategies and practices (ibid.: 350). While levels of vulnerability are influenced by "social, economic and institutional factors […] within a community or nation," they in turn "promote or constrain options for adaptation" (Kelly and Adger 2000, 326), making the two inseparable. Global changes can then be construed to be aggravating the already present challenges for development, making the marginalized more vulnerable. Even those who were previously categorized as non-vulnerable would now be vulnerable: "Climate change acts as a multiplier of existing vulnerabilities in a warming and transforming world" (Mearns and Norton 2010, 2).

South Asia is one of the most vulnerable areas of the world to global change. Apart from the traditional concerns of poverty, the geographical location of its populations makes the impacts more complicated. Nearly 30 per cent of South Asia's population lives in coastal areas. One of the confirmed trends in ecological dynamics is the rise in sea levels and the rise in the surface temperature of oceans (IPCC 2014). In combination with an observed increase in cyclone intensities and storm surges, sea levels are expected to rise by 98 cm by the year 2100 (under high emission scenario), making large segments of populations in India, Bangladesh, Pakistan, and Sri Lanka highly vulnerable.

The other aspect of climate change that has direct implications for South Asia is the expected increase in the intensity of precipitation. The floods in Uttarakhand (2013), Mumbai (2005), and Chennai (2015) are adequate warnings of how poor our rural and urban infrastructure is to deal with extreme events of rainfall and flooding in the subcontinent.

Indian Society for Ecological Economics (INSEE) held its 7th Biennial Conference on the theme of "Global Change, Ecosystems, Sustainability" with three sub-thematic areas: Understanding Global Change, Managing Ecosystems, and Sustainability: Approaches and Implications. The first sub-theme, "Understanding Global Change," covered biophysical contours of global change including climate change, its social implications, and its governance. The second sub-theme, "Managing Ecosystems," covered institutions at different levels, from local to global. It included de jure as well as de facto institutions and examined the role of political and social movements as part of distributional conflicts over ecological resources across temporal and spatial scales. The third theme, "Sustainability: Approaches and Implications," included the ecological and economic dimensions. Also, it was sensitive to the soft side of sustainable development which includes social and cultural sustainability.

This book brings together a selection of 19 papers. Some of these were presented at the conference and some were specially invited papers for this compilation. The chapters included in this book cover multiple themes, but allocating them into two board sections was felt to be a more efficient classification, depending on the scale and issues discussed in each contribution.

## About the Book

The two broad sections in this book are:

1. Section 1—Making Sense of Global Changes: Macro Dimensions
2. Section 2—Sustainability, Ecosystems, and Institutions: From the Practice

Section 1 addresses the current debates on the drivers, status, direction, and magnitude of global changes, as well as methods that would enhance our understanding on global changes and their impacts both in theoretical as well as empirical terms. Besides, there is an engagement with the institutional challenges that sustainability poses vis-à-vis the present development pathways and the possible policy interventions. In particular, it deals with the following: the kind of challenges brought about by the global changes in the sustainability of economic development (Chapter 2), the theoretical and empirical challenges in measuring sustainability of economic development (Chapters 3–5), how to bring scientific credibility to the international policy discourse on environmental matters (Chapter 6), how the value judgements on the part of the author appear at various levels in the works that attempt to integrate ecological matters with economics (Chapter 7), how energy transitions can influence the development trajectories (Chapter 8), and the challenges posed by the present process of appropriation of surplus energy which is embedded within a particular form of socio-economic organization (Chapter 9).

Section 2 addresses, among others, the complex interaction between nature, scale, and intensity of vulnerabilities, and the corresponding adaptation and mitigation strategies across people, communities, or groups. The responses are studied at macro, meso, and micro levels, across specific occupations and spatial locations. Besides, a few chapters in this section identify possible drivers behind the non-sustainability of specific ecosystems, and the related issue of appropriate institutional choice of responding to sustainability challenges. These studies have been carried out in different agro-climatic regions in South Asia, from the hills and forested regions of Assam (Chapter 10), West Bengal (Chapter 18), Meghalaya (Chapter 19), Odisha (Chapter 20), and Nepal (Chapter 12) to coastal tracts of Sundarbans (Chapter 11), Odisha (Chapter 13), Kanyakumari (Chapter 16), and Gujarat (Chapter 17) to wetlands of Bangladesh (Chapter 15) and arid expanses of Uttar Pradesh (Chapter 14). Methodically, most of these studies have used primary data collected through specific field surveys. The authors cover issues of coping strategies towards "livelihood adjustment" against natural calamity in a fragile ecosystem (Chapter 11), appropriateness of awareness campaigns in influencing human behaviour towards adaptation against extreme events (Chapter 13), relative influence of socio-economic or biophysical variables on vulnerability of farming (Chapter 14), institutional interventions for managing ecosystems in terms of resource stock (Chapter 18) or towards sustaining livelihood (Chapter 15) or avoiding extreme events (Chapter 12), effectiveness of statutory institutional interventions to sustainably manage ecosystems and in ensuring livelihood (Chapter 16), institutions for facilitating adoption of resource conserving technologies (Chapter 17), and impact of economic (mining) activities on vulnerability of ecosystems and sustainability of livelihoods (Chapters 19 and 20).

## Making Sense of Global Change: Macro Dimensions

One of the persisting themes in ecological economics has been finding alternative pathways for sustaining the development process given the additional constraints posed by the global changes. Nilanjan Ghosh offers a trajectory of advances in economic thought on the changing dimensions of what constitutes "development" (Chapter 2). He is sensitive to the necessity of life-support systems provided by nature for the development process and its finiteness at the same time. Towards operationalizing sustainable development that reconciles the apparent trade-off amongst achieving economic growth, ensuring social development, and maintaining ecological sustenance, he suggests ecological economics to play the role of a "critical enabler" through influencing the public policy discourse.

It is not enough to suggest that our goal should be sustainability; but what measures sustainable economic development should also be enunciated. M.N. Murty asks whether it is income or wealth that is to be considered as a measure of well-being (Chapter 3). This has important consequences on the corresponding accounting prices. In a steady state, this choice may be inconsequential, but as the world is not in a steady state, this choice does matter. The other item to choose is the accounting price. Should we use marginal benefit or marginal cost of abatement as the former is likely to be higher in suboptimal economies? Murty argues for using the marginal maintenance cost as shadow prices along the sustainable non-optimal developmental paths of economy. This is a more practicable solution from the viewpoint of empirical feasibility and tractability, given the problems associated with measurement of benefit-based shadow prices in general. It showcases an empirically feasible path towards testing whether a country is able to augment its wealth (and, hence, well-being) or not; it is left to other researchers to tread along this empirically challenging yet socially relevant path, which will be of interest to the policymakers as well.

This has implications for green accounting. India has made a start in this direction with a set of studies commissioned by the Central Statistical Office (CSO; MOSPI 2014). It was followed up by a committee headed by Sir Partha Dasgupta (MOSPI 2013). Haripriya Gundimeda highlights the contrasting picture of United Nations' Satellite System of Integrated Environmental and Economic Accounting (SEEA) Framework and the conceptual framework defined in the Dasgupta Committee Report towards operationalizing sustainable development (Chapter 4). Based on her experience, Gundimeda identifies some of the key challenges in implementing this framework for India, one of which is the availability of reliable and quality ecological data.

The preparation of a green national accounts as outlined in MOSPI (ibid.) requires a step-wise effort: first, developing a more complete national balance sheet that includes environmental assets and flows; second, periodic collection and compilation of data for this purpose; and third, identifying the principles for valuing them. Kanchan Chopra (who, like Haripriya, was a member of the Dasgupta-chaired committee) being "privy" to the working of this committee (Chapter 5) shares her concern on the progress in preparing green accounts in India, which is a long-term intervention in the sustainability policy. Chopra finds that such efforts are often overtaken by more immediate policy concerns and the onus of moving forward must lie with the concerned academics and policymakers.

The process that informs policymaking in matters connected with environment can fall short of ensuring the accepted level of scientific credibility. Anantha Kumar Duraiappah, based on his engagements at the international policymaking space, locates a number of structural reasons behind the problem (Chapter 6). One problem is the opaqueness in the process for selection of scientists leading to asymmetrical representation across different geographical regions, generations, and disciplines. He suggests an alternative akin to a "managed commons" approach with a few guiding principles to ensure scientific credibility, while ensuring transparency in selection, scientific independence, inclusiveness, and cost-wise efficiency at the same time. A simplified version of this approach was applied to prepare the background document for developing the conceptual framework for IPBES. Duraiappah argues that the IPBES experience was positive enough to be replicable on a larger scale.

The interface of ecology and economics has seen the application of diverse approaches and frameworks. Vikram Dayal provides a critical review of such models with a particular emphasis on theoretical and statistical models (Chapter 7). Dayal argues that the ways in which various attributes of both types of models have been used and applied in economic analysis show a surprisingly diverse—if not plural—analytical paths. In more than one way, the chapter reinvents and re-emphasises the "methodological pluralism" a la Norgaard (1989) in economics and not just in ecological economics. The list of attributes that were analysed is exhaustive: assumptions and axioms, inclusion and exclusion of variables (in theoretical models) and appropriateness of instrumental variables (in statistical models), applicability of techniques, suitability of frameworks, and use and applicability of regression models and causality tests. Each attribute, as practised in ecological economics, was examined against their respective theoretical roots along with appropriate illustrations. Dayal cautions against taking either of the extreme positions—of placing models in an altar or not considering them at all.

One of the talking points in the development world has been the comparison of India and China's growth strategies. China is ahead of India on numerous indicators and policymakers in India often talk about emulating the Chinese path. Anke Schaffartzik and Marina Fischer-Kowalski caution against such a strategy as the consequences of this could be catastrophic (Chapter 8). Schaffartzik and Fischer-Kowalski make their analysis by connecting shifts across socio-metabolic regimes with the trajectories of development. They looked at the historical transitions in these two countries using biophysical, economic, and demographic indicators over a period of one and a half centuries. The countries had a broadly similar picture till around 1950, after which their paths were divergent. Post 1950, while the fossil fuel energy consumption per unit of GDP for China was falling, for India it was rising, even though they are nearly equal now. For the long-term interests, Schaffartzik and Fischer-Kowalski recommends China to drift away from the present exponential growth of fossil energy carrier use and India not to emulate such a development path.

The link between energy and economic development is explored in the historical context by Sagar Dhara (Chapter 9). He examines the generation, distribution, and accumulation of surplus energy that is present across "ages" or "class societies." He distinguishes between eras of anthropo-energy, bioenergy, and fossil fuel ages accounting for the manner in which energy resources are owned, harvested, and used. Dhara warns against global problems of gigantic proportion, signs of which are already visible in the form of "tipping points," "peak oil," temperature rise, etc. Questioning the ability of capitalism to be sustainable and inclusive, Dhara advocates "eco-socialism" as an alternative system.

## Sustainability, Ecosystems, and Institutions: From the Practice

The impact of climate change is examined by Utpal Kumar De in the state of Assam (Chapter 10). He examines the changing pattern of climate variables over the last four decades and finds an erratic nature of rainfall and significant interregional variations. De points out that monsoon rainfall has been declining significantly in the region over the years, while the proportion of pre- and post-monsoon rainfall has been rising. Along with this, both maximum and minimum temperature has been increasing and the trend rate of minimum temperature has been higher than that of maximum temperature. De argues that these changes are already having important consequences for the livelihood of those who are dependent on natural resources.

Livelihoods are affected by climate change directly as De has noted, but there could be indirect effects too. As we know, climate change is increasing the frequency of extreme events which could in turn affect livelihood. Santadas Ghosh examines household response to one such extreme event—cyclone Aila in May 2009 that struck the Sundarbans which is one of the largest mangrove forests in the world (Chapter 11). He surveyed 800 households in three repeat surveys between 2010 and 2012 to track changes in the livelihood choices. Ghosh's objective was to understand the coping strategies and "livelihood adjustments" subsequent to the cyclone Aila. The study finds a fascinating set of responses vis-à-vis choices of livelihood, starting with a dependence on surrounding open-access natural resources, and eventually migrating outside the region as labourers. Most interestingly, Ghosh found that even after the restoration of productivity of farmlands, a significant number of households had continued to migrate contrary to expectations.

A calamity that has been a serious concern in forest areas in South Asia is forest fires. These are sometimes naturally occurring and sometimes triggered by human activities. Nepal's community forestry programme is probably one of the most widely studied resource management institutions. This programme is considered to have been very successful in forest regeneration in Nepal. Lok Mani Sapkota critically examines the model of community management of forests in the Central Shivalik region of Nepal in the specific context of managing forest fires in this region (Chapter 12). Labour intensive but technically weak methods such as suppression and exclusion, and an ineffective regulatory framework have been found to be the most serious causes. Sapkota argues that establishing legal rights may be necessary but are not sufficient to effectively manage natural resources. Awareness campaigns and capacity building of community forest users can prove to be effective enablers.

Another extreme event that is increasingly being encountered is "heat waves." Saudamini Das and Stephen C. Smith study the autonomous adaptation as a response strategy to heat waves in Odisha (Chapter 13). Das and Smith evaluate the effectiveness of awareness campaigns carried out across multiple mediums. These campaigns undertaken by the State Disaster Management Authority in Odisha help people to understand adaptation options during heat waves. They analyse district-level death toll due to heat stroke for the period 1998–2010 in treatment and control areas to see the effectiveness of the campaigns.

It is now well understood that climate change can exacerbate existing vulnerabilities. Amarnath Tripathi studies how significant the socio-economic factors are in influencing the vulnerability of the farmers faced with climate change (Chapter 14). Tripathi's study is based in Uttar Pradesh, the largest producer of many food and non-food crops. To assess farmers' vulnerability to climate change, 23 biophysical and socio-economic variables against exposure, sensitivity, and adaptive capacity were considered. Five socio-economic variables, namely, urbanization, share of non-farm employment, share of small and marginal landholdings, rural population density, and average size of landholdings were identified as the most relevant ones explaining agricultural vulnerability to climate change in the area under study. However, how to address such structural matters remains as an open question as it requires intervention at a broader level, including macroeconomic policies affecting agriculture and farmers.

The threat to livelihoods comes not only from nature and extreme events but can also be anthropogenically induced. Md Hafiz Iqbal explores strategies for sustainably managing Tanguar Haor, a wetland, located in Northeastern Bangladesh (Chapter 15). This wetland is a Ramsar Site but presently under a degraded state. It provides livelihood support to more than 50,000 people. The degradation is triggered by a lack of legal entitlements to fisherfolk, prompting them to overfish the resource. In order to conceive a sustainable management plan, Iqbal considered the fishers as key agents in the system and carried out a choice experiment with 418 households neighbouring the Haor, covering a variety of policy options: fishing control, plantation, payment for only fishing permit, and both fishing and grazing permits. Economic welfare effects were arrived at in two alternative scenarios that highlighted the importance of sustaining the resource base for the fishers.

The role of anthropogenic pressures is explored also in the context of coastal ecosystem services in India by Priya Parasuram, Rajakumari S., and Ramachandra Bhatta (Chapter 16). Data from the demographic census for 1991, 2001, and 2011 were combined with satellite images and Marine Census data for 2005 and 2010 to capture the demographic, physical, and socio-economic changes in 11 selected coastal fishing villages in

Kanyakumari, Tamil Nadu. The spatial focus was on the section of the coast lying within 500 m from the high tide line (HTL) and some of its neighbouring zones. Priya et al. find that between 1991 and 2011, the average per capita area available for an individual fisher has declined by 5 times in this zone. On the other hand, the Coastal Regulation Zone (CRZ) Notification, 1991, and the revision of 2011 could reduce the rate of growth of the commercially built area within the area of its jurisdiction (<500 m) compared to the area just outside CRZ (>500 m–1 km).

Two chapters in this book explore individual behaviour in a community setting. In Gujarat, there have been a number of irrigation schemes aimed at using groundwater more efficiently. Chandra Sekhar Bahinipati and P.K. Viswanathan explore adoption and diffusion of Micro-irrigation across the state (Chapter 17). They find that in recent years there has been a rapid rise in the adoption rate across farm size, agro-climatic regions, and water-stressed dark-zone talukas. Bahinipati and Viswanathan attribute the rapid adoption rates in the recent years to the nature of the scheme which has a differentiated subsidy disbursement favouring socio-economically weaker caste-groups located in groundwater-wise "dark" blocks. Unfortunately, as the authors point out, this mechanism covers only 10 per cent of the cultivated area and therefore leaves concerns of sustainability and rejuvenation of aquifers.

Does an individual's identity play a role in determining natural resource management outcomes? This is the question posed by Biswajit Ray, Promita Mukherjee, and Rabindra Nath Bhattacharya (Chapter 18) when they examine two kinds of identity: gender and caste. Ray et al. used primary data collected from 341 households in the forest areas managed by seven Joint Forest Management Committees (JFMCs) of West Midnapore and Jalpaiguri (presently known as Alipurduar) districts in India. The study examines whether the differences in outcomes of natural resource management can be attributed to differences in an individual's identity. They find strong influence of social identities in both creation and use of social capital as well as in the maturity of community-based institutions for natural resource management.

Mining has been an area of contest between the State large corporates, and communities. Two chapters in this book examine this issue. Lekha Mukhopadhyay provides a framework to examine the consequences of economic activities on adaptive capacity, vulnerability of the ecosystem, and sustainability of livelihoods (Chapter 19). Mukhopadhyay presents a synthesis of two well-known frameworks—Driver–Pressure–State–Impact–Response (DPSIR) and Sustainable Livelihood—and applies them to study "rat-hole" coal mining in Jaintia Hills, Meghalaya, India. There has been a shift from agro-based to coal-based livelihoods in this region. Export of coal was identified as the most important driver of degradation. The chapter finds that the negative economic impact on rice and fish seed production could not be compensated by the increase in income from coal mining, thus violating the "weak" Heal–Solow–Dasgupta–Hartwick criterion for sustainable development.

The second study on mining is based in Sundergarh district, Odisha (Chapter 20). Narendra Nath Dalei and Yamini Gupt studied the impact of mining on livelihood and welfare of indigenous and forest dependent communities over a period of time. The state of forest ecosystem was classified into four phases. Welfare levels in each phase were calculated in terms of discounted net present value derived from extraction of forest resources. By using multinomial logistic regression analysis, Dalei and Gupt found that the welfare across different phases was affected significantly.

The underlying and dominant concern has been that human interaction with nature has breached the capacity of the latter to regenerate itself. While rapid technological progress and availability of resources have made it possible to intensify the use of natural resources towards production of goods and services, the matters related to non-substitutability of "natural capital" by other forms of capital is well acknowledged. Even while the studies and methods to address these concerns may not be easy in the light of complexities, but the consensus around the current and perceived changes including extreme changes warrants prioritization of measures based on sound principles for scientific management of the ecosystems. Additional concern is on the hurdles that prevent the creation of appropriate institutions and adoption of effective instruments towards achieving these ends. The connection between specific interventions and development strategies takes place through the complex social and economic processes in the locations differentiated by physical diversities, from the fragile hills and coastal areas to river valleys and metropolises. Thus, both global/macro-level changes and micro-level ecosystem-based studies are warranted to address the diverse (un)sustainabilities. Such attempts have been made in the subsequent chapters. It is hoped that both practitioners and policymakers alike would find the book valuable.

# References

Adger, W. Neil, Suraje Dessai, Marisa Goulden, Mike Hulme, Irene Lorenzoni, Donald R. Nelson, Lars Otto Naess, Johanna Wolf, and Anita Wreford. 2009. "Are There Social Limits to Adaptation to Climate Change?" *Climatic Change* 93 (3): 335–54.

Brandt, Patric, Anna Ernst, Fabienne Gralla, Christopher Luederitz, Daniel J. Lang, Jens Newig, Florian Reinert, David J. Abson, and Henrik von Wehrden. 2013. "A Review of Transdisciplinary Research in Sustainability Science." *Ecological Economics* 92 (August): 1–15.

Dasgupta, Partha. 2010. "The Place of Nature in Economic Development." In *Handbook of Development Economics*, Vol. 5, edited by Dani Rodrik and Mark Richard Rosenzweig, 4977–5046. Amsterdam/Boston: Elsevier/North-Holland.

Dasgupta, Partha, and Karl-Goran Maler. 1995. "Poverty, Institutions, and the Environmental Resource-base." In *Handbook of Development Economics*, Vol. 3, Part A, edited by J.N. Breman and T.N. Srinivasan, 2371–463. Amsterdam/Boston: Elsevier/North-Holland.

Füssel, H.-M. 2007. "Adaptation Planning for Climate Change: Concepts, Assessment Approaches, and Key Lessons." *Sustainability Science* 2 (2): 265–75.

IPCC. 2014. *Climate Change 2014: Impacts, Adaptation, and Vulnerability. Contribution of Working Group II to the Fifth Assessment Report of the Intergovernmental Panel on Climate Change.* United Kingdom and New York: Cambridge University Press.

Kates, Robert W., William C. Clark, Robert Corell, J. Michael Hall, Carlo C. Jaeger, Ian Lowe, James J. McCarthy, Hans Joachim Schellnhuber, Bert Bolin, Nancy M. Dickson, Sylvie Faucheux, Gilberto C. Gallopin, Arnulf Grübler, Brian Huntley, Jill Jäger, Narpat S. Jodha, Roger E. Kasperson, Akin Mabogunje, Pamela Matson, Harold Mooney, Berrien Moore III, Timothy O'Riordan, and Uno Svedin. 2001, April. "Sustainability Science." *Science* 292 (5517): 641–42. doi: 10.1126/science.1059386

Kelly, P.M., and W. Neil Adger. 2000. "Theory and Practice in Assessing Vulnerability to Climate Change and Facilitating Adaptation." *Climatic Change* 47 (4): 325–52.

Maddison, Angus. 2001. *The World Economy: A Millennial Perspective.* Appendix B, p. 28. Paris: OECD.

McCarthy, James J., O.F. Canziani, N.A. Leary, D.J. Dokken, and K.S. White, eds. 2001. *Climate Change 2001—Impacts, Adaptation, and Vulnerability: Contribution of Working Group II to the Third Assessment Report of the Intergovernmental Panel on Climate Change.* Cambridge, UK; New York: Cambridge University Press.

Mearns, Robin, and Andrew Norton. 2010. "Equity and Vulnerability in a Warming World: Introduction and Overview." In *Social Dimensions of Climate Change Equity and Vulnerability in a Warming World*, edited by Robin Mearns and Andrew Norton, 1–44. Washington, DC: World Bank.

MOSPI. 2013. *Green National Accounts in India: A Framework.* New Delhi: Central Statistical Office, Ministry of Statistics & Programme Implementation, Government of India. Available at: http://mospi.nic.in/mospi_new/upload/Green_National_Accouts_in_India_1may13.pdf (accessed on 26 April 2017).

———. 2014. *Compendium of Environment Statistics India 2014.* New Delhi: Central Statistical Office, Ministry of Statistics & Programme Implementation, Government of India. Available at: http://mospi.nic.in/mospi_new/upload/COMPEN_ENVR_STAT_31jan2014/CHAPTER_TWO_13feb14.pdf (accessed on 26 April 2017).

Nelson, Donald R., W. Neil Adger, and Katrina Brown. 2007. "Adaptation to Environmental Change: Contributions of a Resilience Framework." *Annual Review of Environment and Resources* 32: 395–419.

Norgaard, Richard B. 1989. "The Case for Methodological Pluralism." *Ecological Economics* 1(1): 37–57.

Smit, Barry, and Johanna Wandel. 2006. "Adaptation, Adaptive Capacity and Vulnerability." *Global Environmental Change* 16 (3): 282–92.

Smit, Barry, and Mark W. Skinner. 2002. "Adaptation Options in Agriculture to Climate Change: A Typology." *Mitigation and Adaptation Strategies for Global Change* 7 (1): 85–114.

# SECTION 1

# Making Sense of Global Change:
# Macro Dimensions

# 2

# Ecological Economics: Sustainability, Markets, and Global Change*

## Nilanjan Ghosh

## Introduction

Ecological economics, as is practised today, often marks a paradigm shift from the ways neoclassical environmental economics was initially conceived. Yet, the embedment of the present day ecological economics in the traditional and critical developmental issues cannot be ignored. The origin of the development discourse traces back to the notions of economic growth defined in the form of expansion of the social basket of goods and services, and has eventually reached a stage where governments and academics are more concerned with more holistic notions of development than merely talking of reductionist growth. Though growth-fetishism persists in large parts of policy thinking in the developing world, sustainable development, eventually, has become a very important notion of the day and provides a more comprehensive definition of development, linking ecosystem services and quality of life with economic growth. Such a paradigm shift in less than a century is no less than a revolution. Expectedly, this shift has been marked by cognitive dissonance, bitter debates, and scholastic antagonism.

## The Days of Classical Political Economy

With political economy evolving out of the writings of Adam Smith and David Ricardo, the scope of economics as a discipline got defined in the confinements to find and explain the "nature and causes" of economic development. The scenario was neither simple nor comfortable for modern economists of the post-Keynesian era; it has always been considered a maverick field, lurking somewhere in the background but not really thought of as real economics, rather as an amalgam of sociology, anthropology, history, politics, and all-too-often is based on ideological constructs of political thoughts and normative principles from ethics.

---

* Modified version of the presidential address delivered at the Seventh Biennial Conference of the Indian Society for Ecological Economics, Tezpur University, Tezpur, Assam, 5–8 December 2013.

Though it has often been claimed that economic development as a branch of economic science emerged only in the 1950s, there is no doubt that the notion of development existed even in the classical economic thought processes, albeit by a different name. The recognition of development economics as a sub-discipline over the past 50 years earmarked the changes in understanding of development. The wealth of experiments so far has revealed that there are clearly no sure-fire formulas for success; if there were, there would have been many more successes than there are today. Economic theory has, in fact, evolved to account for both successes and failures.

Nonetheless, few of the greatest economists actually ignored it outright. Those belonging to Classical School, starting with Adam Smith, were undoubtedly concerned with "economic development." However, their notion of economic development was quite different from what is defined as development today by development theorists. This difference gets reinforced in Smith's *Wealth of Nations* (1776), and Ricardo's *Principles of Taxation* (1817), and goes on till Schumpeter's classic *Theory of Economic Development* (1911). The German Historical School—and its English and American counterparts—could very well be deemed as part of "development economics," though it was thoroughly geared towards the theory of economic growth, as was known then.

However, the primary focus of economic research remained confined to developed nations till the 1930s. It was Colin Clark's quantitative study in 1940 that made economists realize that most of humankind did not live in the advanced capitalist economic systems. Yet the early concern was still Europe, namely, post-war European reconstruction and the industrialization of its eastern fringes as exemplified by the pioneering article by Paul Rosenstein-Rodan (1943) and Kurt Mandelbaum's book (1947). It was only sometime after the war that economists really began to show their concerns for Asia, Africa, and Latin America.

To this end, decolonization was an important catalyst. Faced with a plethora of new nations whose standards of living and institutions were so different from the European way of life, modern development theory—by which we mean the analysis of not only growth but also of institutions that could induce, sustain, and accelerate growth—began in earnest to change its focus and rearrange its referential. After the Second World War, academes began to think of ways and means of effectively dealing with poverty and destitution that heavily weighed upon two-thirds of the human race (Pakdaman 1994).

The post-war formation of the United Nations and its attendant agencies, such as the World Bank, the International Monetary Fund (IMF), the International Labour Organisation (ILO), and various regional commissions, provided an impetus to the shift in focus and perceptions. The commissioning of numerous studies by these institutions led to the emergence of a non-academic strand of development theory.

# Post-war Period: Stage Theory of Growth and Capital Formation

Post-war development was primarily looked at from the viewpoint of growth and capital formation. Even before that developing nations looked at development primarily as a process of industrialization. This resulted in the concept of a Third World consisting of Latin American, Asian, and African countries, which were to be mostly viewed as "underdeveloped" countries. It was believed that they were in the early stages of development; and with time, they would be able to transcend the various stages of underdevelopment and move up the ladder. This was contingent upon the way in which capital was being formed, industrialization was taking place, and GDP growth occurred.

This thought culminated in the "stage" theory of development, made famous by Rostow (1960) and Gerschenkron (1962). The stage theory assumes certain linearity in the development patterns of economies and argues that "underdevelopment in some of the economies will be converted to development over time."

A few of the Asian, African, and Latin American countries lagged behind the developed nations in terms of the time taken for development. Interestingly, to view development, capital formation, and technological change as linear functions of time is an assumption that is reductionist and that does not incorporate social and political variables that might result in differential and varying growth trajectories.

However, the role of capital formation as a crucial component that accelerates development was not only recognized by Rostow and Gerschenkron but also by Nurkse (1953) and Lewis (1955). Early Keynesians, such as Kaldor (1940 and 1961) and Robinson (1953), attempted to call attention to income distribution as a determinant of savings and growth. Even modern Marxists like Dobb (1951 and 1960) focused on the formation of savings. And even orthodox Marxists have had no conflict on this issue. Lewis and even Keynesians have argued that savings can be manipulated through government intervention (Myrdal 1957; Singer 1950). Thus, government involvement—whether by planning, socio-economic engineering, or effective demand management—was regarded as a critical tool of economic development.

## Post-war Marxist Thinking

A number of emigrant economists in Britain, influenced by their personal experience of late industrialization in Central and Eastern Europe, developed plans for the post-war transformation of underdeveloped regions. The contributions of Michael Kalecki, Kurt Mandelbaum, Joseph Steindl of Oxford University, and Paul Rosenstein-Rodan of the Royal Institute of International Affairs laid the basis of development economics as a formal sub-discipline. These Central European economists were more familiar with Marx than with Keynes, and the success of the Soviet five-year plans played a significant role in their approaches to developmental planning. It is well known that Kalecki's (1955, 1956) model of an economy with underutilized resources of labour and capital was similar to Keynes' but presented in Marxist rather than the more familiar Anglo-Saxon analytical categories. In fact, Kalecki's contribution to planning for economic development deserves to be widely acknowledged.

Newly formed economies like India also followed the planning processes, as was done in the USSR, and their initial growth models were based on the USSR–Soviet experience. It was generally accepted that the State must play a central role in economic transformation because the private sector was either dominated by landed and commercial oligarchies with vested interest in the status quo or was simply too weak and disorganized. The degree of State involvement in the economy varied across countries, but basic public infrastructure and its financing was universally undertaken by the State, which was accompanied by some form of long-term economic planning. In the first three post-war decades, countries were able to privilege domestic agriculture and industry by discretionary access to credit and foreign exchange, subsidies, and a variety of protective commercial policies. The principle of sovereignty regarding natural resources, and more generally the sovereign right of nations to formulate fiscal, monetary, commercial, and all other aspects of government policy, was not questioned, although in practice it was often violated (Pakdaman 1994). Homer-Dixon (1991, 1994), Ghosh and Bandyopadhyay (2009), and many others have presented cases of such violations and conflicts in the context of various developing nations.

This was the time (at the end of first three post-war decades) when the new orthodoxy emerged around the notion of balanced growth with the works of Lewis and Nurkse. However, it never took much time for an antithesis to emerge in the notions of unbalanced growth with the works of Hirschman (1963, 1981) and Streeten (1959). They were of the view that balanced growth is not possible as the theory assumes that a modern sector would be superimposed on an old and traditional one. In the process, the balanced growth theory lost its focus from the processes of change, which, in fact, should have been the real focus of development theory.

# Neoclassical Growth Theory

Neoclassical development theorists have emphasized the important role that international trade plays as a substitute for low domestic aggregate demand. They argue that governments should act as facilitators to promote international trade between economies. In the process of positioning the economy on an autonomous, sustained growth path, the government has to remove barriers to international trade in commodities. Comparative advantage, combined with the Hecksher–Ohlin theorem, can then take care of the rest. Subsequent amendments to this position require the removal of price distortions in domestic factor and commodity markets ("getting prices right"); this is in addition to the list of government actions that are required to induce suitable movements of factors of production across sectors, encourage the adoption of appropriate technology, and increase capital accumulation. In this view, domestic and international liberalization programmes suffice to bring about sustained economic growth and structural change.

Many economies have revealed considerable faith in this framework and have relied extensively on export-oriented growth. This has been the main characteristic of Southeast Asian economies and the present-day China. To a certain extent, even developing economies such as India and Brazil have also subscribed to this thought process. Interestingly, export facilitation in many of the Southeast Asian economies resulted in pegged exchange rate regimes and free international mobility of capital. Although phenomenal economic growth has been achieved, yet there have often been problems of capital flight caused by the lowering of interest rates as currencies were devalued to promote exports. Hence, in developing economies like India, where full capital account convertibility has been discussed and debated for long, words of caution have always been forwarded to go slow at this front.

# From Economic Growth to Economic Development

Capital formation remained an important component of growth for centuries, and even today, its importance remains undiminished. However, over time, its connotation has changed. Schultz (1963, 1971) was the first to recognize the need for human capital formation as an important appendage to physical capital formation. This led to an emphasis on education and training as prerequisites of growth and the identification of the problem of "brain drain" from the Third World to the First.

Lewis (1965) and Singer (1965) also subscribed to Schultz's thesis. Their argument was focused towards social development as a whole, which could be brought about by education, health, fertility, etc. Improvement in human capital thus began to be considered as a necessary pre-requisite for economic growth. In this view, industrialization, if it came at the cost of social development, could never be self-sustaining.

According to Singer (1965, 5), "[d]evelopment is growth plus change, and… change is not only economic but also social and cultural." He pointed out that growth had not resolved the problem of poverty, and suggested "poverty-biased policies" to affect the lives of the poorest. Till this time, all arguments, even those in favour of development, were growth-centric.

The growth obsession of development theory received a huge jolt when Seers (1969) published a seminal essay where development was construed as a social phenomenon rather than merely being defined in the reductionist mode of per capita income growth. Development, in Seers' opinion, involved the movement towards the social goals of poverty reduction, employment, and equality.

Myrdal (1968) also supported Seers' views. In his presidential address at the 11th Conference of Society for International Development at New Delhi, Seers (1969, 2) presented a more succinct statement of development with distinction: "[i]t is very slipshod for us to confuse development with economic development, and economic development with economic growth." Haq (1971, 6) was galvanized by Seers' call to redefine economic development, when he stated, "[w]e were taught to take care of our GNP as this… [would] take care of poverty. Let us reverse this and take care of poverty as this will take care of GNP."

Thus, structural issues, such as dualism, population growth, inequality, urbanization, agricultural transformation, education, health, and unemployment, began to be reviewed on their own merits, and not merely as appendages to an underlying growth thesis. Eventually, there was an emerging debate on the very desirability of growth, which was led by the extremely provocative publication by Schumacher (1973) where he argued against the desirability of industrialization and inscribed the merits of handicrafts economies.

The social positions of development became even more prominent with the adoption of Human Development Index (HDI) as a somewhat rough measure of development by academics and multilaterals in the 1990s. The HDI measures life expectancy, literacy, education, and standard of living for countries worldwide. This provides an indicative measure of the impact of economic policies on the quality of life. The index was developed in 1990 by Amartya Sen and Mahbub ul Haq with help from Gustav Ranis of Yale University and Meghnad Desai of the London School of Economics. Ever since its development, the United Nations Development Programme (UNDP) uses it as a standard measure for categorizing development of a nation in its annual *Human Development Reports*. Though a "vulgar measure," as described by Sen because of its limitations, it nonetheless brings forth the broader aspects of development than the per capita income measure it supplanted and provides a pathway for researchers to delve into the wide variety of detailed measures contained in the *Human Development Reports*. Even other multilateral agencies like the World Bank have started focusing their attention on social attributes like poverty. As a result, whether in policymaking or in academic research, social variables began to be factored in and became an integral part of development economics.

Yet the debate between growth and development continued and took a new twist in the late 1980s and became more prominent in the 1990s when the very sustainability of economic development was being questioned by environmentalists because of grave concerns about the growing environmental crisis. Environmental pollution was seen as an externality of mindless developmental policies. The questions that loomed large were: Growth? At what cost?

## Sustainable Development

Around three and a half decades ago, a group of academics known as the Club of Rome put forth the "limits to growth" theory, predicting disaster for humankind unless natural resources depleting economic and technological progress were abandoned. Such pessimistic calls were, indeed, extreme in nature. However, the global recognition of the linkage between environment and development came as late as 1980 when the International Union for the Conservation of Nature (IUCN) published the *World Conservation Strategy* and used the term "sustainable development."

The concept came into general use following the publication of the 1987 report of the Brundtland Commission—formally the World Commission on Environment and Development (WCED). Set up by the United Nations General Assembly, the Brundtland Commission coined what was to become the oft-quoted definition of sustainable development: "Development that meets the needs of the present generation without compromising the ability of future generations to meet their own needs" (WCED 1987: 41). This definition, despite being lauded as the first formal attempt to delineate sustainable development, has met with a lot of resistance and cognitive dissonance.

However, there is a misconception that sustainable development is all about environment and ecology. There cannot be anything more disastrous than conceiving such a reductionist scope of this notion. Rather than focusing solely on environmental issues, sustainable development policies broadly encompass three areas: economic, environment, and social. In support of this, several United Nations texts, most recently the 2005 World Summit Outcome Document, refer to the interdependent and mutually reinforcing pillars of sustainable development as economic development, social development, and environmental protection.

Among many subsequent definitions, the sustainable development triangle in Figure 2.1 shows one of the widely accepted explanations proposed by Munasinghe (1992) at the 1992 Earth Summit in Rio de Janeiro.

All the available documents on sustainable development acknowledge the interlinkages between the three domains and have argued that environmental changes (e.g., in ecosystem services like food production and water purification) not only influence economic growth in the short and the long run but also institutions and culture (Munasinghe 1992, Munasinghe and Reid 2005). Changes in social values and behaviour influence economic development and environmental management. And critically, economic growth and distribution of wealth and welfare influence both social and ecological attributes.

Sustainable development, eventually, led to the recognition that life-support systems that are crucial to human development are given by nature and can be finite, diminishing, yet replenishable at times. In the context of non-replenishability, there is an utmost need to look for alternative sources so that the exploitation of such resources is diminished. It also gave recognition to the fact that a given stock, composition, and productivity of society's capital—natural, man-made, and human—can contribute towards meeting basic human needs in a sustained manner over time, but only up to a maximum limit (Sengupta and Sinha 2003).

Yet the debate still rages. Despite various attempts to define "sustainable development," in terms of pathways, values, indicators, goals, practice, etc., a clear, fixed, and immutable definition remains elusive (Kates, Parris, and Leiserowitz 2005). It has also led some to infer that sustainable development is an oxymoron: "development" and "sustainability" cannot be reconciled. Kates et al. (2005, 20) state,

Sustainable development draws much of its resonance, power, and creativity from its very ambiguity…its malleability allows it to remain an open, dynamic, and evolving idea that can be adopted to fit these very different situations and contexts across space and time. Likewise, its openness to interpretation enables participants at multiple levels, from local to global, within and across activity sectors, and in institutions of governance, business, and civil society to redefine and reinterpret its meaning to fit their own situation.… Despite this creative ambiguity and

**Figure 2.1**
*Elements of sustainable development*

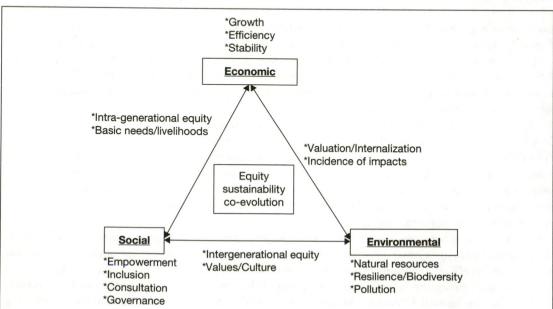

*Source:* Munasinghe and Reid (2005).

openness to interpretation, sustainable development has evolved a core set of guiding principles and values, based on Brundtland Commission's standard definition to meet the needs, now and in the future, for human, economic, and social development within the restraints of life-support systems of the planet.

Hence, no ambiguity can deter one from concluding that sustainable development is probably one of the most powerful and holistic thought processes that has enriched the development discourse, by challenging the reconciliation of what apparently seems to be the irreconcilable trinity of economic growth, social development, and environmental sustenance, thereby providing opportunities for a healthier and sustainable future.

## Is Sustainable Development Opposed to Economic Growth?

Sustainable development has sometimes been treated as a notion emerging from the communistic thought processes, and sometimes as a tool used by antagonistic ecological and environmental activists. Both of these are widespread misconceptions about the notion. Rather, the notion is much more objective than being treated as inclined towards a particular tradition. The concrete challenges of sustainable development are at least as heterogeneous and complex as the diversity of human societies and natural ecosystems around the world. Unfortunately, both socialistic thought processes and ecological antagonism have used this notion as a powerful tool to talk against economic growth, and this has even deterred many market-oriented thinkers from adopting this notion. It needs to be remembered that sustainable development is not opposed to economic growth or development; rather, it talks of sustaining the process of growth and development over generations.

On the contrary, the relationship between economic growth and indicators of air and water quality indicates that growth does not always contribute to environmental degradation. The connection is highly dependent on income levels: there seems to be a U-shaped relationship between income and environmental quality. This statement in favour of reconciliation of growth and ecological sustainability is best reflected in the Environmental Kuznets' Curve (EKC).[1] The EKC presents a relation between various indicators of environmental degradation and income per capita. In the early stages of economic growth, degradation and pollution increase, but beyond a threshold level of per capita income the trend reverses, so that at high-income levels economic growth leads to environmental improvement.

The EKC concept emerged in the early 1990s with Grossman and Krueger's (1993) path-breaking study of the potential impacts of NAFTA, and Shafik and Bandyopadhyay's (1992) background study for the 1992 *World Development Report*. However, the idea that economic growth is necessary for environmental quality to be maintained or improved is an essential part of the sustainable development argument promulgated by the WCED (1987). However, the EKC remained as an empirical phenomenon, despite research papers on the topic being inflicted by weak econometrics.

In the context of the EKC, it is easy to interpret that the levels of suspended solids and toxic metals in air and water increase rapidly as incomes approach middle-income levels, but thereafter they decrease. The link between income and pollution arises because the composition of output changes with growth in favour of newer, cleaner technologies. The EKC also presents a powerful statement on the political dimension of the economy–ecology linkage. Because of better education and awareness, citizens in higher income economies articulate their demands for a cleaner environment in a more effective manner than those in lower income nations. Hence, it is the concern of "environment" as a "good" being featured in the "utility bundle" of the consumer that acts as a prime driver in the scheme of things.

On the other hand, the convincing statements made by Munasinghe (1992, 2005) and the recently published Millennium Ecosystem Assessment (2005a) and TEEB (2010) on ecosystem services affecting economic behaviour reveal that ecological services and economic development cannot be dissociated or disintegrated, and that the causality flows from both directions.

Developing countries have often perceived pollution abatement as being opposed to their development aspirations. An implausibly high level of technical progress in energy use would be needed if these were to result in the stabilization of emissions. Incidentally, in consonance with the EKC phenomenon, most developing countries are still well below the peaks of their pollution so that global environmental damage is likely to increase substantially before it declines. Does that imply that growth needs to be sacrificed for this? Rather, sacrificing on growth would aggravate the problem, accelerating population growth, slowing the adoption of cleaner technologies, and frustrating the development of democratic institutions. Pollution tends to be related to population, and population growth is inversely related to income growth. Higher average income and output levels are only good for the environment when associated with policies that lessen demographic pressures by reducing personal risk and the need for large families. Improvements in the security of employment, education and training, pension policies, social security, and the employment of women are especially important.

Measurement of environmental costs and benefits is a key first step to the development of appropriate policies. The failure of current estimates of the net national product to account for the depreciation of environmental resources amounts to imputing this depreciation to be zero, biasing investments and technological choices. If full account were taken of environmental depreciation, profits and national output would be lower. In Costa Rica, for example, it is estimated that the depreciation of forests amount to around 10 per cent of GDP and over a third of gross capital accumulation (Salzman 2005). Biases like these have severe consequences everywhere, but are particularly pernicious in poor countries where small fluctuations in income or growth levels can spell the difference between famine and survival. Small changes in techniques of measurement, production, and lifestyle are likely to prove sufficient to preserve the options for future generations. Investments in environmental maintenance are likely to lead to barely significant declines in income growth (under 1 per cent) in the short term; in longer term, they should facilitate more rapid and globally equitable development (Salzman 2005). Policies which facilitate growth and lead to the appropriate pricing of natural resources provide the basis for enhanced environmental management. The establishment of a pricing structure for natural resources which reflects their true value will also be invaluable. The failure to price natural resources, such as water, at their economic cost means that degradation of natural resources by the present generations may undermine the basis for future economic growth.

Trade liberalization offers a particularly powerful impetus to growth and is entirely compatible with sustainable development. Indeed, trade distortions are a primary explanation for environmental degradation, as shown by the high dependence on subsidized dirty fuels in China and Eastern Europe. To the extent that trade policies may have an adverse effect on the environment, it is up to governments to initiate policy changes. Improved minimum standards and global cooperation for environmental management are a vital step to ensure that the benefits of economic growth may more quickly and effectively be reflected in an enhanced environment. Not only is growth sustainable, but it is a necessary condition for improved environmental management.

# The Role of Markets

From the discussion so far, it is clear that from the viewpoint of policymaking, a development path that is sustainable should also take into consideration institutions that will be conducive to greater participation of citizens at various levels. One of the critical elements that have been implicitly pointed out in this debate is the crucial role of market mechanism. Markets have traditionally been one of the mechanisms of social adaptation to scarcity. There are others as well. To understand the determinants of social adaptation to scarcity, Homer-Dixon (1995) defines "ingenuity" as society's ability to supply enough ideas.

Unfortunately, the role of market in sustainable development has not received much attention, and rather, in many cases, the same has been criticized by communist groups. Therefore, it is only pertinent here to talk of a few market phenomena that have emerged and might prove conducive to sustainable development.

## Trading in Ecosystem Services: A Market for Nature

It has often been argued that ecosystems services should be viewed as a natural capital, investment in which can prove more effective than that in the built capital to deliver key services. As an example, consider the case of flood control. One can address floodwaters through built capital, such as engineered works (e.g., construction and maintenance of dikes and levees) or through natural capital, such as landscape management (e.g., restoration of wetlands in flood plains). In some instances, perhaps many, landscape management may prove a better public and private investment strategy for providing flood control, once one accounts for the positive externalities of improved water quality, wildlife habitat, and recreational amenities (Salzman 2005). Many solutions have been proposed to halt environmental degradation and reverse the downward trend in ecosystem services. Some have been successful, while others have failed. An assessment of response strategies undertaken by the Millennium Ecosystem Assessment (2005b) highlighted the potential of market-based strategies to mitigate the degradation of ecosystem services.

At one point in time, it was thought that nature is endowed with resources in abundance. Anything that is supplied in abundance eventually has no value, and no market. However, over time, with human intervention in the working of the environment, there has been degradation and depletion of the resources. With the decline in their *supply*, a traditional response has been to turn to governments for continued supply of ecosystem services, through regulations, cost sharing, and other related mechanisms. This is what has been done for public goods and utilities so far. The status of the ecosystem is really a cause for more serious concern than that of public goods and utilities. The Hardin-initiated parable of "The Tragedy of the Commons" demonstrates how free access and unrestricted demand for an open-access natural resource doom the resource through overexploitation (Hardin 1968). This happens as none of the beneficiaries from the resource are willing to take up the responsibility of restoration and maintenance, because the individual cost of doing so is perceived to be much higher than the benefits that accrue. According to the Millennium Ecosystem Assessment (2005a), if the current trends continue, ecosystem services that are freely available today will cease to be available or become more costly in the near future. The higher costs that primary users may face will be passed downstream to secondary and tertiary industries and will transform the operating environment for all businesses.

Since monitoring and regulation of the ecosystem services is difficult and expensive for the government, the need for creating markets and market values assumes importance. Ecosystem services affect the well-being of individuals and the performance of firms. Yet this is rarely reflected in the financial incentives that ecosystem participants get. Typically, those who reduce ecosystem services do not bear all the costs they impose on others, nor those who supply such services are rewarded for the benefits they provide to others. In the absence of non-existent markets, allowing participants to act in their own private interest can result in fewer ecosystem services than is optimal for the society as a whole. Markets work well at providing rewards, and hence, markets are a way of encouraging resource managers to properly manage natural resources by offering them incentives.

When one looks at the value chain of any marketed commodity, one realizes that goods extracted from ecosystems have long been traded in markets (i.e., can be bought and sold at established prices). The services provided by ecosystems have been used for just as long, but have remained beyond markets and largely unpriced. The problem of open access hinges on the fact that property rights over certain resources (including forests, water, or grasslands) are either poorly defined or undefined. Hence, if their use is not regulated, they can be accessed by all and used until exhaustion. But just as in any market, an emerging scarcity can make them tradable.

There have been establishment of markets for ecosystem services, and as argued by many, payments for ecosystem services can help in rural poverty alleviation and the process of conservation simultaneously (Uddhammar and Ghosh 2006, Ghosh 2007, Ghosh and Uddhammar 2013). Economists have also been instrumental in devising tools like environmental valuation to assess the value of the benefits accrued to human civilization by the environment (e.g., Chopra and Adhikari 2004; Costanza et al. 1997). This has often helped in devising rules of compensation for environmental damages that cause economic losses to backward communities (e.g., Ghosh and Shylajan 2005).

There was a consequent expansion of markets for other environmental services that suggested that they may rapidly become a central point of sustainable development financing, representing tens of billions of dollars annually within the next 10–15 years. All these moves towards markets have been triggered by two major drivers that include conscious national environmental policy movements towards market-based instruments, and rising demand for environmental goods and services from public authorities, private entities, and consumers. On the one hand, there are new public regulations along with the establishment of market-based instruments, and on the other, it has become quite lucrative and fashionable for private players to show initiatives towards efforts of biodiversity protection. Consumer demand for derivatives of healthy ecosystems in the form of organic foods, fair trade products, and ecotourism has also increased over time. Its positive incidence on human health and overall welfare is also being steadily documented.

## The Failure of Markets

Lately, however, the failure of environmental markets point out to a different perspective on markets. The failure is more visible in the context of crash of the markets on carbon trading, especially the Certified Emission Reduction (CER) markets after the financial market crash of end 2008 and the consequent global slowdown.

As one may see in Figure 2.2, the CER futures prices dropped from USD 23 during 2008 to USD 0.4 during 2016. This market crash brings us to a different perspective on markets. Let us go into the fundamentals of the markets to explain this. Essentially, with the assumption of the efficient market hypothesis, the price of CER (or its derivatives) is supposed to reflect on the value loss due to a ton of carbon emission. When viewed from another angle, the price will also reflect the shadow value generated by the forest through a ton of carbon sequestration. This is an important regulating service of the forest. Now, the situation is

**Figure 2.2**

*Settlement price of CER futures at international exchange (USD)*

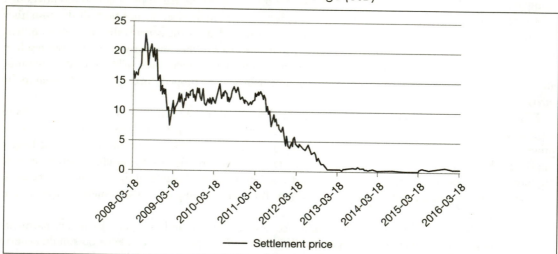

*Source:* www.theice.com

such that due to decline in demand for carbon credits by industries and related sectors, mostly because of the global slowdown, the CER prices have dropped to abysmal levels. Does that imply that the value of the forest ecosystem services in the form of carbon sequestration declines during the times of slump, as compared to the times of economic boom? Of course, this is the age-old paradox of economic theory that views all values through the prism of the markets, and there is no denying of the fact that markets are inefficient. As this example clearly shows, the markets have failed to acknowledge the true value of the underlying ecosystem services. Possible imperfections also exist in the derivatives markets, where it has essentially turned out to be a market of speculation.

## Emerging Markets and Sustainability

Even with its inherent imperfections, markets are important. They need to be regulated to be put to right use. One may not deny the fact that market institutions make the common person understand the value of the services that the ecosystem provides to the economy as a whole, the incidence of economic activity on the ecosystem, and finally, its possible repercussions on the quality of life. This dictates the supply-side phenomenon of an economy, including human health, welfare, and eventually, labour markets. At the same time, trade in ecosystem services has the potential to become the new growth industry. Areas and projects where such trade is possible are likely to generate significant secondary benefits, such as ecotourism, with multiplier effect on incomes and employment. The potential for synergies among various initiatives, therefore, is plenty. Not only can an economy fulfil its obligations under the various environmental conventions to combat desertification, biodiversity degradation, and global climate change, but the possibility also exists to engage various rural communities in formal market transactions, reducing thereby the extent and magnitude of poverty.

# Ecological Economics and Global Change

Global change refers to planetary-scale changes in the earth system. The system consists of the land, oceans, atmosphere, poles, life, the planet's natural cycles, and deep Earth processes. These constituent parts influence one another. The earth system now includes human society, so global change also refers to large-scale changes in society. At Indian Society for Ecological Economics (INSEE), we debated on why we need to include global change as a theme of this conference. What is the relevance of global change in ecological economics? In terms of explicit scope delineation, ecological economics emerged over the last three decades, as a trans-disciplinary domain of academic research in an attempt to address the critical interface between the nature, economy, and society. In the process, ecological economics recognized the spatio-temporal co-evolutionary interactivity of the human economy and the natural ecosystem. Environmental economics, on the other hand, is explicitly recognized in the mainstream economic analysis as an embodiment of the neoclassical framework. Ecological economics saw the economy as embedded in, and supported by, natural systems, whereas environmental economics treated nature as a pool of resources that act as factors in the foundation of economic activity. Ecological economists sought to provide scientific arguments for preserving the natural world not only by integrating models from ecology and economics, but also by looking at the interplay of various other socio-ecological and institutional factors that governed an economic system (Ropke 2004; Sagoff 2011).

In a recently published article in the *Breakthrough Journal*, Sagoff (2011) postulates, "Ecological economics aimed to be revolutionary, but it is now ignored by the sciences it had hoped to transform. Both ecology and economics have changed, but not because of the rise of ecological economics." This position, however, is not true, as a large component of Sagoff's arguments are based on the contention that ecological economics has essentially attempted to place a price tag on the ecosystem services and functions. This position would have been true if we indeed accepted ecological economics as another off-shoot of the traditional school of economics that deals with the issues of values and market prices. Neoclassicism, essentially, entailed a methodological breakthrough within the traditional school of economics that was obsessed with the working of various forms of markets, with varying powers of the stakeholders. Rarely, however, neoclassicism thought of evaluating institutions, and even if it did so, the traditional cost-benefit approaches with the present value of monetized net benefits were used for decision-making.

Sagoff (2011) was, however, right in pointing out the lack of advances made in this domain, as also the inherent reductionism that dominated the policy and academic spheres, because of the adherence to these measures. What Sagoff has completely missed out in his argument is the advancement of ecological economics in the other direction that is independent of cost-benefit analysis of ecosystem services and functions. This is where Ostrom (2005, 2009) opened a new horizon for ecological economics. With the institutional analysis and development framework, she showed how the working of institutions can be evaluated without really resorting to neoclassical methods of valuation. Moreover, Ostrom also took a departure from looking at ecosystems as merely providing services (provisioning, regulating, supporting, and cultural) to human society, as has been envisaged by the early works of many ecological economists. She has looked at the society as an integral component of the social–ecological system. This approach was missing from the body of ecological economics. Sagoff, unfortunately, in his criticism, has indeed failed to capture this emerging dimension in the study of ecological economics.

By studying "global change" and setting it as a theme in its seventh biennial conference, INSEE has essentially attempted to understand the broader linkage of the human society with the changes taking place in the global system. This encompasses a wide range of issues entailing population, climate, the economy, resource use, energy development, transport, communication, land use and land cover, urbanization, globalization, atmospheric circulation, ocean circulation, the carbon cycle, the nitrogen cycle, the water cycle and other cycles, sea ice loss, sea-level rise, food webs, biological diversity, pollution, health, over fishing, and more. One needs to appreciate here the circular causality between the various forces. In the context of ecological economics in South Asia, while it is important to initiate the causal thought process, it is also important to recognize the exogenous stimuli working on the dynamics of the various forces. This can render a better and more holistic understanding of the social–ecological systems.

## Concluding Remarks

Sustainable development, by all means, is an all-encompassing notion involving parameters of human health, labour, education, industrialization, and demand-side factors along with the recognition of the contribution of nature to the economy. Such a paradigmatic shift to a holistic concept of development from a reductionist notion in less than a century is no less than a revolution.

The quality of life indicators (see Oswald 1997), rather than simply growth, have increasingly become important for governments and academics, as disciplines are being transcended. As the biophysical constraints of land, soil, and water put an upper limit on the carrying capacity of nature, there is the utmost need to develop institutions like markets to manage the limited resources efficiently, ensure equity in the distribution of these resources, allow substantial time for replenishment of the resources, and find alternatives to guarantee sustainability. This would simultaneously require a trans-disciplinary knowledge base,[2] public action, and design of appropriate macro and sectoral policies. More critically, the entire discourse of public policy needs to be viewed in the wider context of inclusive development, including those of future generations. Ecological economics is definitely the critical enabler of this process.

# Notes

1. EKC is named after Simon Kuznets (1955), who hypothesized that income inequality initially rises with per capita GDP and then falls as economic development proceeds beyond a threshold level.
2. Sustainomics has been suggested by Munasinghe (1992) as a trans-disciplinary knowledge base emerging out of knowledge of economics, ecology, and society.

# References

Chopra, K., and S.K. Adhikari. 2004. "Environment Development Linkages: Modelling a Wetland System for Ecological and Economic Value." *Environment and Development Economics* 9 (1): 19–45.

Clark, C. 1940. *Conditions of Economic Progress.* London: Macmillan.

Costanza, R., R. d'Arge, R. De Groot, S. Farber, M. Grasso, B. Hannon, K. Limburg, S. Naeem, R.V. O'Neill, J. Paruelo, R.G. Raskin, P. Sutton, and M. Van den Belt. 1997. "The Value of the World's Ecosystem Services and Natural Capital." *Nature* 387: 253–60.

Dobb, M. 1951. *Some Aspects of Economic Development.* Delhi: Ranjit.

———. 1960. *An Essay on Economic Growth and Planning.* London: Routledge and Kegan Paul.

Gerschenkron, A. 1962. *Economic Backwardness in Historical Perspective: A Book of Essays.* Cambridge: Belknap Press of Harvard University Press.

Ghosh, N. 2007. "Trading in the Ecosystems Services: A Market for Nature." *Commodity Vision* 1(2): 92–99.

Ghosh, N., and J. Bandyopadhyay. 2009. "A *Scarcity Value* Based Explanation of Trans-boundary Water Disputes: The Case of the Cauvery Basin in India." *Water Policy* 11 (2): 141–67.

Ghosh, N., and C.S. Shylajan. 2005. "Coastal Mangrove Ecosystems, Fishermen's Welfare and Anthropogenic Externalities: Compensatory Payments Through Mangrove-Fishery Linkages." In *Biodiversity and Quality of Life*, edited by N. Sengupta and J. Bandyopadhyay, 294–315. New Delhi: Macmillan Publishers.

Grossman, G.M., and A.B. Krueger. 1993. "Environmental Impacts of a North American Free Trade Agreement." In *The Mexico–U.S. Free Trade Agreement*, edited by P. Garber. Cambridge, MA: MIT Press.

Haq, M. 1971. "Employment and Income Distribution in the 1970s: A New Perspective." *Development Digest* 9 (4): 3–8.

Hardin, G. 1968. "The Tragedy of the Commons." *Science* 162 (3859): 1243–48.

Hirschman, A.O. 1963. *The Strategy of Economic Development.* New Haven and London: Yale University Press.

———. 1981 "The Rise and Decline of Development Economics." In *Essays in Trespassing: Economics to Politics and Beyond*, edited by A.O. Hirschman. Cambridge: Cambridge University Press.

Homer-Dixon, T.F. 1991. "On the Threshold: Environmental Changes as Causes of Acute Conflict." *International Security* 16 (2): 76–116.

———. 1994. "Environmental Scarcities and Violent Conflict: Evidence from Cases." *International Security* 19 (1): 5–40.

———. 1995. "The Ingenuity Gap: Can Poor Countries Adapt to Resource Scarcity?" *Population and Development Review* 21(3): 1–26.

Kaldor, N. 1940. "A Model of the Trade Cycle." *Economic Journal* 50 (197): 78–92.

———. 1961. "Capital Accumulation and Economic Growth." In *The Theory of Capital*, edited by F.A. Lutz and D.C. Hague, 177–222. London: Macmillan.

Kalecki, M. 1955. "The Impact of Armaments on the Business Cycle After the Second World War." Reprinted in *Collected Works of Michael Kalecki: Vol. II. Capitalism: Economic Dynamics*, edited by Jerzy Osiatynski, 351–73. Oxford: Clarendon Press, 1991.

———. 1956. "The Growth of Investment and National Income in a Socialist Economy." Reprinted in *Collected Works of Michael Kalecki: Vol. III. Socialism: Functioning and Long-Run Planning*, edited by Jerzy Osiatynski, 131–44. Oxford: Clarendon Press, 1992.

Kates, R.W., T.M. Parris, and A.A. Leiserowitz. 2005. "What is Sustainable Development? Goals, Indicators, Values and Practice." *Environment: Science and Policy for Sustainable Development* 47 (3): 8–21.

Kuznets, S. 1955. "Economic Growth and Income Inequality." *American Economic Review* 49 (1): 1–28.

Lewis, W.A. 1955. *The Theory of Economic Growth*. London: Allen & Unwin.

———. 1965. "A Review of Economic Development." *American Economic Review* 55 (2): 1–16.

Mandelbaum, K. 1947. *Industrialisation of Backward Areas*. London: Blackwell.

Millennium Ecosystem Assessment (MA). 2005a. *Ecosystems and Human Wellbeing: Synthesis*. Washington, DC: Island Press.

———. 2005b. *Ecosystems and Human Wellbeing: Opportunities and Challenges for Business and Industry*. Washington, DC: Island Press.

Munasinghe, M. 1992. "Environmental Economics and Sustainable Development." Paper presented at the UN Earth Summit, Rio De Janeiro, and reprinted by the World Bank.

———. 2009. *Sustainable Development in Practice: Sustainomics Methodology and Applications*. Cambridge: Cambridge University Press.

Munasinghe, M., and W. Reid. 2005. "The Role of Ecosystems in Sustainable Development." In *Biodiversity and Quality of Life*, edited by N. Sengupta and J. Bandyopadhyay. New Delhi: Macmillan.

Myrdal, G. 1957. *Economic Theory and Underdeveloped Regions*. London: University Paperbacks, Methuen.

———. 1968. *Asian Drama: An Enquiry into the Poverty of Nations*. New York: Twentieth Century Fund.

Nurkse, R. 1953. *Problem of Capital Formation in Underdeveloped Countries*. Oxford: Basil Blackwell.

Oswald, A.J. 1997. "Happiness and Economic Performance." *Economic Journal* 107, 1815–31.

Ostrom, E. 2005. *Understanding Institutional Diversity*. Princeton: Princeton University Press.

———. 2009. "A General Framework for Analyzing Sustainability of Social-Ecological Systems," *Science* 325 (5939): 419–22.

Pakdaman, N. 1994. "The Story of Developmental Thinking." In *The Uncertain Quest: Science, Technology and Development*, edited by J. Salomon, F.R. Sagasti, and C. Sachs-Jeante. Tokyo: United Nations University.

Ricardo, D. 1817. *On the Principles of Political Economy and Taxation* (reprinted by Batoche Books in 2001).

Robinson, J. 1953. "The Production Function and the Theory of Capital." *Review of Economic Studies* 21 (2): 81–106.

Ropke, I. 2004. "The Early History of Modern Ecological Economics." *Ecological Economics* 50 (3–4): 293–314.

Rosenstein-Rodan, P. 1943. "Problems of Industrialisation of Eastern and South-Eastern Europe." *Economic Journal* 53 (210–11): 202–11.

Rostow, W.W. 1960. *The Stages of Economic Growth: A Non-communist Manifesto*. Cambridge: Cambridge University Press.

Sagoff, M. 2012. "The Rise and Fall of Ecological Economics: A Cautionary Tale." *The Breakthrough*. Available at: https://thebreakthrough.org/index.php/journal/past-issues/issue-2/the-rise-and-fall-of-ecological-economics (accessed on 30 June 2016).

Salzman, J. 2005. "Creating Markets for Ecosystem Services: Notes from the Field." *New York University Law Review* 80 (600): 101–84.

Schultz, T.W. 1963. *The Economic Value of Education*. New York: Columbia University Press.

———. 1971. *Investment in Human Capital: Role of Education and Research*. New York: Free Press.

Schumacher, E.F. 1973. *Small is Beautiful: Economics as if People Mattered*. New York: Harper and Row.

Schumpeter, J.A. 1911. *The Theory of Economic Development: An Inquiry into Profits, Capital, Credit, Interest, and the Business Cycle*. Translated from German by Redvers Opie (1961). New York: Oxford University Press.

Seers, D. 1969. "The Meaning of Development." *International Development Review* 11 (4): 2–6.

Sengupta, R., and A. Sinha. 2003. "Population, Life Support, and Human Development." In *Challenge of Sustainable Development: The Indian Dynamics*, edited by R. Sengupta and A. Sinha. New Delhi: Manak Publications.

Shafik, N., and S. Bandyopadhyay. 1992. "Economic Growth and Environmental Quality: Time Series and Cross-country Evidence." Background paper, *World Development Report*. Washington, DC: The World Bank.

Singer, H.W. 1950. "Gains and Losses from Trade and Investment in Underdeveloped Countries." *American Economic Review* 40 (2): 473–85.

———. 1965. "Social Development: Key Growth Factor." *International Development Review* 7 (1): 3–8.

Smith, A. 1776. *An Inquiry into the Nature and Causes of the Wealth of Nations* (reprinted by Liberty Classics in 1981).

Streeten, P.P. 1959. "Unbalanced Growth." *Oxford Economic Papers* 11 (2): 167–90.

TEEB. 2010. *The Economics of Ecosystems and Biodiversity (TEEB) Ecological and Economic Foundations*. Edited by Pushpam Kumar. London and Washington: Earthscan.

Uddhammar, E., and N. Ghosh. 2006. "Ecotourism and Development in East Africa and India: Biodiversity Changes and Institutional Designs in Four Protected Areas." Paper presented at the Ninth Biennial Conference of International Society for Ecological Economics, ISEE, New Delhi, 16–18 December.

WCED. 1987. *Our Common Future*. Oxford: Oxford University Press.

# 3

# Accounting Prices for Measuring Environmental Changes*

## M.N. Murty

## Is Income or Wealth a Measure of Well-being?

Current and past research on green accounting provides insights into choice between income and wealth as a measure of well-being. National income or net national product (NNP) of a country is calculated by adding the nation's consumption to its net investment. Does the NNP has welfare significance? Does it represent the maximum attainable level of consumption or well-being as defined in the more recent literature that could be maintained forever? Samuelson (1961) has argued that the rigorous search for a meaningful welfare concept leads to a rejection of all current income concepts like NNP and ends up with something closer to a "wealth magnitude," such as the present discounted value of future consumption. More recently, Arrow et al. (2012) and Dasgupta Committee Report (Dasgupta 2013) on "Green National Accounts in India: A Framework" has provided conceptual foundations and very convincing arguments for choosing wealth as a measure of intergenerational well-being.

Weitzman (1976, 2003) has shown that in theory the NNP, an income measure, is a proxy for the present discounted value of future consumption, a wealth measure, only if the economy considered is in a steady state. Dasgupta Committee Report also observed that income, an index of the determinants of flow of societal well-being, and wealth, an index of determinants of intergenerational well-being, would move in the same way over time, provided the economy is under a steady state. However, the two will differ outside the steady state. The flow of societal well-being is an ingredient of international well-being, but it is not a substitute for it.

The recent literature on measuring well-being has developed in the following ways:

1. United Nations (UN) Methodology of System of Environmental and Economic Accounting (SEEA; United Nations 2014)
2. European Union (EU) Methodology of Extended Input–Output Tables for Accounting of Environmental Externalities (EXIOPOL; European Commission 2012)
3. World Bank Methodology of Measuring Genuine Savings of Countries (Hamilton and Clemens 1999)
4. Methodology of Dasgupta Committee Report on Green National Accounts in India (Dasgupta 2013)

---

* A different version of this chapter has appeared in Economic and Political Weekly XLLX (35), August, 2014.

The UN methodology of SEEA suggests the preparation of physical accounts of natural resources and their monetary counterparts as satellite accounts to the conventional System of National Accounts (SNA). The EU methodology of extended input–output tables suggests the development of these accounts considering natural resources as inputs and emissions as outputs of each sector as satellites accounts of conventional input–output tables. The World Bank methodology of Genuine Savings suggests measurement of wealth formation during an accounting period as the value of changes in man-made capital stocks, human skill capital, and the natural resource stocks. Dasgupta Committee Report provides a methodology for developing detailed physical asset accounts of natural resources and monetary counterparts of them to measure what it regards as the intergenerational well-being—a measure of wealth of nations.

Preparation of physical accounts of natural resources in the form of stocks and flows accounts is a common ingredient of all these methodologies with the Dasgupta committee methodology requiring minutely detailed accounts of health capital, human skill capital, the natural resource stocks, etc. However, there could be differences in the preparation of monetary accounts depending upon the particular methodology aiming to measure well-being as income or wealth. It is because the accounting prices or shadow prices differ depending on whether it is income or wealth to be measured. In the case of contribution of an asset to income, the accounting price is the price or value of flow of services an additional unit of it provides during an accounting period. However, in the case of asset's contribution to wealth, the accounting price is the present value of flow of services provided by a unit added to the stock during its lifetime. In the terminology of the Dasgupta Committee Report, the accounting price of a unit stock of an asset is its contribution in the form of the present value of societal well-being during its lifetime or its contribution to the intergenerational well-being.

In a steady state economy, improvements of income or wealth have the same consequences for intergenerational well-being. In this case, it would be enough to measure the accounting price of a resource stock as the value of flow of services a unit increase in its stock provides during an accounting period. The steady state economy is the ideal configuration of the economy which is normally not found in actual situations. Therefore, we have to know about what could be the accounting prices of natural resource stocks in a non-steady state or suboptimal economies. The accounting price of a natural resource could be either cost based (marginal cost of restoration of a depleted resource, or marginal cost of pollution abatement) or benefit based (marginal benefit of preservation of water or air quality or forest conservation). These could be measured either as a flow becoming part of income or the present value becoming part of wealth. In a steady state, the choice between these measures does not matter because resource stocks are maintained such that the marginal abatement cost is equal to marginal benefit along the optimal developmental path. However, these choices really matter in non-steady state economies.

# Shadow Prices of Environmental Resources in the Economy Under a Steady State

Consider urban air quality as an environmental resource. It is both a consumption good and a producer good. As a consumption good, it provides utility benefits to urban dwellers, and as a producer good, it provides waste disposal services to firms. In a steady state economy, the shadow price of air quality could be derived given the constraints on the use of man-made physical capital and environmental capital, that is, the air quality. This could be done as discussed in Murty (2014) or according to the different descriptions of technology of polluting firms. Given the environmental regulations, firms choose a combination of technologies comprising end of pipe treatment, process changes in production, changes in the quality of products, and input choices. The pollution load accepted by the environmental media may be regarded as environmental inputs that the industry receives. The environmental inputs can be considered as productive inputs along with conventional inputs. The demand for environmental services can be interpreted as a derived demand arising out of use of certain inputs in the production of a commodity. Alternatively, the firm can reduce pollution load by reducing its production implying that the pollution load is not freely disposable. This could be a case in which the technology of a polluting firm can be described as one of joint production of good and bad outputs, the bad output being pollution load.

It is shown in the literature that in the steady state economy, the well-being is considered as wealth in the form

$$\int_0^\infty U(C_t, dS/dt)\, e^{-rt} dt, \tag{1}$$

where $C_t$ is the consumption and $dS/dt$ is the change in air quality, and r is the rate of discount and the well-being considered as income representing Hamiltonian

$$H_t = C + \dot{K} + P_s \cdot dS/dt \tag{2}$$

Here $\dot{K}$ is the change in man-made physical capital and $P_s$ is the shadow price of air quality moving in the same direction with respect to changes in control variables, consumption, and air quality in a solution to the planning problem. The marginal cost of pollution abatement (MCA) or demand price of industry for waste disposal services and marginal willingness to pay (MWP) or supply price of environmental services of society are equal in a first best or steady state economy. Therefore, either MCA or MWP could be considered as a shadow price or accounting price of air quality in a steady state economy.

The economy under a steady state is an ideal configuration for sustainable development. In the famous report on humanity's dependence on nature, the Brundtland Commission (World Commission on Environment and Development 1987) defined sustainable development as "development that meets the needs of the present without compromising the ability of future generations to meet their own needs."

However, the economies practically observed are generally not on paths of sustainable development due to various constraints on markets to operate competitively and provide for Pareto optimal resource allocations. Therefore, in more realistic economies the following considerations become pertinent in the economics of sustainable development:

(a) Whether income is a measure of well-being or wealth is a measure of well-being?
(b) Whether an accounting price of a resource is measured as income or measured as wealth?, and
(c) Whether an accounting price is marginal benefit or marginal cost of restoration or abatement?

It is important to examine the problem of measuring well-being from both theoretical and empirical points of view. In the economies that are on an unsustainable path of development, many conceptual and empirical issues surface in the measurement of well-being.

In the context of considering income as a measure of well-being as required by SEEA or EU methodology of extensions of input–output tables, the choice between marginal cost and marginal benefit as an accounting price of an environmental resource assumes importance from the empirical point of view. Many countries trying to implement SEEA methodology have stopped short of developing physical accounts of environmental resources because of lack of reliable estimates of accounting prices. In suboptimal economies, marginal benefits could exceed marginal cost in resource management. Therefore, estimates of well-being based on either marginal benefit or marginal cost as an accounting price of a resource will form a range.

Estimating MWP as the accounting price of an environmental resource using conceptually well-developed non-market (revealed or stated preferences) methods of environmental valuation is empirically challenging. Given rather inadequate knowledge about the empirical estimates of marginal-benefit-based accounting prices of environmental resources, it is not possible to use these prices to prepare reliable estimates of monetary accounts of environmental assets for India or for that matter for any other country as per SEEA methodology. Instead, MCA-based estimates of accounting prices could be obtained more accurately given the current database of Indian economy and empirically feasible attempts to improve the database through well-organized industry, farm, and household surveys. In one of the earlier versions of SEEA, marginal-cost-based accounting prices were recommended with an accounting method called maintenance cost. This was carried out in recognition of difficult conceptual and empirical problems associated with estimating MWP using non-market methods of environmental valuation.

Maintenance cost could be considered as the cost of environmentally sustainable development incurred as defensive expenditures by various economic activities to comply with second best environmental regulations like the pollution tax standards. These could be estimated as the monetary value of changes in stocks of environmental assets such as air and water quality and forest cover evaluated at marginal costs of abatement or afforestation. This cost has to be deducted from a conventional measure of national income for arriving at an income measure of well-being.

## Accounting Prices and Wealth as a Measure of Well-being: The Dasgupta Committee Report

Income is an index of the determinants of the flow of societal well-being $B(C(t))$, where $C(t)$ is the flow of consumption goods and services in period t. On the same token, wealth could be an appropriate index of the determinants of the stock of intergenerational well-being $V(t)$:

$$V(t) = \sum_{u=t}^{T} B(C(u))/(1+r)^{(u-t)}, \quad r \geq 0, \quad u \geq t, \tag{3}$$

where r is the rate of discount and T is the planning period. The societal well-being and hence intergenerational well-being at time u depends on the stock of assets $K(t)$ at time t where $u \geq t$:

$$B(C(u)) = B(C(K(t))), \quad \text{for } u \geq t \tag{4}$$

$$V(t) = V(K(t)) \tag{5}$$

The shadow price of an asset as a flow in terms of societal well-being could be defined as

$$Q_i(t) = \partial B(C(K(t)))/\partial K_i(t) \tag{6}$$

The shadow price of an asset (i) as a stock in terms of intergenerational well-being could be defined as

$$P_i(t) = \partial V(K(t)))/\partial K_i(t) \tag{7}$$

If the economy is under a steady state, both $B(C(K(t)))$ and $V(K(t))$ would move in the same way over time since the shadow prices of assets relative to one another remain the same over time. Also, the shadow prices expressed as flow and stock, $Q_i(t)$ and $P_i(t)$ respectively, move in the same way over time with $P_i(t)$ becoming a scalar multiple of $Q_i(t)$ as shown in Equation (9). The shadow price $P_i(t)$ could be interpreted as the present value of the marginal increase in societal well-being during the planning period (T–t) due to one unit increase in asset $K_i(t)$ at time t:

$$P_i(t) = \sum_{u=t}^{T} Q_i(u)/(1+r)^{(u-t)}, \quad u \geq t \tag{8}$$

If $Q_i(u) = \alpha Q_i(u-1)$, $Pi(t)$, $\alpha > 0$ could be written as

$$P_i(t) = \left[ \alpha^{(T-t)} \sum_{u=t}^{T} 1/(1+r)^{(u-t)} \right] Q_i(t) \qquad (9)$$

Wealth, $W(t)$ is the social value of capital assets in the economy in year t which could be written as

$$W(t) = \sum_i [P_i(t) K_i(t)] \qquad (10)$$

Wealth, $W(t)$, and intergenerational well-being, $V(K(t))$, track one another, with $W(t)$ increasing if and only if $V(K(t))$ increases. However, outside steady states, the choice between $B(C(K(t)))$ and $V(K(t))$ becomes important. To reiterate, the flow of societal well-being is an ingredient of intergenerational well-being, but is not a substitute for it.

However, sustainable or growing time paths of intergenerational well-being could exist in a non-steady state or suboptimal economies. In non-optimal economies, planning for sustainable development has to be assessed in terms of intergenerational well-being or wealth but not in terms of societal well-being. Suppose there is a perturbation in the economy introduced in the form a new investment project. This involves redeployment of assets with probably some additions to assets. The social value of change in asset portfolio given on the left-hand side of Equation (11) represents change in wealth. The right-hand side of the equation represents the present discounted value of benefits of the project expressed in the form of a change in intergenerational well-being:

$$\Delta V(t) = \sum_i [P_i(t) \Delta K_i(t)] \qquad (11)$$

A project contributes to intergenerational well-being if and only if it increases wealth. Then the question next to be addressed is "What are the shadow prices of environmental assets in the second-best economy?" This could be defined as the present value of increase in societal well-being due to one unit addition to the asset stock at time t (for example, increase in forest stock by one hectare at the margin) during asset's lifetime as given in Equation (8).

# Forecasts of Incremental Benefits from Environmental Changes and Shadow Prices

Shadow price of an environmental resource is the contribution of a unit addition to asset stock to intergenerational well-being. Estimation of it requires the forecast of $\partial B(C(K(t)))/\partial K_i(t)$ during the life of an asset. What constitutes this forecast? It consists of estimates of user and non-user values and option value benefits that one hectare of forest land provides every year during its lifetime. The current state of knowledge about estimates of these values is inadequate in any country, developed or underdeveloped. There are many conceptual and empirical difficulties in arriving at reasonable estimates of these even for the initial year of asset's life, even if the matter of forecasting is left aside.

Environmental benefits of an asset are expected to grow over time with increase in incomes, growth of population (public goods), and improvements in technology and knowledge (quasi-option value). Assume that the estimate of initial year benefits from a hector of forest land, $Q_i(u)$, is known. If these benefits are known to grow at the rate $\beta$ during asset's lifetime due to reasons mentioned earlier, a forecast of ($Q_i(u)$, $Q_i(u+1)$,............ $Q_i(u+T)$) could be obtained as

$$Q_i(t) = Q_i(u) (1+\beta)^{(t-u)} \text{ for } t > u, \ t = u+1, \ldots\ldots u+T; \quad \beta \geq 0 \tag{12}$$

Using Equations (8) and (12), the accounting or shadow price of the $i^{th}$ environmental resource stock could be obtained as

$$P_i(t) = Q_i(u) \sum_{u=t}^{T} \{(1+\beta)/(1+r)\}^{(t-u)}, \quad \text{for } t > u, \quad r \geq 0, \quad \beta \geq 0 \tag{13}$$

Given an estimate of initial year environmental benefits of one unit of asset at the margin, an estimate of rate of growth of these benefits during asset's lifetime, and the rate of discount, the shadow price of an environmental resource stock could be estimated using Equation (13). This could greatly simplify otherwise very difficult problems; but the larger problem of estimating initial year's benefits still remains.

Another important question to be answered is "How one can proceed in measuring wealth as intergenerational well-being with having practical environmental policy instruments like pollution tax standards and pollution permit standards on the background?" If standards are normally fixed for air and water pollution, taking into account the assimilative capacity of environmental media, they are fixed along the path of sustainable development. Even if environmental resource stocks are fixed, the value society places on them may change over time because changes of tastes and preferences and incomes of people, growing population, and technological changes along the developmental path. Also, if environmental standards have to change along the sustainable development path, the case for measuring wealth along the development path arises.

In the context of fixed environmental standards as part of policy for sustainable development, the cost of maintaining the standards along the developmental path has consequences for the measurement of wealth of a nation. Suppose river quality standards are set for cleaning the river Ganges in India. The ongoing Ganga Action Plan (GAP) could be considered the investment project to achieve these standards with a time stream of costs incurred along the developmental path of Indian economy. Similarly, if a hectare of forest land has been lost in the development process, compensating by adding a hectare of forest by afforestation to meet the standards is a marginal investment project with a time flow of costs along the developmental path. The present value of costs of these projects is a measure of wealth which may be called the maintenance cost of environmental standards or environmental resource stocks. The present value of costs of marginal projects for pollution reduction, afforestation, etc., may be defined as a stock measure of shadow prices. Environmental resource stocks as per the standards could be valued at these shadow prices in estimating the contribution of these stocks to national wealth or intergenerational well-being. In Equation (11), depletion of environmental resource stocks ($\Delta K_i(t)$) implies that the value of depleted stocks valued at marginal maintenance cost defined earlier contributes negatively to wealth or intergenerational well-being.

Presence of irreversibility in resource use could be a problem in considering the marginal maintenance cost as an accounting price of environmental resource stocks. A lost hectare of pristine forest with (in)valuable biodiversity cannot be restored by compensatory afforestation. The cost of rehabilitation of a highly polluted lake or aquifer can be prohibitively high. Therefore, the compensating marginal investment projects mentioned earlier are not feasible in the presence of irreversibility in resource use. Given the difficulties of measuring benefit-based shadow prices, an empirically feasible method of measuring wealth of a nation could be to use the marginal maintenance cost as shadow price in general and benefit-based measure in the special cases where irreversibility is present.[1]

## Summary and Conclusions

Accounting prices are either a flow or a stock measure depending upon the state of the economy. In an economy under a steady state, both measures of accounting prices move in the same direction as income and wealth measures of societal well-being do. In a non-steady state economy, the choice matters. Some recent studies convincingly argue that wealth is the appropriate measure of societal well-being in economies with non-optimal development paths. Therefore, stock measures of accounting prices as defined in this chapter are appropriate asset prices to estimate wealth.

In a steady state economy, the marginal cost of pollution abatement or restoration of lost resource stocks is the appropriate shadow price to measure societal well-being along the developmental path. In the competitive market economy with many firms and many consumers and pollution externality, pollution tax equal to MCA along the path of sustainable development will keep the economy in a steady state. However, practical second best environmental policy instruments such as permits, taxes, and standards for sustainable development will move the economy out of the steady state equilibrium path. Sustainable non-optimal developmental paths could be obtained in economies out of a steady state using second best environmental policy instruments mentioned earlier. In such situations, wealth is the appropriate measure of well-being, which some recent studies refer to as intergenerational well-being.

Along the sustainable non-optimal developmental paths of economy, the choice between benefit-based or cost-based accounting prices for measuring wealth assumes importance from the point of empirical feasibility and tractability. The presence of irreversibility in resource use could be a problem in considering the marginal maintenance cost as an accounting price of environmental resource stocks. Given the difficulties of measuring benefit-based shadow prices, an empirically feasible method of measuring wealth of a nation could use marginal maintenance cost as the shadow price in general and the benefit-based measure in the special cases where irreversibility is present.

## Note

1. See Murty (2010), Haque, Murty, and Shyamsundar (2012), Murty and Surrender Kumar (2004), and Markandya and Murty (2000) for empirical studies of environmental valuation in India and South Asia.

## References

Arrow, K.J., P. Dasgupta, L.H. Goulder, K. Mumford, and K. Oleson. 2012. "Sustainability and the Measurement of Wealth". *Environment and Development Economics* 17 (3): 317–53.

Dasgupta, P. 2013. "Green National Accounts in India: A Framework." A Report of Expert Group Convened by National Statistical Organization, Government of India, New Delhi, March.

European Commission. 2012. "A New Environmental Accounting Framework Using Externality Data and Input Output Tools for Policy Analysis (EXIOPOL)." Accessed at: http://www.feem-project.net/exiopol/scheda.php?ids=45 (accessed on 24 April 2017).

Hamilton, K., and M. Clemens. 1999. "Genuine Savings Rates in Developing Countries." *World Bank Economic Review* 13 (2): 333–56.

Haque, A.K.E, M.N. Murty, and Priya Shyamsundar, eds. 2012. *Environmental Valuation in South Asia*. Cambridge: Cambridge University Press.

Markandya, A., and M.N. Murty. 2000. *Cleaning Up Ganges: The Cost Benefit Analysis*. New Delhi: Oxford University Press.

Murty, M.N. 2010. *Environment, Sustainable Development and Well-being: Valuation, Taxes and Incentives*. Delhi: Oxford University Press.

Murty, M.N. 2014. "Measuring Well-being and Accounting Prices of Environmental Resources." *Economic and Political Weekly* XLLX (35, August): 64–69.

Murty, M.N., and Surendar Kumar. 2004. *Environmental and Economic Accounting for Industry*. New Delhi: Oxford University Press.

Samuelson, P.A. 1961. "The Evaluation of 'Social Income': Capital Formation and Wealth." In *The Theory of Capital*, edited by F.A. Lutz and D.C. Hague. London: MacMillan.

United Nations. 2014. "System of Environmental Economic Accounting 2012—Central Framework." Accessed at: http://unstats.un.org/unsd/envaccounting/seeaRev/SEEA_CF_Final_en.pdf (accessed on 24 April 2017).

Weitzman, M. 1976. "On the Welfare Significance of National Product in a Dynamic Economy." *The Quarterly Journal of Economics* 90 (1): 156–62.

———. 2003. *Income, Wealth, and the Maximum Principle*. Cambridge, MA: Harvard University Press.

World Commission on Environment and Development. 1987. *Our Common Future*. New York: Oxford University Press.

# 4

# Green National Accounting Framework for India: Summary of the Report of Partha Dasgupta Committee

Haripriya Gundimeda

## Introduction

Economic evaluators turn to the national accounts to understand the state of the economy for assessing the performance as well as prescribing policy. However, if the evaluator is asked "whether the development is likely to be sustainable," s/he does not have the answer. By meaning sustainable, here we mean the development path along which the intergenerational well-being does not decline. The existing System of National Accounts (SNA), though provides a comprehensive accounting framework, is extremely narrow as it does not have a mechanism to evaluate the status, use, and future of natural environment.

The objective of this chapter is to present the key findings of the report on green national accounts in India (Dasgupta 2013). We discuss here the framework, feasibility, and challenges involved in implementing green national accounts which requires constructing physical accounts, estimating shadow prices, and integrating the monetary accounts into the existing system. We illustrate the feasibility of implementation with special reference to forests and mineral resources. The policy uses of developing green national accounts are also discussed.

## SNA and the SEEA

The SNA comprises of a sequence of accounts, comprising of current accounts (records production of goods and services, and the generation, distribution, and use of income), accumulation accounts (changes in assets, liabilities, and worth), and balance sheets (static measure of wealth, stock of wealth, liabilities, and net worth of the country). The three aggregates important for accounting for the environment are the net domestic product, consumption expenditures, and aggregate investment. Net domestic product is the gross domestic product minus the depreciation of the produced capital. GDP is computed using the production approach

(GVA=value of output less the value of intermediate consumption), income approach (use of primary factors of production), and the expenditure approach (purchase of final goods and services). Changes in wealth of the country are established through the accumulation accounts (capital and financial accounts).

The production boundary of the SNA is limited to the marketed goods and services. There is inconsistency in the way investments are treated in the national accounts. The expenditure incurred in conversion of natural resources into alternate uses, for example, is recorded as gross capital formation while the accounts are completely silent on the value of natural resource per se. Defensive expenditures, especially those relating to investments to improve the quality of natural resources, are treated as increases in income, which clearly gives wrong signals, as the evaluators would not be able to know whether the economy is growing because of repairing the damages already caused. National accounts do have balance sheets for produced capital and some natural capital but are incomplete when it comes to valuing the stock changes of natural assets that are considered within the asset boundary. The national accounts do not capture the natural resources in their use as intermediate consumption or treat natural resources as capital assets. Thus, the GDP may increase even when the natural capital stock depletes or when the quality of environment deteriorates.

Keeping in view the limitations of the existing SNA, the United Nations has adopted the Satellite System of Integrated Environmental and Economic Accounting Framework (SEEA framework), which enabled the extension of the current boundaries of the SNA and also provided the scope for recording the use and depreciation of natural capital. The latest version of SEEA comprises three parts: the central framework, experimental ecosystem accounts, and extensions and applications. The central framework describes the interactions between the economy and the environment, and between the stocks and changes in the stocks of environmental assets. The SEEA experimental accounts describe both the measurement of ecosystems in physical terms and the valuation of ecosystems in so far as it is consistent with the market principles. SEEA extensions give the applications to the policy. There are key differences in terminologies between the SNA and SEEA to accommodate for the shortcomings of the SNA. The SEEA central framework has been adopted as a statistical standard, and work is still progressing and evolving.

## Conceptual Framework—What It Means for Operationalizing?

The report (Dasgupta 2013) provides a framework for estimating the comprehensive wealth (adjusted for the distribution of wealth in the economy), not per capita GDP. Comprehensive wealth is defined as the social value of an economy's stock of capital assets comprising physical capital, reproducible capital, human capital, natural capital, and social capital. It measures the productive base of the economy. It is the change in wealth per capita that determines the intergenerational well-being and is used for evaluating sustainable development. Sustainable development in this chapter refers to the positive increase in the aggregate net investment per capita, where per capita investment is the social value of change (called shadow price) in per capita stock of assets.

The report postulated that well-being is derived from different assets and the changes in wealth are the prime objects of interest to understand the sustainability analysis. An economy's development is sustainable over time only if over the period its wealth increases. However, the effective limiting factor in measuring the well-being is the availability of internally consistent reliable periodic data. Especially, this is a huge problem for countries like India that do not even have national balance sheets yet. The valuation approach should be consistent with that of the methods for produced assets. The bases of evaluating all forms of wealth are the shadow prices. In the case of produced assets, the stock is valued at historic prices and assumes that the market price is equivalent to the shadow price at all points of time.

Measuring social worth has its own challenges. It is not possible to derive the shadow prices in the absence of flow accounts and without integrating the flow accounts with the existing SNA. The sustainability of development based on the net investment can be examined if the stock boundary is extended to also include other forms of assets and integrate the changes in the assets with the other flows in the economy. To fully integrate the environment flows with the SNA, it is necessary to develop the physical and monetary supply use tables for various institutional sectors. NDP, which also includes the depletion of natural capital, can in fact provide a compact descriptor of growth in immediate well-being. In making this operational, the committee concluded that the GDP should be left untouched and only the current components of consumption of natural capital arising out of production should be taken into account.

## Illustrating the Green National Accounting Framework for India—Some Key Results

The report illustrates how by using quick estimates it is feasible to estimate changes in wealth as well as the flows for three resources (land, forests, and minerals). The framework is consistent with the wealth accounting approach and SEEA framework. In the process, the report does not use latest data but makes use of the estimates already existing earlier (and where available uses new estimates) to discuss the framework, methodology, data availability, and data gaps. The approach has been to measure the stock of assets at the beginning of the accounting period and account for all changes that occurred during the accounting period to estimate the closing stocks using physical and monetary terms. Opening stocks and closing stocks are measured as the economically exploitable quantity of reserves or stocks available at the beginning and end of the accounting period. Changes in quantity are brought about by the direct economic use/exploitation of the asset. The following identity between the opening stocks and closing stocks should hold.

Quality changes can be recorded where appropriate data is available.

Opening stocks + Additions to stocks (renewable resources) − Depreciation of the stock (economic use/ exploitation) +/− other stocks changes (revaluations/natural processes) = Closing stock.

The challenging issue is valuation of the stock changes. National accounts advocate the use of market prices. However, many of the environmental resources do not have well-established markets and there is no price signal that can act as an indicator. However, several non-market valuation techniques do exist which can be used to value the environmental stock changes. These non-market techniques would be more relevant for those that cannot be proxied or approximated by market prices. Various valuation techniques are used to estimate the value of the stock and the flows of environmental resources considered.

The monetary accounts are derived from the physical accounts by applying market prices or estimated market values to the physical stocks and stock changes in natural resources. As the intention is to follow the SEEA central framework, only those natural resource goods and services which have market prices or can have market prices are considered. Finally, the monetary estimates are integrated with the main national accounting aggregates. The integration should ensure that the following three components are addressed: (a) figures for the production of natural resource adjusted for unreported production; (b) adjusting the capital account to expand capital formation (that includes accumulation of natural assets and their depletion or degradation), which increases GDP or NDP; and (c) consumption of capital to include the cost of depletion and degradation of natural resources which decreased NDP.

Integrating with the main accounting aggregates allows for the computation of depreciation of the resource in question by computing a new aggregate through adjusting the net state domestic product to reflect the depletion of natural capital. The new depletion-adjusted indicator could guide policy to evaluate the wealth impact of the previously unaccounted damage and also evaluate the trade-offs in land use and resource use.

# Recommendations for Implementing Environmental Accounting for India

Environmental accounting is practical, feasible, and useful. Some data exists, and some more data is required so that the internal consistency of the SNA is not violated and the data is accurate. The transition to a comprehensive set of national accounts can be done in a phased manner. The following are the short-, medium-, and long-run recommendations for implementation.

1. Prepare physical supply use tables (PSUTs) and asset accounts for land, forests, and minerals (short run).
2. Prepare monetary Supply use tables (MSUTs) for land, forests, and minerals and PSUTs for soil, water, carbon, and energy (medium term).
3. Develop medium-term plan for identifying data sets, getting data in place, valuation methodologies, and developing NDP (to include the capitals mentioned above as well as the defensive expenditures).
4. Develop long-term plans for institutionalizing mechanisms for periodic collection of data and for organizing periodic studies and surveys, estimating shadow price ranges.

# Reference

Dasgupta, P. 2013, March. "Green National Accounts in India: A Framework." A Report of Expert Group Convened by National Statistical Organization, Government of India, New Delhi.

# 5

# Towards Green National Accounting: Government of India Expert Group (2011–13), INSEE Conference Panel (December 2013) and the Way Forward

Kanchan Chopra

## The Expert Group Report and INSEE Conference Panel

Economists interested in the environment come in all kinds of hues. The optimistic among them think they can impact the economic policy to take nature into account. Efforts at doing this exist through a range of studies focusing on conceptual frameworks, valuation, pricing, intervention through legal and economic instruments, and so on. Studies on these lines have been going on at the micro level in India and elsewhere, with some impact on policy. The even more optimistic have tried to frame macroeconomic indicators which would attract popular attention and be instrumental in driving policy in specific directions.

Governments, however, are typically conservative in introducing change, particularly if it is not driven by a vote bank. So the setting up of the Expert Group (EG) on Green National Accounting in India in August 2011 was itself a great step ahead by the then government. The EG also had access to considerable time and human resources in the course of its deliberations. It was headed by the noted economist Partha Dasgupta and submitted its report in April 2013 (Anant et al. 2013). The report constituted an attempt to lay out a road map for the implementation of a schema which would take nature into account in the regularly published macroeconomic indicators, dominated as they are by "the tenacious hold that the GDP has on our economic sensibilities."

It was in this background that in the Seventh Biennial Conference of the Indian Society for Ecological Economics (INSEE) held at Tezpur in December 2013, a panel on Green National Accounting was organized. Apart from two members of the EG (other than the chair of the panel who was also a member of the EG), the panel included an international voice, a view from within the government, and an academic from outside the EG.[1]

Haripriya Gundimeda presented the findings of the EG (also referred to as the Partha Dasgupta Committee). T.C.A. Anant gave an overview of the felt need within the Indian Government and also the challenges faced in the likely follow-ups. M.N. Murty traced the history of green national accounting in India with alternative approaches which also pointed in the same directions of implementation. As two other chapters in this book cover a large part of this matter, I shall in this write-up dwell on the experiences of the EG from 2011 to 2013 and on lessons for green national accounting in institutional frameworks inherent in it.

The EG had several unique advantages from the outset. It chair had impeccable credentials internationally as an economic theorist and an environmental economist. It was set up at a time when the United Nations had adopted the Satellite System of Integrated Environmental and Economic Accounting Framework (UNSEEA Framework) and its affiliated international agencies were developing further extensions to it. It had the chief statistician of India as its member-convenor and the Central Statistical Organisation (CSO) as the coordinator of its activities. The entire spectrum from theory (internationally) to practice (in India and elsewhere) had been covered by the broad sweep of expertise of the members of the EG.

In the strengths, however, also lay the challenges. A look at the process followed by the report is of some interest. From the beginning, there was agreement on viewing economic growth as growth in wealth per capita, not GDP per capita. The EG reiterated that development could be sustained over a period of time if and only if aggregate net investment was positive, where net investment stood for the social value of the change in per capita stock of assets. This understanding was built on the large body of theoretical literature showing that development and long-term growth depends on the wealth of a nation, where wealth is broadly defined to include produced capital, natural capital, human and institutional capital, and net foreign financial assets (see Arrow, Dasgupta, and Mäler 2003, Dasgupta 2001, Dasgupta and Mäler 2000, Hamilton and Clemmens 1999). If wealth is decreasing, for example, from depletion or degradation of natural capital, then a country will not be able to sustain its current level of income. However, estimating stocks of wealth (capital) is hard work. Not sufficient attention is given to even initiating this in policy discussions.

Picking up the threads from the end of existing practice in India, the EG next listened to presentations from and had interaction with organizations working in the area of data collection and analyses on environmental and natural resource issues. An array of government and non-governmental institutions (from the Indian Council of Agricultural Research, the Forest Survey of India, the Botanical and Zoological Surveys, among several) outlined their activities from the environmental point of view. Simultaneously, a member of the EG, G. Haripriya, in her presentation gave a comparative list of data requirements and availability with respect of the sectors, land, forests, and mines.

The later meetings were intense, often contested, with discussions on changes required in the System of National Accounts (SNA) to take into account the theoretical position taken by the EG. Some of the requirements were identified as extending the asset and production boundaries and determining the national shadow prices of resources from existing and future studies. However, there remained a few contentious issues. These related to the integration of environmental asset use and degradation into the existing SNA based as it is on a system of double accounting. The accountants' principles of double entry were certainly not amenable to extensions to ecosystems whose services were often outside the pale of money income and/or expenditure. The group noted that it was perhaps on account of this that the UNSEEA had also conceived of the following two-tier framework for extension of national income accounts:

1. SEEA Central Framework which starts from the perspective of the economy and its economic units, and
2. SEEA Experimental Ecosystem Accounting which links ecosystems to economic and other activities.

This approach understands and states upfront that placing ecosystems in an accounting context requires the disciplines of ecology, ecological economics, and statistics to come together and think of measurement and policy issues in new ways. It does not give precise instructions on how to compile ecosystem accounts but it represents a strong and clear movement towards a convergence across the disciplines on many core aspects.

The EG then decided to identify the way forward in the Indian context in a step-by-step fashion. In doing so, it took note of the work earlier carried out by CSO on national environmental income accounting through eight national institutions that had adopted a slightly different perspective.[2] The details were presented in the panel (and in this book) by M.N. Murty.

## The Way Forward

The central issue is, What is doable in the short run and what could be aimed at in the longer run?

Particularly, as the canvas to be covered is large and uncertainties of different kinds exist in this area, range estimates were to be preferred to point estimates of parameters. The way ahead for government institutions working in this area was then charted out.[3] Additionally, it was pointed out that the steps outlined in the way forward would require initiating exploratory research in two areas: the development of a more complete balance sheet for the nation and the identification of principles for valuing and periodically collecting and compiling data on environmental assets and flows. A long-term plan for an institutional mechanism for ensuring that this is undertaken would need to be set up.

Three years down the line, it is not clear whether much progress has been achieved on this count, within government or within research institutions. Be that as it may, the report of the EG put together a state of the art document that can be delved into for guidance as and when policymakers are ready for it.

## Notes

1. The panel consisted of T.C. Anant, A. Duraiappah (who eventually could not make a presentation), G.D. Haripriya, and M.N. Murty with Kanchan Chopra as the chair.
2. See Murty and Panda (2012).
3. See the chapter by Haripriya Gundimeda in this book.

## References

Anant, T.C.A. (Convenor), K. Basu, K. Chopra, P. Dasgupta (Chair), N. Desai, H.P. Gundimeda, V. Kelkar, R. Kolli, K. Parikh, P. Sen, P. Shyamsundar, E. Somanathan, and K. Sundaram. 2013. "Green National Accounts in India: A Framework." Report by an Expert Group Convened by the National Statistical Organisation, Ministry of Statistics and Programme Implementation, Government of India, New Delhi. Available at: http://mospi.nic.in/Mospi_New/upload/Green_Accouts_in-India-1may13.pdf (accessed on 24 April 2017).

Arrow, K.J., P. Dasgupta, and K.-G. Mäler. 2003. "Evaluating Projects and Assessing Sustainable Development in Imperfect Economies." *Environmental & Resource Economics* 26 (4): 647–85.

Dasgupta, P. 2001. *Human Well-being and the Natural Environment.* Oxford: Oxford University Press.

Dasgupta, P., and K.-G. Mäler. 2000. "Net National Product, Wealth and Social Well-being." *Environment and Development Economics* 5 (1): 69–93.

Hamilton, K., and M. Clemens. 1999. "Genuine Savings Rates in Developing Countries." *World Bank Economic Review* 13 (2): 333–56.

Murty, M.N., and M. Panda. 2012. *Generalized National Income Accounts for Measuring Green GDP for India: A Review of Indian and International Experience.* Report submitted to the Central Statistical Office, Government of India, New Delhi.

# 6

# Linking Science and Policy: Using the Crowd in the Cloud*

Anantha Kumar Duraiappah

## Introduction

Should our policies be guided by credible science? And what does credible science mean? In this chapter, I shall address the latter and make the assumption that the answer to the first is a strong affirmation for credible science. This can be easily substantiated for environmental policy, in particular, by the large number of scientific assessments[1] that are conducted by scientific subsidiary bodies of environmental conventions such as the SBSSTA (CBD 2005). The same, however, cannot be said for social and economic policies (ICSU, ISSC 2015). While the latter can definitely be a topic for another paper, I would like to focus in this chapter on defining what constitutes credible science in the field of environment-related development policymaking. This would of course include the social sciences but within the context of policymaking in the field of environment-related development policies.

In this chapter, I shall draw on the experience of the Intergovernmental Science-Policy Platform on Biodiversity and Ecosystem Services (IPBES) in my attempt to answer what credible science means. The insistence by the scientific community of the complex nature of the issue at hand and the need for credible and independent science to inform policymaking at multiple levels were primary reasons for going ahead with the establishment of the IPBES (UNEP 2012). Another and a more sobering reason for it was the recognition of the existence of a large number of biodiversity and ecosystem services-related multilateral environmental agreements (MEAs) that were undertaking scientific studies with varying levels of scientific rigour (Perrings et al. 2011). A common science–policy platform was expected to strengthen these MEAs by providing highly credible science in a periodic and timely manner for policymaking at multiple levels of governance.

But the IPBES is not the first example of an attempt to bring credible science to environment-related development policymaking. The Intergovernmental Panel on Climate Change (IPCC) was established in 1988 to bring the best climate science to investigate if the rapid increase in global greenhouse gases (GHGs) might cause a rise in global temperatures leading to climate change. In 1992, based on the first report from the IPCC, negotiations for a framework on climate change—the United Nations Framework Convention on Climate Change (UNFCCC)—began in earnest. This is a classic example of how science was brought

---

* Much of the information presented in this chapter is reproduced from two of my earlier papers (Duraiappah 2014; Duraiappah et al. 2012).

to bear on international environmental and development policymaking. But recent questions of the validity of some of the platform's scientific findings have come under scrutiny as lapses were found in reporting the science underlying the analysis (Banerjee and Collins 2010). An independent report by the Inter Academy Panel (IAP) of the IPCC recommended a number of steps to be taken to prevent lapses of scientific scrutiny over the platform's findings (IAP 2010). Many of these have been considered in this chapter in the ensuing discussion and recommendations.

## Key Gaps in the Existing Science–Policy Platforms

Many of the MEAs had overlapping mandates. For example, the Convention on Biological Diversity (UNCBD) was established to protect the world's biodiversity. The Convention to Combat Desertification (UNCCD) also had as part of its mandate to protect the biodiversity in lands facing desertification pressures. The scientific understanding on the root causes of biodiversity loss should ideally have been similar under both the conventions. However, this was not found to be true (Duraiappah and Bharadwaj 2007). There might have been many reasons for this dichotomy but a major factor was the lack of uniform scientific tests for verifying robustness and/or consistency across the various scientific studies (Duraiappah 2014).

For example, in the Millennium Ecosystem Assessment (MA), the key assumptions underlying the socio-economic systems in an integrated socio-economic-ecological model were found to be very different across different science-based studies leading to different outcomes. The following key gaps were identified as critical for ensuring scientific credibility (UNEP 2009):

1. Lack of an accepted level of scientific credibility: The presence of a wide range of science–policy interfaces working in an ad hoc manner with little strategic thinking led to incoherent scientific findings, which were poor in quality as well. For example, the rigour of the peer review process across scientific studies was not standardized leading to varying qualities of outputs.
2. Lack of a common and shared knowledge base: Although there was an extensive scientific knowledge base, there were no common conceptual frameworks, methodologies, and common understanding among the many scientific studies undertaken. Moreover, much of the knowledge collected was dependent on the scientists who were involved in the studies and no attempts were made to reach out to the broader group of scientists who could not be included for a variety of reasons.
3. Selection of scientists: Many of the existing science–policy interfaces follow a selection process, which is heavily influenced by politics and ideologies.

## Ensuring Credible Science?

A key feature of the present approach to assessment is what we call the "closed peer assessment" (CPA), which includes a selected, closed group of "experts" (see Figure 6.1). This current process generally calls for a "leader" to invite participants who are already known, or have "distinguished" themselves in some way, to participate. This often implies drawing on familiar network of colleagues, many of whom have worked together before and are likely to have similar ideological orientations and perceptions towards the problems to be assessed. These experts are traditionally nominated and selected by the governments or in some cases by special science-based organizations approved by the governments. Deliberations are largely carried out through email chains (and attachments), punctuated occasionally by face-to-face meetings. Over time, the

**Figure 6.1**
*The managed commons*

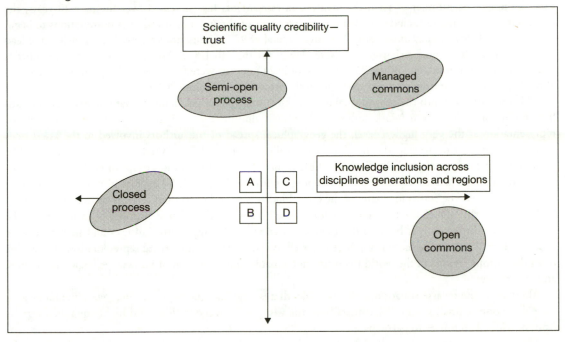

*Source:* Duraiappah et al. (2012).

original team dwindles down to a much smaller number of members and, generally, a small cadre of scientists produces the final document.

Moreover, because of cultural differences, most scientists from certain parts of the world—where open dialogues and confrontations are frowned upon—usually shy away from active participation and deliberations. The counterpart of CPA is known as the closed peer review (CPR), which is adopted for the subsequent review process.

This form of collaboration is not only inefficient but also ineffective in drawing out the best ideas from the large pool of knowledge-holders who are keen to contribute. This collaborative process by its very nature has trouble supporting more than 15 participants; in most cases, around five to eight authors can be said to have had direct involvement in the production of the final document. We have to ask ourselves as scientists if this is good enough or should we try to find more inclusive processes to get the broader community involved.

The process described above is not so different for many of the existing non-intergovernmental assessment initiatives. For instance, the MA was completed by a selection of authors chosen by a science panel and endorsed by the MA board. The same was done in the selection of reviewers, though in this case an independent review board oversaw the selection and implementation of the review process. In some assessments, the review process has been opened to a larger community for comments and reviews. We call this an open peer review process. Both these options have some serious drawbacks worth discussing in more detail as we deliberate on the assessment processes for the IPBES (see section "A Managed Commons Approach" later in this chapter).

There are four primary concerns with the CPA and CPR models: (a) limited and low rates of participation, (b) long process durations (important when considering policy relevance), (c) cost and efficiency, and (d) limited scalability. These have been discussed as follows.

## Limited and Low Rates of Participation

First, although the number of scientists involved in assessments has increased over the past 20 years, the process itself has come to exclude many more, giving an air of elitism. The number of nominations to begin with is relatively low. For example, only 258 out of a total of 977 nominations received for coordinating lead authors, lead authors, and review editors were chosen for the 5th IPCC Assessment Report. 44 countries were represented in total, and of the 258 authors, only 24 per cent were from developing countries. There is also a lack of representation of social scientists in the assessments (Hulme 2010).

This leads directly into the second weakness of the current paradigm, namely that scientists from established, developed country networks still overwhelmingly dominate participation. Even if there is regional representation at the very highest level, the geographical spread of the authors involved in the assessment itself is skewed towards developed countries—specifically, Europe and the United States. As an example, The Economics of Ecosystems and Biodiversity (TEEB) included in its working group on ecological and economic foundations just 10 experts from developing countries, along with 54 experts from developed countries. The same can be stated for many of the other biodiversity and ecosystem services-related assessments.

But why is this? Does the low representation arise because of the limited number of experts from the developing countries or is it because the transaction costs of working across cultures and newcomers are much higher? Whatever be the reason, there is a need to address the asymmetrical representation of scientists from the various regions of the world to ensure an equitable representation of knowledge, views, ideologies, and experiences.

Alternately, the reverse situation is also possible, that is, regional quotas in an intergovernmental process may allow only a small group of scientists from the vast pool of very credible and highly qualified experts from developed countries to participate.

Third, it is too easy for a small, unrepresentative group of scientists to commandeer and dominate the closed discourse, potentially resulting in a biased process and assessment. The recent controversy surrounding the IPCC reports on the melting of the Himalayas and then the renewable energies scenarios analysis episode attest to this danger (Banerjee and Collins 2010). Although reputable scientific organizations such as the American Association for the Advancement of Science (AAAS) and the Union of Concerned Scientists (UCS) have since exonerated those involved in the controversies, their reports nevertheless highlighted the need for transparency and openness in the assessment process.

## Process Duration—Too Slow to Be Relevant

The IPCC takes approximately five years to complete an assessment cycle. The MA took five years. The long durations of these processes lead to the real danger that results—and the following policy prescriptions—may become dated or obsolete by the time they are released. For example, when the MA was released, food prices were not considered to be a major driving variable in the assessment and yet within a year of its release, food prices sky rocketed and set into motion a string of events that the MA had missed.

The challenges presented by environmental change demand decisive action and thus thorough, yet expeditious, advice from the scientific community. Even if the IPBES has by virtue of its work programme the flexibility to carry out thematic assessments, the present style of assessment implementation still implies a relatively long time period before findings are released. And even if times are reduced in the current framework, it is at the expense of bringing together a large group of experts to bear on the issue and provide a scientifically credible product free of bias.

## Cost and Efficiency

Traditional assessments are expensive and, ironically, environmentally unfriendly. In a conventional assessment process, a number of scientists selected primarily by governments physically meet for about a week or so, discuss key points, and make presentations, before returning to their respective countries, after which point work is continued via electronic means. The cost of MA was about USD 25 million, excluding the time of the 1,400-odd scientists involved. Costs for IPCC assessments are in the same range, if not higher, again excluding the time of the scientists involved. Adding these costs together with the carbon emissions of all these meetings held all over the world seems to point towards the need for more effective and carbon-friendly ways to undertake assessments.

There is no doubt that face-to-face meetings are inevitable; the challenge is to minimize these such that both efficiency and effectiveness are increased. Moreover, because the scientists from developed countries have a larger pool of funds to use in supporting travel to these meetings, many of these meetings inadvertently become dominated by them. This brings into question the issue of equity in the assessment process.

## Scalability: Meetings and Conferences Cannot Support Wider Participation

It has become clear that the present mechanisms for global collaboration on assessments—characterized primarily by face-to-face meetings and email chains—will not be sufficient to include the increasing number of active stakeholders involved. Either we can expect the costs for carrying out needed assessments to increase drastically or, worse, we may see these assessments increasingly carried out in an ad hoc manner, taking advantage of participants' proximity to each other or by "piggybacking" onto other meetings bringing like-minded experts together—both yielding suboptimal outcomes. Neither of these scenarios would bode well for our ability to organize and carry out global collaboration on assessments of critical issues, the first presenting insurmountable financing challenges and the second leading to serious sacrifices in quality, scope, and representation.

# A Managed Commons Approach: Crowding It in the Cloud

Figure 6.1 shows comparative differences in quality and inclusiveness of the various approaches under consideration. The present system (quadrant A), as with the IPCC, is a semi-open process in which nominations are restricted by the plenary. The fact that there is some scrutiny over the experts nominated and selected gives this system a relatively high score on credibility but low on the inclusiveness of multiple disciplines and knowledge systems.

This is in contrast to other existing biodiversity-related assessments, which utilize a closed system (quadrant B), whereby nominations are not solicited and an executive body selects authors. The process is not open to outside experts and the entire process is limited to within the selected group. We score this process pretty low on scientific credibility, as there is no systematic mechanism to ensure experts' suitability for the tasks involved. It also scores low on inclusiveness due to the decreased likelihood of opposing ideological viewpoints within closed processes.

Quadrant C depicts a system in which there is no formal system of nomination or selection of authors. It is a completely open process, with all processes taking place virtually on an online platform. All are invited to present their work, which is then vetted by essentially anyone interested in doing so. This process mirrors Wikipedia in its operation. It, thus, also provides no guarantee of scientific credibility and, because it is not managed at all, could be either inclusive or exclusive of particular scientific fields, groups, or regions.

Quadrant D depicts a so-called managed commons. In this model, an initial group, nominated by governments and involved scientific bodies, is selected to oversee the process. This to a large extent ensures the political legitimacy of the process, while allowing for a reviewable input from a wider group of experts. This mechanism is similar to that utilized by private sector actors to "crowd-source" input into product design processes.

Our experience with the managed commons approach has so far been positive. A simplified version of the managed commons approach was used in preparing the background document for the development of the conceptual framework for the IPBES (UNU-IHDP 2011, 2012). A group of authors were selected based on their expertise in biodiversity and ecosystem services.[2] This group of experts used an online platform to facilitate inputs and responses. All records of discussions and document revisions were maintained and archived as a part of the online platform. While this initial discussion was not opened up to a broader group of scientists, it demonstrated the utility of the online platform for ensuring transparency and high levels of interaction.

The success of the online process was evident during the face-to-face workshop meeting that took place after a relatively detailed document had been developed. The speed at which approximately 25 experts— many who have had never before interacted with each other—were able to collaborate and produce a final document with which all of them were comfortable demonstrated a positive process. A three-day face-to-face finalization would have been impossible under previous processes. The next step would be to attempt a fully managed commons assessment and review system as suggested in the steps outlined as follows:

Step 1: Establish an online collaboration platform in the "clouds" to "crowd source" initial inputs.

Step 2: Identify coordinating lead authors through normal intergovernmental processes or any other formal process to secure legitimacy.

Step 3: Open process to wider scientific community but under clear and well-defined criteria for participation, managed by the group established in step 2.

Step 4: Establish author groups based on quality of inputs sourced from the crowd in the clouds, while paying attention to regional, gender, and disciplinary composition.

Step 5: Establish an oversight expert panel to oversee inputs from the commons to ensure quality and transparency of the whole process.

Step 6: Open review process.

Step 7: Establish a review board to oversee and mange review comments and ensure that they are addressed in a fair and transparent manner.

# Guiding Principles for Scientific Credibility

Ensuring the highest quality of science is a necessary condition for all assessment platforms including the IPBES (Farrell and Jäger 2005; Miller and Edwards 2001). One of the reasons cited for the establishment of the IPBES in some of the early documents was the lack of consistency in the quality of science across the assessments landscape.

## Principle 1: Transparency in Selection of Scientists and Reviewers

There are two key processes to ensure high science standards. The first involves the selection of the scientists for the platform and the second revolves around the reviewing process of the scientific outputs from the platform. In both cases, there needs to be a clear and open process whereby scientists can be nominated by all relevant parties including accredited scientific organizations and not just governments as in the case of most assessments. The final selection of the scientists has also been proposed by the scientific community to be overseen by an independent scientific body based on a set of criteria agreed by the plenary of the platform with final approval by the plenary. The same level of openness and transparency is suggested for the review process with an independent science body overseeing the review process of the outputs of the platform.

## Principle 2: Scientific Independence

Assessments done by the IPBES must be independent of any political and/or special interest. This will require making the negotiation process separate from the scientific work undertaken by the platform. One way of ensuring the independence is to establish two subsidiary bodies within the IPBES (UNU-IHDP 2011): the first (a bureau) is to focus on the administrative and political process within the platform while the second (science panel) will work primarily on the science. This would mean establishing a bureau which is tasked with overseeing the mandate of the platform on behalf of the plenary while the science panel co-chaired by a prominent natural and social scientist will focus solely on implementing the work programme of the platform with upmost scientific rigor and independence.

## Principle 3: Inclusiveness

The high degree of interconnectivity and interdependence among biodiversity, ecosystem services, and human well-being requires a trans-disciplinary approach to be taken by the IPBES. The platform needs to bring together a range of disciplines ranging from natural sciences to social sciences and humanities. But in addition to disciplines, there is also a need to include different knowledge systems. The important and relevant knowledge held by traditional and/or local knowledge on biodiversity and ecosystem services also requires the IPBES to embrace these knowledge systems within its various work components (UNU-IHDP 2012). But equally important is to include scientists with different ideologies and perspectives on the issue addressed. This is, in particular, critical among the social scientists involved in the study.

## Principle 4: Bottom-up Approach

The spatial-location-based nature of biodiversity and ecosystem services and their corresponding impacts on human well-being suggest a bottom-up approach to be taken up with a focus beginning at the regional and subregional scale. There was consensus among governments to build regional building blocks upon which the periodic global assessment would draw on and synthesize. It was also felt that this approach will suit the needs of the respective regions more closely than global activities in all areas of IPBES activities such as knowledge generation, policy support, and capacity building where the needs can be site- and context-specific.

# Conclusion

The rapid increase in information and communication technologies (ICT) and the growing use of the Internet to store and search for information makes it a viable tool for scientific research and collaboration. The former is already underway but the latter is still in the infant stages. This is especially true when it comes to the science–policy nexus.

The traditional method of limiting the selection of scientists to a few selected experts usually nominated and selected by the political community, instead of expanding the selection to the huge pool of scientists available, already constitutes a conflict of interest. The credibility of the science delivered cannot be guaranteed and it finally boils down to a hit or miss with the quality of the final outputs.

The rapid improvements in ICT and the use of the Internet have reduced the barriers to bringing together larger groups of scientists to work on any specific issue. There are a variety of ICT tools that can facilitate online discussions in a relatively cost-effective and efficient manner. Scientists can be brought together from remote places to centrally located common nodes and then connected to the online discussions. This will cut down travel expenses as well as make it more environment-friendly than the mega meetings bringing together over 1,000 scientists to share, discuss, and produce findings relevant to policy.

The uses of such modern technology also go towards bringing more scientists to the discussion and ensure quality and transparency in the process leading to final findings. In a similar manner, the review process can also be opened to an online process whereby scientists not involved in the process can provide their comments and suggestions for improving the final findings. This is critical as the mass of knowledge grows exponentially and the ability of covering this huge amount of literature by a selected few is humanly impossible.

There is scope for improving credible science that is urgently a need to address many of the social–economic–ecological problems societies face all over the world. The traditional system of producing policy-relevant scientific findings fails to bring together the full breadth of scientific knowledge available and more importantly fails to bring the different perspectives and views of scientists—in particular, social scientists—to the scientific process. This has in part played a role in weakening the role of science in the policy arena. The improvement of ICT tools and the rapid development of the Internet now makes these challenges manageable and improves the prospect of improving the credibility of scientific findings in the guidance of policy design and implementation.

In conclusion, this chapter would recommend the managed commons model for future scientific studies and assessments for the following reasons: (a) Such a model would allow experts from all levels to participate, bringing with them vast amount of knowledge that might otherwise have been lost. This is in particular relevant for the IPBES, which due to the nature of biodiversity and ecosystem service issues requires an extraordinarily broad input of knowledge and experience; (b) The process would be more transparent and inclusive—generationally, geographically, and among various disciplines—while preserving high scientific standards and quality control mechanisms; and (c) It is significantly more cost-effective than other comparable methods.

## Notes

1. Sciences in this chapter include natural as well as social sciences, which in the broadest sense include economics and the humanities.
2. Based on the analytical indicators such as number of relevant publications and involvement in science–policy activities.

## References

Banerjee, Bidisha, and George Collins. 2010. "Anatomy of IPCC's Mistake on Himalayan Glaciers and Year 2035." *Yale Climate Connections*. New Haven, CT: Yale School of Forestry and Environmental Studies, Yale University.

Convention on Biological Diversity (CBD). 2005. "Report of the Subsidary Body on Scientific, Technical and Technological Advice on the Work of Its Eleventh Meeting." Available at: http://www.cbd.int/doc/meetings/cop/cop-08/official/cop-08-03-en.doc (accessed on 26 April 2017).

Duraiappah, A.K. 2014. "Strengthening the Science–Policy Interface: Lessons from the Intergovernmental Platform on Biodiversity and Ecosystem Services." In *Handbook on the Economics of Biodiversity and Ecosystem Services*, edited by P. Nunes, P. Kumar, and T. Dedeurwaerdere. Cheltenham, UK, and Northampton, MA: Edward Elgar.

Duraiappah, A.K., and A. Bhardwaj. 2007. "Measuring Policy Coherence Among the MEAS and the MDG's." International Institute for Sustainable Development (IISD) Working Paper Series, IISD, Winnipeg, Manitoba.

Duraiappah, A.K., Martin Thormann, Jaya Sinnathamby, and Carmen Scherkenbach. 2012. "IPBES: Beyond Rhetoric." In *Dimensions: House of Cards*. Bonn, Germany: UNU-IHDP.

Farrell, A.E., and J. Jäger, eds. 2005. *Assessments of Regional and Global Environmental Risks: Designing Processes for the Effective Use of Science in Decision-making*. Washington, DC: RFF Press.

Hulme, Mike. 2010. "IPCC: Cherish It, Tweak It or Scrap It?" *Nature* 463 (7282): 730–32.

IAP. 2010. *Climate Change Assessments: Review of the Process and Procedures of the IPCC*. Netherlands: Inter-Academy Council.

ICSU, ISSC. 2015. *Review of the Sustainable Development Goals: The Science Perspective*. Paris: International Council for Science (ICSU).

Miller, C., and P.N. Edwards, eds. 2001. *Changing the Atmosphere: Expert Knowledge and Environmental Governance*. Cambridge: MIT Press.

Perrings, C., A.K. Duraiappah, A. Lariguarde, and H. Mooney. 2011. 'The Biodiversity and Ecosystem Services Science–Policy Interface." *Science* 331 (6021): 1139–40.

UNEP. 2009. *Report of the Second ad hoc Intergovernmental and Multi-stakeholder Meeting on an Intergovernmental Science Policy Platform on Biodiversity and Ecosystem Services*. UNEP/IPBES/2/4/Rev.1. Nairobi: UNEP/IPBES.

———. 2012. *Report of the Second Session of the Plenary Meeting to Determine Modalities and Institutional Arrangements for an Intergovernmental Science Policy Platform on Biodiversity and Ecosystem Services*. UNEP/IPBES.MI/2/9. Panama City: UNEP/IPBES.

UNU-IHDP. 2011. *Summary of Results from the International Science Workshop on Assessments for IPBES*. UNEP/IPBES. MI/1/INF/12. Nairobi: UNEP/IPBES.

———. 2012. *Summary of Results from the Second International Science Workshop on Assessments for IPBES*. UNEP/IPBES.MI/2/INF/10. Panama City: UNEP/IPBES.

# 7

# Traversing Diverse Paths in Ecological Economics with Enigmatic Models

Vikram Dayal*

> *The Econ tribe occupies a vast territory in the far North.... The dominant feature, which makes status relationships among the Econ of unique interest to the serious student, is the way that status is tied to the manufacture of certain implements, called "modls."*

Leijonhufvud (1973, 327–28)

## Introduction

"Shallow or deep economics?" asks Spash (2013, 351), while taking stock of ecological economics. He (ibid.) places a diverse scholarship in ecological economics in different, somewhat overlapping, camps and wants ecological economists to adopt an approach radically different from mainstream economics. Spash (ibid., 351) worries that

> Ecological economics and its policy recommendations have become overwhelmed by economic valuation, shadow pricing, sustainability measures, and squeezing nature into the commodity boxes of goods, services and capital in order to make it part of mainstream economic, financial and banking discourses. There are deeper concerns which touch upon the understanding of humanity in its various social, psychological, political and ethical facets.

Spash (ibid., 35) focuses on examining philosophies and approaches, rather than models, but he does state that, "Teaching economics via mathematical formalism as an exclusive approach positively rejects deep reflection and questioning by bounding concepts within a narrow language of presumed logic and unwarranted objectivity."

Lele (2009) reflected on interdisciplinarity in environmental economics in India. He recognized that "environmental economics is not considered synonymous with ecological economics in the West. Fortunately,

* I thank the organizers of the INSEE conference held in Tezpur University in December 2013 for inviting me, and the ecological economists present there. Nandan Nawn gave me several useful comments on an earlier draft of this chapter.

in the Indian context, this divide is not very sharp—the Indian Society for Ecological Economics includes economists of both hues" (ibid., 303). He discussed two kinds of crossings over disciplinary boundaries: (a) ecologizing economic analysis, and (b) socializing economic analysis. Lele focused on the barriers posed by embedded values and conflicting models.

In comparison with the papers by Spash (2013) and Lele (2009), this chapter has a relatively modest objective: It reflects on one aspect of ecological economics—the way we use theoretical and statistical models in the craft of ecological economics. However, the contents cover modelling aspects of ecological economics broadly defined, but draw on various other sub-disciplines of economics in seeing how such modelling aspects are approached and debated. In their everyday practice, whether in research or teaching, economists use and grapple with models. And ecological economists, faced with important questions of great significance such as the importance of ecosystems, or modifying the measures of national income of a country, or the relationship between dams and poverty, also use models to study and debate these issues.

First, I present a framework for thinking about theoretical and statistical models in terms of their attributes. Then I present different ways in which these attributes interplay in different analytical paths, first with theoretical models and then with statistical models. I use cases specific to ecological economics and also illustrate the argument with quotations from diverse scholars including Nobel laureates in economics. The ideas of the Nobel laureates are surprisingly more plural and sceptical than those in typical textbooks.

# A Framework for Thinking About Theoretical and Statistical Models

We make use of models (M) in environment and development economics: both theoretical models (T: $\underline{M}$) and statistical models (S: $\underline{M}$). I claim that these interact in different ways, but before we consider their interaction, I propose a framework (Figure 7.1) to help us think about these enigmatic objects that economists create and use. I use the word enigmatic deliberately here; indeed, it is one of the key points I would like to make. On closer inspection of models, they turn out to have aspects to them that are not immediately obvious. Also, economists not only use theoretical and statistical models, but there is also a distinct manner in which they do so.

## Theoretical Models

We can think of a theoretical model (T: $\underline{M}$) as having a list of attributes—variables (T: $\underline{V}$), axioms and assumptions (T: $\underline{A}$), and technique (T: $\underline{TE}$). The technique used could be mathematical or verbal. Assumptions and

**Figure 7.1**
*Attributes of theoretical and statistical models*

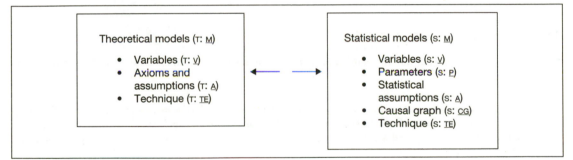

axioms are to some extent tied to the technique—constrained optimization techniques in neoclassical micro-economics use the axiom of rationality (Bromley 2006). Over a long period, an average economist invests in such techniques, so such axioms may become part of the economist's mental reflexes. The set of variables (T: $\underline{v}$) varies from problem to problem. In neoclassical economics, the set of variables (T: $\underline{v}$) usually includes prices and quantities.[1]

## Statistical Models

We can think of a statistical model (S: $\underline{M}$) as having the following list of attributes: a set of variables (S: $\underline{v}$), a causal graph (S: $\underline{CG}$), a set of parameters that are to be estimated (S: $\underline{P}$), a technique (S: $\underline{TE}$), and statistical assumptions (S: $\underline{A}$). We would have data on the variables (S: $\underline{v}$), which is connected with an implicit, default causal graph or an explicit causal graph. When we use regressions, the parameters we estimate include the coefficients and their standard errors. Often, attention is centred on the "significance" (often equated with statistical significance) of S: $\underline{P}$, S: $\underline{A}$, and not so much on S: $\underline{CG}$.

A particular economic analysis addresses a specific problem, by harnessing elements of a theoretical model (T: $\underline{M}$) and/or elements of a statistical model (S: $\underline{M}$). A problem may be framed in a new way by mapping a model used for a different purpose to the phenomenon being studied—we may use models of investment not just for the stock of machinery but also for investment in human capital (education), or nature (forest preservation). Our starting point may be the results of a regression (S: $\underline{M}$) of sulphur dioxide on per capita income, leading us to the metaphor of the Environmental Kuznets Curve, and we may then subsequently develop a theoretical model (T: $\underline{M}$) to explain the empirical finding. Or we may go from a theoretical model (T: $\underline{M}$) of monetary valuation of air pollution to a statistical model (S: $\underline{M}$).

I now consider how different attributes of theoretical and statistical models come into play in economic analysis and are used by economists to traverse different analytical paths; I use the notation for the attributes of these models as set out in the framework above.

# Attributes of Theoretical Models and Economic Analysis

Nobel Laureate Robert Solow wrote (1956, 65), "All theory depends on assumptions that are not quite true. This is what makes it theory. The art of successful theorizing is to make the inevitable simplifying assumptions in such a way that the final results are not very sensitive."

Varian (1989) provides several examples of the use of economic theory: A theoretical model (T: $\underline{M}$) can guide us when we do not have data on the effects of a new tax; a theoretical model can tell us what parameters (S: $\underline{P}$) we need to estimate to shed light on the claim that taxes can be increased by decreasing the tax rate. Varian (ibid.) also suggests that theory helps us with computations, and economics gives us numerical support for decision-making. However, since models require assumptions, we turn to consideration of assumptions (T: $\underline{A}$).

## Axioms and Assumptions (T: $\underline{A}$)

Bromley (2006, 87), who could be regarded as a critic of standard economics, reflects on how economists fix belief:

> The standard approach to economics is embedded in the hypothetico-deductive method. On this approach, primitive axioms (covering laws) inform the search for particular assumptions and applicability postulates that will then suggest hypotheses to be tested against data from the "real" world. The axioms entail postulates of rationality,

self-interest, stable preferences, and the alleged desire to maximize utility. Indeed, the core axioms of economic theory are rarely subjected to tests of their veracity.

As early as 1955, Nobel Laureate Herbert Simon had also written about the assumptions about economic man (Simon 1955, 99):

> This man is assumed to have knowledge of the relevant aspects of his environment which, if not absolutely complete, is at least impressively clear and voluminous. He is assumed also to have a well-organized and stable system of preferences, and a skill in computation that enables him to calculate, for the alternative courses of action that are available to him, which of these will permit him to reach the highest attainable point on his preference scale.

As we saw earlier, Bromley mentions "standard" economics, but, of course, what is "standard" changes over time—behavioural economics has emerged in recent years. Devarajan (2014, 353) in his comments on a study, estimating the value of statistical life, points out the shadow cast on the usual theoretical assumptions (T: A):

> [T]he past decade has seen a burgeoning… "behavioural economics" literature—that questions whether individuals do in fact behave according to the rational-agent model…. This compelling evidence in the behavioural economics literature leads one to ask: are the estimates derived from standard WTP estimates, which assume agents are following neoclassical assumptions, valid under alternative behavioural models?

Nobel Laureate Kahneman, closely associated with behavioural economics, was involved in contingent valuation studies. Some environmental economists believe that contingent valuation has a vital role in such diverse settings as the preservation of species and the value of sickness due to air pollution. Contingent valuation method (CVM) gained great momentum when it was used in the US courts for assessments of damage. Interestingly, Kahneman in a paper with Knetsch investigates one of the key issues in CVM, that of embeddedness:

> Another problem for CVM is an effect that we call embedding, also variously labeled as a part-whole effect, symbolic effect, or disaggregation effect… the same good is assigned a lower value if WTP for it is inferred from WTP for a more inclusive good rather than if the particular good is evaluated on its own…. This result appears to invalidate a basic assumption of CVM: that standard value theory applies to the measures obtained by this method…. Our tentative conclusion is that the factor that controls the magnitude of the embedding effect is not the distinction between public goods that have use value and those that only have non-use value. A more important distinction could be between public goods for which private purchase is conceivable and other goods for which it is not. (Kahneman and Knetsch 1992, 57–69)

These observations from eminent economists do plant a seed of doubt on some axioms that underlie constrained optimization models; however, we may still rely on constrained optimization models because models by their nature are useful abstractions, but we should not lose sight of the context in which we are applying them.

## Constrained Optimization is a Flexible Technique, but We Need to Keep in Mind the Context

Economists frequently use theoretical models that use the technique of constrained optimization (T: TE)—an objective function is maximized subject to one or more constraints. According to Screpanti and Zamagni (2005, 381), "Samuelson's argument, that all the problems faced by economics (in the neoclassical approach) can be reduced to problems of constrained maximization, was very important."

We can move from successive domains of applicability with the same mathematical technique of constrained optimization, but the context is changing and how much we are stretching the applicability of the model is a matter of judgement, perhaps of taste. Surely, we can distinguish between the following contexts:

- A simple choice by a consumer between two simple commodities that they can understand reasonably well: tea and coffee, butter and jam, etc.
- An inter-temporal choice by a consumer: current and future consumption, etc.
- Very difficult choices: Should I put all my wealth into paying for a risky surgery for one of my four children?
- Choices in the public realm: Should I pay for the preservation of a bird species?

Nobel Laureate Vernon L. Smith (1998) suggests that it is important to

> distinguish impersonal market exchange and personal exchange. Noncooperative behavior in the former maximizes the gains from exchange, the basis of specialization and wealth creation. Cooperative behavior in personal exchange is based on reciprocity—trading gifts, favours, and assistance across time—which maximizes the gains from social exchange. That people can be both cooperative and noncooperative is corroborated in laboratory experiments and is postulated to stem from a self-interested propensity for exchange in markets and friendships.

We generally use optimizing models to capture the choices or behaviour of people. But within a household, norms and identity may be influencing choices, not necessarily optimizing models. This issue is considered in section "Reinterpreting the Instrumental Variable to Think About the Theoretical Model" later in this chapter. There we will see that if the role of norms and identity are acknowledged, one way ahead is to incorporate them in the theoretical model, as done for example by Akerlof and Kranton (2010). Sethi and Somanathan (1996) examined the evolution of social norms using an evolutionary game-theoretic framework. And in section "Game Theory Models Give us Very Different Insights," I briefly consider how game theory gives us very different insights from models, which don't incorporate strategic interaction.

## Choosing Variables in the Theoretical Model to Fit the Context

Models using constrained optimization (T: TE) are extremely flexible, and by suitably selecting variables in the theoretical model (T: V), we can make them fit a context. The economic models used by analysts in developed countries to examine the benefits of reducing air pollution are aimed at modern pollution. Often, however, people in developing countries experience the worst of both traditional air pollution resulting from the use of biomass fuels for cooking and the air pollution resulting from industry and transport.

Das et al. (2009) aimed to understand and evaluate the total exposure to air pollution in the mining regions of Goa, India. Das et al. (ibid.) adapted the standard air pollution valuation model as presented in Freeman's (1993) book. Das et al. (2009) developed a model drawing on health production models (Harrington and Portney 1987), agricultural household models (Singh, Squire and Strauss 1986), and a branch of environmental health sciences, "Total Exposure Assessment" (Smith 1993). A key consideration was the correspondence between the theoretical model (T: M) and the statistical model (S: M). Therefore, variables in the theoretical model (T: V) had to correspond to variables in the statistical model (S: V).

I now compare a few features of the basic theoretical model in terms of variables (T: V) used to value reduction in morbidity due to air pollution in Freeman (1993) with Das et al. (2009).

In Freeman (1993), sickness $S = S(C, a, b)$, where C is the concentration, a is averting activity, and b is mitigating activities. On the other hand, in Das et al. (2009), sickness of an individual depends on total exposure to pollution of that individual (which can vary between persons in a household) E, consumption of cooked food (CF), doctor visits (D), individual characteristics ($Z_i$), and household characteristics ($Z_{hh}$): $S_i = S_i(E_i, CF_i, D_i; Z_i, Z_{hh})$. Total exposure incorporates time spent in different micro-environments, but unlike in some western cities where people may avoid going outdoors on bad days, here the concentration indoors, particularly in the kitchen, may be high. Here, the only mitigating activity considered is doctor visits.

A marked contrast between Freeman (1993) and Das et al. (2009) is the more detailed treatment of total exposure, $E_i$, by Das et al.:

$$E_i = t_o{}^i C_o + t_k{}^i C_k + t_w{}^i C_w + t_{in}{}^i C_{in},$$

where d denotes time, i indexes individuals, o is for outdoor, k for the kitchen, w for work, in for outdoor, and C denotes concentration. So Co, that is, outdoor concentration is not assumed to be the dose as in Freeman (1993), but is only one component of total exposure.

Another difference in the two models is the utility functions. In Freeman (1993), this is U(X, f, S), where X, f, and s are consumption, leisure, and sickness, respectively. In Das et al. (2009), $U=U(S^C, S^{AM}, S^{AF}, X^{NF})$, where S is sickness and X denotes consumption. The key difference is that in Das et al. (2009) children (C), adult males (AM), and adult females (AF) are distinguished.

Finally, in Freeman (1993), time spent working is a choice variable, but in Das et al. (2009), there is a choice between time spent in several activities and associated micro-environments, including, in the case of adult females, cooking, and gathering biomass for fuel. Thus, the model used by analysts in the developed world was modified to better suit the context of the mining villages of Goa, India. Not including cooking, for example, would be like not including smoking in an epidemiological study of the effects of air pollution in the developed world.

## Moving to the Imperfect Aggregate Economy in Resource Accounting

Resource accounting aims to measure sustainability, providing corrections to conventionally measured measures of the aggregate economy. Resource accounting is often based on theoretical models in which a representative agent conducts a dynamic optimization (T: TE) exercise over time. The theoretical model (T: TE) is used to guide and interpret the accounting, whereas the data come from the messy real world. Nobel Laureate Solow (1994) comments on models that use inter-temporally optimizing representative agents: "Maybe I reveal myself merely as old-fashioned, but I see no redeeming social value in using this construction, which Ramsey intended as a representation of the decision-making of an idealized policymaker, as if it were a descriptive model of an industrial capitalist economy."

Dasgupta and Maler (2009) incorporate the role of institutions, in contrast to the usual theoretical model of sustainability, including their own previous work (Dasgupta, Kristrom, and Maler 1997), which leaves out institutions. I compare two models: DM2 (Dasgupta and Maler 2009) with DKM1 (Dasgupta, Kristrom, and Maler 1997); we can use mathematical techniques innovatively to frame an issue differently.

In both DM2 and DKM1, welfare over time is very similar. In DM2, welfare at time t is

$$W_t = \int_t^\infty U(C_\tau)e^{-(\tau-t)}d\tau,$$

where C is the aggregate consumption. In DKM1 current social welfare, U is a function not only of C but also of the environment and labour.

The key difference between DKM1 and DM2 is the use of α—a resource allocation mechanism—by DM2. The co-evolution of institutions and the state of the economy is reflected in α. This means that C, resource flows R, and capital stocks K, are functions of α. The value function V can be written as

$$V(K_t, \alpha_{,t}) = W_t, \text{ where } W_t \text{ is given by the expression above.}$$

DKM1 use optimal control theory (T: TE) to derive what adjustments should be made to obtain the net national product (NNP)—this is common in theoretical models dealing with this issue—and the model is silent about institutions. DM2 innovatively define sustainable development as a path where $dV_t/dt \geq 0$. By using the value function directly, and assuming that $\alpha$ is autonomous, DM2 show that $dVt/dt = \Sigma p_{it} \, dK_{it}/dt = I \geq 0$ on a sustainable development path.

The different approaches have significantly different implications. DM2 argue that sustainable development requires examining wealth and not gross national product (GNP) or even NNP, whereas in DKM1, they derived results for adjustments to NNP.

## Game Theory Models Give us Very Different Insights

We can use the technique (T: TE) of constrained optimization, with assumptions of rationality (T: A), and in the case of a perfectly competitive market, individual and social rationality coincide. Game theory, a different technique (T: TE), can be used to model other situations. Game theory helps us model interdependent decisions for more than one person. If we consider two persons, each person's decision depends on the other's. While game theory seems to be a purely technical extension of single person optimization, it often leads to different insights. Notably, game theory can show the tension between individual and social rationality and its resolution through collective action.

Garett Hardin (1968) portrayed the over-exploitation of the commons as an inexorable tragedy. We can capture the essence of the idea of the tragedy of the commons by modelling the use of the commons as a Prisoner's Dilemma game with two players, who could conserve or plunder (Wydick 2008). In the Hardin story, the tragedy is almost inevitable and the actors are trapped in the Prisoner's Dilemma. However, the essence of collective action is transforming the game itself. If either the state or the community imposes a substantial fine whenever an actor plunders the commons, the game is transformed. Now the Nash equilibrium is where both actors conserve—the game is no longer a Prisoner's Dilemma. Thus, the tragedy of the commons is not inevitable.

## Frameworks Can Be More Inclusive than Models

We can think of frameworks—which are more general than models (T: M)—and include more elements of reality. A framework may include more than one model. Nobel Laureate Elinor Ostrom developed the Institutional Analysis and Development framework. In this framework, the context influences the action arena and interactions, which lead to outcomes. Outcomes can feed back into the context and the action arena and interactions. Some action arenas and interactions may be represented by a game theory model. Among the contextual or exogenous variables are rules or institutional arrangements. Thus, we have a more inclusive view—institutions can help resolve social dilemmas represented by game theory models.

Ostrom (2005, 5–7) wrote,

> Can we dig below the immense diversity of regularized social interactions in markets, hierarchies, ... and other situations to identify universal building blocks used in crafting all such structured situations? ... While the usefulness of a universal *model* of rational behavior is challenged ... the assumption of a universal framework composed of nested sets of components within components for explaining human behavior is retained throughout ... the approach presented here encompasses contemporary game theory as one of the theories that is consistent with the IAD framework. Also included, ... are broader theories that assume individuals are fallible learners trying to do the best they can in the long term by using norms and heuristics in making their immediate decisions.

Ostrom (2009) used the Institutional Analysis and Development framework to synthesize studies of 47 irrigation systems and 44 fisheries. She found that farmer-managed irrigation systems performed better than government irrigation systems, and informal fishery groups allocated space, time, and technology to reduce over-harvesting. The studies by her and other scholars of common pool resources are of critical importance to the question of sustainability in developing countries.

# Attributes of Statistical Models and Economic Analysis

How do the theoretical model (T: $\underline{M}$) and statistical model (S: $\underline{M}$) relate? There is a tension between a theoretical model and a statistical model—a theoretical model is a thought experiment abstracting from all but a few key features of reality, whereas a linear regression, for example, needs to include relevant variables or it might lead to omitted variable bias. In the earlier stage of the development of econometrics, theory (T: $\underline{M}$) held sway over the statistical model (S: $\underline{M}$); but over time, the idea that there should be feedbacks from the statistical model gained acceptance (Maddala and Lahiri 2009). And, as we shall see, in several studies today the theoretical model may be verbal or even insignificant. While this may dismay purists, I think the greater role of statistical models today has led to a greater diversity of phenomena studied.

The different components of a statistical model are closely related; the nature of the dependent variable (S: $\underline{V}$) plays a key role in the statistical technique (S: $\underline{TE}$), the statistical variables included (S: $\underline{V}$) or excluded change the estimated parameter values (S: $\underline{P}$), etc. Manski (2013) has highlighted the key roles of assumptions in deriving conclusions from data. Manski (ibid.) states his law of decreasing credibility: As researchers make stronger assumptions, they get sharper results, but at the cost of lower credibility.

## Ingeniously Combining a Simple Valuation Model with a Data-based Ecology Simulation Model

Chopra and Adhikari (2004) simulated ecology–economy interactions in the Keoladeo National Park. In my interpretation, they go beyond the variables suggested by the theoretical travel cost model (T: $\underline{V}$) in the set used in their simulation model. This is critical in linking ecology with the economy. They use time series data on the ecology of the park and carry out a dynamic numerical simulation. Their analysis is distinct from both static valuation exercises and typical dynamic but stylized mathematical bioeconomic models that rely on dynamic optimization.

In traditional recreational valuation, the number of trips is a function of travel cost incurred and household characteristics; in Chopra and Adhikari (ibid.), the number of trips is also a function of the ecological health of the park. The ecological health of the park was parametrized (S: $\underline{P}$) by using medium- or long-run time series data (S: $\underline{V}$) and by modelling the wetland system (S: $\underline{M}$). Upstream demand for water influences the ecological health of the wetland. Changing stocks of water, biomass, and birds in it determine the state of the wetland. Thus, the short-term value is linked to the long-term value (Figure 7.2).

Chopra and Adhikari (ibid.) made projections for key variables for 23 years on a monthly basis. They found that (from the travel cost model) the visits by tourists were not responsive to private costs. The direct and indirect income from the park depended on ecological health indices. Further, the response or elasticity of income was more at high values of the ecological health indices. In other words, not only was the ecological health a significant determinant of income from the park but the relationship also was marked by a non-linearity as the ecological health indices varied over time. Although mathematical bioeconomic models often incorporate various non-linearities, Chopra and Adhikari (ibid.) bring in ecological complexities into the valuation exercise, in contrast to static valuation models that often abstract from ecological complexity.

**Figure 7.2**
*The link between static value and ecological dynamics*

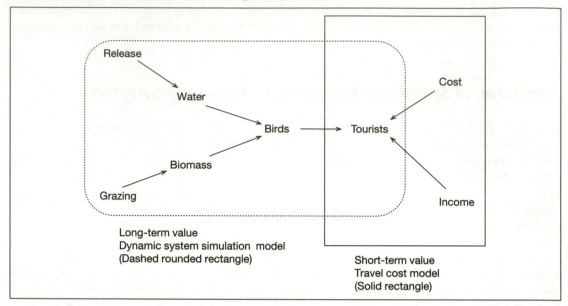

*Source:* Chopra and Adhikari 2004.

## Using Structural Break Techniques to Empirically Examine Ecosystem Flips

Another use of statistical models (s: M) is studying sudden, catastrophic changes in ecosystems. According to Scheffer et al. (2001, 591), "Nature is usually assumed to respond to gradual change in a smooth way. However, studies on lakes, coral reefs, oceans, forests and arid lands have shown that smooth change can be interrupted by sudden drastic switches to a contrasting state." Ecology is complex—it is non-linear, dynamic, and often not easily controlled or predicted.

According to Andersen et al. (2008), ecologists should draw on other disciplines when they study regime shifts, for example, draw on tests of structural breaks developed in econometrics. We see the role of a statistical technique (s: TE) here. Since 1990, econometric tests of deterministic versus stochastic trends, and structural breaks have been developed. A trend is a persistent long-term movement of a variable over time. Modern econometrics distinguishes between stochastic and deterministic trends. A deterministic trend is a non-random function of time (e.g., a clearly visible steady growth of 5%/year). A stochastic trend is random and varies over time (Stock and Watson 2010). In addition to a stochastic or a deterministic trend, a time series variable may have a structural break. A structural break is a change in the parameters of a model characterizing the variable (e.g., slope or level). The distinction between a stochastic and a deterministic trend break is based on how frequent the shocks to the trend are (Hansen 2001). In a stochastic trend, shocks occur frequently, while in the case of a deterministic trend with a break, shocks occur at the break. The statistical tests for a stochastic trend are sensitive to the presence of structural breaks. Hence, both stochastic trends and breaks should be tested.

## Regression Models and Causality

I now turn to an enigmatic aspect of statistical models—causality. Issues of causality become very important from a policy perspective. Nobel Laureate Herbert Simon (1953, 56) used an arrow to designate cause:

"A→B if and only if A is a direct cause…of B"; and provides an example from economics: "poor growing weather → small wheat crops → increase in price of wheat." In more recent years, Judea Pearl has built on the basic device of a causal graph to represent causality.

In the following quotation, Pearl (1999, 1) emphasizes the distinction between causal thinking and probability theory, which he suggests is key to gaining insight into the enigma of causality:

> The word cause is not in the vocabulary of standard probability theory. It is an embarrassing yet inescapable fact that probability theory, the official language of many empirical sciences, does not permit us to express sentences such as "Mud does not cause rain"; all we can say is that the two events are mutually correlated, or dependent—meaning that if we find one, we can expect to encounter the other. Scientists seeking causal explanations for complex phenomena or rationales for policy decisions must therefore supplement the language of probability with a vocabulary for causality, one in which the symbolic representation for the causal relationship "Mud does not cause rain" is distinct from the symbolic representation for "Mud is independent of rain."

To summarize, we use probability for empirical work, but causal thinking requires a directional arrow: rain → mud. The arrows in the causal graph (s: CG) show us the subset of statistical assumptions (s: A) that are "causal" in nature; or, that are required for a causal interpretation.

If we want to explore the effect of X on Y, following Morgan and Winship (2007), we can list the key ingredients of causal graphs (s: CG) as follows:

- Common cause (controlling for M, the common cause, will block the path): X←M→Y. Here, M causes X as well as Y.
- Mediator (controlling for Z will block the path): X→Z→Y. Here, X causes Z and Z causes Y.
- Collider (controlling for B opens the path): X→B←Y. Here, X and Y are both causes of B.

If we should control for a variable depends on whether it is a common cause, a mediator, or a collider. However, we need to see the causal graph (s: CG) as a whole. Figure 7.3 illustrates three specification options for studying the effect of X on Y, given the causal graph.

**Figure 7.3**
*Causal graph and regression options*

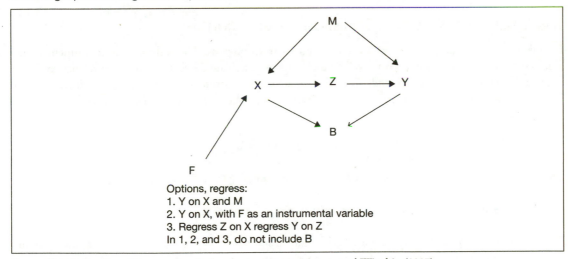

Options, regress:
1. Y on X and M
2. Y on X, with F as an instrumental variable
3. Regress Z on X regress Y on Z
In 1, 2, and 3, do not include B

*Source:* Based on various figures and and related exposition in Morgan and Winship (2007).

If we wish to study the causal effect of X on Y, we can also experimentally vary X and see how the outcome of the experiment, Y, varies between the "treatment" and the "control" group. In this case, we free X from the influence of M if our experiment is carefully designed.

However, although experiments are increasingly being used by economists, they are often not feasible, and so we might need to use a theoretical model (T: M) or detailed knowledge to enlighten us about causality.[2] But Hoover (2012, 92) draws our attention to a perennial conundrum in this context: "[I]f we know the true theory, we can dispense with empirical study; but how do we know that the theory is true?"

## Effects of a Cause Versus Causes of Effects

One can ask, "What are the causes of an effect or what are the effects of causes?" (Holland 1993). At the first glance, this may appear to be a play on words; actually, it is significant. It is far more difficult, and vague, to find out about the causes of deforestation than to ask whether a certain intervention resulted in an effect on the forest cover.

How do we compare the efficacy of state and community forest management? Somanathan, Prabhakar, and Mehta (2009) studied the long-run effects of transfer of management of some areas of the state-managed forest to local communities in the central Himalayas of India. The authors found that village council management cost an order of magnitude less per unit area and did no worse in terms of conservation than state management.

Separating out the effects of decentralization from other factors affecting forests is difficult (ibid.). The authors compared the costs of managing state forests with village council forests. They used government data for state forest costs and survey data for the costs of village council forests. The costs of managing state forests were at least seven times more per hectare compared to the costs of managing village council forests.

We now consider the variables used (s: V). The authors used the percentage of crown cover to compare state- and village council-managed forests. Since the devolution of state forests to council management was done in 1930, the authors went through historical records; they found that the areas kept as state forests were systematically different from those devolved to village councils. To account for this initial difference in assignment of areas, the authors controlled for aspect and population density in their regressions.[3]

As a check on their results, they also used the method of matching (s: TE)—comparing satellite image polygons of village council lands and state forests that were as close to each other as possible. They concluded that state forests did not have greater forest cover than comparable village council forests. Only such a careful statistical study credibly establishes the credentials of community management of forests.

## The Enigmatic Nature of Statistical Assumptions

I think statistical assumptions (s: A) are subtle and far from obvious. The technique of instrumental variables (s: TE) is magical when it works well, allowing us to glean causal effects from observational data, and overcoming endogeneity. As a prelude to discussing enigmatic instrumental variables and their use in some interesting case studies, I describe the statistical assumptions behind using instrumental variables.

Let our regression equation be

$$Y_i = \beta_0 + \beta_1 X_i + u_i, i = 1,\ldots,n$$

and let $X_i$ be correlated with $u_i$ because of simultaneous causality (i.e., X and Y cause each other).

We could use an instrumental variable Z to estimate the effect $\beta_1$ of X on Y.

The conditions for a valid instrument are (a) instrument relevance: the correlation between Z and X should not be zero and should be high, and (b) instrument exogeneity: the correlation between Z and u should be zero.

We can test for instrument relevance statistically, but exogeneity is subtle—we need to use thinking and judgement. If we have more than one instrument, we can use a statistical test to aid our thinking and judgement, but it is "incumbent on both the empirical analyst and the critical reader to use their own understanding of the empirical application to evaluate whether this assumption is reasonable" (Stock and Watson 2010, 454).

Nobel Laureate Deaton (2010, 31) distinguishes between variables that are external (whose variables are not set or caused by the variables in the model) and those that are exogenous (orthogonal to the error term). He writes:

> Failure to separate externality and exogeneity—or to build a case for the validity of the exclusion restrictions—has caused, and continues to cause, endless confusion in the applied development (and other) literatures. Natural or geographic variables … distance from the equator, … land gradient (as an instrument for dam construction in explaining poverty, Duflo and Rohini Pande 2007), … are not affected by the variables being explained, and are clearly external.… Whether any of these instruments is exogenous (or satisfies the exclusion restrictions) depends on the specification of the equation of interest, and is not guaranteed by its externality. And because exogeneity is an identifying assumption that must be made prior to analysis of the data, empirical tests cannot settle the question.… Passing an overidentification test does not validate instrumentation.

As I see it, statistical models are enigmatic, not only because we require judgement with respect to their assumptions (s: A) but also because we need to use judgement with respect to the tests of statistical assumptions.

## Damning Dams with an Instrumental Variable?

Dams are controversial development projects. Environmentalists often criticize dams. Advocates suggest that they help growth and therefore are needed in developing countries to alleviate poverty. And yet, protests by those who will lose control over natural resources because of a dam are a part of what Ramachandra Guha (2005) and Martinez-Alier (2014) call the "environmentalism of the poor." How would we assess the effect of dams?

A comprehensive cost-benefit analysis would look at the costs (e.g., displacement) and the benefits (e.g., increased agricultural production). Usually, the project agency prepares a document suggesting diverse effects. Typically, the analyst uses this and other information to guess at the effects; such an exercise is a bundle of implicit causal claims. Moreover, underlying the welfare calculations is a theoretical model (T: M). However, in statistical evaluation, the outcome of some intervention is assessed statistically, with careful attention to causality. Instead of implicit causal claims, we make statistical assumptions (s: A) that are often subtle.

According to Duflo and Pande (2007), by 2000, 19 per cent of the world's electricity and 30 per cent of its irrigated area were accounted for by dams. But dams had displaced over 40 million people. There was no systematic empirical evidence on how the average large dam affected the poor. They study this question for India.

Duflo and Pande's paper is notable for harnessing the combined power of several data sets for different sets of variables—dam location, river gradient, agricultural production, and rural poverty. The authors paid careful attention to biophysical features of dams, and used this knowledge to estimate the causal effects of dams. The unit of analysis is a district, which is a sub-state administrative tier in India. They distinguish between districts upstream of a dam and those downstream of a dam.

Duflo and Pande argue that dams and agricultural production simultaneously influence each other—dams can affect agricultural production, but states with high agricultural production can build more dams. Duflo and Pande use river gradient as an instrumental variable to overcome simultaneity.[4] They find that dam construction significantly increases agricultural production (0.34%) and yield (0.19%) in the downstream districts. However, each dam is associated with a significant poverty increase (headcount ratio) of 0.77 per cent in its own district. Although poverty decreases in downstream districts, the poverty reduction in downstream districts is insufficient to compensate for the poverty increase in the dam's own district.

## Reinterpreting the Instrumental Variable to Think About the Theoretical Model

I now offer a reinterpretation of the instrumental variable that was meant to unpack causality (s: <u>CG</u>) using the air pollution study by Das et al. (2009), discussed earlier. The authors of the study tried to examine the effect of total exposure to air pollution (i.e., indoor plus outdoor pollution weighted by the time spent). They knew they had measurement error and they suspected simultaneous causation; the authors struggled to overcome these problems. Exposure is a cause of sickness which is a cause of the inability to work, which in turn affects the allocation of time to different activities and exposure to air pollution. A paper by Pitt, Rosenzweig, and Hassan (2005) on the health effects of indoor air pollution, which used female hierarchy as an instrumental variable, helped them establish the causal effect of exposure on sickness.

In the theoretical model (T: <u>M</u>) that they used, as with Pitt et al. (ibid.), Das et al. (2009) assumed that the household was optimizing utility, which guided the empirical research. Following Nobel Laureate Friedman's (1953) ideas about "The Methodology of Positive Economics" broadly, Das et al. (2009) did not worry much about whether the household was actually optimizing; what mattered to them most was the prediction or getting the regression "right." But the efficacy of the instrumental variable—female hierarchy, in this instance—should make us reflect because it lends support to a view of the household which is in tune with the role of norms and identity. Nobel Laureate Akerlof and co-author Kranton (2010) argue that gender matters in the workplace in the United States, and suggest that careful observations rather than statistical tests are more enlightening in studying identity. Akerlof and Kranton (ibid.) seek to modify, rather than abandon, formal theoretical models. They modify the utility function, so central in microeconomic theoretical models, to incorporate identity.

## Granger Causality or Precedence?

At times appearances may be deceptive. Is Granger causality—a relatively easily implementable statistical technique (s: <u>TE</u>) developed by Nobel Laureate Clive Granger—about precedence rather than causality?

Govindaraju and Tang (2013) claim that "in the case of India...policymakers can be confident that there will not be any long run implication of the energy conservation policies for India." The basis of their assertion is the result of their econometric analysis that "we could only find evidence of uni-directional Granger causality running from real GDP growth to growth of coal consumption in the short run." Govindaraju and Tang make causal claims on the basis of a Granger causality test.

Hendry and Mizon (1999) review Granger causality comprehensively and sympathetically, and write:

> Granger causality is both pervasive, and important, in econometric modelling.... but many of its effects do not in fact depend on the role that Granger causality was initially designed to play, namely testing for actual causality. Moreover, finding Granger causality in an empirical model does not necessarily entail causal links—in the sense of genuine influences in the real world—nor does the empirical absence of Granger causality entail no link.

They provide the definition of Granger causality, distinguishing between Granger causality and its empirical implementation:

> If, in the universe of information, deleting the history of one set of variables does not alter the joint distribution of any of the remaining variables, then the omitted variables were defined...not to cause the remaining variables.... In practice, many authors have applied the idea to eliminating variables from a small set, as in bivariate modeling for example. Without the untenable assumption that the small set of variables selected is indeed the universe of relevant information, nothing about causality in the DGP can be deduced from the empirical evidence.

Leamer (1985) had earlier questioned the definition: "I strongly object to the use of the words Granger causality when precedence or its equivalent more accurately communicates the concept."

Often, Granger causality is applied via the technique (s: TE) of a reduced form vector autoregression (VAR):

$$y_t = \pi_{11} y_{t-1} + \pi_{12} x_{t-1} + v_{1t}$$

$$x_t = \pi_{21} y_{t-1} + \pi_{22} x_{t-1} + v_{2t}$$

The reduced form does not include the contemporaneous values of y and x that are there in the structural form. Or, the reduced form abstracts from the causal graph (s: CG), $x_t \rightarrow y_t$ and $y_t \rightarrow x_t$. If this is a reduced form VAR, because we have no $x_t$ on the right-hand side of the first equation and no $y_t$ on the right-hand side of the second equation, then in order to say anything about the causal effect of x on y we need a structural VAR. Or, we cannot ignore the causal graph. We, therefore, need to use an instrument, or an "exogenous" variable that appears in one equation and not in the other. To use the example of supply and demand, weather could shift the supply curve and help us identify the demand curve. According to Stock and Watson (2001), "VARs are powerful tools for describing data…. Whether 20 years of VARs have produced lasting contributions to structural inference and policy analysis is more debatable."

In other words, VARS help us explore data to see the pattern of correlations as variables affect each other over time. But in order to say how an intervention on a variable will affect the values, over time, of another variable we need to take a structural approach, and this will mean either drawing on some information on the structure, or making causal, as distinct from statistical, assumptions.

## Conclusions

This chapter discussed ways in which theoretical (T: M) and statistical models (s: M) are used in ecological economics. Faced with complex systems and trying to answer ambitious questions, we turn to models. Perhaps we should avoid two extremes—of taking models either too seriously or not at all seriously (Fox 2008)—and exercise our judgement allied with what Norgaard (1989) called methodological pluralism. Or, we may recognize that models may both help us see beyond the surface appearance of reality and also filter our vision so that we miss out on key aspects of reality. Keynes (1938) wrote, "Economics is a science of thinking in terms of models joined to the art of choosing models which are relevant to the contemporary world." The art of choosing models, requiring judgement and wisdom, is far more difficult than the science of thinking in terms of models.

## Notes

1. While it is true that it is not only neoclassical economists who include prices and quantities, neoclassical economists greatly emphasize these variables (Benham 2008), and also use these variables along with the axiom of rationality, etc.
2. I have referred earlier to Vernon Smith's work. Work in experimental economics has led to a more nuanced approach to rationality by economists.
3. In physical geology, aspect is the compass direction that a slope faces.
4. We saw earlier that Deaton (2010) has expressed reservations about this instrumental variable.

# References

Akerlof, G.A., and R.E. Kranton. 2010. *Identity Economics: How Our Identities Shape Our Work, Wages, and Well-being*. Oxford: Princeton University Press.

Andersen, T., J. Christensen, E. Hernandez-Garcia, and C.M. Duarte. 2008. "Ecological Thresholds and Regime Shifts: Approaches to Identification." *Trends in Ecology and Evolution* 24(1): 49–57.

Benham, L. 2008. "Licit and Illicit Responses to Regulation." In *Handbook of New Institutional Economics*, edited by C. Menard and M.M. Shirley, 591–608. New York: Springer.

Bromley, D.W. 2006. *Sufficient Reason*. Princeton, NJ: Princeton University Press.

Chopra, K., and S.K. Adhikari. 2004. "Environment Development Linkages: Modelling Wetland System for Ecological and Economic Value." *Environment and Development Economics* 9 (1): 19–45.

Das, S., V. Dayal, A. Murugesan, R. Uma, M. Sehgal, and S.K. Chhabra. 2009. "An Integrated Empirical Model of Health Effects of Air Pollution: The Case of Mining in Goa, India." IEG Discussion Paper, Institute of Economic Growth, Delhi.

Dasgupta, P., B. Kristrom, and K.G. Maler. 1997. "The Environment and Net National Product." In *The Environment and Emerging Development Issues*, Vol. 1, edited by P. Dasgupta and K.G. Maler. Oxford: Oxford University Press.

Dasgupta, P., and K.G. Maler. 2009. "Some Recent Developments." In *Oxford Handbook of Environmental Economics in India*, edited by K. Chopra and V. Dayal. New Delhi: Oxford University Press.

Deaton, A. 2010. "Instruments, Randomization, and Learning about Development." *Journal of Economic Literature* 48 (June): 424–55.

Devarajan, S. 2014. Comments on "Estimating the Value of Statistical Life." In *Environment and Development Economics: Essays in Honor of Sir Partha Dasgupta*, edited by S. Barett, K.-G. Maler, and E.S. Maskin. Oxford: Oxford University Press.

Duflo, E. and R. Pande 2007. "Dams." *Quarterly Journal of Economics* 122(2): 601–46.

Fox, J. 2008. *Applied Regression Analysis and Generalized Linear Models*. New York: SAGE Publications.

Freeman, A.M. 1993. *The Measurement of Environmental and Resource Values: Theory and Methods*. Washington, DC: Resources for the Future.

Friedman, M. 1953. "The Methodology of Positive Economics." In *Essays in Positive Economics*, edited by M. Friedman. Chicago, IL: University of Chicago Press.

Govindaraju, V.G.R.C., and C.F. Tang. 2013. "The Dynamic Links Between $CO_2$ Emissions, Economic Growth and Coal Consumption in China and India." *Applied Energy* 104 (2013): 310–18.

Guha, R. 2005. "The Environmentalism of the Poor." In *Debating the Earth: The Environmental Politics Reader*, edited by J.S. Dryzek and D. Schlosberg. New York: Oxford University Press.

Hansen, B.E. 2001. "The New Econometrics of Structural Change: Dating Breaks in US Labor Productivity." *Journal of Economic Perspectives* 15 (4): 117–28.

Hardin, G. 1968. "The Tragedy of the Commons." *Science* 162 (3859): 1243–48.

Harrington, W., and P.R. Portney. 1987. "Valuing the Benefits of Health and Safety Regulation." *Journal of Urban Economics* 22 (1): 101–12.

Hendry, D.F., and G.E. Mizon. 1999. "The Pervasiveness of Granger Causality in Econometrics." In *Cointegration, Causality and Forecasting*, edited by R.F. Engle and H. White. Oxford: Oxford University Press.

Holland, P.W. 1993. "Which Comes First, Cause or Effect?" In *A Handbook for Data Analysis in the Behavioural Sciences*, edited G. Keren and C. Lewis, 273–82. Hillsdale, MI: Lawrence Erlbaum.

Hoover, K.D. 2012. "Economic Theory and Causal Inference." In *Philosophy of Economics*, edited by Uskali Mäki, 89–113. San Diego, CA: North Holland.

Kahneman, D., and J.L. Knetsch. 1992. "Valuing Public Goods: The Purchase of Moral Satisfaction." *Journal of Environmental Economics and Management* 22 (1): 57–70.

Keynes, J.M. 1938. "Letter to Harrod." Available at: http://economia.unipv.it/harrod/edition/editionstuff/rfh.346.htm (accessed on 9 December 2015).

Leamer, E.E. 1985. "Vector Autoregression for Causal Inference?" *Carnegie-Rochester Conference Series on Public Policy* 22 (1985): 255–304.

Leijonhufvud, A. 1973. "Life Among the Econ." *Western Economic Journal* 11 (3): 327–37.

Lele, S. 2009. "Reflections on Interdisciplinarity in Environmental Economics in India." In *Handbook of Environmental Economics in India*, edited by K. Chopra and V. Dayal, 303–23. Delhi: Oxford University Press.

Maddala, G.S., and K. Lahiri. 2009. *Introduction to Econometrics*. Delhi: Wiley.

Manski, C. 2013. *Public Policy in an Uncertain World: Analysis and Decisions*. London: Harvard University Press.

Martinez-Alier, J. 2014. "The Environmentalism of the Poor." *Geoforum* 54 (July): 239–41.

Morgan, S.L., and C. Winship. 2007. *Counterfactuals and Causal Inference*. Cambridge: Cambridge University Press.

Norgaard, R.B. 1989. "The Case for Methodological Pluralism." *Ecological Economics* 1 (1): 37–57.

Ostrom, E. 2005. *Understanding Institutional Diversity*. Princeton, NJ: Princeton University Press.

———. 2009. "Beyond Markets and States: Polycentric Governance of Complex Economic Systems." Nobel Prize Lecture, Stockholm, Sweden, 8 December 2009.

Pearl, J. 1999. "Graphs, Causality and Structural Equation Models." In *Research Methodology in the Social, Behavioral and Life Sciences*, edited by H.J. Ader and G.J. Mellenbergh. London: SAGE University Press.

Pitt, M.M., M.R. Rosenzweig, and M.N. Hassan. 2005. "Sharing the Burden of Disease: Gender, the House-hold Division of Labor and the Health Effects of Indoor Air Pollution." CID Working Paper No. 119, Center for International Development, Harvard University, Boston, MA.

Scheffer, M., S. Carpenter, J.A. Foley, C. Folke, and B. Walker. 2001. "Catastrophic Shifts in Ecosystems." *Nature* 413 (11): 591–96.

Screpanti, E., and S. Zamagni. 2005. *An Outline of the History of Economic Thought*. New Delhi: Oxford University Press.

Sethi, R., and E. Somanathan. 1996. "The Evolution of Social Norms in Common Property Resource Use." *The American Economic Review* 86 (4): 766–88.

Simon, H.A. 1953. "Causal Ordering and Identifiability." In *Studies in Econometric Methods*, edited by W.C. Hood and T.C. Koopmans, 49–74. New York: John Wiley & Sons.

———. 1955. "A Behavioral Model of Rational Choice." *Quarterly Journal of Economics* 69 (1): 99–118.

Singh, I., L. Squire, and J. Strauss, eds. 1986. *Agricultural Household Models: Extensions, Applications and Policy*. Baltimore: Johns Hopkins University Press.

Smith, K.R. 1993. "Fuel Combustion, Air Pollution Exposure, and Health: The Situation in Developing Countries." *Annual Review of Energy and Environment* 18: 529–66.

Smith, V.L. 1998. "The Two Faces of Adam Smith." *Southern Economic Journal* 65 (1): 1–19.

Solow, R.M. 1956. "Contribution to the Theory of Economic Growth." *The Quarterly Journal of Economics*, 70 (1): 65–94.

———. 1994. "Perspectives on Growth Theory." *Journal of Economic Perspectives* 8 (1): 45–54.

Somanathan, E., R. Prabhakar, and B.S. Mehta. 2009. "Decentralization for Cost-effective Conservation." *PNAS* 106 (11): 4143–47.

Spash, C.L. 2013. "The Shallow or the Deep Ecological Economics Movement?" *Ecological Economics* 93 (C): 351–62.

Stock, J.H., and M.W. Watson. 2001. "Vector Autoregressions." *Journal of Economic Perspectives* 15 (4): 101–15.

———. 2010. *Introduction to Econometrics*. Boston: Addison-Wesley.

Varian, H.R. 1989. "What Use is Economic Theory?" Available at: http://people.ischool.berkeley.edu/~hal/Papers/theory.pdf (accessed on 21 December 2015).

Wydick, B. 2008. *Games in Economic Development*. Cambridge: Cambridge University Press.

# 8

# A Socio-metabolic Reading of the Long-term Development Trajectories of China and India

Anke Schaffartzik and Marina Fischer-Kowalski

## Introduction

In this chapter, we will make an effort to compare India and China, the two most populated countries that may be expected to mould the world's future in the long run. We utilize databases built up in the course of our efforts at Long-term Socio-ecological Research (LTSER, see Singh et al. 2013), our analyses of the global course of energy transitions (e.g., Fischer-Kowalski, Krausmann, and Pallua 2014a; Fischer-Kowalski and Schaffartzik 2015), and our more recent interest in the interrelation between energy transitions and social revolutions (Fischer-Kowalski et al. 2014b). We observe these two countries, given very different political and cultural traditions, to have taken an astonishingly similar course during the past three centuries in terms of their socio-ecological macro features. Our time frame, depending on interpretation, covers two major socio-ecological transitions: the transition from biomass-based agrarian economies to fossil fuel-based industrial capitalist economies. It also covers, in essence, a transition beyond the fossil fuel-based regime. We seek to describe and to explain the similarities these two countries exhibit in their transitions and also the differences by which the most recent decades are marked. Our toolbox is small: we do not aspire to a full-blast socio-ecological, even less a historical reconstruction (e.g., for India, see Singh et al. 2012). But we do make the effort to capture, with a few critical variables, some bifurcations that may matter a lot, not only for these two countries but also for the world's future trajectory.

## The Transition from a Biomass-based to a Fossil Fuels-based Socio-metabolic Regime

Even when it appears as an earth-shattering event in hindsight, the most far-reaching societal changes are gradual as they occur. Modern (i.e., fossil) energy first came into large-scale use in India and China in the second half of the nineteenth century. Its implementation as the major energy source for the gradually developing industrial regime took more than a century and is far from completed. In both countries, the period which we can identify as the onset of this transition was marked by revolutionary movements and events in both countries, spanning from the turn to the twentieth century to the years immediately following the Second World War. Explicit goals of the revolutionary movements were to achieve national sovereignty and freedom from global imperialism, expropriate the domestic feudal class of large landowners in favour of a more equal distribution of landed property and a more social equality altogether, and to turn towards a scientifically based industrial mode of production (Guha 2011; Snow 1937).

We look upon this transition as a shift from one socio-metabolic regime to another. We use the term *socio-metabolic regime* (Krausmann and Fischer-Kowalski 2013) to refer to a particular mode of societal organization which is not only socio-economically but also socio-ecologically distinct from other possible forms of societal organization. Following Sieferle (2003), we distinguish between three socio-metabolic regimes, namely hunting and gathering, agrarian, and industrial. Hunting and gathering as well as agriculture are biomass-based regimes and rely on the ability of plants to perform photosynthesis, that is, to transform solar energy, carbon dioxide, and water into carbohydrates, including sugars and starches. Pre-industrial societies obtain 99 per cent of the energy they use from biomass sources, with human nutrition and animal feed accounting for the dominant fractions of this use. Burning biomass provides heat (for cooking, heating, and some technical processes) and light. In agrarian societies, a very limited amount of process energy is gained from wind and water (Smil 2008). Mechanical energy needs to be exerted by humans and their livestock and is strictly limited therefore.

The "passive" use of solar energy by hunting and gathering usually only allows for very low population densities and, as a rule, does not lend itself to a sedentary mode of living. Agrarian systems, in contrast, "actively" use solar energy by transforming and maintaining land in such a way that it is useful to human societies (colonization), and by selecting and breeding plants for cultivation. The specific characteristics of an agrarian socio-metabolic regime depend on the topography, soil, seasonal temperature, and precipitation cycles, as well as population density and societal organization such as landownership and other forms of hierarchy. As a form of subsistence, the agrarian regime requires a positive energy yield or energy return on investment (EROI, see Hall, Cleveland, Kaufmann 1986): more energy in the form of harvested biomass must be produced than is invested in human and animal labour. The size of any surplus has important consequences for the possibilities of social differentiation by allowing for the provision of non-agrarian segments of society (e.g., urban areas, animal-powered transport systems, landowners, and their staff) with energy. The production of surplus, thus, allows for additional social complexity but cannot be infinitely extended: Commonly, 10 families actively engaged in agrarian production can sustain 1–2 non-agrarian households (Krausmann and Fischer-Kowalski 2013). Under the agrarian regime, production can be increased via expansion of cropland (either through deforestation or through annexation of territory) or, where this is not possible, through intensification via higher human labour inputs. Both strategies, however, ultimately face physical limits—the first in the availability of land area, and the second in the decreasing marginal utility of human labour and the associated high fertility rates. The resulting interplay between the socio-metabolic mode and demographic development was investigated by Boserup (1965); through the high demands on human labour, intensification in the agricultural regime eventually leads to a decrease in the material and energy available per person.

As we have discussed, some social differentiation and, therefore, also urbanization is possible under the agrarian regime but the share of the population which can live in cities is ultimately limited not only by the ability of rural areas to produce the necessary surplus but also by the limits to the transport system (Fischer-Kowalski, Krausmann, and Smetschka 2013). Where transport is fueled by human and/or animal power, it is only feasible over distances at which both the commodities to be traded and the biomass required as energy input can be carried. Given the comparatively low energy density of biomass, these distances are typically not very far. Larger urban areas could, therefore, only develop along waterways which provided some relief from this limit to transport. While the agrarian system does mobilize significantly higher amounts of energy and material than do hunters and gatherers, their abilities to harness and distribute energy remain ultimately constrained. Nonetheless, the agrarian regime was and is associated with environmental problems, among which widespread deforestation is most prominent. In conjunction with the interference of humans in the water and nutrient cycles, this change to the land cover can be linked to erosion and loss of soil quality. Since the latter is one of the prerequisites to agricultural production, this presents a quintessential sustainability problem. In order to be sustainable, agrarian societies must achieve a long-term balance between population and soil fertility. In all agrarian societies, cultural regulations of reproduction serve to address the population issue and include (legal) restrictions of marriage and sexual taboos (especially concerning the pre- or extra-marital sexual activity of women). At the same time, high fertility within marriage is considered a blessing, and it is indeed in the sense of sharing the ever-increasing workload in agriculture. This high fertility becomes part of a vicious cycle, regulated mainly by increased mortality: high fertility leads to high food demand which requires higher labour input per unit area and, in turn, more labour power (and more children) (Ringhofer, Singh, and Fischer-Kowalski 2014).

The longer the agrarian regime persists and matures in a territory, more territory becomes trapped in a pattern of high population density, a high demand for human labour power (and concomitant high fertility rates), threatened soil fertility, and social inequality with a small number of privileged landowners[1] and city inhabitants competing to appropriate whatever little surplus is produced by the agricultural system. There is hardly any room to manoeuvre on distributional issues, unless by violent means and/or if mortality is raised by suppression, civil strife, wars, or epidemics.

At this point, the introduction of even small amounts of additional energy resources makes a huge difference. To relieve cities of their need for the increasingly rare firewood by providing coal creates the opportunity for traders, for example, to sustain their families on profits from (international) trade rather than from local agrarian surplus. It creates the opportunity for employing wage labour absorbing agrarian population surplus, and it generates a new well-to-do class competing with landowners for political privileges. All this happens quite a while before proper industrial innovations allow for the transformation of heat into work. This change is based on the use of fossil energy carriers. Therefore, we regard the share of fossil energy in primary energy use as the key indicator—and fortunately, an indicator that can be quantified much more easily than technical innovations—for the industrial transition. A small rise of free additional energy triggers, as we show elsewhere (Fischer-Kowalski et al. 2014b), a "critical phase" of industrial transformation that is not "industrial" in the common sense of technological innovation, but rather a social transformation: creating and empowering new social groups and classes to force open the constraints of the agrarian regime towards manufacture and trade, a departure from traditionalism towards enlightened forms of experimenting and learning, and growing urban infrastructure. In the industrial mode, human settlements are no longer directly dependent on land to the extent that this is true for the other two modes. Much higher population densities become possible, fostering a growing urban population.[2]

From the United Kingdom of the eighteenth century and Europe eventually spreading to other parts of the world, the use of the coal-fired steam engine was decisive for the industrial transformation in the more common understanding of the word. While Pomeranz (2009) has argued that the early industrial transition could also have occurred in China, Figure 8.1 shows that a fossil fuel-based industrial transition did not take off there until the twentieth century. At that time, modern energy sources were already the main component of the energy system in the United Kingdom and the Netherlands, and also in France and Japan, where the transition had started much later. The uptake of these new energy sources and technologies is not simply a matter of natural availability and technological imitation, but of a major societal change. Such a change is very difficult in agrarian empires increasingly trapped in a vicious cycle of high population density, a culture of high fertility in response to extremely high agricultural workloads of the large, and poor majority of the population being controlled by a small privileged (largely unproductive) elite sustaining itself on the extraction of the scarce surplus. Some countries, such as the United Kingdom, the Netherlands, France, and Japan, gained freedom for change of various degrees through colonialism, which permitted them to expand the area from which they could draw surplus. India and China, in contrast, were among the countries forced to share their surplus with colonial powers. Thus, their room to manoeuvre was very limited, indeed.

**Figure 8.1**

*Per cent of modern energy in domestic energy consumption (DEC) in China, India, the United Kingdom, France, Japan, and the Netherlands between 1600 and 2005*

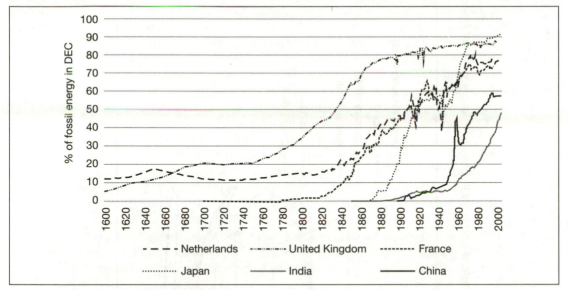

*Source:* Data for the figure taken from Pallua (2013).

As their early take-off in the energy transition occurred in the late nineteenth and early twentieth century, India and China were under colonial rule, struggling to liberate themselves from it. During this phase, they were marked, like many other countries, by a series of revolutionary uprisings (Fischer-Kowalski et al. 2014b). New energy sources enabling new productive activities to emerge require new forms of social organizations, and challenge the traditional order established under the agrarian mode. In China, the revolutions of 1911 and 1949 are examples of such challenges. In India, the independence movements from the late nineteenth century until 1947[3] prepared the ground for fundamental societal changes and opening the pathway towards the industrial transformation.

This societal change included liberation from colonial dependence, and at least partial disempowerment of the ruling feudal classes, new forms of governance, and urbanization. As can be gathered from Figure 8.2, the level of fossil fuel use at which the revolutionary events occurred in India and China was very low (barely 2 Gigajoules per capita and year [GJ/cap/a]). They have this level in common with other countries which had their revolutions during the nineteenth century and before (Figure 8.2). In all cases, revolutions followed the first phase of fossil fuels use (with annual growth rates between 2% and 3%, albeit at very low absolute levels), but after the revolutionary events a major take-off in fossil fuel use took place (with annual growth rates between 5% and 6%).[4]

# Development Trajectories in China and India

We will now compare and contrast the macro-indicators for the socio-ecological development trajectories of China and India, tracing the more general properties of energy transitions from an agrarian to an industrial regime. In the course of this analysis, we will demonstrate that the combination of the macro-indicators we have chosen to include biophysical data in addition to the economic and demographic indicators more

**Figure 8.2**

*Fossil fuel use in gigajoules per capita and year (GJ/cap/a) in the 50 years before and after the key revolutionary event (year of revolution: 0)*

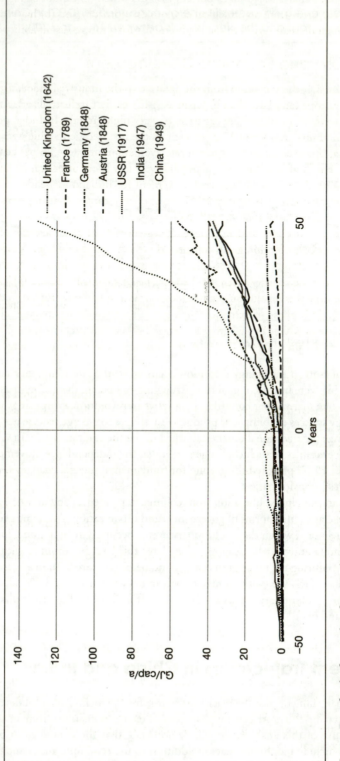

United Kingdom (1642)
France (1789)
Germany (1848)
Austria (1848)
USSR (1917)
India (1947)
China (1949)

*Source:* Data for the figure taken from Fischer-Kowalski et al. (2014b, 25).

commonly used in policy analysis leads to important insights which (a) cannot be replicated without the use of biophysical data (i.e., stem from an ecological economics approach) and (b) have important implications as to what we can conclude with regard to the requirements for a future sustainability transition.

## Socio-metabolic and Economic Development

As illustrated in Figure 8.1, the transition from the agrarian to the industrial mode began later in China and India than it did in Europe (and later than in Japan as Asia's earliest industrializer). At very low rates of per capita use, absolute levels of fossil fuel use experienced very high growth. In India, per capita fossil energy carrier use grew at an annual average of 17.2 per cent in the first decade in which we can document its use (1853–63). In China, this average annual growth rate even amounted to 43.6 per cent (between 1900 and 1910; Pallua 2013). This high growth rate at comparatively low levels of per capita energy use is typical for take-off situations. With the rise of an organized movement for Indian independence in the late nineteenth century and until the partition of Bengal in 1905, fossil energy carrier consumption per capita grew at an annual average rate of 8 per cent and by 1905 had reached 0.7 GJ/cap/a. Growth was noticeably slower during the following period of the Indian independence movement at an average of 2 per cent per year. Since then, fossil energy consumption again accelerated (at an average of 4% per year until 2000) and with much larger absolute gains (Figure 8.3). In China, the uprisings that led into the Xinhai Revolution (1911) began around the turn of the century when fossil energy carriers contributed 0.2 GJ/cap/a (0.1%) to energy consumption. By the time this revolution occurred, consumption had quadrupled to 0.8 GJ/cap/a (3.9% of energy consumption). This phase of extremely high growth rates with relatively small absolute increments was followed by a phase in which annual growth averaged 3 per cent per year throughout the Chinese Civil War and up to the revolution of 1949. By 1948, the consumption of modern energy carriers amounted to 1.8 GJ/cap/a.

In the phase of the industrial transition in China and India between 1900 and 1950 (Figure 8.3, top), increasing use of fossil energy clearly preceded a rise of economic output (measured as gross domestic product [GDP] in 1990 international Geary–Khamis dollars [GK$]). In 1950, China used 1.0 EJ of fossil fuels per year, while India used 0.7 EJ/a, equivalent to an energy consumption of 1.9 GJ/cap/a in both countries. Up to 1950, the trajectories of both countries look very much alike, with the same pattern of rapidly rising fossil fuels use and much slower GDP growth leading to more or less the same economic and energetic outcome in both countries. From 1950 onwards, fossil energy consumption and GDP follow a pattern of growth in both countries with a much steeper trajectory on both indicators in China than in India (Figure 8.3, bottom): between 1950 and 2005, China's GDP grew at an average of 6 per cent per year, while India's grew at 5 per cent; fossil energy consumption grew at an average of 8 per cent per year in China and 7 per cent in India. While research on industrial societies has long indicated a link between energy use and GDP (see, e.g., Coers and Sanders 2013), other factors must be taken into account to analyse energy use in pre-industrial societies or those in the early phase of industrialization.

## The Role of Population Dynamics

That the development trajectory of China and India could be decisive for the whole world was already apparent in 1900; already then, these were the two most populous countries. The (moderate) population growth during the long agrarian era had, by 1900, led China to a population size of over 400 million and India to one approaching 300 million (Figure 8.4). Together, they accounted for approximately 40 per cent of the world population. The share of population living in urban areas[5] was still similarly low in both countries at 6.6 per cent in China and 5.2 per cent in India. The low levels of fossil energy use and the related high dependence on land for the provisioning of biomass-based energy did not allow for a higher urban share in the population at this point.

**Figure 8.3**

*GDP in trillion 1990 international GK$ and fossil energy carrier use in exajoules per year (EJ/a) in China and India between 1900–50 and 1950–2005*

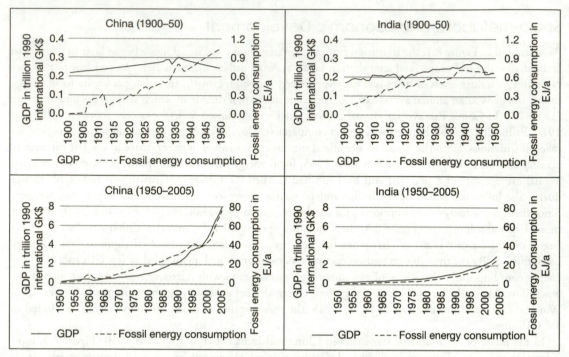

*Source:* Data for the figure taken from Pallua (2013) and Schaffartzik et al. (2014).

With the transition towards fossil energy use (Figure 8.3), the growth in population and the urbanization rate accelerated in China and India, a development that can be considered typical for this phase of the energy transition (Fischer-Kowalski et al. 2014b). Average annual population growth rates increased in both countries until the 1970s[6] and were, in most years, slightly higher in India than in China. In China, the decline in annual population growth clearly preceded the formal introduction of the one-child policy but coincides with the political turn from a natalist position to the encouragement of antinatalist measures. From a policy

**Figure 8.4**

*Population in million capita and urbanization rate in percentage in China and India between 1900 and 2000*

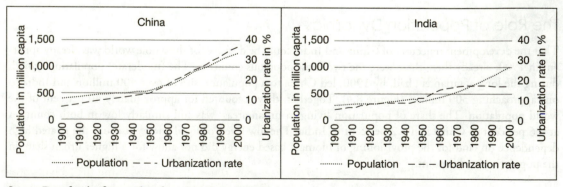

*Source:* Data for the figure taken from Livi-Bacci (2012).

of male sterilization implemented in the 1970s to a greater focus on the education of women and girls thereafter, the declining population growth rate in India also coincided with the rise of antinatalist positions.

With such similar patterns in population growth, the most distinct difference in the demographic development of China and India lies in the patterns of distribution of the respective large populations on the national territory. In 1900, the average population density on the territory of the Indian Empire was already approximately twice as high as in Qing dynasty, China. By 1960, an average of 70 people per square kilometre ($km^2$) in China compared to 150 people per $km^2$ in India.[7] By 2000, India's population density had reached more than 350 people per $km^2$, while China's grew to approximately 130 people per $km^2$. By international comparison, India's population density was and is quite high. In 1960, it was higher than that of many central European countries and in 2000, India was more densely populated than for example Japan or the Philippines. It is important to consider this high average population density in India when comparing the urbanization rates of the two countries. In China, from 1950 onwards (and in conjunction with policies seeking to curb urban growth), the share of the urban population grew at the same rate as the overall population. In India, the urban share began to stagnate from the mid-1970s onwards. By the year 2000, 37 per cent of the Chinese compared to 17 per cent of the Indian population lived in urban areas (Livi-Bacci 2012).

Rather than interpreting this difference in urbanization rates as the cause of a slower pace of the industrial transition in India as compared to China, we propose that it may be the slower pace of the energy transition which lends itself to lower urbanization rates. By comparing India and China, we find that not only is a greater share of the Chinese population living in urban areas, the population remaining in the rural areas also appears to have transitioned or be transitioning to fossil fuel-based energy more quickly than is the case in India. China boasts an electrification rate of almost 100 per cent in its rural regions, while the rate in India is slightly above 50 per cent (Niez 2010). Yet even in China, the rural energy regime still differs from that found in urban areas, most notably because non-commercial energy carriers remain the most important source of energy for cooking and heating; in India, 90 per cent of rural households use biomass for cooking energy (Pachauri 2004; Pereira et al. 2011). The difference in rural energy use between China and India seems to have little impact on the overall fossil energy use. The fossil energy consumption per urban population (in 2000, 86 GJ/cap in China and 81 GJ/cap in India) is much more similar than the fossil energy consumption per capita of the total population (in 2000, 32 GJ/cap in China and 14 GJ/cap in India).

At this point in our analysis, it already becomes apparent that if India were to, as has recently been the subject of governmental declarations, follow the Chinese development trajectory, the environmental impact would be far-reaching. Whether India, however, is already locked in to such a development still remains a topic for discussion. Before we turn to this question, we want to add some more detail to the underlying reasons for the different speeds at which the energy transition occurred in the two countries. Why is it that India and China shared, for such a long period of time, basic socio-metabolic, economic, and demographic patterns of development (see Figures 8.1–8.4), and from about 1950 onwards each display a different trajectory? And what does this mean for their future, and indeed for the future development of the world?

## Steel and Cloth: Legacies of Industrialization Campaigns in China and India

After taking power in China in 1949, Mao Zedong introduced major agrarian reforms. He expropriated the landed gentry and redistributed their land, equipment, and animals to the three hundred million poor or landless peasants. These reforms were very successful in increasing food production and improving rural standards of living and doubling the income share of the poorest 20 per cent of the peasants (Selden 1993, 72). They were also successful in creating surplus for industrialization, as is apparent in the rise of fossil fuel use from 1950 onwards (Figure 8.5). To further accelerate this process, farms were collectivized and the "Great Leap Forward" campaign (1958–61) was initiated that would industrialize the rural areas of China through the construction of millions of "backyard" steel mills across the country, using the labour power of the farm collectives. While this campaign was initially successful in raising steel production (and coal

**Figure 8.5**

*The impact of the "Great Leap Forward" in China on fossil fuel use (in gigajoules per capita and year [GJ/cap/a]) and GDP (in trillion international Geary–Khamis dollars [GK$]), 1940–65*

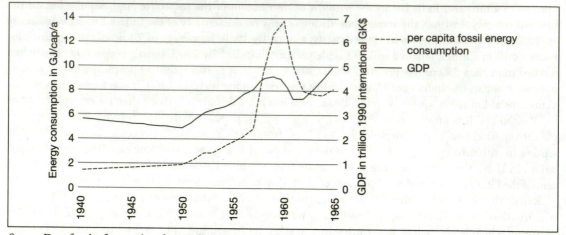

*Source:* Data for the figure taken from Pallua (2013).

consumption, see Figure 8.4), it deprived agriculture of labour power for food production and led to a great famine with millions of deaths in consequence.[8] Thus, this extremely forceful and socially costly effort met its boundaries but still seems to have led to a steeper trajectory of transition than we can see for India in the same period (Figures 8.1 and 8.3). Galtung and Nishimura (1978) emphasize the empowerment effect of this policy initiative. This type of decentralized industrialization required training millions of peasants to handle industrial technologies, necessitating the collaborative finding of local solutions to novel technical problems, without being able to rely on expert help.

In India, the movement for independence from the United Kingdom also led to a concept for decentralized development. Mahatma Gandhi mobilized Indians, as part of the civil disobedience movement, to boycott British textiles and other industrial goods that had harmed domestic industry. He envisioned putting an end to the exploitation of India's rural population by empowering them to produce cloth for themselves and for the people of India. With a spinning wheel in every home, Gandhi proposed that the impoverished peasants would be able to produce enough cloth to sell a surplus to the urban population, thus alleviating their poverty. In contrast to Mao's campaign in China, Gandhi's vision to support the "cottage industries" of rural India was much less capital-intensive, more labour-intensive, and even more decentralized. The "backyard" steel mills required quite some initial investment in technology and the constant availability of coal to fire them as well as the aforementioned cooperation of the peasants-turned-workers in running them. The spinning wheel was a comparably cheap object which ran on human labour alone and did not require more than one person to spin yarn. Although Gandhi acknowledged the need for large-scale heavy industries, he sought to protect village life from them. Gandhi's follower and leader of the independence movement, Jawaharlal Nehru, who became India's first prime minister in 1947, emphasized modernization and heavy industry in urban centres, emulating the top-down policies of the Soviet model. Even though India's five-year-plans in the second half of the twentieth century called for the development of the heavy industries capable of producing capital (rather than consumer) goods, agriculture was prioritized (Misra 1995). The land-reform policies of this period had two specific objectives:

The first is to remove such impediments to increase agricultural production as arise from the agrarian structure inherited from the past.... The second object, which is closely related to the first, is to eliminate all elements of exploitation and social injustice within the agrarian system, to provide security for the tiller of soil and assure equality of status and opportunity to all sections of the rural population (Government of India 1961 as quoted by Appu 1996).

Agricultural production was, thus, even prioritized over the improvement of living conditions for the rural population which had been Gandhi's motivation. As a result of the continuous focus on agriculture, the capital goods required for further industrial development were lacking.[9]

## The Impact of Neo-liberal Policies

In India and China, the phases focusing on government-led industrialization around the middle of the twentieth century were followed by the rise of neo-liberal economic policies. China's development during this phase was marked by an opening beyond the country's borders. Isolation had already melted away under Mao's reign,[10] allowing China to borrow from international banks and to attract foreign investors. After Mao's death, Deng Xiaoping took over as the country's leader in 1978 and continued to pursue an increased openness vis-à-vis the outside world while simultaneously implementing reforms aimed at promoting economic growth. By devaluing its currency and maintaining comparatively low wages, China became very attractive for foreign investment and managed to firmly establish its commodities on the world market years before it finally joined the World Trade Organisation (WTO) in 2001[11] (Figure 8.6). Average annual growth rates of physical trade volumes increased markedly with each decade. In terms of fossil fuel use and GDP (Figure 8.3), China's development from 1980 onward constituted a "great acceleration," very similar to the take-off of Western Europe and the United States after the end of the Second World War.

**Figure 8.6**
*Physical trade flows of China and India in megatonnes per year (Mt/a) between 1950 and 2010*

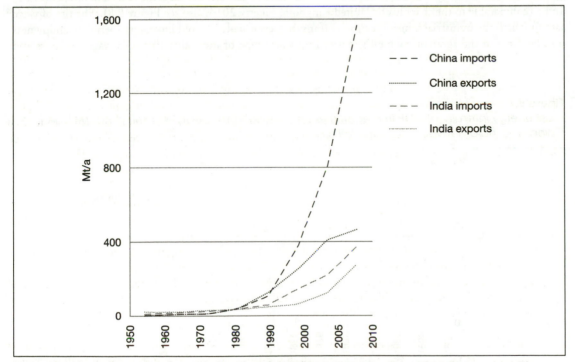

*Source:* Data for the figure taken from Schaffartzik et al. (2014).

No such great acceleration happened in India. The country was close to an economic crisis and bankruptcy in 1991 when Narashima Rao became prime minister. Rao initiated a campaign of economic liberalization, dismantling of the license system, reducing tariffs, and ending import quotas (Singh et al. 2012). These policies can be related to some growth in trade volumes (Figure 8.6), although during this period of liberalization in the 1990s, growth rates were not nearly as pronounced as they were in China. In contrast to the marked increase in China's GDP and energy use in response to liberalization measures, no such change in trajectory can be detected in the same indicators for India (Figure 8.3). Agriculture still employs 57 per cent of the workforce, while industry and services, the typical corollaries of the industrial transition, employ 19 per cent and 25 per cent, respectively, the latter contributing a very high share, namely 54 per cent, to India's GDP (Singh et al. 2012).

The unchanged long-term trajectory of India's energy use and GDP translates into an energy intensity of GDP (measured here as fossil energy carrier consumption per unit of GDP) which increased steadily throughout the second half of the twentieth century (Figure 8.7). In China, on the other hand, the phase of liberalization is clearly associated with GDP growth surpassing the considerable growth in fossil energy consumption, leading to decreasing energy intensity of GDP to the point that this indicator is comparable for China and India early in the twenty-first century. While this intensity indicator is, thus, highly informative in terms of understanding the relative development of GDP and energy use in each of the countries, we are also able to show here that the same performance, as far as this indicator goes, can be the result of very different patterns of development. From our analysis, we know that India and China are not at the same point of their energy transition, even though the intensity indicator might make it appear to be so.

A development which both countries experienced during their respective liberalization phases is a substantial rise in income inequality after the revolutionary movements had initially been successful in reducing social inequality. However, it seems that India brought a larger burden of inequality "inherited" from colonial times into the industrial transition phase than did China. In 1985, the top 1 per cent earned 4.0 per cent of the total income in China (comparable to the share in Sweden in that same year) and 8.6 per cent in India (comparable to the share in the United Kingdom; Piketty 2014; also see Figure 8.8). The rise of wage labour which the industrial transition entails means that, eventually, the old inequality (between landowners and peasants in the agrarian regime) is replaced by a new type of inequality (between wage labourers and

**Figure 8.7**

*Fossil energy intensity of GDP in megajoules per international Geary–Khamis dollar (MJ/GK$) in China and India between 1950 and 2005*

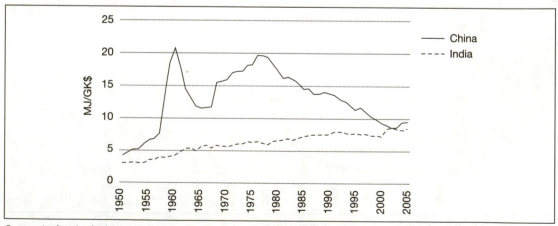

*Source:* Authors' calculations based on data compiled by Pallua (2013).

**Figure 8.8**

*Share of the top 1 per cent and 0.1 per cent of income in total income in India (1925–99) and China (1986–2003)*

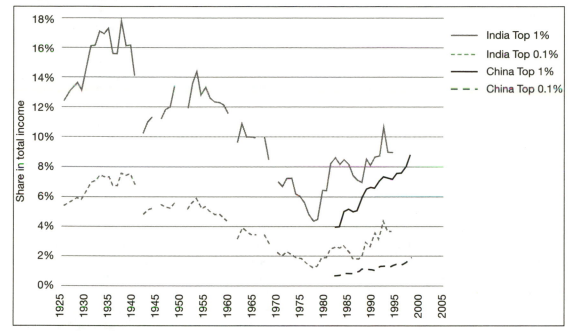

*Source:* Data for the figure taken from Piketty (2014).

capitalists in the industrial regime). Because industrialization both in China and India was realized largely by State-run businesses, it can be expected that the new inequality will manifest itself especially in differences in labour income (as opposed to differences in capital income).

Inequality as reflected by the share of small segments of the population in the total income was highest and increased in India during the phase from 1922 to 1941. In 1938, the top percentile had about 18 per cent of the total income (the top 0.1% had about 8%). Inequality decreased between the late 1950s and the early 1980s and then began to increase again. By 2010, it was as high as around 1947. Piketty (2014, 326) describes the phase between 1950 and 1980 as "more egalitarian." Its development during the twentieth century left China with a much "more egalitarian" starting position, but from the 1980s onwards, inequality increased rapidly and in 2010, the top 1 per cent were estimated to earn 11 per cent of the labour income (comparable to 12% in India) (Piketty 2014).

From energy use and GDP growth to the development of social inequality, the past trajectory of the energy transition in China and India has decisively shaped the present-day situation. The political campaigns pursued in twentieth-century China with their focus on rural industrialization and low fertility led to a radical departure from the agrarian regime with high urbanization and a focus on wage labour. The pattern of industrialization through investment in capital goods such as infrastructure, machinery, and technical equipment has continued so that China's abundant labour force increasingly faces the threat of unemployment in an industrial system capable of producing more with less human labour: the ratio of total wages to total investment is declining, with investments in assets growing much more strongly than employment (Wu 2004). In India, on the other hand, the aim to preserve village life even in the face of industrialization has caused the agrarian regime to figure more prominently, even today. Among India's rural population, ownership of small plots of land still persists and sub-caste groups can provide vital support and mutual insurance

(Munshi and Rosenzweig 2009). In contrast to China where inequality is higher within the rural than the urban setting, India's rural Gini coefficient is lower than the urban one (Pal and Ghosh 2007).

While Asia's "growing giants" share many aspects of their socio-metabolic, economic, and demographic development in the twentieth and twenty-first century, they are nonetheless each faced with a very particular situation today. The recently pronounced goals of India to copy Chinese growth (*The Economist* 2015) could have catastrophic effects on not just the Asian but the global environment. In the final section of this chapter, we therefore want to discuss whether by acknowledging the particularities of the energy transition in both these countries, we might not also be able to draw some conclusions with regards to a sustainability transition.

## Conclusions: Modern Energy for a Sustainability Transition?

If we were to examine the energy transitions in China and India on the basis of socio-economic macro-indicators only, we would find very similar patterns of population growth in both countries and much slower rates of GDP growth in India than in China from the 1970s onwards. We could conclude that more GDP growth is urgently needed in order to increase the average Indian income. We might imagine, given the comparatively low urbanization rate in India, that this growth could be obtained by a far-reaching industrialization effort and the greater expansion of wage labour as the principal source of subsistence. The strong link between GDP growth and fossil energy consumption which both China and India exhibit, especially from 1950 onwards, however, should set off some alarm bells as we contemplate such a scenario.

It is neither in China's interest to continue along a path of exponential growth of fossil energy carrier use—with the associated detriment to its and the global environment, the health of its population, and the looming risks of supply—nor is it in India's interest to emulate China's past development. With its high population density in low-lying coastal areas and its monsoon-dependent agriculture, India is particularly at risk when it comes to the effects of climate change; the pollution impacts of fossil fuel combustion are already troubling its cities as it is.

India could reap multiple benefits from explicitly not following China's lead. Rather than expanding a currently fickle, to say the least, electricity supply based on coal-fired power plants and hydroelectricity from large dams, India might achieve less environmentally destructive and more reliable rural electrification through decentralized renewable solutions (a review of such proposals is provided by Hiremath et al. 2009); in order to be sustainable, however, even an energy provisioning scheme based on renewables would require overall reduction, rather than continuing increase, in energy requirements. In an age in which information technology is the foremost currency of innovation, this pathway could allow for improvements in both the level of technical education and the amount of qualified labour in rural areas, also contributing to a further reduction of fertility. In combination with the large and highly qualified service sector in the cities, this might provide a smoother pathway into a post-fossil energy regime than via the heavy industries-based industrialization with its significant social and environmental price tag. China, alongside its past and current large-scale industrialization that has left it with high and growing fossil energy consumption, is already taking a turn towards renewable energy generation that has no parallel globally (Mathews and Tan 2014).

As we stated in our introduction, our toolbox is deliberately small and we have based our analysis of the energy transition in China and India on a condensed set of economic, demographic, and socio-metabolic data. This dataset does, however, accomplish two very important things: (a) it covers a long period of time and decisive events and phases in the history of both countries; (b) it combines information on the socio-economic development with information on the biophysical development of both countries. By pairing this quantitative analysis with insights from the literature on the history of China and India, we are able to identify important differences in the development path that these countries have been and currently are on.

On this basis, we are not able to prescribe the correct way forward, but we are able to identify important reasons to suggest that what might constitute a move towards greater sustainability is not the same for India as it is for China.

# Notes

1. Possibly, as in the case of India, including foreign colonialists.
2. For an in-depth review and analysis of the relevant literature and data, please see Fischer-Kowalski and Schaffartzik (2015).
3. In the social science literature, there is no general agreement as to which events should be considered social revolutions, nor is it always trivial to assign to them a specific year. This uncertainty applies to India and China in particular, as in both cases there has been an extended phase of revolutionary events. 1947 marks India's long and hotly contested independence from the United Kingdom.
4. This is not to say that whenever there had been a first shift towards fossil fuels use, revolutionary events ensued. Of the 17 countries investigated across the century-long period of their energy transition, we found two without revolutionary events during that period (Sweden and Australia; see Fischer-Kowalski et al. 2014b). With regard to fossil fuel use, they show basically the same patterns as the other countries.
5. The urbanization rate is a tricky indicator in that it depends so strongly on what is defined as urban. We rely here on the data collected by Livi-Bacci (2012) because it is available in a long time series from 1500 to 2000. Urban areas are defined as settlements with a population of 3,000 or greater for all countries. This is an important advantage compared to, for example, the data provided by the United Nations Department of Economic and Social Affairs (UN DESA) which applies the country's definition of urban differing from one country to the next.
6. The famine-induced population decline in China between 1960 and 1961 is, of course, a stark exception to this trend which we discuss in greater detail in the following section of this chapter.
7. India's population density was higher in 1960 than that of many middle European countries was in 2015.
8. The dimension of this catastrophe is contested. Even in the late 1970s, authors sympathizing with Mao's policies attribute the famines to consecutive "natural catastrophes" (Kuntze 1977, 58), while for example Schaeffer (2016), based upon various sources, speaks of 16–29 million deaths as a consequence of famine induced by these policies. UN population statistics show an absolute decline of 7 million people from 1960 to 1961. For some years, China even resorted to a natalist policy to compensate for the loss of labour power (ibid., 159).
9. It appears as a twist of fate that Indian-owned Tata Steel since 2014 is in the process of selling or closing its steel operations in the United Kingdom because the growth of demand for steel, most notably in China, has lagged behind projections causing China to export rather than import steel, resulting in decreasing prices. If no buyer for Tata's UK operations can be found, then this will mark the end of traditional industrial production in the motherland of industrialization.
10. The United States employed China's services in its negotiations with Vietnam. President Nixon travelled to China, met Mao, and ended the United States embargo on China. In 1971, China was admitted to the United Nations (Schaeffer 2016, 160 ff).
11. In contrast to the claim made by Velasco-Fernández et al. (2015) that China's new membership in the WTO can be causally linked to changes in energy consumption and industrial production patterns, we show here that energy consumption and the role of trade had already shifted significantly prior to 2001, setting the stage for China's WTO membership.

# References

Appu, P.S. 1996. *Land Reforms in India: A Survey of Policy, Legislation and Implementation*. New Delhi: Vikas Publishing House.

Boserup, E. 1965. The *Conditions of Agricultural Growth: The Economics of Agrarian Change under Population Pressure*. New Brunswick, NJ: Transaction Publishers.

Coers, R., and M. Sanders. 2013. "The Energy–GDP Nexus; Addressing an Old Question with New Methods." *Energy Economics* 36: 708–15. doi:10.1016/j.eneco.2012.11.015

Fischer-Kowalski, M., Krausmann, and F., Pallua, I. 2014a. "A Sociometabolic Reading of the Anthropocene: Modes of Subsistence, Population Size and Human Impact on Earth." *The Anthropocene Review* 1: 8–33. doi:10.1177/2053019613518033

Fischer-Kowalski, M., F. Krausmann, I. Pallua, and M. Heinz. 2014b. "The Role of Social Revolutions in Major Historical Energy Transitions." In Large Scale Societal Transitions in the Past. The Role of Social Revolutions and the 1970s Syndrome, edited by M. Fischer-Kowalski and D. Hausknost. *Social Ecology Working Paper*, Institute of Social Ecology, Vienna.

Fischer-Kowalski, M., F. Krausmann, and B. Smetschka. 2013. "Modelling Transport as a Key Constraint to Urbanisation in Pre-Industrial Societies." In *Long Term Socio-ecological Research, Human-Environment Interactions*, edited by S.J. Singh, H. Haberl, M. Chertow, M. Mirtl, and M. Schmid, 77–102. Dordrecht, Netherlands: Springer.

Fischer-Kowalski, M., and A. Schaffartzik. 2015. "Energy Availability and Energy Sources as Determinants of Societal Development in a Long-term Perspective." *MRS Energy Sustainability—A Review Journal* 2. doi:10.1557/mre.2015.2

Galtung, J., and F. Nishimura. 1978. *Von China lernen?* [Learning from China?] Opladen: Westdeutscher.

Guha, R. 2011. *India After Gandhi: The History of the World's Largest Democracy*. Hampshire: Pan Macmillan.

Hall, C.a.S., C.J. Cleveland, and R.K. Kaufmann. 1986. *Energy and Resource Quality: The Ecology of the Economic Process*. New York: Wiley Interscience.

Hiremath, R.B., B. Kumar, P. Balachandra, N.H. Ravindranath, and B.N. Raghunandan. 2009. "Decentralised Renewable Energy: Scope, Relevance and Applications in the Indian Context." *Energy for Sustainable Development* 13: 4–10. doi:10.1016/j.esd.2008.12.001

Krausmann, F., and M. Fischer-Kowalski. 2013. "Global Socio-metabolic Transitions." In *Long Term Socio-ecological Research, Human-Environment Interactions*, edited by S.J. Singh, H. Haberl, M. Chertow, M. Mirtl, and M. Schmid, 339–65. Dordrecht, Netherlands: Springer.

Kuntze, P. 1977. *China—Revolution in der Seele* [China—Revolution in the Soul]. Frankfurt/Main: Fischer TB.

Livi-Bacci, M. 2012. *A Concise History of World Population*. Hoboken: John Wiley & Sons.

Mathews, J.A., and H. Tan. 2014. "Economics: Manufacture Renewables to Build Energy Security." *Nature* 513: 166–68. doi:10.1038/513166a

Misra, O.P. 1995. *Economic Thought of Gandhi and Nehru: A Comparative Analysis*. India: M.D. Publications.

Munshi, K., and M. Rosenzweig. 2009. "Why is Mobility in India so Low? Social Insurance, Inequality, and Growth." Working Paper No. 14850, National Bureau of Economic Research, Cambridge, MA.

Niez, Alexandra. 2010. "Comparative Study on Rural Electrification Policies in Emerging Economies: Keys to Successful Policies." Information Paper, International Energy Agency, Paris.

Pachauri, S. 2004. "An Analysis of Cross-sectional Variations in Total Household Energy Requirements in India Using Micro Survey Data." *Energy Policy* 32: 1723–35. doi:10.1016/S0301-4215(03)00162-9

Pal, P., and J. Ghosh. 2007. "Inequality in India: A Survey of Recent Trends." DESA Working Paper No. 45, United Nations Department of Economic and Social Affairs, New York.

Pallua, I. 2013. "Historische Energietransitionen im Ländervergleich. Energienutzung, Bevölkerung, Wirtschaftliche Entwicklung." [A Cross-country Comparison of Historical Energy Transitions. Energy Use, Population, Economic Development] Social Ecology Working Paper No. 148, Institute of Social Ecology, Vienna.

Pereira, M.G., J.A. Sena, M.A.V. Freitas, and N.F. da Silva. 2011. "Evaluation of the Impact of Access to Electricity: A Comparative Analysis of South Africa, China, India and Brazil." *Renewable and Sustainable Energy Reviews* 15: 1427–41. doi:10.1016/j.rser.2010.11.005

Piketty, T. 2014. *Capital in the Twenty-first Century*. Cambridge, MA: Harvard University Press.

Pomeranz, K. 2009. *The Great Divergence: China, Europe, and the Making of the Modern World Economy*. Princeton, NJ: Princeton University Press.

Ringhofer, L., S.J. Singh, and M. Fischer-Kowalski. 2014. "Beyond Boserup: The Role of Working Time in Agricultural Development." In *Ester Boserup's Legacy on Sustainability, Human–Environment Interactions*, edited by M. Fischer-Kowalski, A. Reenberg, A. Schaffartzik, and A. Mayer, 117–38. Netherlands: Springer.

Schaeffer, R.K. 2016. *Understanding Globalization: The Social Consequences of Political, Economic, and Environmental Change*, 5th ed. London: Rowman & Littlefield.

Schaffartzik, A., A. Mayer, S. Gingrich, N. Eisenmenger, C. Loy, and F. Krausmann. 2014. "The Global Metabolic Transition: Regional Patterns and Trends of Global Material Flows, 1950–2010." *Global Environmental Change* 26: 87–97. doi:10.1016/j.gloenvcha.2014.03.013

Selden, M. 1993. *The Political Economy of Chinese Development*. Armonk: M.E. Sharpe.

Sieferle, R.P. 2003. "Sustainability in a World History Perspective." In *Exploitation and Overexploitation in Societies Past and Present*, edited by B. Benzig, 123–42. Münster: LIT Publishing House.

Singh, S.J., H. Haberl, M. Chertow, M. Mirtl, and M. Schmid., eds. 2013. *Long Term Socio-ecological Research*. Dordrecht, Netherlands: Springer.

Singh, S.J., F. Krausmann, S. Gingrich, H. Haberl, K.-H. Erb, P. Lanz, J. Martinez-Alier, and L. Temper. 2012. "India's Biophysical Economy, 1961–2008. Sustainability in a National and Global Context." *Ecological Economics* 76: 60–69. doi:10.1016/j.ecolecon.2012.01.022

Smil, V. 2008. *Energy in Nature and Society: General Energetics of Complex Systems*. Cambridge, MA: MIT Press.

Snow, E. 1937. *Red Star Over China—The Rise of the Red Army*. Left Book Club. Reprinted with revisions, notes and annotations added, in New York: Grove, 1968.

*The Economist*. 2015. "Catching up with China." *The Economist*, 10 October. Available at: http://www.economist.com/news/asia/21672359-prime-minister-wants-india-grow-fast-over-next-20-years-china-has-over-past-20 (accessed on 19 May 2017).

Velasco-Fernández, R., J. Ramos-Martín, and M. Giampietro. 2015. "The Energy Metabolism of China and India Between 1971 and 2010: Studying the Bifurcation." *Renewable and Sustainable Energy Reviews* 41: 1052–66. doi:10.1016/j.rser.2014.08.065

Wu, F. 2004. "Urban Poverty and Marginalization Under Market Transition: The Case of Chinese Cities." *International Journal of Urban and Regional Research* 28: 401–23. doi:10.1111/j.0309-1317.2004.00526.x

# 9

# The Central Role of Surplus Energy in Human Development and a Class-divided Unsustainable Society

## Sagar Dhara

## Introduction

Energy flows power all abiotic (e.g., the revolving of planets around the sun and the movement of continents on earth) and biotic processes (e.g., photosynthesis and evolution). Without energy flows all processes will stop.

Surplus energy, the difference between the energy humans invest to harvest an energy source and the energy yield of that source (see section "Surplus Energy Generation"), has been the locomotive engine for human development from hunting-gathering till today. No species other than humans generates surplus energy as humans are the only species that possess the ability to create knowledge of energy conversion, or technology. The main course of human history has been the quest for maximizing the generation of surplus energy.

In the last 100,000 years, humans expanded their technological capacity manifold, drawing increasing amounts of energy resources from nature. The per capita energy draw of modern man is greater than 25 times that of his ancient forefather, the hunter-gatherer, and human population has increased more than 2,000-fold since then. Humans have overdrawn energy from nature, to the detriment of the environment and other species. Consequently, human society has become unsustainable and faces the tipping points of global warming and peak oil.[1]

Surplus energy was distributed more or less equally amongst all members of hunting-gathering bands. With the advent of class society, initially in the form of slavery and subsequently in the form of feudalism and capitalism, surplus energy was distributed unevenly, with a small minority getting a bulk of the harvested surplus energy and the vast majority getting only a small fraction of it. Unequal distribution of surplus energy has caused enormous conflict throughout human history.

Two ideologies have contributed to the making of a human society that is unsustainable and unequal. Anthropocentrism prioritizes energy draws from nature by humans over that of all other users—biotic and abiotic. Privatization of nature and its products has allowed class society to grow legitimized inequality. For a sustainable, equal, and peaceful human society, anthropocentrism, privatization of nature, and the institutions that support them will have to be discarded.

**Table 9.1**
*Atmospheric constituents and temperature on selected planets*

|  | $CO_2$ (%) | N (%) | $O_2$ (%) | Temperature (°C) |
|---|---|---|---|---|
| Venus | 96 | 3.5 | <0.01 | 477 |
| Mars | 96.5 | <1.8 | <0.01 | −53 |
| Earth without life | 98.0 | 1.9 | Trace | 290 |
| Earth with life | 0.03–0.04 | 78 | 21 | 13–14 |

*Source:* Williams (2016).

This chapter explores the central role that surplus energy has played in a class-divided society, and whether such a society can become sustainable and inclusive.

# Human Interference in the Carbon Cycle

Since its birth, earth has had three atmospheres. The first, made primarily of hydrogen, helium, and a little carbon, formed 4.5 Giga[2] years ago (Gya), was short-lived as both gases are light and probably escaped into space during random thermal fluctuations.

The second atmosphere formed in 4.4 Gya when the earth's crust solidified and volcanoes ejected steam, carbon dioxide ($CO_2$), and ammonia. Earth's atmosphere, like that of Venus and Mars, was predominantly a superheated (290°C) mixture of $CO_2$ and small quantities of nitrogen and oxygen (Table 9.1).

The $CO_2$ gradually dissolved in the oceans and precipitated as carbonates. About 3.5 Gya the first life forms (archaea) emerged, and by ~2.7 Gya, oxygen-producing phototropic organisms (cyanobacteria) slowly began to suck $CO_2$ from the atmosphere and released oxygen. This process, known as photosynthesis, used $CO_2$ to make complex organic compounds.

In the next half a billion years, photosynthesis and silicate rock weathering transformed Earth's atmosphere from an anoxic to an oxic (oxygen-containing) state and cooled the earth to an average temperature of ~13°C, making it habitable. This did not happen on Venus or Mars as they lacked photosynthetic organisms.

Heterotrophic creatures (e.g., mammals) that developed after photosynthetic organisms use oxygen to burn organic compounds made by the latter and release $CO_2$. Both photosynthetic and heterotrophic organisms die, and decomposers break down dead organic matter to release carbon dioxide, which eventually recirculates its way back into the food web.

The complete traverse of carbon through land, water, and air constitutes the carbon cycle (Table 9.2). The carbon cycle has been in equilibrium for millennia, with ~169 Peta[3] grams per year of carbon ($PgCyr^{-1}$) exchanged both ways between the atmosphere and the earth's surface (land and oceans).

Carbon is stored in land (rocks—limestone, dolomite and chalk; soil—organic matter and vegetation; and fossil fuels), water (as calcium carbonate in shells and corals), and in the atmosphere. Rocks store the maximum carbon and vegetation the least (Table 9.3).

Animate and biomass energies, the primary energy sources prior to 1700, were replaced by fossil fuels (coal, oil, and gas) after the Industrial Revolution. Humans have already used 37 per cent of the original fossil fuel stock. About 65 per cent of the carbon released from used fossil fuels into the carbon cycle has accumulated in the atmosphere, increasing its carbon stock by 45 per cent over the pre-1750 stock of 529 PgC (Johansson et al. 2012).

The total carbon on earth being constant, the additional carbon being pumped into the active carbon cycle comes largely from burning fossil fuels in which carbon was locked away for 300 million years. A smaller fraction comes from land use change. Fossil fuel use and deforestation add 4 Pg of carbon to the

**Table 9.2**
*Carbon flux changes between land, water, and air*

|  |  | *Pre-1750* | *2000–10* | *Difference* |
|---|---|---|---|---|
|  |  | $PgCyr^{-1}$ | $PgCyr^{-1}$ | $PgCyr^{-1}$ |
| **Net per annum flux to atmosphere from oceans and land** |  | 169 | 207.1±1.4 | 38.1±1.4 |
| From oceans |  | 60.7 | 78.4 | 17.7 |
| From land | Respiration & fires | 107.2 | 118.7 | 11.5 |
|  | Volcanism | 0.1 | 0.1 |  |
|  | Freshwater outgassing | 1.0 | 1.0 |  |
|  | Fossil fuels & cement production | ~0 | 7.8±0.6 | 7.8±0.6 |
|  | Net land use change | ~0 | 1.1±0.8 | 1.1±0.8 |
| **Net per annum flux from atmosphere to oceans and land** |  | 169.2 | 203.3 | 34.1 |
| To oceans |  | 60 | 80 | 20 |
| To land | Rock weathering | 0.3 | 0.3 |  |
|  | Gross photosynthesis | 108.9 | 123 | 14.1 |
| **Net per annum atmospheric increase*** |  | 0.2 | 3.8±1.4 | 4±1.4 |

*Source:* Ciais et al. (2013).
*Note:*    *Imbalance in fluxes from/to atmosphere as given in the source document. Small imbalances in fluxes may be due to estimation and other errors.

**Table 9.3**
*Carbon stock changes in oceans, land, and atmosphere*

|  | *Pre-1750* | *2000–10* | *Difference* |
|---|---|---|---|
|  | *PgC* | *PgC* | *PgC* |
| **Oceans** | **40,453** | **40,608±30** | **155±30** |
| Surface & deep ocean | 38,000 | 38,155±30 | 155±30 |
| Ocean floor and surface sediments | 1,750 | 1,750 |  |
| Marine biota | 3 | 3 |  |
| Dissolved organic carbon | 700 | 700 |  |
| **Land** (excluding rocks) | **4,652–6,690** | **4,257–6,295±75** | **–395±75** |
| Soils | 1,500–2,400 | 1,500–2,400 |  |
| Permafrost | 1,700 | 1,700 |  |
| Vegetation | 450–650 | 420–620±45 | –30±45 |
| Fossil fuels | 1002–1,940 | 637–1,574±30 | –365±30 |
| **Atmosphere** | **589** | **829±10** | **240±10** |

*Source:* Ciais et al. (2013).

atmosphere every year. This has seriously disturbed the carbon cycle. Global warming and peak oil are consequences of fossil fuel overuse that pose a grave risk to human society.

To understand the relation between disturbance in the carbon cycle, anthropocentrism, and a class society, it is necessary to define and understand the historical process of generation, distribution, and accumulation of surplus energy.

## Surplus Energy Generation

Surplus energy is generated when humans harvest energy from nature, for example, solar energy, fossil fuels, nuclear, wind, and planetary energies. It is the difference between energy yield or return of an energy source and the energy invested by humans to harvest it.

$$\text{Surplus energy} = \text{Energy yield of an energy source} - \text{Energy invested} \\ \text{by humans to harvest the energy source} \tag{1}$$

For example, if 1 Joule (J) of energy is invested by humans to prospect, mine, transport, and refine coal, the energy return to the investor is typically ~30 J. The energy return on energy invested (EROEI)[4] is 30 J and surplus energy is 29 J.

The energy input includes direct energy investment in the form of fossil fuels, animate energy, or other secondary sources such as electricity and embodied energy.[5] The energy return is the theoretical maximum energy yield of the energy source.

The EROEIs of fossil fuels typically range 20–80. An EROEI of 10 or less is not considered to be a good energy source. The EROI of biofuels made from corn are less than 1, hence are not viable (Murphy and Hall 2010).

The creation of an energy source, for example, fossil fuels or vegetation, is an energy conversion process. The laws of thermodynamics require that energy must be conserved in an energy conversion process. Since some energy is lost as waste heat in any energy conversion, energy content of fossil fuels or vegetation must be less than energy input. Written as an equation,

$$\text{Energy yield of an energy source} = \text{Energy input to create the energy source} - \text{Waste heat} \tag{2}$$

The concept of surplus energy does not violate the laws of thermodynamics. To prove that, Equation 1 can be rewritten as:

$$\text{Energy yield of an energy source} = \text{Energy input made by humans to harvest} \\ \text{the energy source} + \text{Surplus energy} \tag{3}$$

and reconciled with Equation 2,

$$\text{Energy yield of an energy source} = \text{Energy input to create the energy source} - \text{Waste heat} \\ = \text{Energy input made by humans to harvest} \\ \text{the energy source} + \text{Surplus energy} \tag{4}$$

The total energy input to create the energy source includes the solar and geothermal energy that nature provides, which comes free of energy cost. Plants use solar energy in photosynthesis and geothermal energy bakes dead phytomass and zoomass to create fossil fuels. Surplus energy is derived from the "free of energy cost" energy that nature provides, that is, energy that nature provides for which no input energy is provided by humans. This energy is not factored in while computing surplus energy. Thermodynamics considers all input energies, but economics considers only energy invested by humans.

Surplus energy is the material basis for the economic categories of surplus value, profit, and capital.

The manner in which surplus energy is generated and distributed in all forms of class society—slavery, feudalism, and capitalism—is the same, only the form varies. The mode of production debate looked at the form in which surplus is generated and not its content.

## Surplus Energy and Human Development

Humans have the unique ability to create energy conversion knowledge and technologies. By improving knowledge and technology, they have continuously increased energy draws.

Without surplus energy, no development occurs. Other species cannot create surplus energy and, hence, do not develop. They only evolve. Humans have created surplus energy throughout their history. Hunter-gatherers transited to farming as they had surplus food which gave them time to domesticate plants and animals. Likewise, surplus energy from agriculture helped them in transiting to industrialism.

### Anthropo-energy Age

The main source of energy humans used was human energy and biomass. Through most of the Palaeolithic and Mesolithic ages (1.8 Mya–10Kya),[6] hunter-gatherers fashioned crude tools from stone and bone—spears, bows and arrows, fishing hooks, and fishing nets—and learned to use fire.

Proto-humans migrated from Africa to Eurasia about 1 Mya, then to Europe around 0.5 Mya. Proto-humans and humans migrated towards regions that yielded maximum energy (food), for example, river valleys and coastal areas. Hunters followed migrating herds or moved after exhausting resources of a region. Gathering food involved everyone in a band, barring the very young, old, and infirm. Hunter-gatherer societies were nomadic people with virtually no hierarchy and no private ownership of energy resources.

The per capita energy availability for hunter-gatherers was between 7.5 and 12.5 GJ/a.[7] The average EROEI of hunting-gathering societies for all regions was 10–20. This was adequate for making tools, organizing bands, and for some leisure. Without surplus energy, hunter-gatherers would not have transited to the next stage, that is, primitive agriculture and pastoralism.

### Bioenergy Age

Bioenergies consist of animate energy and biomass. In the bioenergy age, human-power and domesticated animals were used as prime movers.

Agriculture developed and gradually replaced hunting-gathering as the prime activity that created the maximum surplus energy in the Neolithic age; it remained so for a very long time, 10–0.5 Kya. Throughout its history, agriculture provided food, fodder, and fibre for humans.

#### Primitive Agriculture

Primitive agriculture appeared independently in at least five places between 10 and 5 Kya—Mesopotamia, China, Mesoamerica, the Andes and Amazon, and Eastern America. Secondary domestication of local crops happened in 9–5 Kya in the Indus Valley, Egypt, and Europe. Domestication of animals, except dogs, happened almost simultaneously at the same sites as crops. This helped humans make the shift to agriculture faster. Domestic animals provided milk, meat, farm manure, draught power for farming and transport, hides and wool for clothing, and other utilities.

This period also saw the development of simple wooden ploughs and other agricultural implements, harnesses for draught animals, wheeled vehicles, roads, and square-sailed ships. To reduce the risk of crop loss, primitive agriculturalists also did some hunting-gathering.

The per capita energy consumption of primitive agriculturalists ranged 18–24 GJ/a. Energy returns for shifting agriculture ranged 11–15-folds for small grain, 20–40-folds for root crops and good corn yields, and 70-fold for legumes in rich farmlands (Smil 1994, 2008). These surpluses helped primitive agriculture move on to the next stage of development, that is, traditional agriculture that was more settled and permanent.

While primitive agricultural societies inherited the largely egalitarian structure of hunter-gatherer societies, surplus food and larger populations triggered the beginning of the division of labour and a settled way of life in villages. Bands became tribes and tribes required some minimal administration to maintain intra- and inter-tribal order and harmony, which elders did. In due course they became chiefs, whether appointed by selection or by hereditary. They required help to do their job, which saw the beginnings of a bureaucracy. A bureaucracy requires upkeep, so voluntary contributions to the chief gradually became compulsory tax or forced tribute. An incipient class society and state came into being.

## Traditional Agriculture

Biomass and animate energy remained the primary energy sources during the period when traditional agriculture was the primary economic activity. Wind and water became secondary energy sources around 1 Kya. Traditional agriculture progressed very gradually by extending the cropped area and through farm intensification. Farm intensification was done gradually by improving farm tools, irrigation, crop rotation, use of fertilizers, and replacing human labour with animal power. Better connectivity between places helped indirectly in raising the energy surplus.

The per capita energy consumption was ~30–50 GJ per annum. The EROEI for wheat crops was about 20 in the Roman Empire, ~40 during Medieval Period, and greater than 150 at the beginning of the nineteenth century (Smil 1994, 2008).

Societies and their administration became complex. Chiefdoms became kingdoms, and kingdoms became empires. Kings appointed chiefs who were responsible for tax collection, maintaining law and order, and contributing manpower and money for wars waged against other kingdoms. Greater food surplus meant more division of labour. A range of new craft and administrative vocations were created—craftsmen, traders, intellectuals, bureaucrats, soldiers—and this division played a major role in moving the society to the fossil fuel age.

# Fossil Fuel Age

Fossil fuels became the primary energy sources in it. The fossil fuel age consists of two periods—from the sixteenth century when coal began to be used in Britain till the Industrial Revolution began in the eighteenth century, and the last 250 years of industrial society.

## Pre-industrial Society

Though coal began to be used in pre-industrial society, animate energy and biomass remained the primary energy sources. Wind (sail ships and windmills) and water (watermills) power were used in many parts of the world. Wind's contribution to the total energy consumption was small, but its importance lay in moving sail ships that were used for trade and discovering and colonizing new lands from where vast amount of energy was harvested by the imperial powers. Innovation in windlasses, capstans, and gearwheels increased energy conversion efficiencies and set the tone for the shift to fossil fuels.

## Industrial Society

Ever since the Industrial Revolution began 250 years ago, fossil fuels have become the primary energy source. They have a very high energy density (gas has 50–52 MJ/kg, oil ~80 per cent of that, and coal ~50 per cent) and are easy to transport and store. This has allowed larger energy throughputs to flow through the economy, and consequently generate higher surplus energy.

Coal was used to power several eighteenth- and nineteenth-century inventions—the steam engine and the railway locomotive. Since then there has been a flood of inventions—automobiles, aeroplanes, inorganic fertilizers, diesel pumps, etc.—that use petroleum products. Oil has become indispensable for meeting our daily needs.

Oil was first extensively drilled in Pennsylvania in 1860. The oil rush over the next 30 years paralleled the earlier gold rush in "wild west" America. Oil was first used to provide lighting to replace the scarce whale oil. Oil became the route to quick fortune for the enterprising. Rockefeller made his millions in the latter half of the nineteenth century by integrating oil production with refining and marketing, and edging out competition.

The last 150 years of global politics has been dominated by the need for access and control over oil. At the turn of the twentieth century, Churchill, the then British defence secretary, ordered the Royal Navy to replace coal-fired boilers in warships with oil-fired ones to gain speed. He also secured assured oil supplies from Persia. This allowed the Royal Navy to maintain superiority at sea in the First World War. It was between the two world wars that the automobile and aircraft industries grew rapidly, and so did the demand for oil products, in particular for gasoline.

Fossil fuels played an important role in the Second World War. Japan had no fossil fuels. To get coal, Japan invaded Manchuria in the early nineteen thirties. After attacking Pearl Harbour, Japan invaded Indonesia for its oil and gas, and Germany invaded Russia to gain control of the Baku oil wells. Finally, Japan and Germany ran out of oil and lost the war (Yergin 2008).

Gas is a more recent fossil fuel that has come into use. While gas today meets 21 per cent of human primary energy requirements (IEA 2016), it has not influenced global politics to the same extent as oil as the latter's contribution to primary energy supply is significantly greater than that of gas, can be transported and stored easily, and has more end products.

# Surplus Energy Acquisition and Distribution

Only in hunter-gatherer societies was surplus energy distributed more or less equally. In all class societies—slavery, feudalism, and capitalism—it is distributed unequally.

## Ownership of Energy Resources

It took nature 300 million years to bake coal from dead plants and animals of the Carboniferous Period. Humans created private ownership rights over coal when in fact they played no part in making it. The same logic holds for other natural resources. Humans, therefore, have no ownership claim over nature or its products. At best, like other species, they have a usufruct claim, and such rights should be equal for all humans.

Since slavery began 5,000 years ago, private ownership of nature and energy resources has created and perpetuated a class society, and consequently this has led to inequitable distribution of surplus energy. Today capitalism justifies private ownership of natural resources as an ideology that works best for human development.

By claiming ownership of energy resources, surplus energy was appropriated by a small class of people (slave and feudal lords and the bourgeois). By virtue of a small investment that slave and feudal lords and the bourgeois make in harvesting energy sources, they acquire and claim ownership over the energy source and all the energy it contains. In the example mentioned earlier (p. 85), by making an investment of 1 J, the investor claims ownership of 30 J, of which 29 J are surplus.

In slave societies, the slave-owner provides a certain amount of energy, direct and embodied, as food, housing, etc., to the slave. The grain that the slave produces on the owner's farm and other services s/he performs are appropriated by the slave-owner as s/he owns the slave. In feudalism, a serf provides energy inputs into land as animate and embodied energies (tools). The farm output, whose energy content is greater than its input, is shared with the feudal lord, who provides no energy inputs but owns land. In capitalism, because the EROEI of fossil fuels ranges 20–80, the capitalist is able to get a much higher return than his/her investment.

In post-capitalist societies (USSR, China, and Vietnam), the State appropriates the surplus energy and distributes it on the principle of "each according to his ability." In practice, this was never followed completely. The distribution of surplus energy on the principle of "each according to his need" never happened as abundance of surplus required for this never existed.

## Ownership Though Conquest, Colonization and Privatizing Global Commons

Surplus energy in the form of embodied energy was often acquired through conquest. The conqueror gained ownership of surplus energy generated and accumulated by the conquered. Land and water act as host energy sources because photosynthesis occurs in plants that grow on land or in water. Harvesting energy and marking boundaries is the easiest on land. It was, therefore, privatized from the times of antiquity. Harvesting energy and marking boundaries is more difficult in water, so it was privatized only recently. The energy in air is low; therefore the atmosphere was not privatized. The Kyoto Protocol is now attempting to privatize air as a preferential $CO_2$ dumping ground for the developed countries.

# Surplus Energy, Class Society, Inequality, and Conflict

## Class Society

Slave and feudal lords and the bourgeoisie can use the surplus energy they acquired in any manner they wished—conspicuous consumption or by reinvesting it in a virtuous cycle to harvest more energy and, therefore, generate more surplus energy. The accumulation of surplus energy happens in the hands of a class of society that lays claim to ownership over energy resources, that is, slave and feudal lords and the bourgeoisie.

Accumulation of surplus energy takes the form of direct ownership of energy resources as well as that of embodied energy, that is, goods. The continuous accumulation of surplus energy in the hands of one class results in inequality.

## Inequality

Inequality manifests itself between and within countries. Energy consumption today across regions is highly unequal. While developed countries may have a per capita consumption of 3–7 toe/year,[8] developing countries consume 0.2–0.6 toe/year (see Table 9.4).

Intra-country energy inequality is quite high. Many in India may be consuming as little as 0.1 toe per annum, while a few may be consuming as much as 200 toe per annum.

## Conflict

Human conflict is driven by human perception of the potential difference in energy access and control between people. In the last century, just three types of conflicts—interstate, colonial, and civil wars were responsible for over 100 million deaths (Leitenberg 2006). About a tenth of our global energy consumption

**Table 9.4**

*Per capita energy consumption inequality between countries*

| Country/Region | Total primary energy supply 2013 Mtoe/Year | Per capita energy consumption 2013 Toe |
|---|---|---|
| USA | 2,220 | 6.94 |
| EU | 1,680 | 3.29 |
| China | 2,780 | 2.04 |
| World | 13,460 | 1.88 |
| India | 780 | 0.64 |
| Cambodia | 5.3 | 0.34 |
| Bangladesh | 31.3 | 0.21 |
| Ethiopia | 34 | 0.39 |

*Source:* IEA (n.d.).

today, that is, 50 EJ,[9] or the equivalent energy yield of one million Hiroshima-sized atom bombs,[10] is expended to keep the global war machine up and running (Smil 2008). Conflicts between people were largely around the capture of lands that yielded high energy levels.

## Surplus Energy and Anthropocentrism

Anthropocentrism is the belief that humans are the most important species on earth and the rest of nature is for their use and enjoyment. It is epitomized in v 1:26, *Book of Genesis,*

> And God said, Let us make man in our image, after our likeness: and let them have dominion over the fish of the sea, and over the fowl of the air, and over the cattle, and over all the earth, and over every creeping thing that creepeth upon the earth.

Anthropocentrism legitimizes unbridled exploitation of nature for human use. As an ideology, anthropocentrism drives the creation of increasing amounts of surplus energy by overdrawing energy from nature.

Eight thousand years ago, forests covered 40 per cent of the world's landmass, that is, 60 million km², a third of which has been colonized by humans (FAO 2015), that is, over six times India's land area, to make way for agricultural lands and pastures. The energy used to cut that forest is estimated to be greater than 8 ZJ,[11] or the energy in 160 million Hiroshima-sized nuclear bombs[12] (20,000 bombs/year × 8,000 years).

Human appropriated net primary production (HANPP; a measure of human usurpation of phytomass) is estimated to be 24 per cent of all new phytomass produced annually (Haberl et al. 2007), that is, the energy contained in ~8 million Hiroshima-sized atomic bombs.[13] The doubling of HANPP in the last century has caused the species extinction rate to jump by 1,000–10,000-fold (Chivian and Bernstein 2008). Amongst large mammals, the Tasmanian tiger, California grizzly bear, Bali tiger, Newfoundland wolf, Indian cheetah, Pyrenean ibex, Baiji, and the Zanzibar leopard have disappeared for good in just the last century.

A consequence of anthropocentrism is environmental degradation. Humans have exploited the environment for their benefit to such an extent that its life-support systems—air, water, and land—have been badly degraded.

Air pollution has caused extensive injury to human health, crop yields, water bodies, forests, and monuments. Air pollution is estimated to cause 235 million asthma cases a year (WHO 2013). Air pollution causes an estimated 15–40 per cent crop yield loss in a 60–70 km radius around large Indian cities (Ashmore and Marshall 1997).

Two recent continuous drought years in South Asia and consequent water shortages have caused over 2,000 deaths in the summer 2015 heat wave. Contaminated water causes an estimated 3.4 million deaths annually (WHO 2015).

Unsustainable land use has caused unprecedented land degradation—deforestation, desertification, soil erosion, nutrient depletion, soil salinity, soil moisture reduction, chemical contamination, and biological cycle disruption. Drylands, 90 per cent of which are in developing countries, cover 40 per cent of earth's land surface and support a third of the world's population. They are at great risk of desertification.

Capitalism and societies that attempted to move beyond capitalism, that is, USSR, China, and Vietnam, were both anthropocentric.

## Energy Growth

In the last 10,000 years, the pursuit of maximizing surplus energy has led to a massive growth in energy draw. The capita energy consumption of the industrial man is more than 100 times greater than the 0.075 toe/year of the hunter-gatherer. Global energy consumption today is 50,000-fold greater than it was during the Anthropo-energy era (Figure 9.1).

Because of fossil fuels, the growth rate of energy consumption jumped from 0.1 per cent per annum before the Industrial Revolution to 1.4 per cent per annum after. Global energy consumption today is 13.5 Gtoe/year, of which fossil fuels contribute 81 per cent (IEA 2016).

Global energy use, which is growing at a rate of 2 per cent per annum today, has doubled in the last four decades. If it maintains this growth rate, energy use would be 50,000 times the current energy consumption

**Figure 9.1**
*Per capita energy use*

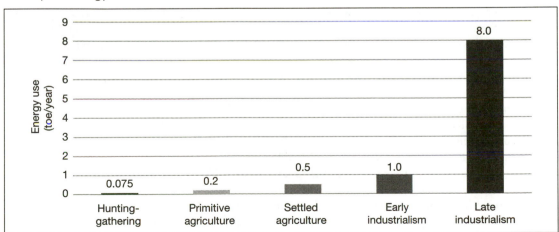

*Source:* Projections made from data available in Smil (1994, 2008).

**Figure 9.2**

*Recent past and future global energy use (Gtoe) at 2 per cent per annum growth*

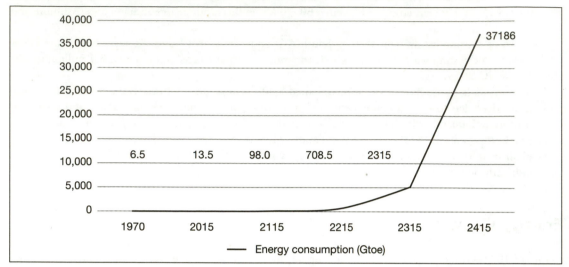

*Source:* Projections made from data available in IEA (2016).

in about 550 years (Figure 9.2). Human society already faces the tipping points of peak oil and global warming after the first 50,000-fold increase in energy use. The impact of next 50,000-fold increase, even if that energy was available, is unimaginable.

# Tipping Points

## Impending Energy Crisis

As developing countries try to catch up with the developing ones, energy demand is projected to grow rapidly. Fossil fuels cannot fulfil this demand. About 50 per cent of the original oil reserves and 30 per cent of coal and gas reserves have already been consumed (Table 9.5). Oil production has peaked and will start declining in the near future. This phenomenon is known as "peak oil." If the current production levels are maintained, oil will exhaust in about 40–45 years, the recent production of shale oil notwithstanding. Gas and coal will also exhaust within this century.

As oil becomes scarcer, prices will increase, triggering demand destruction and a possible global economic crisis and social collapse, with lawlessness spreading—armed brigands controlling neighbourhoods—and the reformation of fiefdoms.

In the twentieth century, Global North developed by using massive quantities of fossil fuels either stolen (e.g., coal acquired by Japan from China and Indonesia) or available cheaply (e.g., low-priced oil from the Middle East) from the Global South. These sources are no longer available to Southern nations as none of carbon- and hydrocarbon-rich countries are colonies nor will they sell fossil fuels cheaply anymore. Even if the technical issues related to renewable energies were solved, they cannot offer the EROEI[14] as the fossil fuels do, and hence cannot play the same role that fossil fuels did for North nations. The Global South cannot develop to become like the Global North.

**Table 9.5**

*Fossil fuel reserves*

| Fuel | Original resource* | | Remaining reserves | Current annual consumption | R/P** |
|------|--------------------|--------------------|--------------------|----------------------------|-------|
| | *ZJ*** | *% used* | *ZJ* | *ZJ/Year* | *Years* |
| Coal | 26.2 | 31 | 18.1 | 0.17 | ~106 |
| Oil | 13.7 | 54 | 6.3 | 0.17 | ~37 |
| Gas | 9.8 | 29 | 7.0 | 0.13 | ~54 |

*Source:* Compiled based on data from Johansson et al. (2012).

*Notes:* * Estimates of resources and reserves are closely guarded information; hence, figures for original resources and current reserves are approximations.

** Reserve to current production ratio.

*** Zeta ($10^{21}$) Joules.

Declining energy resources have grave implications for the future human society as it has the potential to cause economic crises, and even cause civilizational regress or collapse. The oil price shock after the 1973 Yom Kippur War triggered a global stock market crash, soaring inflation and high unemployment rates. Energy collapses were responsible for many civilizational collapses in the past, for example, Mayan, Roman, and Polynesian civilizations; but such collapses remained local as economies were not integrated across boundaries.

In today's globalized economy, a collapse will be worldwide and we are not far from there. As the global economy's EROEI drops to less than 10, supporting an industrial civilization will become difficult because an increasing amount of energy has to be invested to harvest a fixed amount of energy. The global EROEI is around 16–17 today and is dropping (Murphy 2014).

## Global Warming

For 10,000 years prior to the Industrial Revolution, $CO_2$ concentrations were stable between 260 and 280 ppm (Bjørke and Seki n.d.). Massive use of fossil fuels and deforestation has raised the concentration of atmospheric $CO_2$ to 400 ppm (NOAA n.d.). Concentrations of other important greenhouse gases (GHG)—methane, nitrous oxide, and tropospheric ozone—have also risen in the last 250 years. The impact of the warming that GHGs will cause is expected to be devastating.

Prior to the UN Framework Convention on Climate Change (UNFCCC) meeting held in Paris in December 2015, 184 countries submitted voluntary pledges to tackle global warming. The UNFCCC (2015), the UN Environment Programme (UNEP 2015), and several researchers in recently published assessments, for example, Climate Action Tracker, indicate that the pledges are inadequate. Even if they are fully implemented, temperature rise by 2100 will exceed 2°C, and is likely to be in the range 3–4°C (Climate Interactive n.d.). Some researchers put the temperature rise at up to 5°C (Reilly et al. 2015).

The impact of an average global 3–4°C temperature rise could cause unprecedented heat waves over land; alter precipitation patterns; increase the frequency and intensity of extreme weather events (these impacts will be unevenly distributed); raise sea levels; flood many coastal areas; result in climate refugees; shrink glaciers and reduce the Arctic Sea's ice extent; reduce crop yields and cause food shortage, hunger, deprivation, malnutrition, disease, and poverty; severely impact freshwater availability, human health, and biodiversity; and cause large-scale displacement of populations and consequences for human security and economic and trade systems.

Global warming will impact developing countries and vulnerable populations the most, particularly in the tropics, sub-tropics, and towards the poles. Many small islands will not be able to sustain their populations.

# Can Green Energies Replace Fossil Fuels?

Capitalism's solution to tackle the problem of sustainability of human society is to attempt shifting to green energies, materials, and technologies. Several energy sources exist but none of them can replace fossil fuels.

Renewables and nuclear technologies are not in a position to replace fossil fuels. Biomass already provides 10 per cent of the energy people use. It is a widespread resource and can easily be converted to provide energy services. Unfortunately, biomass is already over-harvested—people use 16 per cent of the energy that vegetation produces each year. Further harvesting of biomass will only exacerbate the ugly environmental gashes on the planet that biomass extraction, through deforestation and other land use changes, has already caused.

Hydropower provides 2.4 per cent of the world's primary energy, but 40 per cent of hydropower's deployable potential has been tapped. Resistance to dams has increased because dams destroy upstream forests and agricultural land; downstream areas can flood when excess water is released from reservoirs. Hydropower is unlikely to be expanded much except in some hilly regions.

Nuclear energy, meanwhile, provides about 5 per cent of human beings' energy requirements. But the world is moving away from thermal nuclear energy. It is dirty—uranium mining carries serious health consequences, and about 300,000 metric tonnes of highly radioactive spent fuel (Feiveson et al. 2011) are stored at reactor sites around the world. It is unsafe—already there have been three major accidents at power reactors. It is open to misuse—enriched uranium can be diverted to make bombs. And it is expensive—much costlier than fossil fuels. And uranium ore is finite. The International Atomic Energy Agency (IAEA) and the Nuclear Energy Agency estimate that reasonably assured resources of uranium ore can fuel existing reactors for 150 years (IAEA 2014). But some independent researchers dispute such estimates, arguing that uranium ore will last only half that long (Dittmar 2009).

Photovoltaics and concentrated solar power, along with wind, today provide about 1.4 per cent of global energy (IEA 2016). These sources are growing at 15–40 per cent per annum, but have several drawbacks. They suffer from intermittence. They can only be sited at favourable locations. They cannot be used directly for locomotion. They have environmental impacts that aren't often discussed. Wind facilities and photovoltaic plants require significantly more land than fossil fuel plants do. Realistic estimates suggest that deployable wind energy can satisfy only 5 per cent of today's global energy demand (Castro et al. 2011), and significant amounts of carbon dioxide are emitted in the manufacture of both wind and solar equipment. And these energy sources, without the financial subsidies they receive, are yet more expensive than fossil fuels.

Energy efficiency, meanwhile, is sometimes seen as an easy route to decreasing emissions. But there is a limit to how much can be achieved through efficiency. Moreover, the Jevons' paradox comes into play—if energy availability increases due to greater efficiency, energy will become cheaper and consumption will rise.

# Towards a Sustainable and Equitable Future

Capitalism is based on the principle of continuous generation of surplus, allowing it to be expropriated and accumulated by the bourgeoisie. Continuous growth is its leitmotiv. Anthropocentrism allows capitalism to exploit nature continuously, whereas sustainability requires a steady state. Since natural resources are limited, perpetual growth is impossible. Capitalism, therefore, can never be sustainable.

Capitalism is also based on the principle of private ownership of nature and energy resources. Surplus energy accrues in the hands of the bourgeoisie, creating an unequal class society. While capitalism may allow inequality to reduce, its removal is antithetical to it. Capitalism where everyone is equal is an oxymoron.

If capitalism cannot deliver a sustainable and equal human society, what can? Eco-socialism can. To get there we must replace our current global outlook of "Gain maximization for a few with risk minimization for all species."

We must believe and act in a manner that makes us a part of nature and not apart from it. That shift requires four things to happen:

- Reducing global energy consumption and emissions by 60 per cent.
- Moving into an energy and emissions equality regime.
- Moving away from fossil fuels completely by 2050 and relying on solar, biomass, and animate energy.
- Shifting from non-renewable, abiotic resources, and technologies to renewable and biotic ones; and from high energy to low energy systems.

The road map to get there are hazy. Yet some steps must be taken in that direction as in its quest for maximizing surplus energy, capitalism has already disturbed the carbon cycle beyond immediate repair.

The implications of the above measures are radical; amongst the other measures are that United States and Canada reduce their energy consumption by 90 per cent, Europe, Australasia, and Japan by 75 per cent; destroy weapons of war and of mass destruction; decentralize governance and make it self-administrating; give impetus to localism; dissolve energy differentials between urban and rural areas; guarantee minimum sustenance energy to all and implement a uniform risk and emission standards for all people; trade ownership rights with usufruct rights over nature; put knowledge and energy resources under democratic social control; and discard credit as it operates on the basis of payback from future energy surplus accruals.

Even without phasing out fossil fuels, each of the following three actions has the potential to reduce global energy consumption and $CO_2$ emissions by 10 per cent:[15]

- Move towards soft borders in all parts of the world.
- Shrink cities and re-ruralize.
- Phase out air transport and private surface transport.

With a population of 7.3 billion, equal distribution of energy will give each person 0.75 toe/year of energy, including embodied energy. This is what PPP[16] $ 5,000 can purchase and is adequate for a good life at the current middle-class levels in India, but inadequate for luxury consumption (Dhara 2011). A smaller global population would give each person more energy.

# Notes

1. The maxing of oil production followed by a decline.
2. Giga $= 10^9$.
3. Peta $= 10^{15}$.
4. EROEI $=$ EROEI: Energy return on energy invested. It is the ratio of usable energy obtained to energy invested to obtain it. $=$ Energy output of an energy source $\div$ energy input to tap the energy source.
5. Embodied energy is the total energy—human, fossil fuel, consumed by all the processes associated with the production of a product or service, from the mining and processing of natural resources to manufacture, transport, and delivery. The value of a product or service is proportional to the amount of embodied energy it contains.
6. Mya—million years ago, Kya—Thousand years ago.
7. GJ/a—Giga $(10^9)$ Joules per annum.
8. Tonne of Oil Equivalent, amount of energy released by burning one tonne of crude oil.
9. Exa $(10^{18})$ joules.
10. A Hiroshima-sized bomb contains approximately 50 Tera $(10^{12})$ joules.
11. Zeta $(10^{21})$ joules.
12. Computed by author from embodied energy tables.
13. 1 kg of phytomass has an energy content of 11–19 MJ/kg.

14. Most renewable energies have an EROEIs of less than 10.
15. Per computations made by the author. For example, the fuel used in air transport accounts for 3 per cent of the world's primary energy consumption.
16. Purchasing Power Parity.

# References

Ashmore, M.R., and F.M. Marshall. 1997. "The Impacts and Costs of Air Pollution on Agriculture in Developing Countries." Project number ERP 6289, Final Technical Report Submitted to the Department for International Development, Environment Research Programme, Imperial College of Science Technology and Medicine, London. Available at: http://pubs.iied.org/pdfs/6132IIED.pdf (accessed on 26 April 2017).

Bjørke, S.A., and M. Seki. n.d. "Vital Climate Graphics, GRID Arendal and UNEP." Available at: http://www.grida.no/publications/vg/climate/page/3057.aspx (accessed on 26 April 2017).

Castro, C.D., M. Mediavilla, L.J. Miguel, and F. Frechoso. 2011. "Global Wind Power Potential: Physical and Technological Limits." *Energy Policy* 39 (10): 6677–82.

Chivian, E., and A. Bernstein, eds. 2008. *Sustaining Life: How Human Health Depends on Biodiversity.* New York: Oxford University Press.

Ciais, P., C. Sabine, G. Bala, L. Bopp, V. Brovkin, J. Canadell, A. Chhabra, R. DeFries, J. Galloway, M. Heimann, C. Jones, C. Le Quéré, R.B. Myneni, S. Piao, and P. Thornton. 2013. "Carbon and Other Biogeochemical Cycles." In *Climate Change 2013: The Physical Science Basis. Contribution of Working Group I to the Fifth Assessment Report of the Intergovernmental Panel on Climate Change,* edited by T.F. Stocker, D. Qin, G.-K. Plattner, M. Tignor, S.K. Allen, J. Boschung, A. Nauels, Y. Xia, V. Bex, and P.M. Midgley. Cambridge/New York, NY: Cambridge University Press.

Climate Interactive. n.d. *UN Climate Pledge Analysis.* Available at: https://www.climateinteractive.org/programs/scoreboard/ (accessed in April 2016).

Dhara, S. 2011. "How Much Energy can Humans Have to be Sustainable." Available at: https://www.academia.edu/7164929/How_much_energy_can_human_society_have_to_be_sustainable (accessed on 26 April 2017).

Dittmar, M. 2009. *The Future of Nuclear Energy: Facts and Fiction.* Zurich: Institute of Particle Physics.

Feiveson, H., Z. Mian, M.V. Ramana, and Frank von Hippel. 2011. "Managing Spent Fuel from Nuclear Power Reactors: Experience and Lessons from Around the World, International Panel on Fissile Materials." Available at: http://fissilematerials.org/library/rr10.pdf (accessed on 26 April 2017).

Food and Agricultural Organization of the United Nations (FAO). 2015. "Global Forest Resource Assessment 2015." Available at: http://www.fao.org/3/a-i4808e.pdf (accessed on 26 April 2017).

Haberl, H., K.H. Erb, F. Krausmann, V. Gaube, A. Bondeau, C. Plutzar, S. Gingrich, W. Lucht, and M. Fischer-Kowalski. 2007. Quantifying and Mapping the Human Appropriation of Net Primary Production in Earth's Terrestrial Ecosystems." *Proceedings of the National Academy of Sciences of the United States of America* 104 (31): 12942–47.

International Atomic Energy Agency (IAEA). 2014. "Nuclear Fuel Cycle and Materials." Available at: http://www.iaea.org/OurWork/ST/NE/NEFW/Technical-Areas/NFC/uranium-production-cycle-redbook.html#RedBook (accessed in April 2016).

International Energy Agency (IEA). n.d. "Sankey Diagram." Available at: http://www.iea.org/Sankey/ (accessed in April 2016).

———. 2016. "Key World Energy Statistics." Available at: https://www.iea.org/publications/freepublications/publication/KeyWorld2016.pdf (accessed on 26 April 2017).

Johansson, T.B., N. Nakicenovic, A. Patwardhan, and L. Gomez-Echeverri, eds. 2012. *Global Energy Assessment.* Laxenburg, Austria: International Institute for Applied Systems Analysis.

Leitenberg, M. 2006. "Deaths in Wars and Conflicts in the 20th Century 3rd Ed." Occasional Paper No. 29, Peace Studies Programme, Cornell University. Available at: http://www.clingendael.nl/sites/default/files/20060800_cdsp_occ_leitenberg.pdf (accessed on 26 April 2017).

Murphy, D.J. 2014. "The Implications of the Declining Energy Return on Investment of Oil Production." *Philosophical Transactions of the Royal Society A: Mathematical, Physical and Engineering Sciences* 372: 20130126. Available at: http://dx.doi.org/10.1098/rsta.2013.0126 (accessed on 26 April 2017).

Murphy, D.J., and C.A.S. Hall. 2010. "Year in Review—EROI or Energy Return on (Energy) Invested." *Annals of the New York Academy of Sciences* 1185 (2010): 102–18.

National Oceanic and Atmospheric Administration (NOAA). n.d. "Global Greenhouse Gas Reference Network." Earth System Research Laboratory: Global Monitoring Division, U.S. Department of Commerce. Available at: https://www.esrl.noaa.gov/gmd/ccgg/trends/global.html (accessed in April 2016).

Reilly, J., S. Paltsev, E. Monier, H. Chen, A. Sokolov, J. Huang, Q. Ejaz, J. Scott, J. Morris, A. Schlosser. 2015. "Energy and Climate Outlook Perspectives from 2015." MIT Joint Programme on Science and Policy of Global Change, Massachusetts Institute of Technology. Available at: https://globalchange.mit.edu/sites/default/files/newsletters/files/2015 per cent20Energy per cent20 per cent26 per cent20Climate per cent20Outlook.pdf

Smil, V. 1994. *Energy in World History.* Boulder, CO: Westview press.

———. 2008. *Energy in Nature and Society: General Energetic of Complex Systems.* Cambridge, MA: The MIT press.

United Nations Environment Programme (UNEP). 2015. "Emissions Gap Report 2015: Executive Summary." Available at: http://uneplive.unep.org/media/docs/theme/13/EGR_2015_ES_English_Embargoed.pdf (accessed on 26 April 2017).

United Nations Framework Convention on Climate Change (UNFCCC). 2015. *Synthesis Report on the Aggregate Effect of Intended Nationally Determined Contributions.* New York, NY: UNFCCC.

Williams, M. 2016. "Astronomy Guide to Space: What Is the Atmosphere Like on Other Planets?" https://www.universetoday.com/35796/atmosphere-of-the-planets/ (accessed on 25 August 2017).

World Health Organization (WHO). 2013. "Asthma Fact sheet No. 307." Available at: http://www.who.int/mediacentre/factsheets/fs307/en/ (accessed on 26 April 2017).

———. 2015. "World Water Day Report." Available at: http://www.who.int/water_sanitation_health/takingcharge.html (accessed on 26 April 2017).

Yergin, D. 2008. *The Prize: The Epic Quest for Oil, Money and Power.* New York, NY: Free Press.

# SECTION 2

# Sustainability, Ecosystems, and Institutions: From the Practice

# 10

# Changing Weather Pattern in Sub-Himalayan Northeast India and Interrelations Among the Weather Variables

## Utpal Kumar De

## Introduction

The climatic condition and the livelihood pattern of human beings in any region are intricately related. On the one hand, changes in the climatic condition have serious impacts on the biodiversity, availability of water, and hence the agricultural practices of the concerned people. On the other hand, the livelihood patterns of masses necessitate human interactions with environmental resources such as soil, forests, watercourses, and vegetation. The outcomes of the interactions emerge as intense in the hilly region because of its fragility, and for this reason we observe frequent landslides, soil erosion, and changes in the watercourses, ultimately affecting the livelihood of inhabited population in and around (Shrestha et al. 1999). A thorough study of changes in weather variables and their interlinkage may help to understand the complexities of the weather change pattern and their interrelations so as to frame policies for improving the socio-economic condition of the people living in the region (Metz, Davidson, Swart, and Pan 2001; Pathak, Gajurel, and Mool 2010; Whiteman 2000).

The weather pattern and its change in the Indian Subcontinent and particularly in Northeast India is highly conditioned by the presence of Himalayan ranges in the north and the sub-Himalayan range in the east and partly by the Bay of Bengal, Indian Ocean, and the Arabian Sea on the south and west. The entire region and particularly Assam, thus, recorded high rainfall and temperate weather conditions (Clemens et al. 1991; Johnson and Houze 1987). The Himalayan ranges in the north and the sub-Himalayan ranges in the east help in generating high rainfall, by concentrating the southwest monsoon current emerging from the Arabian Sea and Bay of Bengal during the summer. The Himalayan and the sub-Himalayan ranges also block the northeasterly wind during the winter and control the temperature and humidity of the area.

Despite this positional advantage, the temperature of the region has recorded a sharp increase over the years in tune with the other regions of the globe (De, Pal, and Bodosa 2015). It was reported that in some places of the region, water used to freeze in winter in the early morning even a few decades back. In recent years, the global warming scenario has clearly been reflected by the shortened winter span and the changes in the type of clothing worn by the people and increasing use of electric fans in the region.

Apart from the secular trend, short-term erratic changes in the behaviour of weather have been noticed in the form of occurrences of high rainfall, before as well as after the usual monsoon. Human interventions, such as deforestation, mining, industrialization, changes in the agricultural practices, and resettlement of human population could be the possible reasons for such often occurrences of extreme weather conditions. Northeast India recorded frequent floods of different intensity and timing in the previous years.

The pattern of rainfall, relative humidity, and the temperature in the state of Assam in Northeast India vary across its various zones due to the geographical positions and altitudes (Barry and Chorley 2003). There are colder zones in the hilly areas and warmer zones in the plain lands. The mighty Brahmaputra, full of water from rain and glacial melt, passes through the northern part of the state and the Barak flows through the Cachar zone, with numerous tributaries contributing to the local climatic condition. Despite being an agriculture-based economy, the state of Assam experiences distressed diversification of occupational activities, which have put pressure on its forests cover and land use patterns. The rise of petty services sectors including the transport sector has visible impacts on the environment. Changes in the agricultural pattern are, however, subject to the adaptability of the farmers with the changing weather patterns over the years (Ye et al. 2013).

Meteorological records have shown a rise in the mean temperature by 0.74°C in the past 100 years (1906–2005) in the Eastern Himalayas (IPCC 2007). Indian monsoon exhibited a slight negative trend during 1871–2009 and it is associated with high spatial variation (GoI 2010; Sen, Roy, and Balling 2004). Inter-temporal and spatial variation of rainfall across the season in India, rising surface temperature, decrease in the number of rainy days and increase in the intensity of rainfall, and extreme climatic behaviour (e.g., cyclonic storms) are well-warranted in some studies (Ranuzzi and Srivastava 2012). High rate of growth of temperature in recent years has a link with the glacial retreat, which varies across the Himalayan region and could be one of the reasons for the variability in the monsoon intensity (Karma et al. 2003).

Experiences across regions of India reveal that because of changing rainfall patterns and depletion of water resources, the existing cropping pattern is becoming less productive (Guiteras 2009; Pachauri 2009; Sivanandan 1983; Venkateswarlu 2009). Thus, intensification of crops through mixed cropping and integration of high-value crops such as horticultural production are gaining prominence as a climate change adaptation strategy, especially in the hill regions. Here, dry seeding short-period paddy, wheat, maize by shifting cultivation, and some horticulture crops help in reduced water use with reasonable agricultural output (De 2015, 30–41).

All the components of weather are also supposed to be interrelated. A change in one aspect of weather is expected to alter the other factors. Thus, change in temperature is not confined to itself. It is related to rainfall and other aspects such as moisture content of the soil, humidity pattern, and evapotranspiration. Rainfall, in turn, has impact on agricultural output, vegetation, and livelihood patterns of people. Thus, it is necessary to examine the changes in the climatic pattern in order to have an idea of future trends.

There are a few studies on the linkage between human intervention and climate change in the neighbourhood (Deka, Baruah, and Bhuya 2011; Dev 2011). Also, some studies examine the effect of rising climatic uncertainty and extremes in weather condition on the economic activities, performance, livelihood conditions, and food security, as well as adaptive measures required for the sustenance of people (CESPR, RGVN, and INECC 2012; Howitt, Azuar, and MacEwan 2010; Pathak et al. 2010; TERI 2003; UNESCO 2012; Weitzman 2009). There are a number of studies on the trend and pattern of climate change (Ananthapadmanabhan, Srinivas, and Gopal 2007; Christensen et al. 2007; Cruz et al. 2007; World Bank 2008). However, these studies have not explained the relationships among the major weather components, that is, precipitation, temperature, and humidity, at the local level. Precipitation in an area may depend on temperature and evaporation levels and prevalent winds, and may affect the local temperature and humidity. In this chapter, we shall mainly concentrate on examining the complex interplay of these three major weather factors.

This study attempts to examine the spatio-temporal variation in the weather pattern in the state of Assam and analyse whether there has been any significant relation among various components of weather, namely, temperature, rainfall, and humidity. Also the causal relationship among these variables has been examined.

## Materials and Methods

Data on maximum and minimum temperature, morning and evening humidity, and rainfall for last six decades have been collected from the India Meteorological Department (IMD) and Government of Assam. At first, we have computed the quinquennial (five year) moving average of maximum and minimum temperatures of the bi-monthly average and that of rainfall from 1950–54 to 2006–10. Temporal changes in climatic variables are examined by comparing both the 10 and 30 years averages of month-wise variation at different periods. Also, trend in the month-wise and region-wise variation is plotted against the over-time change in the average figure in order to examine the seasonal and spatial variation over time.

We have tried to check the stationarity of time series processes and compared the trend coefficients of various weather variables using the Augmented Dickey–Fuller (ADF) method and Akaike information criterion (AIC) for appropriate lag length (Dickey and Fuller 1979). In addition, to have a better idea about the extremity of the climatic characters, the movements of the gap between the maximum and the minimum temperatures was studied. Thereafter, the causality between temperature and rainfall is examined by the Granger test for all the regions (as mentioned below) for which relevant data was available (Granger 1969). Finally, vector auto-regression and co-integrating relationships among the three relevant climate variables were examined (Watson 1994). Co-integration vectors were estimated by Johansen (1988).

At present, Assam constitutes 27 districts. But data on various aspects of agriculture is not available for all these districts throughout the period as many of them were created time to time carving out from 10 districts. Thus, for analytical purpose, available information on all current districts is aggregated to the erstwhile undivided 10 districts.

## Observations and Analysis

The climatic conditions in the state changed significantly over the years and that to some extent led to the variation in crop cultivation but was not observed to be in line with the growth process as expected from a progressive agricultural economy (De 2015, 30–41). Here, temporal variation in three major weather components such as rainfall and maximum–minimum temperature over six decades of time is observed.

The 10 and 30 years' month-wise average figures show a rise in minimum temperature in the range of 0.6–1.3°C (Figure 10.1). Monthly average maximum temperature also increased from 0.7°C to 1.8°C (Figure 10.2) though it has been more erratic. Also, inter-month variation in the average minimum temperature is on the decline at a significant rate along with the temporal rise in the yearly average minimum temperature. Thus, an inverse relation is revealed between the yearly average and seasonal variation in the minimum temperature. It is an indication of gradual convergence of seasonal temperature with global warming in the state (Figure 10.3a). However, there is insignificant change in month-wise variation in the maximum temperature with a rising trend, which is subject to significant uncertainty in prime monsoon months that start little early than the normal monsoon season in the Indian mainland (Figure 10.3b). Zone-wise variation in the minimum temperature has also been rising at a faster rate than the maximum temperature. This growing regional variation is also associated with increasing fluctuation, which is reflected from Figures 10.4a and 10.4b.

Annual rainfall also declined during last six decades. Its seasonal pattern has also been undergoing significant changes over the years. Monthly rainfall reaches its peak alternately in June, July, or August. The

**Figure 10.1**
*Variation in month-wise average minimum temperature in Assam since 1951*

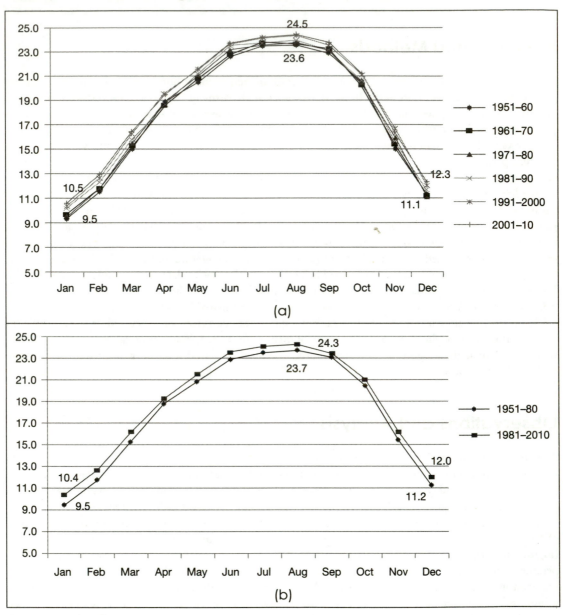

*Source:* IMD, Guwahati.

**Figure 10.2**
*Variation in month-wise average maximum temperature in Assam since 1951*

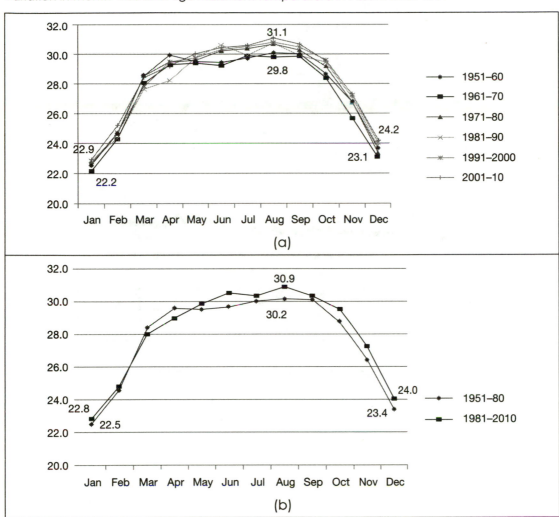

*Source:* IMD, Guwahati.

**Figure 10.3**

*Trend of annual average temperature (minimum and maximum) and their cofficient of month-wise variation in Assam since 1950*

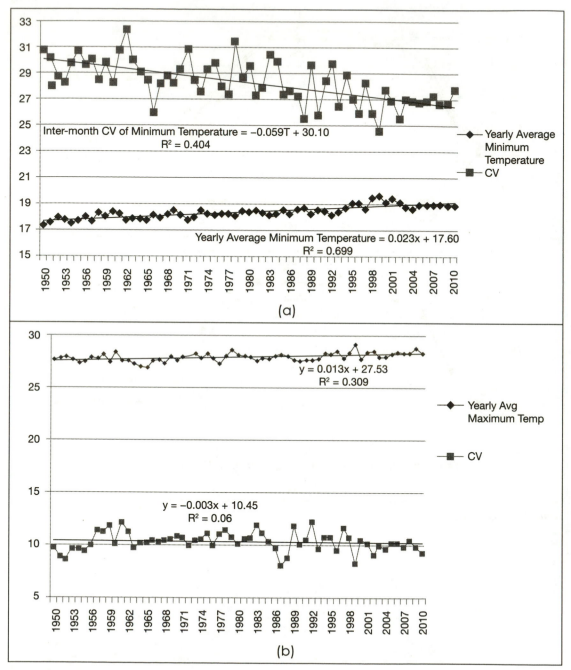

(a)

(b)

*Source:* IMD, Guwahati.

**Figure 10.4**
*Changing inter-zonal variability of minimum and maximum temperature in Assam since 1950*

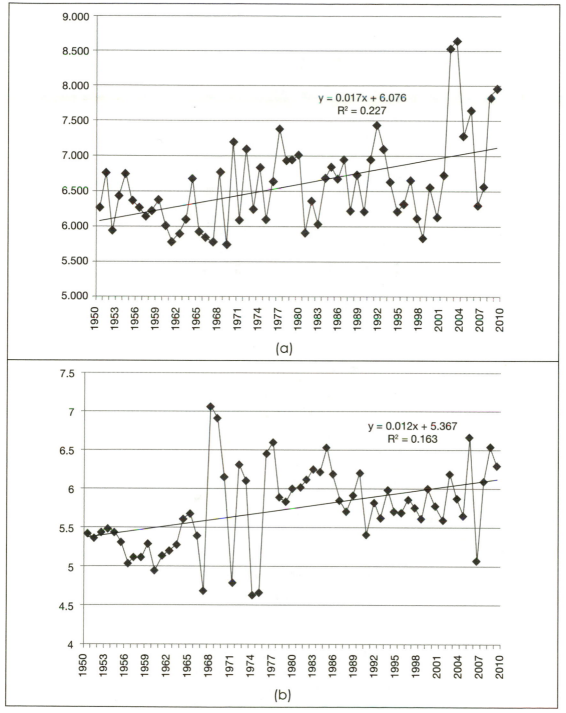

Source: IMD, Guwahati.

**Figure 10.5**

*Changing rainfall (monthly averages) since 1950 in Assam*

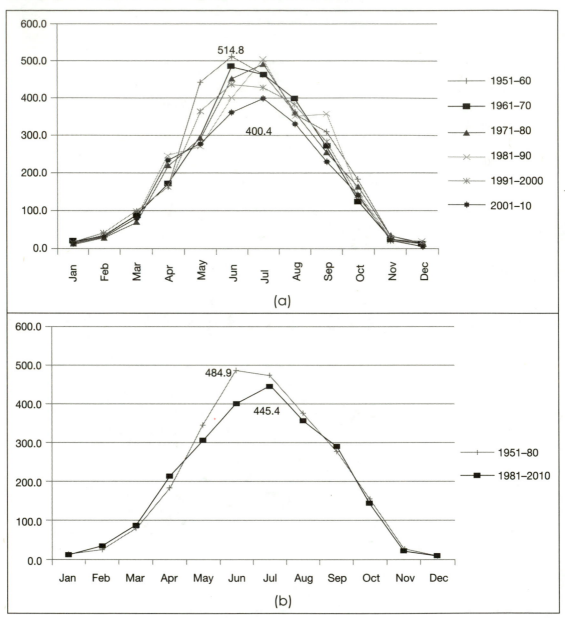

(a)

(b)

*Source:* IMD, Guwahati.

30-years average shows that the rainfall in the peak month declined from 484.9 mm during 1951–80 to 445.4 mm during 1981–2010. However, the incidence of flood became erratic owing to heavy concentration of rainfall in a few days when the maximum portion of rainfall of the month/year occurs (Figure 10.5). Figure 10.6a also shows a significant decline in annual rainfall and that the share of the annual rainfall that occurred during the peak monsoon months declined over the years (Figure 1.06b). Though, the overall trend in low rainfall zones is not significant, it declined significantly in the relatively high rainfall zones, and rising zonal variability is also clear from Figure 10.7.

**Figure 10.6**
*Trend in annual rainfall and share of various seasons in Assam*

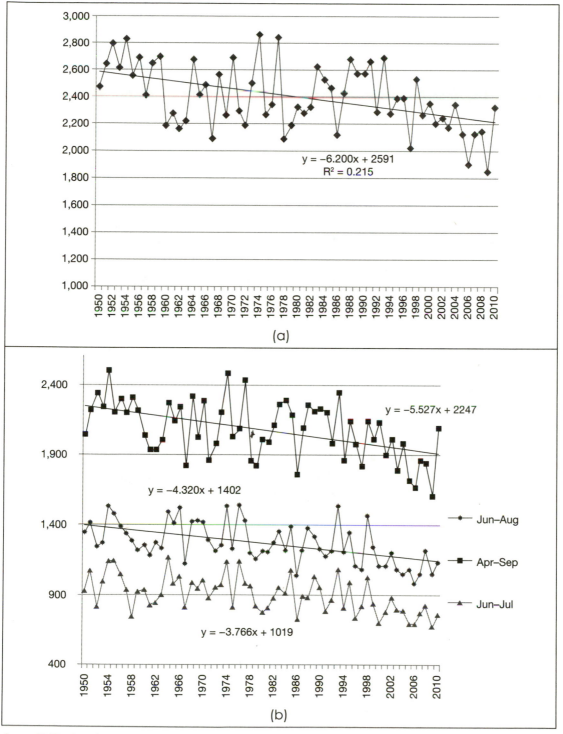

**Figure 10.7**

*Trend in annual rainfall of various zones of Assam and its CV*

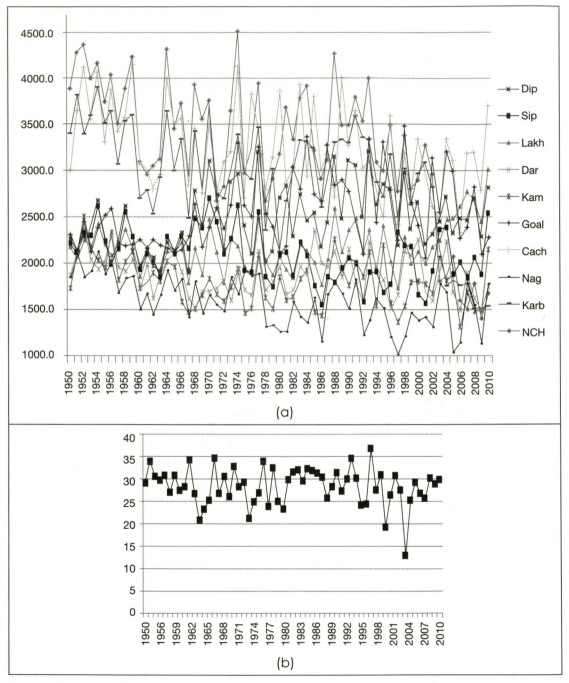

(a)

(b)

*Source:* IMD, Guwahati.

**Figure 10.8**
*Changes in yearly average max–min temperature gap and its coefficient of variation across the month in Assam*

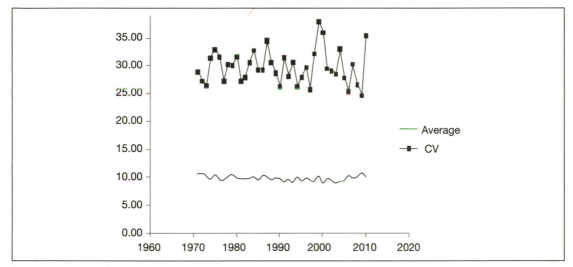

*Source:* IMD, Guwahati.

**Table 10.1**
*Unit root test for stationarity of climatic components in Assam during 1950–2010*

| Variable | Level | | | | First Diff. | | | | Comment |
|---|---|---|---|---|---|---|---|---|---|
| | *Coeff.* | *AdjR²* | *LogLikelihood* | *F* | *Coeff.* | *AdjR²* | *LogLikelihood* | *F* | |
| MaxTemp_Kh | −0.038* | 0.16 | −579.9 | 6.51 | −2.68** | 0.66 | −581.90 | 64.72 | I(0) |
| MaxTemp_Rabi | −0.059* | 0.21 | −645.02 | 15.23 | −2.14** | 0.71 | −649.08 | 142.56 | I(0) |
| MinTemp_Kh | −0.049* | 0.13 | −505.04 | 15.19 | −1.76** | 0.66 | −509.19 | 233.16 | I(0) |
| MinTemp_Rabi | −0.079* | 0.22 | −516.54 | 10.36 | −2.38** | 0.71 | −521.55 | 85.87 | I(0) |
| Rain_Kh | −0.10** | 0.27 | −3286.3 | 56.50 | −2.06 | 0.74 | −3293.7 | 573.66 | I(0) |
| Rain_Rabi | −0.228** | 0.453 | −2642.7 | 70.90 | −5.81** | 0.82 | −2604.7 | 186.15 | I(0) |

*Source:* IMD, Guwahati.
*Note:* ** and * indicate that the coeff. is significant at 1 per cent and 5 per cent level of significance, respectively.

On an average, the minimum temperature has been rising at faster rates than the maximum temperature except at a few erratic locations and, thus, the maximum-to-minimum gap shows a marginal decline across the seasons. However, the coefficient of variation in the monthly maximum–minimum temperate gap shows more variability over the years (Figure 10.8).

We can now summarize the findings by stating that rainfall has a negative trend, whereas minimum temperature and maximum temperature have a significant positive trend. Also, all the seasonal variables such as maximum temperature, minimum temperature, and rainfall in both the kharif (March–September) and rabi seasons (October–February) of the year are mostly stationary (Table 10.1). Some consequences should follow from these findings. Firstly, the increase in temperature and the decrease in the rainfall should make the atmosphere drier. Possibly, there are other variables, which are active here. The agricultural production is affected significantly, both in quality and in variety. The rising intensity of floods in the recent past, thus, cannot be fully associated with the rainfall pattern in the area. The floods in this downstream area have

**Table 10.2**

*Testing of pair-wise Granger causality between various components of weather in Assam*

| Null hypothesis | F-Stat. | Prob. |
|---|---|---|
| MinTemp does not Granger cause rainfall | 93.59 | 6.E-35 |
| Rainfall does not Granger cause MinTemp | 64.82 | 1.E-25 |
| MaxTemp does not Granger cause rainfall | 98.69 | 2.E-36 |
| Rainfall does not Granger cause MaxTemp | 158.57 | 2.E-53 |
| Humidity does not Granger cause rainfall | 64.36 | 2.E-25 |
| Rainfall does not Granger Cause Humidity | 96.48 | 7.E-36 |
| MaxTemp does not Granger Cause MinTemp | 1.74 | 0.1759 |
| MinTemp does not Granger Cause MaxTemp | 238.31 | 3.E-72 |
| Humidity does not Granger Cause MinTemp | 16.99 | 8.E-08 |
| MinTemp does not Granger Cause Humidity | 139.07 | 3.E-48 |
| Humidity does not Granger Cause MaxTemp | 99.39 | 9.E-37 |
| MaxTemp does not Granger Cause Humidity | 152.45 | 8.E-52 |

*Source:* IMD, Guwahati.

been mostly due to heavy rainfall within a shorter period in the higher upstream areas. Glacial melt in the high mountains may also cause flood in the downstream or foothill area. On the other hand, shortened low rainfall in the zone may at times cause sudden landslides and droughts. The rising pre-monsoon minimum temperature appears to be associated with depressions and rising early rainfall or advancement of rainfall season and low rainfall in the main rainfall months.

## Interrelations Between the Variables

Rainfall depends on the moisture flow from its source, far from the place of precipitation. Rainfall, temperature, and glacial movement in the upstream areas affect the level of humidity in an area. On the other hand, humidity and rainfall affect the temperature in a short time. Looking at the trend and stationarity pattern as described in Table 10.1, it appears that there is a close relationship between rainfall and temperature. The bivariate causality has been examined by Granger causality test. The result reveals that there is both-way causality between any two weather variables (Table 10.2). Here, we have also included average humidity as another variable for examining causality, assuming that changing humidity level can also affect temperature and rainfall, and vice versa.

Vector auto-regression with two period lag yields the following results:

$$Rain = -757.04^* + 0.084 \ Rain_{(-1)}^* \quad -0.296 \ Rain_{(-2)}^* + \ 28.705 \ MinTemp^* + 6.318 Hum^*,$$
$$(-9.458) \quad (1.775) \qquad (-7.037) \qquad (18.09) \qquad (6.22)$$

$R(bar)^2 = 0.640$, $F = 213.12$, Log-likelihood $= -2954.78$, AIC $= 12.384$

$$MinTemp = -18.28^* \ +0.536 \quad MinTemp_{(-1)}^* \quad -0.422 \ MinTemp_{(-2)}^{**} \quad +0.0057 \ Rain^* + 0.972 \ MaxTemp^* + 0.0825 Hum^*$$
$$(-9.201) \quad (11.613) \qquad (-14.903) \qquad (12.30) \qquad (17.34) \qquad (4.69)$$

$R(bar)^2 = 0.944$, $F = 1615.203$, Log-likelihood $= -805.062$, AIC $= 3.394$

$$MaxTemp = 17.21^* \ +0.243 \ MaxTemp_{(-1)}^{**} \ +0.163 \ MaxTemp_{(-2)}^* \quad -0.0022 \ Rain^* +0.495 \quad MinTemp^* -0.122 \quad Hum^*$$
$$(35.02) \quad (8.10) \qquad (6.76) \qquad (-6.44) \qquad (32.93) \qquad (-14.19)$$

**Table 10.3**
*Results of linear regression of different endogenous variables on various explanatory variables*

| | Endo. Variables | MinTemp | MaxTemp | Rainfall | Humidity |
|---|---|---|---|---|---|
| | Constant | 5.839 | 18.946 | 121.258 | 46.186 |
| | Rainfall | 0.005 | −0.001 | – | 0.005 |
| | MinTemp | – | .403 | 35.029 | 0.684 |
| | MaxTemp | 0.895 | – | −20.62 | −2.16 |
| | Humidity | 0.123 | −0.176 | 6.955 | – |
| Coefficients of Variables | Rainfall(−1) | 0.005 | – | 0.218 | −0.006 |
| | MinTemp(−1) | 0.413 | 0.145 | −7.407 | 0.538 |
| | MaxTemp(−1) | −0.51 | 0.265 | – | 1.085 |
| | Humidity(−1) | −0.225 | 0.069 | −5.501 | 0.495 |
| | R(bar)², F | 0.946, 1194.85 | 0.924, 971.486 | 0.671, 163.347 | 0.803, 279.054 |

*Source:* IMD, Guwahati.
*Note:* All the coefficients are significant at 1 per cent level of significance.

$R(bar)^2 = 0.922$, $F = 1120.976$, Log-likelihood $= -613.55$, AIC $= 2.592$

$Hum = 34.459^* + 0.635\ Hum_{(-1)}^* + 0.134\ Hum_{(-2)}^* + 0.0053\ Rain^* + 1.056\ MinTemp^* - 1.34\ MaxTemp^*$
    (8.29)  (16.39)    (3.136)    (2.99)    (8.192)    (−7.34)

$R(bar)^2 = 0.584$, $F = 134.86$, Log-likelihood $= -1387.526$, AIC $= 5.831$.

(Figures in the parentheses represent the t-values of the corresponding coefficients and * indicates that the coefficient is significant at 1% level.)

The vector auto-regression reflects the significant positive both-way relationship of minimum temperature and rainfall in the region. Though humidity has a significant inverse impact on the maximum temperature, it has a positive effect on the minimum temperature level. The coefficients of various weather variables of linear regressions on other relevant variables having significant impact on them are presented in Table 10.3. It also describes similar relationships among those weather variables as noted earlier.

The normalized co-integrating relationship among those variables can be written as

$$Rainfall = 79.139 MinTemp^* + 66.234 MaxTemp^* + 15.96\ Humidity^*,$$
        (5.79)        (3.244)        (3.352)

Log-likelihood $= -5555.628$

(Here, * indicates that the coefficient is significant at 1% level. Figures in the parentheses represent t-value of the corresponding coefficient.)

# Concluding Remarks

The whole analysis shows the sustained rise in temperature accompanied by the inter-regional variations in growth, which appears to be due to the geographical position of the respective regions with respect to the Himalayas, and with respect to major rivers in the region. The significant zonal variation in the trend of temperature is also observed. With rising temperature, convergence of both month-wise figures and zone-wise figures has been taking place.

Though minimum temperature recorded a faster upward trend than that of maximum temperature, the variation of extremes of temperature in Assam shows a rising but erratic pattern over the years.

Rainfall follows a declining trend and that varies across the seasons of the year and across the regions. During the prime monsoon season of June–July, a significant declining trend of rainfall was observed, whereas there has been a rising trend in the proportion of annual rainfall occurring during May–June and August–September. In recent years, the highest level of precipitation of the year was observed either in the pre-normal monsoon months of April–May or in August–October. The obvious consequence is the untimely and unexpected devastating floods in the region. In addition, such untimely heavy rainfall in a very short span of time in the mountainous regions, in turn, causes devastation in the form of flash floods causing extensive damage to life and property in lower Assam.

The study also reveals a high degree of causal relationship among the three important weather factors. The results of Granger causality, vector auto-regression, and co-integrating relation suggest high degree of inter-relationships among these weather variables. If a change occurs in any of these variables either due to socio-economic activities or due to a natural phenomenon, it is reflected in the other factors as well. Therefore, the rising uncertainty in the monsoons and rising temperatures call for more preparedness and continuous adaptation in the crop and non-crop activities, reduction in the risk, and the promotion of best possible livelihood practices in the region. Adaptation and disaster mitigation require adequate knowledge, access to suitable technologies, and appropriate policy measures. A failure in adjustment with the changing climatic uncertainty may lead to socio-economic disaster and jeopardize the protection of livelihood.

# References

Ananthapadmanabhan, G., K. Srinivas, and V. Gopal. 2007. *Hiding behind the Poor: A Report by Greenpeace on Climate Injustice*. Bangalore: Greenpeace India Society.

Barry, R., and R. Chorley. 2003 *Atmosphere, Weather, and Climate*, 6th ed. London: Routledge.

CESPR (Centre for Environment, Social and Policy Research), RGVN (Rashtriya Gramin Vikas Nidhi), and INECC (Indian Network on Ethics and Climate Change). 2012. "Impact of Climate Change on the Marginalized Women: An Exploratory Study across Six Districts in Assam." A Research Report. Guwahati, Assam: CESPR, RGVN, and INECC.

Christensen, J.H., B. Hewitson, A. Busuioc, A. Chen, X. Gao, I. Held, R. Jones, R.K. Kolli, W.-T. Kwon, R. Laprise, R.V. Magaña, L. Mearns, C.G. Menéndez, J. Räisänen, A. Rinke, A. Sarr, and P. Whetton. 2007. "Regional Climate Projections." In *Climate Change 2007: The Physical Science Basis. Contribution of Working Group I to the Fourth Assessment Report of the Intergovernmental Panel on Climate Change*, edited by S. Solomon, D. Qin, M. Manning, Z. Chen, M. Marquis, K.B. Averyt, M. Tignor, and H.L. Miller. Cambridge/New York, NY: Cambridge University Press.

Clemens, S., W. Prell, D. Murray, G. Shimmield, and G. Weedon. 1991. "Forcing Mechanisms of the Indian Ocean Monsoon." *Nature* 353 (6346): 720–25.

Cruz, R.V., H. Harasawa, M. Lal, S. Wu, Y. Anokhin, B. Punsalmaa, Y. Honda, M. Jafari, C. Li, and N. Huu Ninh. 2007. "Asia—Climate Change 2007: Impacts, Adaptation and Vulnerability." In *Contribution of Working Group II to the Fourth Assessment Report of the Intergovernmental Panel on Climate Change*, edited by M.L. Parry, O.F. Canziani, J.P. Palutikof, P.J. Van der Linden, and C.E. Hanson, 469–506. Cambridge: Cambridge University Press.

De, U.K. 2015. "Farmer's Response to Changing Climate in North-East India." *AIP Conference Proceeding:* Vol. 1643. *Proceedings of the 2nd ISM International Statistical Conference 2014 (ISM II)*. Melville, NY: AIP Publishing.

De, U.K., M. Pal, and K. Bodosa. 2015. "Global Warming and the Pattern of Overall Climate Changes in Sub-Himalayan Assam Region of North-East India." *International Journal of Ecological Economics and Statistics* 36 (3): 88–105.

Deka, J., C. Baruah, and S.K. Bhuyan. 2011, September. "Impact of Climate Change on Sustainable Livelihood in Deepor Beel: A Case Study of Keotpara, Azara." *NeBIO* 2 (3): 6–8.

Dev, S.M. 2011. "Climate Change, Rural Livelihoods and Agriculture (Focus on Food Security) in Asia-Pacific Region." Working Paper-14, IGIDR, Mumbai. Available at: http://www.igidr.ac.in/pdf/publication/WP-2011-014.pdf (accessed on 27 April 2017).

Dickey, D.A., and W.A. Fuller. 1979. "Distribution of the Estimators for Autoregressive Time Series with a Unit Root." *Journal of the American Statistical Association* 74 (366): 427–31.

Government of Assam. *Directorate of Statistics Economic Survey of Assam.* Various Issues. Manipur: Government of Assam.

Government of India (GoI). 2010. *Climate Change and India: A 4 × 4 Assessment—A Sectoral and Regional Analysis for 2030s.* New Delhi: Indian Network for Climate Change Assessment (INCCA), Ministry of Environment and Forests.

Granger, C.W.J. 1969. "Investigating Causal Relations by Econometric Models and Cross-Spectral Methods." *Econometrica* 37 (3): 424–38.

Guiteras, R. 2009. "The Impact of Climate Change on Indian Agriculture." Mimeo, University of Maryland, College Park.

Howitt, Richard, Josué Medellín-Azuara, and Duncan MacEwan. 2010. "Climate Change, Markets and Technology." *Choices* 25 (3). Available at: http://ageconsearch.tind.io//bitstream/95761/2/Climate%20Change.pdf (accessed on 2 March 2013).

IPCC. 2007. *Climate Change 2007: The Physical Science Basis—Contribution of Working Group I to the Fourth Assessment Report of the Intergovernmental Panel on Climate Change, Summary for Policymakers.* Cambridge: Cambridge University Press.

Johansen, S. 1988. "Statistical Analysis of Cointegration Vectors." *Journal of Economic Dynamics and Control* 12 (2–3): 231–54.

Johnson, R.H., and R.A. Houze. 1987 "Precipitating Cloud Systems of the Asian Monsoon." In *Monsoon Meteorology*, edited by C.P. Chang and T.N. Krishnamurti, 298–353. Oxford: Oxford University Press.

Karma, A., Y. Ageta, N. Naito, S. Iwata, and H. Yabuki. 2003. "Glacier Distribution in the Himalayas and Glacier Shrinkage from 1963 to 1993 in the Bhutan Himalayas." *Bulletin of Glaciological Research* 20 (1): 29–40.

Metz, B., O. Davidson, R. Swart, and J. Pan, eds. 2001. *Climate Change 2001: Mitigation.* Contribution of Working Group III to the Third Assessment Report of the Intergovernmental Panel on Climate Change. Cambridge: Cambridge University Press.

Pachauri, R.K. 2009. *Climate Change and Its Implications for India's Fragile Ecosystems: The Human Impact of Climate Change, Policy Notes for Parliamentarians.* New Delhi: CLRA.

Pathak, D., A.P. Gajurel, and P.K. Mool. 2010. "Climate Change Impacts on Hazards in the Eastern Himalayas. Climate Change Impact and Vulnerability in the Eastern Himalayas." Technical Report 5, ICIMOD, Kathmandu.

Ranuzzi, A., and R. Srivastava. 2012. "Impact of Climate Change on Agriculture and Food Security." ICRIER Policy Series 16, New Delhi: Indian Council for Research on International Economic Relations (ICRIER).

Sen Roy, S., and R. C. Balling Jr. 2004. "Trends in Extreme Daily Precipitation on Indices in India." *International Journal of Climatology* 24 (4): 457–66.

Shrestha, A.B., C.P. Wake, P.A. Mayewski, and J.E. Dibb. 1999. "Maximum Temperature Trends in the Himalaya and Its Vicinity: An Analysis Based on Temperature Records from Nepal for the Period 1971–94." *Journal of Climate* 12 (9): 2775–87.

Sivanandan, P.K. 1983. "Kerala's Agricultural Performances: Differential Trends and Determinants of Growth." M. Phil Dissertation, Centre for Development Studies, Thiruvananthapuram.

The Energy and Resources Institute (TERI). 2003. *Coping with Global Change: Vulnerability and Adaptation in Indian Agriculture.* New Delhi: The Energy and Resources Institute.

UNESCO. 2012. "Education Sector Responses to Climate Change." Background Paper TH/ESD/12/OS/009-E, Bangkok.

Venkateswarlu, B. 2009. *Climate Change and Sustainable Agriculture: Securing the Small and Marginal Farmer in India. The Human Impact of Climate Change: Policy Notes for Parliamentarians.* New Delhi: CLRA.

Watson, M. 1994. "Vector Autoregressions and Cointegration." In *Handbook of Econometrics*, Vol. 4., edited by R. Engle and D. McFadden. Amsterdam: North Holland.

Weitzman Martin, L. 2009, May 7. "Additive Damages, Fat-Tailed Climate Dynamics, and Uncertain Discounting." *Economics: The Open-Access, Open-Assessment E-Journal* 3 (2009-26). Available at: http://www.economics-ejournal. org/economics/journalarticles/2009-26H (accessed on 15 October 2013).

Whiteman, D. 2000. *Mountain Meteorology.* Oxford: Oxford University Press.

World Bank. 2008. "Climate Change Impacts in Drought and Flood Affected Areas: Case Studies in India." Report No: 43946-IN. New Delhi: World Bank.

Ye, L., H. Tang, W. Wu, P. Yang, G.C. Nelson, D.M. D'Croz, and A. Palazzo. 2013, January 7. "Chinese Food Security and Climate Change: Agriculture Futures." *Economics: The Open-Access, Open-Assessment E-Journal.* Available at: http://www.economics-ejournal.org/economics/discussionpapers/2013-2 (accessed on 26 May 2017).

# 11

# Coping with a Natural Disaster: Sundarbans After Cyclone Aila*

## Santadas Ghosh**

## Introduction

This chapter explores household's observed coping behaviour against a large-scale loss of their main livelihood in the Sundarbans islands (India) due to a natural disaster. People in this remote low-lying delta are mainly dependent on rain-fed agriculture which produces a single crop of paddy. A large population lives on these islands with very limited livelihood options in the absence of infrastructural provisions and power-driven industries. Freshwater agriculture on these islands crucially depends on the protective earthen embankments encircling them. Such embankments stand guard against saline water of the surrounding rivers during high tide. Apart from agriculture, another important livelihood option is to exploit the deltaic natural resources. It mainly takes the form of fishing and crab catching in open rivers and mangrove forest creeks, collection of prawn seedlings from rivers to be sold to commercial prawn farms, and occasional honey collection from the reserve forests.

Cyclone Aila, just before the onset of monsoon in 2009,[1] had broken many parts of the embankments on almost every island in the Sundarbans. As a result, the protection against saline water was unavailable for almost all parts of these islands for a varied duration of time. The resultant salt deposits on fields had severely affected agriculture in large areas. Previous local experience showed that such salinity-related productivity loss is fully reversible after two normal monsoon showers. The rains gradually wash out the salt from agricultural fields.

In this backdrop, this study was designed to see how the islands' population has coped with their livelihood loss in the intermediate period. The study has undertaken a detailed survey of 800 sample households over two years (three repeat visits) to find out the ramifications on livelihood in the short run and whether the changes in livelihood practices, if any, showed reversibility along with regaining of soil fertility. It was

* This study is a partial outcome of a research project funded by SANDEE (South Asian Network for Development and Environmental Economics, Kathmandu, Nepal) and hosted by SHODH (The Institute for Research and Development, Nagpur, India).

** I am immensely benefited by various biannual research workshops of SANDEE. I am specifically thankful to Enamul Haque, Priya Shyamsundar, Jeffrey Vincent, E. Somanathan, and Subhrendu Pattanayak for their comments and suggestions at various stages of this study. I am thankful to my university (Visva-Bharati, Santiniketan, India) for allowing me to undertake this research work. My sincere thanks to the anonymous reviewer who painstakingly went through the draft version. The comments have been really helpful.

also interesting to see whether such a disaster has increased the anthropogenic stress on the surrounding natural resources.

Studies with such a backdrop mostly analysed people's livelihood coping behaviour after covariate shocks with a one-shot survey. But it is reasonable to assume that the effect of a widespread disaster on livelihood may not be captured in the short run itself. Rather, it unfolds over a reasonable period of time. Very few studies are found in the literature that tried to uncover a fuller picture by repeat visits to the affected households. This study lives up to that challenge.

# Background

## Natural Disasters and Coping Strategies: Experiences Elsewhere

Natural disasters, both extreme events and periodic shocks, usually result in some change in the livelihood mix, especially in a rural area. In the backdrop of the climate change (CC) scenario, a number of insightful studies across the globe in recent times had analysed the ex post coping behaviour against disaster-induced livelihood loss among the rural poor and forest communities. Literature shows that the coping strategies differ considerably with the available natural resources as well as institutional provisions. Also, the distribution of the disaster-related burden among the asset-holding classes does not follow a unique pattern.

Such studies had been undertaken against a wide variety of events and locations. They vary from relatively rare extreme events like hurricane Mitch (1998, Nicaragua, Honduras), typhoon Harurot (2003, the Philippines) to great floods (1998, Bangladesh), recurrent droughts (1982–95, Zimbabwe; 2002–03, India), and usual climate-related uncertainties in agriculture (Nepal and Brazil). From their findings, it can be said that there is no unique relationship between the nature of the disaster and households' dominant coping strategies against livelihood loss. For most of these studies, the primary effect of a natural disaster had been loss of cultivation. They found that households coped with a variety of strategies depending on local circumstances.

Panel data on a set of households in Zimbabwe, which faced repeated droughts in the decades of 1980s and 1990s, showed that the main private coping mechanism was the sale of livestock (Kinsey, Burger, and Gunning 1998). This behaviour showed consistency over the length of the study period. Consequently, households facing maximum risk were identified as those without significant livestock. Similar observations were made in a study on drought in India (Sivakumar and Kerbert 2004) and in the aftermath of the great flood in Bangladesh in 1998 (Ninno et al. 2001). It was found that mostly the farmers could not plant their usual crops and did not have enough fodder to feed their livestock. Also, in Bangladesh during the post-flood days, many of the farmers found alternative forms of employment, such as boating and fishing. In another study relating to the same event, it was found that households that did not get improved access to credit and insurance facilities after the flood had demonstrated increased incidence of child labour, which was a way of coping with their immediate credit requirement (Alvi and Dendir 2011; Sivakumar and Kerbert 2004). In a rural agricultural area where there is a thriving informal market for small credit, disaster coping might take the route of child labour. This is because both borrowers and lenders are affected by such covariate shocks.

Another key coping strategy mentioned by many studies is an increase in indebtedness. In the Bangladesh flood context, it was also found that households modified their eating habits and reduced the frequency of meals consumed when they suffered income loss and failed to get enough credit to purchase the same amount of food (Ninno et al. 2001). One of its crucial fallout was an increase in households' debts with the traders. Similar phenomenon was observed in a study relating to typhoon Harurot in the Philippines (Huigen and Jens 2006). It was observed that the long-term vulnerability of the individual households was increased, as they had to stop sending their children to school to save money.

There is a strong body of literature that claims, with empirical evidence, that when people are endowed with natural resources like forests in their surroundings, it often acts as a natural insurance against livelihood shocks. In Brazilian Amazon, a study found that forest collection is positively correlated with both agricultural shortfalls (consumption smoothing response) and expected agricultural risks (income smoothing response). It shows that households rely on the forest to mitigate the risks inherent in subsistence agriculture (Pattanayak and Sills 2001). In the Philippines after the typhoon, households living near the edge of the forest were able to cope with their economic loss with income from illegal logging (Huigen et al. 2006).

But the role of natural resources to provide insurance against livelihood shocks is largely determined by the prevailing control regime. A post-Mitch study in Honduras (Mcsweeney 2005) concludes that although reliance on natural resources was predicted to intensify after the hurricane disaster, enforcement of a commercial extraction ban in the forest had actually led to net attrition from forest-based activities. Households that nevertheless continued to sell forest products to self-insure were those who had been unable to recoup their loss vis-à-vis pre-Mitch landholdings. It suggested that household attributes such as land wealth strongly condition how and when forest resources act as safety nets for the rural poor.

Under stricter protection regime of natural resources like forests, one of the most widely observed household coping strategy has been to migrate as a labourer. Using household data from the Chitwan Valley of Nepal, a study found that a decrease in access to firewood increased the likelihood of migration of individuals for work (Shrestha and Bhandari 2007). It showed that environmental insecurity was a significant predictor of migration regardless of its destination. Migration and remittances as significant livelihood coping strategies are also supported by other post-Mitch studies (Carvajal and Pereira 2009). However, a recent study on households' migration behaviour in response to natural disasters in the United States during the 1920s and 1930s has shown that government efforts at disaster mitigation have actually distorted the possible private self-protection behaviour through migration. It found that public investment in rebuilding and protecting flood-prone areas had resulted in in-migration in those areas (Boustan, Kahn, and Rhode 2012).

Also, disaster-induced livelihood shocks are not uniform across households even within the same community. The idea that poor households suffer the most is also not universally true. Under specific circumstances, the immediate livelihood-related distress may be more acute for certain asset-holding classes compared to the asset-poor. Studies showed that in some cases households which are asset-poor had suffered relatively less because they have too little to lose (Morris et al. 2002). But beyond the immediate distress, such events often cause prolonged hardships for the community, and the pattern of changes in livelihood can differ across different asset-holding classes in the long run.

Several livelihood coping strategies are found to be common in varying contexts across the world and there seems to be no general rule for the adoption of a dominant strategy against similar natural disasters. Different case studies stand apart with their own specific geographical and social situations. In this respect, the present study in the Sundarbans attempts to bring out the regional experience after the cyclone Aila.

Following several predictions relating to CC threats over the short and long run, the Sundarbans might be among the first set of casualties due to a sea level rise (SLR) scenario as it belongs to a low-lying delta region. Even the relative SLR is not uniform across all regions as continental land subsidence[2] is also a slow but sure phenomenon. Conducted over a 14-year period till 1998, one study estimated an average increase in the sea level at the rate of 3.14 mm per year for the region that includes the Sundarbans which is larger than the average rate in other parts of coastal India (Hazra et al. 2002). For more than a million inhabitants on the islands in this delta, the more immediate CC-related threat, however, is the forecasted increase in the frequency of cyclones and super cyclones in the Bay of Bengal (Ali 1999; Unnikrishnan et al. 2006).

Cyclone Aila provided a unique opportunity to study the observed coping behaviour across various economic classes in the Sundarbans against salinity-related large-scale crop-loss. This study looks at the coping behaviour of a set of well-dispersed households with diverse asset bases over two years after the event—by the time when resilience of nature was expected to bring back the affected lands to their earlier productive state. In doing so, the study goes beyond capturing just the short-term effects and looks at the longer consequences on surrounding natural resources and local livelihood. Sundarbans is a biodiversity hot spot. A possible increase in anthropogenic stress on this delicate ecosystem due to climate-related disasters calls for appropriately designed interventions from the controlling authority. This study aims to provide some fact-based inputs in this context.

## Sundarbans: Location and Geography

In India, the Sundarbans is located at the southern corner of the eastern state of West Bengal and on the Gangetic delta. Spreading over India and Bangladesh, it is the largest single mangrove forest tract in the world and a declared World Heritage Site. The physiography is dominated by deltaic formations that include innumerable drainage channels. The deltaic islands rise marginally above the sea level with average elevation between 4 and 7.5 m across them. Tidal saline water from the Bay of Bengal sweeps over large parts of the islets twice a day throughout the year.

On the Indian side, out of a total 102 islands, 48 constitute the reserve forest as declared by the Government of India. It is home to the famous Royal Bengal Tiger. The remaining 54 islands are inhabited and contain a large population on them. The reserve forest and the settlements are on two mutually exclusive sets of islands. There is no human habitation inside the forest. The forest lies in the eastern corner while the populated islands are located along its western boundary and further towards the mainland.

Officially, Sundarban Biosphere Reserve (SBR) refers to a region that extends beyond these islands and covers some of the area that is part of the mainland now. It spreads over two southern districts of West Bengal. The region is densely populated (Figure 11.1).

This chapter focuses on that section of the Sundarbans population which reside on the islands. In the absence of any clear estimate from secondary sources, the study estimated the population on such islands at around 1.5 million.[3] Due to remoteness and lack of infrastructural development, their livelihood choices and economic conditions are not similar to those who are generally categorized as "coastal." The people on these low-lying islands are residing within an important and delicate ecological site and a biodiversity hot spot. Their livelihood practices and pattern of exploitation of natural resources have important implications for the sustainability and management of this site.

# Data and Sampling

Following the objective of the study, the selection of sample households has been carefully carried out to ensure reasonable variation in terms of households' remoteness, proximity to natural resources, asset holdings, and the extent of damage to their agriculture. A sample of 800 households were selected by a multistage sampling scheme starting from administrative blocks to villages and then to households. In the first stage, two administrative blocks were chosen purposefully—Gosaba in the northeast and Patharpratima in the south (these two blocks are demarcated by dark grey in Figure 11.1). Gosaba is an entirely island-block, situated on the verge of the reserve forest. Patharpratima, on the other hand, is much away from the reserve forest and close to the sea, with part of it covering the mainland. Apart from differences in their location, these two blocks had also experienced maximum damage from the cyclone as per the official statistics. It may be noted that these two blocks include the maximum number of islands between themselves.

**Figure 11.1**
*Location of the study area*

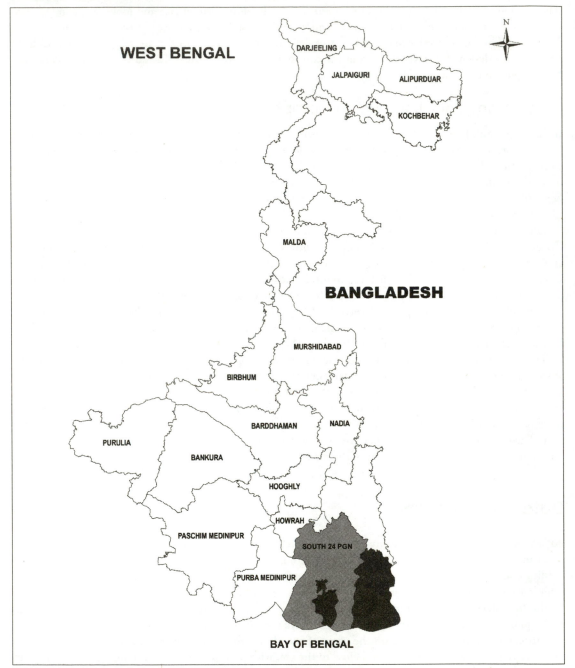

*Source:* Department of Geography, Visva-Bharati University.
*Notes:* 1. The light grey region is the district of South 24 Parganas in West Bengal and the dark areas within it represent the two administrative blocks from which households were selected for primary survey.
2. This figure is not to scale. It does not represent any authentic national or international boundaries and is used for illustrative purposes only.

In the second stage, some primary information from elected representatives of local administrative bodies (panchayats) of each village from these two selected blocks was collected. These are:

- Percentage of cultivable land left uncultivated in the monsoon of 2009 (indicator of the extent of cyclone damage).
- Time taken to reach the block administrative office from the village by the usual mode of transport (indicator of remoteness).
- Length of river embankment in the polling booth area (indicator of proximity to natural resources).

After processing the information, 20 villages from each block were purposively selected ensuring maximum variability in these three aspects. It also ensured that all the 18 islands covered under these two blocks are represented by at least one village located in it.

In the final stage of sample selection, a first-hand list of all village households had been prepared along with their current landholding data for all the 40 selected villages. Then 20 households from each of these villages had been selected as random samples maintaining a fixed proportion from each landholding strata. This way of selecting 800 sample households ensured sufficient variability in households' socio-economic conditions, exposure to natural resources, remoteness, and the extent of livelihood loss due to Aila.

The first round of the detailed survey of these households was carried out between March and June 2010. This survey round collected information on the pre-Aila livelihood activities of the households (by recall), extent of the cyclone damage to its agricultural fields, the state of its own agriculture after the cyclone (monsoon of 2009), and other regular socio-economic data.

The second round of the survey of the same households was conducted during January–March 2011. In this round, information on the state of their agriculture in the previous season (monsoon of 2010) was collected along with changes in livelihood practices between the two visits. This round also collected other regular socio-economic information. The Third round of the survey recorded similar information for the households during January–March 2012.

Out of the 800 households surveyed in the first round, some were dropped off from the final analysis since survey could not be conducted for them in the later rounds. This was due to the fact that no adult member of those households was present during either of the repeat visits. In most of these cases, all the adult members of the sample household temporarily went as migrant labourer outside Sundarbans, leaving the minors in the custody of neighbours or relatives. Altogether, after three rounds of survey, complete information could be recorded for 778 households. The final results of this study, presented in the following sections, are based on this sample size.

# Study Findings

## Endowments

The study area hosts a population that had settled on these islands within the last century, migrating in from neighbouring districts. The region, being adjacent to the international border with Bangladesh, had also received a wave of refugees during the partition of Bengal in 1947.

This special historical background explains why big landowning households are almost absent in the area. Though the initial settlers carved out pieces of land for cultivating, subsequent division and fragmentation of it had created a significant section of marginal farmers. Survey data shows a heavily skewed distribution of land towards marginal and smallholders. A considerable proportion of households were found to be landless. Usually, such households were located close to the riverbanks and used the rivers and creeks for catching fishes and crabs. Also, there is little common land on these islands and usually livestock holding, if any,

**Table 11.1**
*Endowments of survey households*

| | |
|---|---|
| Total number of households surveyed in all three rounds | 778 |
| Average family size | 4.9 |
| Average value of livestock holding (US $)* | 21 |
| % of landless households | 32.4 |
| % of households with landholding between 0 and 0.2 hectare | 29.4 |
| % of households with landholding between 0.2 and 0.4 hectare | 18.8 |
| % of households with landholding between 0.4 and 1.0 hectare | 15.7 |
| % of households with landholding between 1.0 and 2.0 hectare | 3.3 |
| % of households with landholding more than 2 hectare | 0.4 |

*Source:* Primary survey.
*Note:*   * From the first survey round. Value calculated at 2009 prices (conversion factor: US$ 1 = ₹ 55).

mostly caters to the households' own needs. Table 11.1 captures some aspects of the households' physical endowments obtained from the primary survey.

## Livelihood Practices

The livelihood options on these islands comprise a small set and there is no manufacturing industry due to the absence of conventional power supply. Apart from cultivating their own lands, daily labour—both farm and non-farm—is a significant source of livelihood. A small section of households had reported salaried employment as a source of earning. Petty trade and artisanship constitute some other local livelihood options.

The other major livelihood option, particularly engaging the asset-poor, is exploitation of surrounding rivers and forest creeks. Close to a fifth of survey households reported activities like prawn-fry collection and fishing or crab-catching in pre-Aila days. Also, since the region grows only a single monsoon crop in the absence of freshwater irrigation, a large number of working adults adopted the practice of migrating as agricultural workers in the winter season. In more recent times, working as semi-skilled or unskilled labour in large construction projects in distant parts of India has gained momentum. Such workers usually migrate with durations ranging from a few months to more than one year. More than one-fifth of the survey households reported working as migrant labourers before the disaster.

Both these practices, before Aila, had close relation with households' land endowments. Generally, households that were landless or marginal had taken up these two activities. Relatively well-endowed households had resorted to either rivers or forests or even went outside the Sundarbans. Figure 11.2, obtained from the primary survey, captures this phenomenon.

The first round of survey, conducted within one year of Aila, had recorded the set of major livelihood practices of the responding households immediately before and after the disaster. Figure 11.3 gives an idea of the pattern of livelihood changes that were observed within a year of the disaster.

It might be noted that the households often showed a mix of livelihoods. Smallholders mostly augmented their earnings with fishing or other jobs. So, the percentages shown in this figure add up to more than 100.

Figure 11.3 shows that Aila had major adverse effects on agriculture. It had affected labouring activities on farm as well. A marginal increase was seen in the "non-farm daily labour" jobs after Aila. Mostly, it was possible due to new job opportunities created by post-disaster spurt through NGO activities[4] and reconstruction works by government-sponsored rural employment schemes.[5] Such jobs were mostly of livelihood augmenting nature.

**Figure 11.2**

*Natural resource dependents and migrant workers across landholding classes*

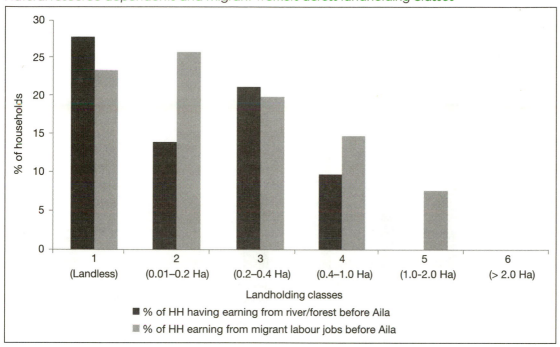

*Source:* Primary survey.

More importantly, the percentages of households depending on river and forest and on migrant labour jobs had increased immediately after Aila. During many group discussions in the field with local affected people, these two livelihood options had been singled out as alternatives against the damage to agriculture. The crop loss, however, was supposed to be temporary and the experienced farmers hoped to regain their land's productivity after two normal monsoon showers. This claim, and the associated dynamics of livelihood adjustment, had been verified with survey data in subsequent sections.

## Cyclone Aila: Differential Damage

Changes in livelihood practices are expected to have a more pronounced relationship with the extent of damage to agriculture, rather than landholding. Since a crucial sample selection criterion was differential damage intensity, it would be interesting to see whether any clear pattern of such change emerges when the households are classified according to the intensity of damage.

Depending on its extent and nature, reconstruction of broken embankments took varied time ranging from a couple of days to more than six months. Agricultural fields in the adjacent area continued to be submerged in saline water during every high tide till the relevant portion of the embankment was repaired. The extent and duration of agricultural loss on a piece of land is directly related to the duration of its exposure to saline water. The more the duration, the more is the amount of salt deposit and its penetration into the soil.

In the first round of the survey, households were asked about the number of days through which such salt water intrusion continued on their cultivable land, if any. It might be noted here that the sample villages had been purposively chosen ensuring sufficient variability across them in terms of damage intensity. As a result, the duration of such submersion, counted in days, had shown enough variation across survey households.

This information was used to classify the households into three categories depending on the duration of water logging in their fields. Also, some of the selected villages were located in the interior of islands and

**Figure 11.3**

*Major livelihood practices before and after Aila*

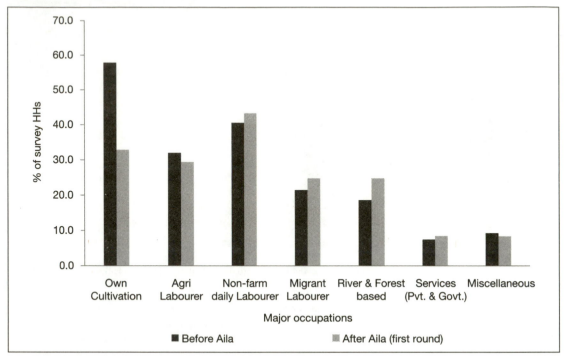

*Source:* Primary survey.

the saline water could not actually reach them. So a fourth category of "unaffected" households was also considered. Table 11.2 describes the distribution of sample households among these four damage categories. The cardinal numbers marking the categories are arranged so to represent the extent of damage to their land. The question of "water staying on land" was only meaningful for the households with some agricultural land. So, the table records a response from 526 landowning households within the sample.

However, landless households also depend on the performance of local agriculture. In the remote villages of Sundarbans, damage to agriculture also greatly affected landless villagers as they lost farm-labour jobs and other related earning activities.[6] So, the landless households are also similarly categorized according to the damage intensity. The average days of water logging in a village, as was computed from the responses

**Table 11.2**

*Definition of damage categories*

| Damage category | No. of days of salt water stay on agricultural land (first round survey data) | No. of landholding households |
| --- | --- | --- |
| 0 | 0 | 141 |
| 1 | 1–7 days | 120 |
| 2 | 8–30 days | 203 |
| 3 | More than 30 days | 62 |
| | Total | 526 |

*Source:* Primary survey.

**Figure 11.4**
*Cyclone damage across landholding classes*

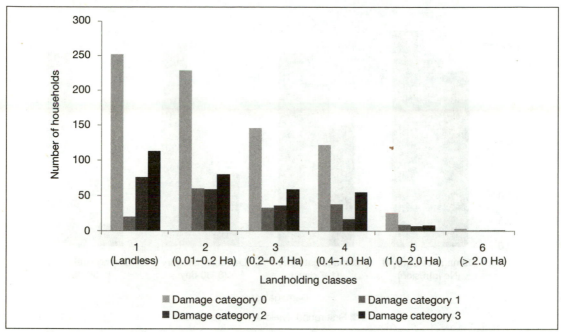

*Source:* Primary survey.

of landed households, has been used as a proxy for the landless respondents to indicate the damage to local agriculture.

The duration of water logging had little to do with the size of respondent's landholding. It depended on the extent of damage to the surrounding embankment and the time taken for its restoration. Within a village, the reported durations showed little variation across households irrespective of their holding size. The variation came mainly across villages. And since the size-class distribution of holdings is similar among the villages, the categories of damage are fairly distributed among all types of landholding classes. This is shown in Figure 11.4.

## Damage to Agriculture and its Recovery

An empirical support to differential damage in agriculture due to varied duration of water logging and nature's resilience in terms of its recovery need to be established before going further. The farmers' claim of two years' recovery time has been checked with productivity data, gathered over three survey rounds and across different damage categories. Figure 11.5 describes the study findings in this regard and the claim is found to be reasonably true.

The figure shows that agricultural productivity loss immediately following Aila (2009) was profound with longer duration of water logging in fields. The damage category "0" (implying no intrusion of water) represents the baseline average productivity in that year.[7] The drop in average productivity compared to this base is visibly more for higher damage categories. Figure 11.5 also describes the pattern of recovery in productivity. The higher the damage, the larger is the extent of recovery in successive seasons. After two monsoon showers, the average productivity in 2011 across all damage categories seems comparable. Interestingly, even productivity for category "0" lands has shown an increase over the three rounds. This can be attributed to better monsoon in following years as this category was unaffected by salinity due to Aila.

**Figure 11.5**

*Loss in productivity across damage categories and recovery over time*

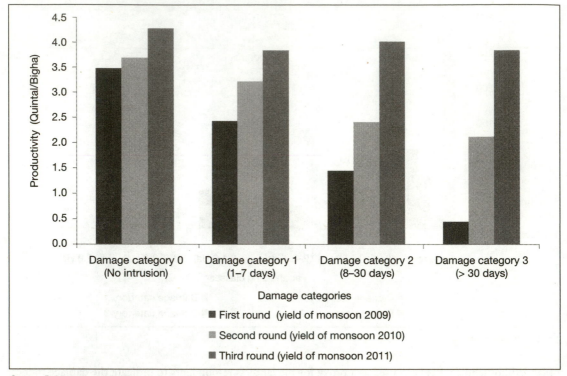

*Source:* Primary survey.

A regression exercise was carried out to statistically verify the significance of damage and recovery in productivity. A simple regression of productivity for landholding households was run on pooled data with dummy variables representing the three survey rounds. The effect of family size (FSIZE), educational qualification of the household head (HDEDU), and the size of landholding (LAND_HOLDING) have been controlled in explaining productivity over three rounds. The crucial damage indicator is the number of days of saline water staying on the field (WATER_STAY). It has been interacted with the dummy variables for survey rounds to see its effect over three years. The regression was run for landholding households with two round-dummies (base round = monsoon 2009) and the interactive terms. The result is described in Table 11.3.

The result shows that the productivity of land is inversely related with the holding size. This might be explained by intensive labour inputs by small and marginal farmers in the study area. It can be noted that the average productivity has increased over the three survey rounds. Compared to monsoon of 2009 (base), the productivity increased by 0.1 quintal/bigha[8] in monsoon 2010 (though it is statistically insignificant) and further in monsoon 2011 it significantly increased by more than 1 quintal/bigha.

More interesting facts are revealed by the estimated coefficients of the interacted terms. The damage indicator (WATER_STAY) shows that in first two rounds, the extent of saline water damage significantly reduced the productivity while in the third round it had no significant effect on productivity. It might be said that the productivity recovered from the impact of salinity in the monsoon of 2011.

The analyses of productivity data across damage categories and across survey rounds reasonably establish the differential damage to agriculture by the cyclone and its recovery. The coping behaviour of the households in the intermediate period against the damage stands to be analysed taking the advantage of differential damage intensities. As already indicated, the main alternatives for the affected households has been to fall back on local natural resources (river and forest) and/or to work outside the region as migrant labourers.

**Table 11.3**

*Regression result for productivity\* differences across damage categories in three survey rounds*

| Dependent variable = "productivity" | | | |
|---|---|---|---|
| Description of regressors | Variable | Coefficient | t-value |
| Base = productivity in survey round 1 (monsoon 2009) | CONSTANT | 3.148 | 17.42*** |
| Size of cultivable land (unit = hectare) | LAND_HOLDNG | −0.452 | −4.54*** |
| Household size | FSIZE | 0.031 | 1.56 |
| Highest educational qualification of the head of the household (Categorical; 1–8) | HDEDU | −0.038 | −1.04 |
| Dummy for survey round 2 (monsoon 2010) | ROUND2 | 0.107 | 0.87 |
| Dummy for survey round 3 (monsoon 2011) | ROUND3 | 1.033 | 8.39*** |
| Interaction of round dummy (ROUND1) with the number of days of water stay (salinity damage indicator) | ROUND1WATER_STAY | −0.075 | −8.14*** |
| Interaction of round dummy (ROUND2) with the number of days of water stay (salinity damage indicator) | ROUND2WATER_STAY | −0.013 | −5.94*** |
| Interaction of round dummy (ROUND3) with number of days of water stay (salinity damage indicator) | ROUND3WATER_STAY | −0.002 | −0.94 |
| No. of observations = 1202; Adj. R-squared = 0.2278 | $F_{(8, 1193)} = 45.28$; Prob > F = 0.000 | | |

*Source:* Primary survey—three rounds.

*Notes:*  1.  Productivity measured in quintal/bigha ("bigha" is the local standard unit for agricultural land = 0.1338 hectare).

   2.  *** represents the 1 per cent level of significance.

## Coping with Natural Resources

As mentioned before, the direct anthropogenic pressure on Sundarbans' ecosystem is caused mainly by activities such as prawn-fry collection on the village side of the rivers, fishing and crab-catching in the open rivers and forest creeks, and seasonal honey collection from the reserve forest. Figure 11.2 showed that such livelihood practices have a clear inverse relationship with landholding.

Data collected in survey rounds has been used to identify the households which had *newly* started such activities after Aila. Figure 11.6 gives us a preliminary idea of the distribution of these new entrants across different damage categories. A household is identified as "new" in this livelihood in the *i*th survey round if none of its members was engaged in any of the above-mentioned activities before Aila, but at least one of them has started it in the *i*th round (*i* = 1, 2, 3).

As every damage category involved a fair distribution of all landholding classes,[9] it can be reasonably assumed that the effect of landholding on livelihood choices, if any, cancels out within each damage category. Increase in the percentage of new entrants in natural-resource-based activities for higher damage categories is, thus, indicative of coping with natural resources in the face of loss in agriculture.

An interesting feature comes out in Figure 11.6. It shows, among other things, that there has been new addition to such activities even for the damage category "0" (unaffected). This is most probably due to the overall livelihood adjustment dynamics in the region in the face of changing socio-economic conditions on those islands. Also, some of the *unaffected* households' earning opportunities might have been adversely

**Figure 11.6**
*Damage intensities and coping with surrounding natural resources*

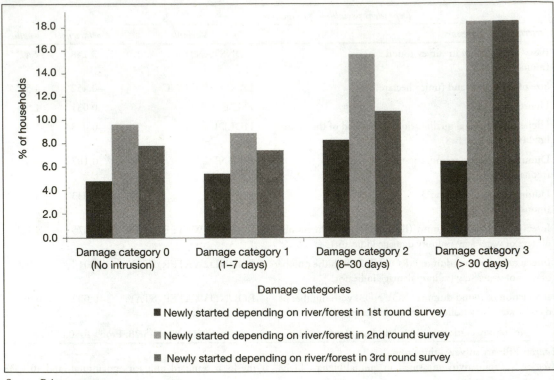

*Source:* Primary survey.

affected through agricultural damage in the neighbouring area. The main point to note here is that the percentage of new entrants is larger for higher damage categories.

## Coping with Migrant Labour Jobs

The story of migrant labour jobs is similar to that of natural resource exploitation. The survey data was used to identify the households which were *new* entrants in this profession after the disaster. Figure 11.7 shows the distribution of such households over survey rounds and damage categories.

Preliminary observations relating to migrant labourers are similar to what was found for natural-resource-based activities. However, there was a significant jump in the percentage of new entrants only in 2010 (second round) for all damage categories. It suggests that there was a time lag before migrant labour activities could be taken up as a coping strategy. This is plausible as one needs some time to prepare before getting into new alternatives. Moving out as a migrant labourer might be a viable option only after some assuring contact is developed through peers or acquaintances working outside. This might explain why the percentage increases were more in second round rather than in the first round itself. What is important to note is that such jumps are more pronounced for higher damage categories.

The jump in the percentage of such households in the second round even for the unaffected category can be attributed to relative backwardness of the study area compared to other growth centres of India. In addition, widespread loss in agriculture in the surrounding area might have restricted earning opportunities of the unaffected households—a logic already put forward for analysing similar phenomenon in the case of natural resource dependence.

**Figure 11.7**
*Damage intensities and coping with migrant labour jobs*

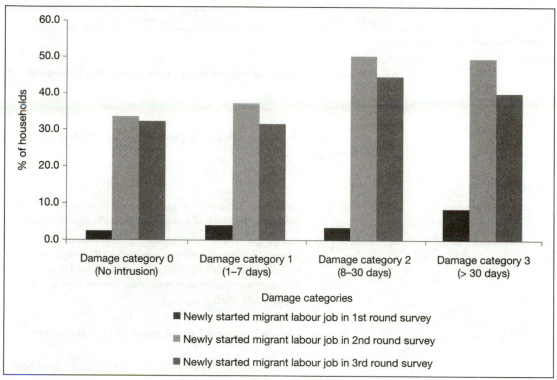

*Source:* Primary survey.

## Determinants of Livelihood Coping: Regression Analysis

This section looks at the possible determinants at household level that shaped the choice of their coping strategies against agricultural damage. The binary variables NRES and MIGR identify a household's status regarding natural resource dependence and migrating behaviour.[10]

These binary outcomes are regressed on a set of household-level variables and attributes such as household's location, exposure to natural resources, physical endowments, and human capital along with the damage intensity. Table 11.4 describes the variables used in the regression exercises.

Among the regressors, location of the household within the Sundarbans delta and educational qualification of the household head (REMOTENESS and HDEDU) are recorded as categorical variables having pre-decided codes. A household's exposure (proximity and availability) to natural resources (EXP2NRES) is also treated as a categorical variable after processing the survey data.[11] Identification of landless households (LANDLESS) and sex of the head of the household (FEMALE_HEAD) are binary variables among the set of regressors. On the other hand, the area of agricultural land (LAND_HOLDNG), number of members in the household (FSIZE), money value of livestock holding (LIVESTOCK), and number of days of work availed by the household members within the last one year through government-sponsored employment schemes (NREG) are recorded as continuous variables. The crucial variable representing the extent of damage caused by soil salinity (WATER_STAY) is also treated as a continuous variable. Table 11.5 provides the summary statistics of the regressors.

Factors affecting households' livelihood choices, before Aila, with respect to two crucial alternatives of natural resource exploitation and migrating have been captured with a probit analysis. However, the choice of these alternatives is not independent as it is constrained by the households' available resources—mainly

**Table 11.4**
*Description of variables used in regression analyses*

| Category | Variable name | Description |
|---|---|---|
| **Dependent variables** | | |
| NRES | (Binary)<br>=1 if any members of the household had earning from river- and/or forest-based activities<br>=0 otherwise | |
| MIGR | (Binary)<br>=1 if at least one member of the household is a migrant worker outside the Sundarbans region<br>=0 otherwise | |
| **Regressors** | | |
| Location/Remoteness | REMOTNESS | Categorical variable (1–4) indicating the distance of the household from the block administrative office (in ascending order) |
| Natural resource availability | EXP2NRES | Categorical variable (0–4) indicating the exposure of the household to natural resource captured by the length of river embankment within the village perimeter divided by the village population (in ascending order; zero indicating not adjacent to a river) |
| Household's productive asset and human capital endowments | LANDLESS | (Binary)<br>=1 if the household does not possess any agricultural land<br>= 0 otherwise |
| | LAND_HOLDNG | Area of household's own cultivable land for landed households (unit=hectare) |
| | FSIZE | Number of members in the household |
| | HDAGE | Age of the head of the household (in completed years) |
| | HDEDU | Categorical (1 to 8) indicating the highest educational qualification of the head of the household (in ascending order) |
| | FEMALE_HEAD | (Binary) Sex of the head of the household<br>0=Male; 1=Female |
| | LIVESTOCK | Money value of household's livestock holding in US $; (conversion rate: US $ 1=₹ 55) |
| Aila damage indicator | WATER_STAY | The number of days through which saline water stayed on the household's agricultural land (reported by the household in first survey round) |
| Access to govt. livelihood programme | NREG | Number of days of paid labour job provided by the government to the members of the household in last one year under the National Rural Employment Guarantee Scheme |
| Dummy variables for survey rounds | ROUND1 | =1 if observation belongs to survey round 1 (monsoon 2009)<br>=0 Otherwise |
| | ROUND2 | =1 if observation belongs to survey round 2 (monsoon 2010)<br>=0 Otherwise |
| | ROUND3 | =1 if observation belongs to survey round 3 (monsoon 2011)<br>=0 Otherwise |

**Table 11.5**
*Summary statistics of the variables used as regressors*

| Variable | Type/Unit | Obs | Mean | Std. Dev. | Min | Max |
|---|---|---|---|---|---|---|
| REMOTNESS | Categorical | 778 | 2.75 | 0.89 | 1 | 4 |
| EXP2NRES | Categorical | 778 | 2.30 | 1.38 | 0 | 4 |
| FSIZE | Integer | 778 | 4.91 | 1.87 | 1 | 15 |
| LANDLESS | Binary | 778 | 0.32 | 0.47 | 0 | 1 |
| LAND_HOLDNG | Hectare | 778 | 0.26 | 0.38 | 0 | 5.6 |
| HDEDU | Categorical | 778 | 2.68 | 1.05 | 1 | 8 |
| HDAGE | Integer | 778 | 46.2 | 13.3 | 20 | 89 |
| FEMALE_HEAD | Binary | 778 | 0.05 | 0.22 | 0 | 1 |
| WATER_STAY | Integer | 530 | 17.05 | 27.10 | 0 | 180 |
| LVSTOCK (round1) | US$ | 778 | 21 | 37 | 0 | 293 |
| LVSTOCK (round2) | US$ | 778 | 87 | 99 | 0 | 1289 |
| LVSTOCK (round3) | US$ | 778 | 89 | 100 | 0 | 785 |
| NREG (round1) | Integer (days) | 778 | 18.9 | 29.5 | 0 | 270 |
| NREG (round2) | Integer (days) | 778 | 7.8 | 16.3 | 0 | 220 |
| NREG (round3) | Integer (days) | 778 | 8.4 | 15.6 | 0 | 110 |

the size of its workforce. So, two probit models for two livelihood choices needed to be estimated jointly. It called for a bivariate probit estimation. Table 11.6 shows the result where NRES and MIGR have been jointly explained by a subset of regressors described earlier.[12]

This result statistically establishes that the uneducated households with little or no landholding had traditionally resorted to natural resources or went out for migrant labour jobs. Both of these occupations are supposed to be dangerous or hazardous for various reasons. So, it is basically lack of alternative earning opportunities and insufficient landholding that forced the households to opt for these activities. Moreover, among this set of households, the probability of resorting to natural resources is significantly more if they are located in close proximity to a river or a forest. For households that are not favourably located, the alternative of migrating is a more probable option. It is evident by the significance of the regressor EXP2NRES for both the regressands, with alternative signs.

Against this background, it is interesting to analyse the livelihood choices after the disaster. Previously, Figures 11.6 and 11.7 indicated some dynamic aspects in livelihood adjustment. In three rounds of the survey, new entrants were coming up or dropping off from these alternatives. A household's choice regarding these options over the three survey rounds after the disaster needs to be jointly analysed for reasons already mentioned. Also, relationship between such choices and the extent of damage (land salinity) need to be statistically established before drawing any conclusion on disaster-induced livelihood coping.

The full set of information collected in three rounds essentially constitutes a panel data set for the study. But in the course of data exploration, it was found that all the variables that came out to be significant determinants for households' livelihood choices had undergone little change over the three survey rounds. So, panel data estimation was of not much additional utility in this context. Instead, a pooled data for three rounds with round-dummies was found to be more informative.

A bivariate probit model has been estimated for the pair of dependant variables NRES and MIGR. Apart from the set of regressors used in Table 11.6, some additional variables are incorporated for explaining the post-Aila scenario. The crucial addition was the damage indicator (WATER_STAY). The livestock

**Table 11.6**
*Determinants of livelihood choices before Aila (bivariate probit regression)*

| Dependent variable: NRES | Marginal effect (dy/dx) | Test statistic (z) |
|---|---|---|
| REMOTNESS | 0.0153 | 1.02 |
| EXP2NRES | 0.0384 | 3.87*** |
| LANDLESS | 0.0633 | 1.72* |
| LAND_HOLDNG | −0.089 | −1.36 |
| FSIZE | −0.0082 | −1.04 |
| HDEDU | −0.0617 | −3.89*** |
| HDAGE | −0.0021 | −1.95* |
| FEMALE_HEAD | −0.0463 | −0.93 |
| *Dependent variable: MIGR* | | |
| REMOTNESS | −0.0044 | −0.26 |
| EXP2NRES | −0.0261 | −2.49** |
| LANDLESS | −0.0407 | −1.15 |
| LAND_HOLDNG | −0.1834 | −2.71*** |
| FSIZE | 0.0102 | 1.21 |
| HDEDU | −0.0328 | −2.09** |
| HDAGE | −0.0002 | −0.2 |
| FEMALE_HEAD | −0.0326 | −0.53 |
| Regression diagnostics | Number of obs=778 | |
| | Log pseudo likelihood=−732.2 | |
| | Wald chi2(16)=74.96; | |
| | Prob>chi2=0.000 | |

*Note:*   *, **, and *** represent the 10 per cent, 5 per cent, and 1 per cent level of significance, respectively.

information, collected in each round, has been added as another variable representing household's physical capital. Two dummies have been used for three survey rounds with the first round (monsoon 2009) being the base. The dynamic effect of damage due to land salinity has been captured by interaction terms of the variable WATER_STAY with dummies for survey rounds.

Regarding the other new regressor NREG, it was assumed that the government-sponsored scheme might have helped people to cope with the crop loss and might have acted as a deterrent for households to enter into new businesses. However, in spite of the "guarantee" in the scheme, the actual number of workdays (with fixed wage rate) made available to a household remained uncertain within a year. It was assumed that the households decided on their alternative choices in one survey year after taking into consideration their "realized" earning through this scheme in the previous year. The variable NREG is, thus, used in the regressions with a one-period lag. The bivariate probit result is given in Table 11.7.

Some patterns of livelihood choice seem to be holding even after Aila, compared to the situation before the disaster. Larger landholding acts as a deterrent for both of these choices even after the calamity. Also, it is the lowly educated households with younger heads that are more probable to venture in these lines of livelihood. Regarding proximity to natural resources (EXP2NRES), the same pattern is visible. That is, such proximity induces the household to opt for natural resource exploitation against opting for migrant labour jobs. LIVESTOCK and NREG are seen to positively affect the choice of natural resource exploitation, while

**Table 11.7**
*Factors explaining coping behaviour after Aila in different rounds (bivariate probit)*

| Dependent variable: NRES | Marginal effect (dy/dx) | Test statistic (z) |
|---|---|---|
| REMOTNESS | −0.0155 | −1.50 |
| EXP2NRES | 0.0504 | 7.70*** |
| LANDLESS | 0.0715 | 3.03*** |
| LAND_HOLDNG | −0.1586 | −3.49*** |
| FSIZE | 0.0022 | 0.43 |
| HDEDU | −0.0491 | −5.16*** |
| HDAGE | −0.0015 | −1.99** |
| FEMALE_HEAD | −0.0799 | −2.52** |
| WATER_STAY | 0.0016 | 3.72*** |
| LIVESTOCK | 0.0003 | 3.04*** |
| NREG (lagged) | 0.0012 | 3.81*** |
| ROUND2 | −0.0124 | −0.49 |
| ROUND3 | −0.0305 | −1.17 |
| ROUND2WATER_STAY | 0.0005 | 0.87 |
| ROUND3WATER_STAY | 0.0008 | 1.26 |
| *Dependent variable: MIGR* | | |
| REMOTNESS | 0.0295 | 2.32** |
| EXP2NRES | −0.0204 | −2.55** |
| LANDLESS | −0.0751 | −2.79 |
| LAND_HOLDNG | −0.1748 | −4.63*** |
| FSIZE | 0.0296 | 4.67*** |
| HDEDU | −0.0839 | −7.31*** |
| HDAGE | −0.0026 | −2.92*** |
| FEMALE_HEAD | 0.0586 | 1.20 |
| WATER_STAY | −0.0026 | −3.21*** |
| LIVESTOCK | −0.0001 | −1.06 |
| NREG (lagged) | 0.0002 | 0.45 |
| ROUND2 | 0.3499 | 11.47*** |
| ROUND3 | 0.3138 | 9.99*** |
| ROUND2WATER_STAY | 0.0030 | 2.85*** |
| ROUND3WATER_STAY | 0.0022 | 2.19** |
| Regression diagnostics | Number of observations = 2334 Wald chi2(30) = 573.88 Prob > chi2 = 0.0000 | |

*Note:* ** and *** represent 5 per cent and 1 per cent level of significance, respectively.

they are not significant determinants of the migration decision. It might indicate that more locally available earning opportunities induce a household towards a local supplementary activity like that of going into rivers and forests.

The household size (FSIZE) turns out to be an important factor favouring the migration decision. Larger household size means more working hands and that, in turn, making it possible to send some of its members outside the Sundarbans for long periods. This, however, is not true for natural resource exploitation, as this is locally practised.

The crucial variable WATER_STAY assumes significance in shaping both of the coping choices, but with alternative signs. While larger value of it (implying larger damage to agriculture) favoured the decision on natural resource exploitation, it acted against labour outmigration. This might be surprising as a larger damage is supposed to trigger more outmigration as well. To solve this puzzle, WATER_STAY has been interacted with different survey rounds.

The round-dummies and their interactions with the damage indicator are not significant for natural resource exploitation, but all are highly positively significant for the migration decision of the households. This finding basically captures the dynamics of livelihood adjustment after the disaster. Larger WATER_STAY induced more natural resource exploitation *only* in the immediate aftermath of the disaster. But its effect is not visible in successive rounds. In contrast, migrating is a decision that is induced by WATER_STAY *only* in later rounds. As was indicated earlier (in section "Coping with Migrant Labour Jobs"), prospective migrants might have needed some preparation time and some arrangement with a personal acquaintance working outside. This decision is also affected by "pull factors" from the rest of the country (higher wage rate in urban growth centres across India during this period). That part is captured by the significance of round-dummies in isolation. But the disaster-inducement is captured by the (positive) significance of the interaction terms. In the short run, however, natural resource dependence might have been chosen by some of the households, who faced larger damage, against the migration decision.

## Summary and Conclusion

Efforts are ongoing at the national and international level for conservation of the Sundarbans' ecosystem. This study shows that anthropogenic pressure on this ecosystem increased with a climate-related disaster and the attendant agricultural loss. Survey data shows that among the households facing larger damage intensity, those with smaller land endowments, lesser education, and larger family size tended to shift to a new livelihood mix. Some of these households used their surrounding open-access rivers as a natural insurance against the loss in the short run. But after some time, the other major coping option for them was migrant labour jobs outside the region. It is seen that even after reasonable restoration of damaged agriculture, a significant number of households had continued with their new livelihood choices.

The coping pattern had revealed that time is an important component in making choices. In the short run, with a widespread loss in major livelihood, the disaster affects almost everyone in a region. Only with passage of time one can observe its lingering effects. A major natural calamity ultimately puts some households in a new trajectory of livelihood. From a policy perspective, it is very important to know who they are and what they have started to do, especially if that implies renewed pressure on a delicate ecosystem.

Such findings are possible only with repeat surveys covering a reasonable time horizon after an event. In this case, the first round of survey alone could not have captured all the aspects of livelihood adjustment. A one-time snapshot in such a context could have been misleading. This study has been undertaken with the aim to fill up such research gaps.

New entrants in natural resource exploitation are harmful for the Sundarbans. Official efforts to protect local agriculture against such future events, in the form of heavy investments in strong embankment building, is not in line with the long-term sustainability of this ecosystems in the face of predicted increase in such events under CC. Instead, helping the local population in getting labour jobs outside can be an alternative way to conserve the ecosystem. The time lag in coping behaviour shows that there is scope for facilitating migration of labour from this region. It might be helpful to generate greater awareness and information regarding job opportunities outside. Some form of subsidizing private costs of migration would also help to steer the workforce of marginal and smallholder families out of the Sundarbans. This might improve the long-run sustainability of the ecosystem as well as provide them with a more certain livelihood option in the face of the CC threats.

# Appendix: Construction of Categorical Variables Used in Regression

1. Remoteness: Within the delta region with a labyrinth of rivers, people mostly commute by boats. In such a context, the distance between places could be meaningfully captured only by measuring the commuting time between them. In the sample selection process, remoteness of a village was recorded in terms of options representing the average time taken to reach the block development office from that village using the usual mode of transport. The four options were (a) less than 1 hour (b) between 1 and 2 hours (c) between 2 and 3 hours and (d) more than 3 hours.

The appropriate option has been recorded by the corresponding number and later this information is used to represent the remoteness of all the households belonging to that village. So, REMOTENESS is an integer between 0 and 4.

2. HDEDU: Highest educational qualification of the household's head has been recorded as one of the eight given options starting from "illiterate" (lowest, recorded as "1") to "post-graduate and above" (highest, marked as "8"). So, this is a categorical variable with ascending values representing higher human capital endowment for the household.

3. EXP2NRES: This is a variable constructed after the collection of survey data. It is invariant for all households within a village and essentially a village-level characteristic. It is intended to represent two dimensions of natural resource availability to the villagers. First, it captured the proximity to natural resources by the length of riverfront (equivalently "length of embankment," as riversides are invariably guarded with embankments) within a village. Second, it considered the degree of competition within the villager for use of that riverfront.

At the village selection stage, data has been collected on embankment length and voter number (adult population) for all villages in the two study blocks. Then, the ratio of embankment length and corresponding voter strength has been calculated. This ratio, representing "per-adult embankment length," has been used as a proxy for villagers' exposure to natural resources.

There are villages for which this value is zero, as they are located in the interiors of an island. The non-zero values, however, represented a continuous variable. It needed to be transformed into a discrete one to arrive at some finite categorization before the selection of sample villages. It was accomplished by calculating quartiles of the non-zero values of that ratio. These quartile numbers were used as categories representing the exposure to natural resource (river) for the village as a whole (i.e., category "1" village representing least exposure to riverfront). So, EXP2NRES had five possible values (0, 1, 2, 3, and 4; with "0" representing "no embankment"). The value of this categorical variable for a village has later been assigned to every household from that village.

# Notes

1. On 25th May 2009.
2. Also called tectonic subsidence, which is the sinking of the earth's crust on a large scale. For more details, see https://en.wikipedia.org/wiki/Tectonic_subsidence
3. The study enlisted the total population of 40 polling booth areas for building a primary sampling frame. The average population of a polling booth area was calculated from this primary information which was multiplied by the total number of polling booths on islands to arrive at the estimate.
4. Most of the NGO activities relates to mangrove protection. It involves creating mangrove nursery and planting and protecting the mangroves on the village sides of the river banks. Also, to win away people from mangrove forest-based activities, alternative livelihood schemes such as poultry farming and goat-rearing are being promoted by NGOs with financial support.
5. National Rural Employment Guarantee (NREG) Scheme: a scheme funded by government of India to provide labour jobs to the rural unemployed.
6. Other related activities include processing of paddy, its transportation, its local trading, and sundry.
7. The only monsoon crop is paddy for all survey households.
8. Bigha is the local reporting unit for land (1 bigha=0.1338 hectare).
9. Already shown in Figure 11.4.
10. For a detailed description of the variables, please refer to Table 11.4.
11. Please refer to the appendix for a detailed description of the categorical variables.
12. LIVESTOCK and NREG data was not available for the recall period (before Aila) and the damage indicator (WATER_STAY) is irrelevant for the pre-disaster period. So, they are dropped from this estimation.

# References

Ali, A. 1999. "Climate Change Impacts and Adaptation Assessment in Bangladesh." *Climate Research* 12 (2–3): 109–16.

Alvi, E., and S. Dendir. 2011. "Weathering the Storms: Credit Receipt and Child Labor in the Aftermath of the Great Floods (1998) in Bangladesh." *World Development* 39 (8): 1398–409.

Boustan, L.P., M.E. Kahn, and P.W. Rhode. 2012. "Coping with Economic and Environmental Shocks: Institutions and Outcomes." *American Economic Review* 102 (3): 238–44.

Carvajal, L., and I.M. Pereira. 2009. "Climate Shocks and Human Mobility: Evidence from Nicaragua." Human Development Report Office (HDRO), UNDP. Available at: https://papers.ssrn.com/sol3/papers.cfm?abstract_id=1599667 (accessed on 11 May 2011).

Hazra, S., T. Ghosh, R. Dasgupta, and G. Sen. 2002. "Sea Level and Associated Changes in the Sundarbans." *Science and Culture* 68 (9–12): 309–21.

Huigen, M.G., and I.C. Jens. 2006. "Socio-economic Impact of Super Typhoon Harurot in San Mariano, Isabela, the Philippines." *World Development* 34 (12): 2116–36.

Kinsey, B., K. Burger, and J.W. Gunning. 1998. "Coping with Drought in Zimbabwe: Survey Evidence on Responses of Rural Households to Risk." *World Development* 26 (1): 89–110.

Mcsweeney, K. 2005. "Natural Insurance, Forest Access, and Compounded Misfortune: Forest Resources in Smallholder Coping Strategies Before and After Hurricane Mitch, Northeastern Honduras." *World Development* 33 (9): 1453–71.

Morris, S. S., O. Neidecker-Gonzales, C. Carletto, M. Munguía, J.M. Medina, and Q. Wodon. 2002. "Hurricane Mitch and the Livelihoods of the Rural Poor in Honduras." *World Development* 30 (1): 49–60.

Ninno, Carlo del, Paul A. Dorosh, Lisa C. Smith, and Dilip K. Roy. 2001. "The 1998 Floods in Bangladesh: Disaster Impacts, Household Coping Strategies, and Response." Research Report No. 122, International Food Policy Research Institute, Washington, DC.

Pattanayak, S.K., and E.O. Sills. 2001. "Do Tropical Forests Provide Natural Insurance? The Microeconomics of Non-timber Forest Product Collection in the Brazilian Amazon." *Land Economics* 77 (4): 595–612.

Shrestha, S.S., and P. Bhandari. 2007. "Environmental Security and Labor Migration in Nepal." *Population and Environment* 29 (1): 25–38.

Sivakumar, S., and E. Kerbert. 2004. "Drought, Sustenance and Livelihoods: 'Akal' Survey in Rajasthan." *Economic and Political Weekly* 39 (January 17): 285–94.

Unnikrishnan, A.S., K.R. Kumar, S.E. Fernandes, G.S. Michael, and S.K. Patwardhan. 2006. "Sea Level Changes Along the Indian Coast: Observations and Projections." *Current Science* 90 (3): 362–68.

# 12

# Fire Environment and Community-based Forest Fire Management in the Central Siwalik Region of Nepal*

Lok Mani Sapkota**

## Introduction

Forest fire is a major disturbance factor and common phenomenon in most of the forests. Availability of ignition sources and flammable material facilitates the occurrence of fire in vegetated area in all ecosystems (Omi 2005). Some forest ecosystems are adapted to fire and require it for nutrient recycling and creating favourable condition for germination and growth of certain native species (FAO 2010; IUCN and WWF 2000). Fire, on the other hand, is also considered as one of the major drivers of deforestation and forest degradation and one of the major sources of greenhouse gases; forest fire has a big share in forestry sector's 17.4 per cent of the total global emissions of greenhouse gases (Barker et al. 2007). Altogether, 63 per cent of the global forest area receives fire every year and forest fire, particularly uncontrolled, causes substantial loss to forest biomass, soil, air, water, and forest functions and services; therefore, forest managers consider it as an important threat to forest management (FAO 2010). Nepal, a South Asian country with the human population of 23 million and area of 14.71 million ha of which nearly 40 forest is forest or shrub land, witnesses fire every year, particularly in dry deciduous forests (DFRS 1999; GoN 2011).

About 90 per cent of the forest area in the tropical region in Nepal is affected with fire annually, most of which is surface fire, which results in the reduced regenerative capacity of forest (ITTO 2009). Forests in the tropical region are under high risk due to a fire-prone fuel and management system. Every year, fire burns large areas consuming lives and property and is considered one of the most important human-induced disasters (FAO 2006a). The damage by forest fire in the year 2009 is burning of 146,742 ha and killing of 43 persons; the estimated total loss by fire excluding the cost of environmental damage, human loss, and destruction of flora and fauna is NRs[1] 134,415,000 (GoN 2010). Altogether, 358 forest fires were detected in Nepal only on 25 April 2009 (PSPL & FECOFUN 2010). This large number of fire on a single day indicates the gravity of the forest fire issue in the country. On the other hand, the Government of Nepal and

* This research is a part of MSc at Asian Institute of Technology (AIT).

** I would like to thank Ganesh P. Shivakoti, Rajendra Shrestha, and Damien Jourdain of School of Environment Resources and Development of Asian Institute of Technology for their invaluable guidance, other great people for assisting me in the field, and the Norwegian Government for financial support in this study.

other stakeholders highlight the success of community-based fire management in preventing and suppressing fire in their forest (FAO 2007).

Nearly quarter of the total forest in the country is managed by communities as community forest (DoF 2010). The Forest Act (1993) of Nepal defines community forest as part of the national forest handed over to users group for the development, protection, and utilization of the forest in the interest of the community and gives community the rights to collectively manage the forest in their vicinity according to the government-approved operational plan (GoN 1995). Communities in Nepal are managing 34.92 per cent of the potential area that can be handed over to them as community forest (DoF 2010). Although the community forests in the Siwalik region are fire-prone and the communities hold responsibility for the protection of their forest, researches, however, report the community lack the required capacity to effectively manage forest fire and their effort is largely limited to the appointment of fire watchers and mobilization of forest guards in the dry period which steps are not sufficient to overcome the damage (FAO 2006b). Nonetheless there is increasing community involvement and interest in the management of fire (FAO 2007).

Fire is regarded as one of the components of the social ecological system—an integrated system of eco-systems and human systems with reciprocal feedbacks and interdependence (Resilience Alliance 2010). Fire management, according to Myers (2006), requires an array of possible technical decisions and actions directed towards preventing, detecting, controlling, containing, and manipulating or using fire in a given landscape to meet specific goals and objectives. Fire itself is a result of fuel, weather, and topography, which are considered as element of the fire triangle (Heikkilä, Gronqvist, and Jurvelius 2007). Fuel for forest fire is the organic material—live or dead—that ignites and burns in, on, or above the ground and comprises dry leaves, twigs, stump, and so on, availability of which is primarily affected by fuel moisture content, wind, and topography (Omi 2005). Weather is not a sole determinant of fire behaviour, yet it is one of the most important factors. It interacts with other factors and results in the actual fire behaviour. The magnitude and seasonal distribution of weather factors such as temperature and precipitation have tremendous impact on fire which influence the drying of forest fuel and in turn determine the availability of fuel for fire (Heikkilä et al. 2007; Omi 2005). Considering these aspects of forest fire management, we conducted this research to assess the fire weather and community response to manage forest fire in the forests in the Central Siwalik region of Nepal.

# Materials and Methods

## Study Area

The study was carried out in the Siwalik area of Makwanpur and Chitwan districts in the Central Development Region in Nepal (Figure 12.1). The area selected for the study is located between 27°21' and 27°46' N latitude and 83°55' and 84°35' E longitude and possesses tropical climate. Forest, mostly of mixed *Shorea robusta*, is the dominant land cover in the area (56.7% in Makwanpur and 62.92% in Chitwan; DDC/Chitwan 2005; DDC/Makwanpur 2010). The study represents the tropical area between the Churiya range in the South and the Mahabharata range in the North in Makwanpur and Chitwan districts. Similarly, the eastern and western boundaries of the study area are Bagmati River and Narayani River, respectively. The area was selected for the study for possessing the following key characteristics (DFO/Chitwan 2011; DFO/Makwanpur 2011):

- High fire susceptibility
- Forest as dominant land cover
- Pioneer districts in community forestry in the physiographic region

**Figure 12.1**
*Map showing study area and studied community forests*

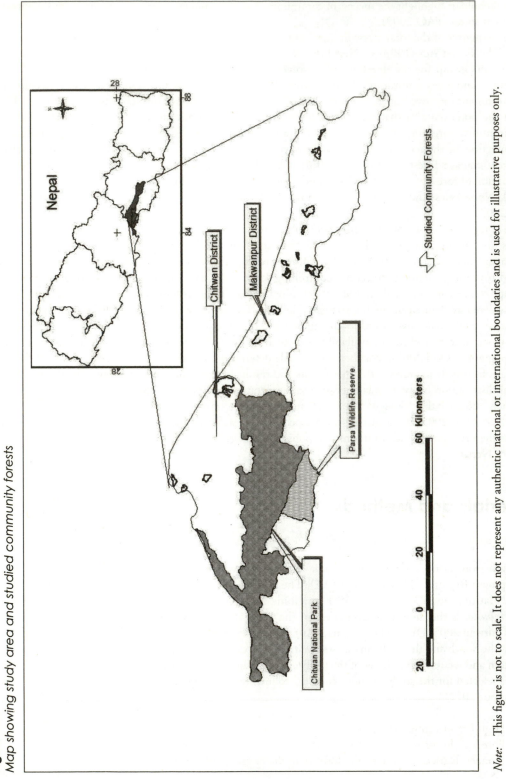

*Note:* This figure is not to scale. It does not represent any authentic national or international boundaries and is used for illustrative purposes only.

## Data Collection and Analysis

Different types of data were collected for the study purpose. Meteorological data were collected from meteorological stations of the Department of Hydrology and Meteorology of the Government of Nepal for 30 years. The data consist of daily precipitation and temperature—maximum and minimum—data collected from eight stations from the year 1981 to 2010. However, due to irregularity of data in six stations, data only from two stations (Hetauda and Rampur) were considered suitable for analysis of temporal change. Hetauda station lies in the Siwalik region of Makawanpur district while Rampur station lies on the Siwalik region of Chitwan district. The temperature data was analysed to get monthly maximum temperatures, yearly maximum, and their trend. Similarly, precipitation data were analysed to get monthly average precipitation, total annual precipitation, annual maximum number of consecutive dry days (days receiving less than 1 mm precipitation), and their trends. T-test was conducted under 0.01 level of significance, where applicable, to assess similarity of the measurement between two stations.

The data on fire occurrence in Nepal for 2001–12 was obtained from the Fire Information for Resource Management System (FIRMS) which generated data on fire spots from MODIS captured satellite images. See, in general FIRMS (2012). The data were supplied in the *.shp format for all the possible points for the whole country which was later clipped for the Siwalik region of Makwanpur and Chitwan districts excluding the protected area (Chitawan National Park and Parsa Wildlife Reserve) using ArcGIS 9.3. The data were classified into three groups as guided by FIRMS. However, only the data points having the confidence level equal to or more than 80 per cent were taken to ensure that only highly likely points are included in the analysis.

Similarly, socio-ecological data were collected from 20 Community Forest User Groups (CFUGs) of the Siwalik area of Makwanpur and Chitwan district (Table 12.1) in five months (from September 2011 to January 2012). The CFUGs were selected so as to represent variability brought about by different locations of CFUGs and activeness of communities in responding to forest fire. District Forest Offices (DFOs) and Federation of Community Forest User Group Nepal at local level helped to select the CFUGs considering the objective of the study. Focus group discussion was carried out in each CFUG and key informant survey with those active in forest management for collecting data on source, timing, location, and trend of fire and fire management practices in their forest.

# Results and Discussion

## Fuel in Community Forest in Central Siwalik

*Shorea robusta* constitutes more than two-thirds biomass of the community forest in the Siwalik region. The species is dominant in all the community forests considered in this study. Users reported that most of leaf shedding of *Shorea* takes place in the short period of less than a month in March. Results of monthly leaf shedding data collected by Bhatta and Shrestha in 2006 and 2007 from the Rani Community Forest, a community in the Siwalik area of Makwanpur district, was accepted by community forest users in this study as well. The amount of leaf shedding in community forest having pole strata of 18 years in Siwalik, leaf of *Shorea robusta* constituted 66 per cent of the total leaf fall in a year, that is, 8.35 tons/ha (Figure 12.2). The leaf fall of *Shorea* takes place within a short period of less than a month in the peak dry season. Also, leaf fall in the forest of Siwalik follows a unimodal pattern with majority of leaf shedding in the short period from February to end of May demonstrating peak in March. Left in the forest floor in the peak dry season, the dried leaf is the main fuel load in the forest (Bhatta and Shrestha 2010).

All the CFUGs reported that the growing stock in their community forest is increasing. They reported that with the increase in conservation effort by the community upon handover of management responsibility and use rights, the growing stock in the forest has increased in every community forest considered in this

**Table 12.1**

*Description of studied CFUGs*

| S. no. | Name of CFUG | Address | Area (ha.) | Number of households | Year of registration |
|--------|--------------|---------|-----------|----------------------|----------------------|
| 1. | Jyamire Kalika | Manahari-7, Makawanpur | 410 | 477 | 1993 |
| 2. | Chanauta | Basamadi-1, Makawanpur | 316.92 | 229 | 1998 |
| 3. | Dangdunge | Hetauda-11, Makwanpur | 196.4 | 400 | 1995 |
| 4. | Neureni Chisapani | Hetauda-7, Makwanpur | 71.13 | 248 | 1990 |
| 5. | Ashok | Hatiya-2, Makawanpur | 137.5 | 193 | 1993 |
| 6. | Mahankal | Phaparbari-7, Makawanpur | 155 | 71 | 1997 |
| 7. | Sundar | Hetauda-1,2, Makawanpur | 109 | 206 | 1995 |
| 8. | Parebashwori | Piple-6, Mahadevtar Chitwan | 1311.9 | 601 | 1996 |
| 9. | Shivapuri | Piple-7, Chitwan | 127 | 261 | 1995 |
| 10. | Pashupati Kailashpuri | Piple-7, Chitwan | 127 | 226 | 1996 |
| 11. | Thakal dada | Basamadi-8, Makawanpur | 99.47 | 130 | 1996 |
| 12. | Ektare | Hetauda-11, Makwanpur | 58.8 | 170 | 1994 |
| 13. | Kalika Chandika | Bhaise-2.3, Makawanpur | 896.75 | 212 | 1998 |
| 14. | Panchakanya | Harnamadi-4, Makawanpur | 516.61 | 211 | 1995 |
| 15. | Namobuddha | Phaparbari-7, Makawanpur | 115 | 170 | 2000 |
| 16. | Pari Pakha Harda dada | Phaparbari-3,4,5, Makawanpur | 163.88 | 222 | 2001 |
| 17. | Ratmate | Churiyamai-3, Makwanpur | 457.28 | 312 | 1997 |
| 18. | Satanchuli | Bharatpur-1, Chitwan | 198.1 | 560 | 1999 |
| 19. | Jaldevi | Bharatpur-2, Chitwan | 189.87 | 982 | 2001 |
| 20. | Rambel | Bharatpur-12, Chitwan | 197 | 1306 | 2001 |

*Source:* Operational plans of studied CFUGs, 2011.

**Figure 12.2**

*Monthly leaf litter fall of Shorea robusta in community forest*

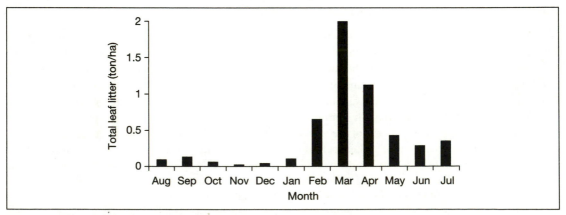

*Source:* Adapted from Bhatta and Shrestha (2010).

study. Similarly, the CFUGs reported an increase in the accumulation of fuel, particularly leaf and twigs and dead herbs on the forest floor due to their protection efforts in recent years.

## Fire Weather

The daily data of 30 years from 1981 to 2010 shows a unimodal distribution of precipitation and scanty precipitation in November, December, January, February, and March in both the stations (Figure 12.3). These months altogether receive less than 4 per cent of the total annual precipitation, that is, 3.42 per cent and 3.73 per cent in Hetauda and Rampur, respectively. Nearly the same distribution pattern of precipitation was observed in both the stations.

Total annual precipitation in the Central Siwalik area is 2,267.3 mm (2,463.5 mm and 2,071.1 mm in Hetauda and Rampur, respectively), which is higher than the national average of 1,600 mm (ICIMOD 2007). T-test, under 0.01 level of significance, revealed that the total annual precipitation in Rampur is significantly higher than that in Hetauda station. However, both the stations witnessed an increasing trend in the total annual rainfall (Figure 12.4).

Maximum number of consecutive dry days (days receiving less than 1 mm of precipitation) in each year from 1981 to 2010 were found to follow no clear pattern. Figure 12.5 shows that the maximum number of consecutive dry days had shown greater fluctuation in recent years than in the past. The diagram points out a number of consecutive dry days over the period ranged from 28 days in 2004 to 141 days in 1999 for Hetauda station, whereas it ranged from 43 days in 1987 and 1995 to 170 days in 2009 in Rampur station. However, t-test under 0.01 level of significance showed no significant difference in the annual distribution of the maximum consecutive dry days in both stations; mean of the maximum number of consecutive dry days in Hetauda and Rampur stations are 71.33 and 74.03, respectively. The trend analysis of both the stations shows an increasing number of consecutive dry days. Likewise, the maximum number of consecutive dry days were mostly observed in the months of November, December, January, and February.

The maximum temperatures in 12 months in 30 years on those stations were found as shown in Figure 12.6. It shows the temperature could reach as high as 43.2°C in Rampur and 40.6°C in Hetauda in the month of May. Although the temperature is significantly higher in Rampur, as depicted by the t-test under 0.01 level of significance with mean temperature 38.41°C and 40.63°C at Hetauda and Rampur, respectively, the pattern of distribution is nearly similar in both the stations. According to the diagram, the maximum temperature reaches its peak in the month of May followed by April, June, and March, respectively.

**Figure 12.3**

*Monthly average precipitation in (a) Hetauda station and (b) Rampur station based on daily precipitation data of 30 years*

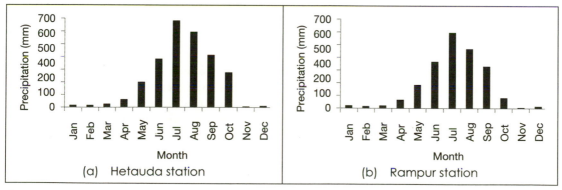

*Source:* Department of Hydrology and Meteorology (2011).

**Figure 12.4**

*Total annual precipitation in (a) Hetauda station and (b) Rampur station based on daily precipitation data of 30 years*

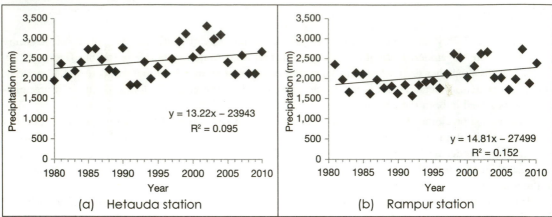

(a)   Hetauda station

(b)   Rampur station

*Source:* Department of Hydrology and Meteorology (2011).

**Figure 12.5**

*Maximum consecutive number of dry days in (a) Hetauda station and (b) Rampur station based on daily precipitation data of 30 years*

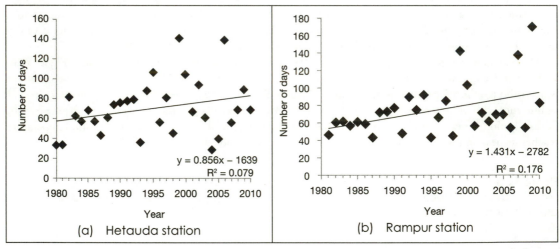

(a)   Hetauda station

(b)   Rampur station

*Source:* Department of Hydrology and Meteorology (2011).

By desiccating all the dead and fallen parts of plants to the maximum level, the higher temperature favours the occurrence and spread of fire in the forest making fuel available for the fire. Despite this, May and June, which are among the hottest months, receive considerable precipitation and are less prone to fire due to unavailability of fuel because of excessive moisture at the period. February was found to have maximum number of consecutive dry days. Therefore, February including March and April was found to have favourable weather for fire to occur.

Likewise, no regular and easily understandable pattern was observed in the yearly maximum temperature distribution in both the stations (Figure 12.7). The maximum temperature ranged from 35.5°C to 40.6°C and from 38°C to 43.2°C in Hetauda and Rampur stations, respectively. According to the t-test, the stations did not show significant difference in the monthly maximum temperature; the mean monthly temperatures at

**Figure 12.6**

*Monthly maximum temperature in (a) Hetauda station and (b) Rampur station based on daily temperature data of 30 years*

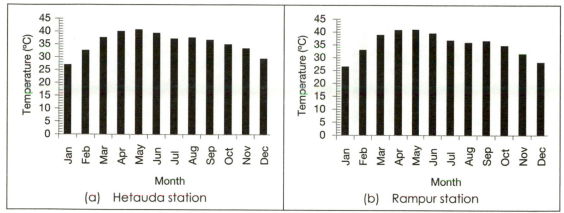

*Source:* Department of Hydrology and Meteorology (2011).

**Figure 12.7**

*Yearly maximum temperature in (a) Hetauda station and (b) Rampur station based on daily temperature data of 30 years*

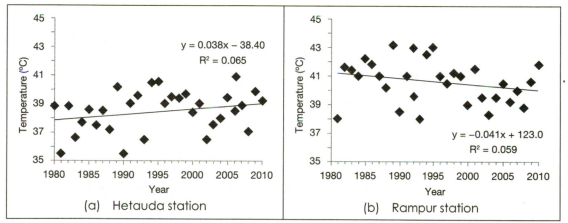

*Source:* Department of Hydrology and Meteorology (2011).

Hetauda and Rampur stations were 35.5°C and 37.3°C, respectively. Surprisingly, the yearly maximum temperature followed an increasing trend in Hetauda station while it showed the opposite trend in Rampur station.

The prolonged period of drought is always favourable for forest fire to occur, given other conditions are constant (Liu, Stanturf, and Goodrick 2010; Ricklefs 2008). The analysis shows that most of the drought occurs during the months of leaf shedding of *Shorea robusta*. Despite an increasing trend of the total annual precipitation, the increasing number of consecutive dry days in each year poses the increasing challenge for management of forest fire.

The temperature in Nepal is rising by 0.05°C/year (APN 2005). Forest fire is robustly connected with weather and climate (Johnson and Miyanishi 2001). In the face of global warming and the complex environment it creates, drought is likely to amplify. Rising atmospheric temperature has an adverse effect on rain factors and wind in Nepal (PSPL & FECOFUN 2010). Important factors such as weather, temperature, and

**Figure 12.8**
*Total number of fire spots detected by MODIS from 2001 to 2011*

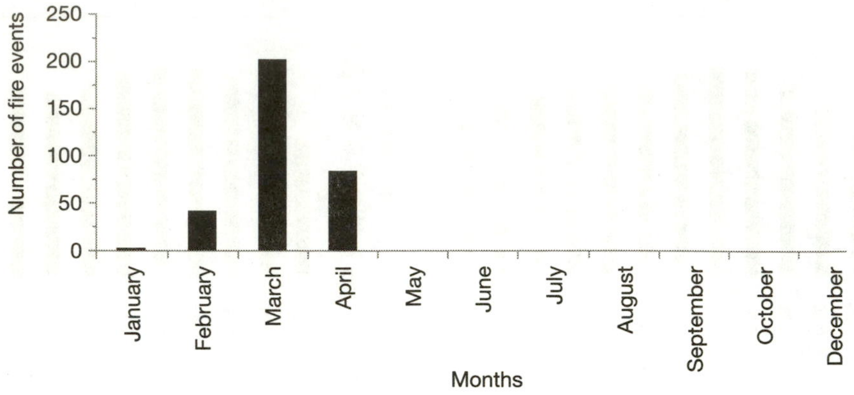

*Source:* Fire Information for Resource Management System (FIRMS), University of Maryland (2012).

rain have serious implication in forest fire. The increase in the drought period and its intensity automatically leads to more fuel availability and more favourable conditions for the forest fire to occur.

## Occurrence of Forest Fire

Remotely sensed data is largely used to detect and monitor forest fire hot spots (Stolle et al. 2004). Data of fire spots received from FIRMS showed that fuel and fire weather have direct association with the number of fire spots in community forests of the Central Siwalik region. As shown in Figure 12.8, 330 fire spots were detected in the study area by MODIS from January 2001 to December 2011; of which 202 fire spots were detected in March alone. April is the second most vulnerable month for forest fire with 83 spots. Likewise, February and January got fire in 42 and 3 spots, respectively. However, for the duration from 2001 to 2012 there were no fires detected in other months.

Similarly, the total number of fires spots from 2001 to 2011 showed fluctuation with occasional peaks. The highest number of fire spots was 59 in 2010, whilst the lowest was five in 2002. However, the total number of fire events in each year shows an increasing pattern in the recent years as presented in Figure 12.9. The synchrony of dry period as indicated by the distribution of consecutive dry days in Figure 12.5, maximum surface temperature in Figure 12.6, and occurrence of forest fire in Figure 12.8 agrees to the finding of Liu et al. (2010) that assessment precipitation and surface temperature provide key information on the potential of forest fire. And their changing scenario as given in Figures 12.4, 12.5, and 12.7 could have some role in increasing fire events as presented in Figure 12.9. Having roughly the same forest type and climate, nearly all forests in Central Siwalik are likely to face this problem (DFO/Makwarnur 2008; FAO 2002).

## Causes Fire in Community Forests

The majority of fires are initiated by human action, and the fire system is the product of social, economic, and biophysical factors operating with feedbacks and interactions across spatial scales (Dennis et al. 2005; Sorrensen 2009). Despite the Forest Act (1993) defines forest fire as a serious crime and other policy documents discourage forest fire, arsonists were rarely caught (GoN 1993, 1995). Moreover, although CFUGs are responsible for controlling fire in community forest, they were unable to exactly identify the cause of

**Figure 12.9**

*Total number of fire spots detected by MODIS in each year from 2001 to 2011*

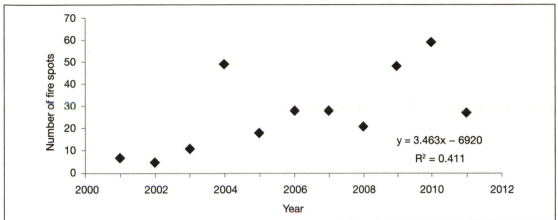

$y = 3.463x - 6920$

$R^2 = 0.411$

*Source:* Fire Information for Resource Management System (FIRMS), University of Maryland (2012).

forest fire in their forest. Discussion with users of CFUGs listed one or many of the causes of fire in their forest from the following list:

Accidental causes
- Children for enjoying
- Source of fire such as cigarette stabs not extinguished properly by trespassers
- Spreading of fire from adjoining forest

Intentional causes
- By shepherds to incite growth of succulent needed for livestock
- By hunters to catch prey such as wild boars and rabbits
- By trespassers to kill insects and snakes on road and ease movement
- By households residing near forest to minimize likelihood of catching fire in difficult situation
- By unsatisfied people to take revenge of punishment from CFUG

We found that the majority of existing studies did not explicitly identify landholders, yet almost all fire in tropical forests is caused by people, and local agents therefore play a significant role in the system (Giri and Shrestha 2000; Kull 2002). The causes of fire in the community forests of Central Siwalik are not very different from the causes of fire in the overall tropical region identified by FAO (2006b). It was found that in user's perception the fire from carelessness, followed by fire set by herders to promote the succulent growth of grass, is the main cause of fire in the community forests of the Siwalik region. Individual users did not differ largely on their understanding about the causes of fire in community forest. Instead, it was found that users were familiar with the causes of fire in their community forest.

## Forest Fire Management in Community Forests

Fire management techniques comprise the activities that can reduce and prevent fire occurrence such as early burning, firebreaks and control lines, and technical management of fires (Heikkilä et al. 2007). All of the CFUGs claimed that their forests were getting more attention and care in reducing the source of fire and escalating suppression effort, although their activeness in doing so and effectiveness, thus achievement, differed. However, the effort of most CFUGs is limited to exclusion and suppression of wildfire as the fire management approach in their respective community forest.

Even though the country is on the way to community-based fire management (GoN 2010), management of fire was not found prioritized in the operational plan of 95 per cent of CFUGs. Only one CFUG was found proactive in managing fire in its forest; it had prepared a detailed fire management plan, arranged firefighting tools, and trained users to manage and fight forest fires. Some others also launched some activities targeting fire management in their forest. The key activities were (a) awareness raising; (b) construction and maintenance of fire line; (c) monitoring and detection of fire; and (d) suppression of fire.

### 1. Awareness raising

Among 20, six CFUGs were found to organize events related to wild fire. The events included training users, dissemination of information via posters, and broadcasting awareness-raising advertisements through local radio stations. Some of the resource poor CFUGs receive forest fire related awareness raising materials such as posters and pamphlets from DFO and use them to aware their members and trespassers as a means to control fire in their forests.

### 2. Construction and maintenance of fire Line

Most common activity of CFUGs to protect their forest from fire was construction of fire line. Among the 20 studied community forests, 12 CFUGs had constructed fire lines. However, the length of fire line in those community forests varied significantly; it ranged from 0.3 Km to 18 km. It was also revealed that the fire line was constructed without adequate planning and was not enough to contain fire. Likewise, not all the CFUGs cleared the fire line before dry season and during leaf litter fall. Instead, some CFUGs reported that the fire line was not effective in controlling fire due to its being covered by large amount of leaf litter during a short leaf-shedding period of *Shorea robusta*.

### 3. Monitoring and detection of forest fire

Users and local people were the only source of forest fire monitoring in community forests. Some financially strong CFUGs appointed and deployed forest watchers to monitor anomalies within the boundary of their community forest. In most CFUGs, the responsibilities of the watchers are not limited to monitoring fire in the forest; they also to control and report other illegal activities within their territory. So, most CFUGs employing the watchers mobilize them for all year around and not only in the dry season. The number of watchers, which ranged from 1–9 in the studied CFUGs, and the number of hours the watchers dedicate for the job depend on the capacity of CFUGs to pay them and also the threat their forests face. Although the forest watchers are employed to detect fire they were not the most common source of information. Because of limited payment they receive from CFUGs in most cases they had to engage in other sources of livelihood, particularly in the evening and night when the fire starts. So, forest watchers are less effective in forest fire detection. In this case, users had to rely on people passing through that area or other villagers for information on occurrence of fire on their forest.

### 4. Suppression of forest fire

It starts with detection of fire and includes communication with the responsible personnel, mobilization of firefighters, and suppression of fire in the forest. Developments in communication technology such as cell phones have proved to be a boon for communication regarding fire. It is used by all the CFUGs in reporting to leaders and mobilizing firefighters for suppression. However, firefighting in community forests in the Siwalik area is a difficult task because of its undulated topography. Firefighting methods and their effectiveness varied across the CFUGs, particularly based on the settlement pattern, topography of the forest, and skill and tactfulness of users.

Very few CFUGs have designed a formal mechanism to communicate the detection of forest fire and to fight it. The CFUGs use either hand mikes or mobile phones, depending upon the settlement pattern and resource availability, to report to leaders and request users, who are often divided in to subgroups based on their settlement pattern, to take part in suppressing fire once they get information on the occurrence of forest fire. Most CFUGs depended on voluntary participation of users in controlling fire. Only one CFUG had designed a firefighting strategy and implemented the plan effectively. In that CFUG, all the firefighting tools such as hand mike, fire swatter, rake, rake hoe, axe hoe, shovel, fire suit, back pack pump, fire boots, and helmet were stored in the office of the CFUG which was near the forest. Most users are trained in using these tools and adopting precautionary and safety measures while fighting fire.

Users are equally active in some other CFUGs but their activities are not organized beforehand. In five CFUGs, all the users available in the village take part in firefighting voluntarily. However, in the case of the other four CFUGs, only users residing near the incident site get mobilized and take part in controlling fire. Likewise, some CFUGs, which have very weak users' participation, have assigned responsibility of fighting fire to some groups such as local youth club by paying in cash or in kind.

## Firefighting Methods in CFUGs

Users of most community forests were not aware of the technical aspect of fire suppression. Extinguishing fire by beating up using green branches was the common approach across all the community forests. However, users reported that beating up of fire was not effective when there were high flames, upward moving fire, or in windy condition. The second most common but more effective method according to users was the exclusion of fuel from fire during fire. At the time of fire, users clear fuel from the surface in a continuous stretch so as to disconnect fire from the dry fuel. However, CFUGs only with high level of participation were successful in using this method as a large number of people is required to carry out this task quickly. Some CFUGs trained by forest staff and other experts practised counter-burning to control forest fire. However, it was found that counter-burning was less known across the community forests.

## Rules for Managing Fire in Community Forests

All the CFUGs have some sort of rule in their operational plan to discourage people from setting fire in their forest. The fine for arsonist in the studied community forest ranged from NRs. 200 to NRs. 2,000 excluding the compensation for the loss. However, discussion with most CFUGs revealed that the rule did not come from users in all CFUGs and, therefore, even executive members of users' committee were also found unaware about the procedure and extent of the punishment to the arsonist. Although nearly all community forest suffered from forest fire set by people only four CFUGs were able to identify and punish arsonists in last few years. The punishments for those identified arsonists were however less than that mentioned in their operational plan. In contrast, users reported that they have been banning users to enter forest with source of fire (such as match box, gas lighter) but that was not found documented in their operational plan. Integrated fire management requires acknowledgement of socio-economic necessities and impacts of forest fire and suggest use of fire also as important component of forest fire management (Myers 2006). However, the rules in the studied CFUGs were biased towards exclusion and suppression of fire.

## Other Initiatives to Reduce Forest Fire Danger

Two CFUGs recently started using *Lantana camara*, another source of fuel in the forests of Siwalik, and other weeds for making bio-briquette. This not only proved to be the source of income for the CFUGs themselves but also reduced the fire hazard by removing fuel from ground level. The initiative of the CFUGs was less than a year old so the effectiveness of the initiative could not be assessed. Likewise, a CFUG had opened its forest to any outsider for collection of leaf litter from its floor with the objective to reduce the amount of fuel from the forest floor. However, the leaf fall during the dry season is so high that the amount of leaf fall largely exceeds the amount removed from forest by users and outsiders.

Likewise, other initiatives included networking of CFUGs for the protection of community forests from threats. This type of network was found in Chitwan district where 10 CFUGs, including three CFUGs under this study, were communicating and cooperating to protect their forests from the threats that might affect many community forests. Another network was found in Makwanpur in the area of the Bhaise range post but this was found passive. But in recent years, CFUGs have started to collaborate to fight against fire and cooperate with nearby security forces and DFOs to control fire in their forests.

## Change in Fire Regime

Fire regime is described in terms of fire frequency, periodicity, intensity, size, pattern of landscape, season of burn, and depth of burn (Kilgore 1987). It acknowledges the concept that characteristics of an ecosystem are consistent with the pattern of behaviour, timing, and interval of fires (Bond and Keeley 2005). The CFUGs reported that out of 5,854.61 ha area of studied community forests, about 1,811 ha got burned annually. Of the studied CFUGs, 90 per cent reported less fire in their forest since they took the reign for the management of the forest. Similarly, in the recent five years, six community forests got their entire area burnt while one community forest reported that it totally excluded fire from its forest.

Among the community forest that suffered from fire, most got two fire events every year. Both fires occurred in the dry season; usually one at the mid of *Shorea* leaf litter fall period and another after the conclusion of litter fall in the year. The community forests having weak a fire control system but abundant fuel were reported to suffer from forest fire up to three times a year. On an average, one part of the community forest is burnt 1.75 times in a year according to data. All of the CFUGs reported that they suffer from surface fire. However, one CFUG having *Pinus roxburghii*-dominated forest strata sometimes suffered from crown fire as well. But all of the CFUGs mentioned that crown fire is very rare in a *Shorea*-dominated forest.

Interaction with CFUGs pointed out that, as shown in Table 12.2, among 20 studied community forests, the extent of the forest fire was reduced significantly in five community forests after handover to the community. Similarly, the extent of fire got reduced, though not significantly, in nine community forests. However, despite the handover to the community, there was no change in the extent of fire in other community forests. Likewise, the frequency of fire was reduced significantly in four community forests, reduced slightly in other seven community forests, while no change in frequency was observed in eight community forests. Surprisingly, the frequency of fire was reported to increase in one of the community forests. The reason for this variation is attributed to the trade–offs between the effort to exclude fire and the increase of pressure of people.

In spite of change in the extent and frequency of forest fire in community forests, the height of flame remained unchanged in most of the community forests. Only one community forest reported reduced height of fire in its forest. Similarly, the intensity of fire was found stable in almost all community forests. It increased only in one community forest with no reduction in any other community forest. Severity also showed the same trend as intensity of fire in the studied community forests (Figure 12.10).

**Table 12.2**

*Impact of changes in fire regime in community forests after handover to community*

|  |  | Percentage of studied community forests | | |
|---|---|---|---|---|
|  |  | *Reduced* | *No change* | *Increased* |
| Components of forest fire regime | Extent | 70 | 30 | – |
|  | Frequency | 55 | 40 | 5 |
|  | Height of flame | 5 | 95 | – |
|  | Intensity | – | 95 | 5 |
|  | Severity | – | 95 | 5 |

*Source:* Field study (2012) (collected from the field by the author during the research).

**Figure 12.10**

*Changes in fire regime in community forests after handover to community*

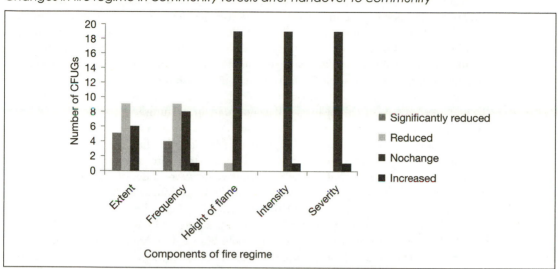

*Source:* Field study (2012) (collected from the field by the author during the research).

## Sustainability of Current Fire Management Approach

Two factors, according to users, are playing a major role in determining the status of fire in community forests. On the one hand, CFUGs are becoming more and more active day by day due to the raised awareness level, increased pressure from forest management offices, stronger capacity of CFUGs with better infrastructure and coordination with other CFUGs, and decreasing dependency of users on forest. Increasing population and, thus, the increasing forest–people interface, anomaly in precipitation and increasing consecutive dry days and temperature in fire-prone seasons, on the other hand, are diluting effectiveness that comes from the increased activeness of the concerned users. All the CFUGs whose activities surpassed the threat of fire had been able to demonstrate decreased fire events and, thus, the damage thereof, while others were suffering more.

Although suppression of fire is largely considered an expensive and unsustainable method of fire management, most CFUGs rely more on suppression of fire than on preventing it (FAO 2007). Despite increased attention of forest users on fire management programmes in recent years, insufficient technical support from line agencies has limited fire management to awareness raising, exclusion, and suppression of fire. As a result the efforts made thereof are technically weak and do not balance the use of fire, its prevention, and its suppression in forest management (Ganz et al. 2003; Myers 2006). Awareness alone reduced 90 per cent of fire outbreaks in India (FAO 2007) but is less effective in Nepal. This could have been the result of inadequate efforts or use of inappropriate methods.

Despite the effort of CFUGs, many CFUGs in Siwalik suffer ground fire every year and are not serious. However, if the seedlings could be protected from unfavourable conditions such as occurrence of fire, the growth of the forest can be rapid (FAO 2002). Therefore, it can be said that the productivity of a forest can be increased by protecting the forest from fire. In the face of increasing precipitation, number of consecutive dry days, growing stock in forest and human pressure, and increasing activeness from CFUG in fire management, the accurate prediction of the future of forest fire is difficult. From the current experience it can be said, unless the fuel accumulates in the forest floor in huge amount for years, any fire may not bring devastation as fire is a common occurrence every year from the historic past. However, any unstudied and not properly planned intervention in the ecosystem has a high risk of being counterproductive, and large gap in data on ecological dynamics, causes, and impacts of fire poses the greatest challenge (FAO 2010).

In spite of some CFUGs reporting that their activity on fire management was severely constrained by their weak financial condition, their activeness is overwhelming. This partly reflects the success in the participation of communities in rehabilitating forests (Chapagain and Banjade 2009). Strong social capital, strong enforcement of rules and sanctions, and greater participation of users in crafting the rules are conducive to increase participation of forest users in forest fire management in Siwalik (Sapkota et al. 2015). There is a need of even more careful consideration over the factors affecting users' participation in the future; only then can anything be said on what type of activity users will demonstrate in the future.

Forests are shaped by environmental variables, where time since fire explains most of them (Drever et al. 2006). Therefore, focusing just on exclusion and suppression of fire ignoring fuel management as a viable option of managing fire makes the future more uncertain. Practices may force the ecosystem to go to the alternative state if practices become successful. The incongruence between causes of fire and management solutions proposed by researchers reflects the complex and spatially scaled interactions of cause and effect in coupled human–environment systems (Wilbanks 2006) and further highlights the need for interdisciplinary research designs and forest fire data management (FAO 2010). As suggested by Butry et al. (2010), a combination of prescribed burning and prevention education would both reduce human-caused ignitions and loss of forest and property. However, lack of resource and capacity is preventing forest users from practising prescribed burning. This, nonetheless, is no surprise for a resource-scare community when globally only 6 per cent of the total forest fire are of the prescribed nature (FAO 2010).

## Conclusion

Different factors work together to determine the fire environment in the community forest of Siwalik in Nepal. The factors affecting fire vary in their direction. Conservation efforts by local communities as a result of community forestry have played a positive role in increasing biomass and, thus, in increasing fuel in the forest. Similarly, precipitation shows a conflicting effect on the Siwalik area; the total amount of precipitation is increasing but the consecutive number of dry days, mostly in fire-prone seasons, is also increasing. Similarly, temperature also show varied patterns; it shows an increasing trend in one part (e.g., Hetauda) whilst a decreasing trend in another part (e.g., Rampur). Nonetheless, very less precipitation and high temperature in the months of February, March, and April provide a very conducive environment for fire in the community forests of Central Siwalik.

Human activity is the source of most of the fires in the community forests of the Siwalik region. Rules itself are not sufficient to keep fire out of forest. Despite banning the setting of fire in community forest by the government and CFUGs, various groups are still using fire in the community forest intentionally and accidentally; however, due to procedural difficulty and mismatching of rules with fire culture, the offenders are rarely identified. Use of fire by forest users aided by favourable conditions created by coinciding and unimodal distribution of leaf litter fall and high drought makes February, March, and April highly fire-sensitive months. Technically, weak and reactive measures not considering fire ecology and culture that CFUGs were practising are not found to be an effective and sustainable forest fire management system.

In sum, weather and human activity has been more favourable for fire to occur in community forests of Central Siwalik, Nepal. However, CFUGs have been largely successful in reducing fire events in community forests in this region. Despite this, effort of communities is limited to exclusion and suppression of fire. Although appropriate use of fire helps in reducing fire danger, serves cultural needs of local people, and plays numerous ecological roles, government regulations and forest management approach discourage use of fire in forests. Given the complexity of the fire system, "cure-all" policy instruments are unlikely to be effective

(Ostrom et al. 2007) although they are repeatedly attempted. The lack of contextual social data in the literature hinders the formulation of management strategies that are aligned to the local reality (Hayes and Rajão 2011). Therefore, the government should play the leading role in paving the way for integrated fire management and should act to remove unfavourable legal conditions and other technological limitations. It should reconsider the total banning of use of fire in forests. Instead, the government should build capacity of the community in that respect and make mechanisms to monitor the use of fire in the community forest to minimize the possible misuse.

## Note

1. Approximately 100 NRs (Nepalese Rupees) = 1 USD (United States Dollar).

## References

APN. 2005. *Enhancement of National Capacities in the Application of Simulation Models for the Assessment of Climate Change and its Impacts on Water Resources and Food and Agricultural Production.* Kobe: Asia-Pacific Network for Global Change Research.

Barker T., I. Bashmakov, L. Bernstein, J.E. Bogner, P.R. Bosch, R. Dave, O.R. Davidson, B.S. Fisher, S. Gupta, K. Halsnæs, G.J. Heij, S. Kahn Ribeiro, S. Kobayashi, M.D. Levine, D.L. Martino, O. Masera, B. Metz, L.A. Meyer, G.-J. Nabuurs, A. Najam, N. Nakicenovic, H.-H. Rogner, J. Roy, J. Sathaye, R. Schock, P. Shukla, R.E.H. Sims, P. Smith, D.A. Tirpak, D. Urge-Vorsatz, and D. Zhou, 2007. Technical Summary. In *Climate Change 2007: Mitigation. Contribution of Working Group III to the Fourth Assessment Report of the Intergovernmental Panel on Climate Change,* edited by B. Metz, O.R. Davidson, P.R. Bosch, R. Dave, and L.A. Meyer. Cambridge and New York, NY: Cambridge University Press.

Bhatta, B., and L.S. Shrestha. 2010. *Removal of Nutrients from Community Forest of Makwanpur District through Litter Collection.* Hetauda, Nepal: Tribhuvan University.

Bond, W.J., and J.E. Keeley. 2005, July. "Fire as a Global Herbivore: The Ecology and Evolution of Flammable Ecosystems." *Trends in Ecology and Evolution* 20 (7) : 387–94.

Butry, D.T., J.P. Prestemon, K.L. Abt, and R. Sutphen. 2010. "Economic Optimisation of Wildfire Intervention Activities." *International Journal of Wildland Fire* 19 (5): 659–72.

Chapagain, N., and M.R. Banjade. 2009. "Community Forestry and Local Development: Experiences from the Koshi Hills of Nepal." *Journal of Forest and Livelihood* 8 (2): 78–92.

DDC/Chitwan. 2005. *District Profile.* Makawanpur: District Development Committee, Government of Nepal.

DDC/Makwanpur. 2010. *District Profile.* Makawanpur: District Development Committee, Government of Nepal.

Dennis, R.A., J. Mayer, G. Applegate, U. Chokkalingam, C.J.P. Colfer, I. Kurniawan, H. Lachowski, P. Maus, R.P. Permana, Y. Ruchiat, and F. Stolle. 2005. "Fire, People and Pixels: Linking Social Science and Remote Sensing to Understand Underlying Causes and Impacts of Fires in Indonesia." *Human Ecology* 33 (4): 465–504.

DFO/Chitwan. 2011. *Community Forest User Group Monitoring and Evaluation Report.* Chitwan: District Forest Office, Government of Nepal.

DFO/Makwanpur. 2008, January. *Forest Fire Management Plan.* Makwanpur: Makwanpur District Forest Office, Government of Nepal.

———. 2011. *Annual Report.* Makwanpur: Makwanpur District Forest Office, Government of Nepal.

DFRS. 1999. "Forest Resources of Nepal 1999." Publication No. 74, Department of Forest Research and Survey, Nepal.

DoF. 2010. "Hamro Ban." Annual Report of Fiscal Year 2065/66 B.S. Published in Nepali, Department of Forest, Government of Nepal.

Drever C.R., C. Messier, Y. Bergeron, and F. Doyon. 2006. "Fire and Canopy Species Composition in the Great Lakes—St. Lawrence forest of Te´miscamingue, Que´bec." *Forest Ecology and Management* 231 (2006): 27–37.

FAO. 2002. "Fire Situation in Nepal." *International Forest Fire News* (26, January): 84–86.

FAO. 2006a. "Participatory Forest Fire Management: An Approach." *International Forest Fire News* (34, January–June): 35–45.

———. 2006b. "Forest Fire in the Terai, Nepal: Causes and Community Management Interventions." *International Forest Fire News* (34, June): 46–54.

———. 2007. "Fire Management—Global Assessment 2006." FAO Forestry Paper 151, Food and Agriculture Organization of the United Nations, Rome.

———. 2010. "Global Forest Resources Assessment." Main Report, FAO Forestry Paper 163, Food and Agriculture Organization of the United Nations, Rome.

FIRMS. 2012. Shapefile of Burnt Area Supplied by Fire Information for Resource Management System, University of Maryland, USA (from 1 February 2001 to 4 April 2012 Acquired by MODIS). Available at: http://firefly.geog.umd.edu/download/tmp/firms12351308074670.zip (accessed on 5 April 2012).

Ganz, D., P. Moore, D. Reeb, D. Ganz, W. Hall, P. Moore, B.B. Sindangbarang, and D. Reeb. 2003. "Community-based Fire Management Case Studies from China, the Gambia, Honduras, India, Lao People's Democratic Republic and Turkey." *Community-based Fire Management*. Food and Agriculture Organization of the United Nations, Regional Office for Asia and the Pacific, Bangkok, pp. 1–9.

Giri, C., and S. Shrestha. 2000. "Forest Fire Mapping in Huay Kha Khaeng Wildlife Sanctuary, Thailand." *International Journal of Remote Sensing* 21 (10): 2023–30.

GoN. 1993. *Forest Act, 1993*. Kathmandu: Government of Nepal.

———. 1995. *Forest Regulation, 1995*. Kathmandu: Government of Nepal.

———. 2010. *Forest Fire Management Strategy, 2010*. Kathmandu: Ministry of Forests and Soil Conservation, Government of Nepal.

———. 2011. National Population and Housing Census 2011 (National Report). Government of Nepal, Central Bureau of Statistics, Kathmandu, Nepal. Available at: http://cbs.gov.np/image/data/Population/National%20Report/National%20Report.pdf (accessed on 19 May 2017).

Hayes, N., and R. Rajão. 2011. "Competing Institutional Logics and Sustainable Development: The Case of Geographic Information Systems in Brazil's Amazon Region." *Information Technology for Development* 17 (1): 4–23.

Heikkilä, T.V., R. Grönqvist, and M. Jurvélius. 2007. *Wildland Fire Management: Handbook for Trainer*s. Helsinki: Development Policy Information Unit, Ministry of Foreign Affairs of Finland.

ICIMOD. 2007. *Nepal Biodiversity Resource Book*. Kathmandu: International Centre for Integrated Mountain Development.

ITTO. 2009. "Outline of the 'Development of a Policy, a Strategy and Building Capacities in Local, National and Transboundary Forest Fire Management for Nepal'." PP-A/35-140A. International Tropical Timber Organization. Available at: http://www.fire.uni-freiburg.de/GlobalNetworks/South_Asia/ITTO-Project-Outline.pdf (accessed on 12 May 2017).

IUCN and WWF. 2000. *Global Review of Forest Fires*. Switzerland: The World Conservation Union & World Wide Fund for Nature.

Johnson, E.A., and K. Miyanishi. 2001. *Forest Fires: Behavior and Ecological Effects*. California: Academic Press.

Kilgore, B.M. 1987. "The Role of Fire in Wilderness: A State-of Knowledge Review." In *Wildland Fire in Ecosystems: Effects of Fire on Flora*—Vol. 2. General Technical Report RMRS-GTR-42, December, 2000. Ogden, UT: United States Department of Agriculture.

Kull, C.A. 2002. "Madagascar's Burning Issue: The Persistent Conflict over Fire." *Environment* 44 (3): 8–19.

Liu, Y., J. Stanturf, and S. Goodrick. 2010. "Wildfire Potential Evaluation During a Drought Event with a Regional Climate Model and NDVI. *Ecological Informatics* 5 (5): 418–28.

Myers, R.L. 2006, June. *Living with Fire-Sustaining Ecosystem and Livelihoods Through Integrated Fire Management*. Arlington, VA: The Nature Conservancy, Global Fire Initiative.

Omi, P.N. 2005. *Forest Fire: A Reference Handbook*. Santa Barbara, CA: ABC-CLIO.

Ostrom, E., M.A. Janssen, and J.M. Anderies. 2007. "Going Beyond Panaceas." *Proceedings of the National Academy of Sciences of the United States of America* 104 (39): 15176–78.

PSPL and FECOFUN. 2010. *REDD Strategy Options in Nepal*. Practical Solution Consultancy Nepal and Federation of Community Forestry Users Nepal. Kathmandu, Nepal.

Resilience Alliance. 2010. *Assessing Resilience in Social-Ecological Systems: Workbook for Practitioners*. Revised version 2.0. Resilience Alliance.

Ricklefs, R.E. 2008. *The Economy of Nature*. New York: W.H. Freeman and Company.

Sapkota, L.M., R.P. Shrestha, D. Jourdain, and G.P. Shivakoti. 2015. "Factors Affecting Collective Action for Forest Fire Management: A Comparative Study of Community Forest User Groups in Central Siwalik, Nepal." *Environmental Management* 55 (1): 171–86.

Sorrensen, C. 2009. "Potential Hazards of Land Policy: Conservation, Rural Development and Fire Use in the Brazilian Amazon." *Land Use Policy* 26 (3): 782–91.

Stolle, F., R.A. Dennis, I. Kurniwan, and E.F. Lambin. 2004. "Evaluation of Remote Sensing-based Active Fire Datasets in Indonesia." *International Journal of Remote Sensing* 25 (2): 471–79.

Wilbanks, T. 2006. *How Scale Matters: Some Concepts and Findings*. In *Bridging Scales and Knowledge Systems: Concepts and Applications in Ecosystem Assessment*, edited by W.V. Reid, F. Berkes, T. Wilbanks, and D. Capistrano, 21–36. Washington, DC: Island Press.

# 13

# Can Educational Campaigns Promote Successful Adaptation to Climate Change? Evidence from a Heat Wave Awareness Programme in Odisha*

Saudamini Das and Stephen C. Smith

## Introduction

Heat waves are defined as an extended period of abnormally hot and humid weather extending from more than one day to several days. The temperature threshold for declaring a heat wave varies from region to region in accordance with local norms (Meehl and Tebaldi 2004). Whereas temperatures above 28 °C can be considered heat waves in Denmark, such thresholds are as high as 45 °C for tropical or semi-tropical countries such as India. Heat waves have been a prominent human killer in recent years and are projected to worsen with climate change (IPCC 2007; Kunkel et al. 2008). The World Meteorological Organization (WMO) predicts that heat-related fatalities will double in less than 20 years. Under these circumstances, adaptation is a key response strategy to minimize the potential impacts and adverse effects of heat waves on health (Menne and Ebi 2006).

During a heat wave, the dissipation of metabolic heat from the human body through the evaporation of body perspiration is constrained; and the body has to work extra hard to maintain normal temperature. Thus, the core body temperature goes up due to heat stress and if it exceeds a threshold (normally 40–42 °C), a person may collapse or may suffer hyperthermia (Sherwood and Huber 2010; Mehnert et al. 2000). Heat waves affect both developed and developing countries. In India, the coastal states of Odisha, Gujarat, Telangana, and Andhra Pradesh have been the worst affected ones.

* This chapter draws on Das and Smith (2012), "Awareness as an Adaptation Strategy for Reducing Mortality from Heat Waves: Evidence from a Disaster Risk Management Program in India." *Climate Change Economics* 3(2). doi: 10.1142/S2010007812500108, Copyright @ 2012 World Scientific publisher. We thank Pranab Mukhopadhyay for valuable comments and the journal *Climate Change Economics* and its editor, Professor Robert Mendelsohn for permission to adapt and use these sections.

This chapter discusses some of the interventions by the Odisha state government to help people adapt to these extreme conditions. Many national and local governments issue heat wave warnings during high-risk periods. Some also undertake awareness campaigns to help citizens prepare for and survive worsening regional heat waves. Such campaigns have been an integral part of Odisha government's heat wave management strategy. In the campaigns, the Information, Education, and Communication (IEC) material included "dos" such as carrying a water bottle and oral rehydration solution, wearing head cover, eating food with high water content such as cucumber, onion, and curd before going out, attending to young children and old people, learning symptoms of heat stroke, and utilizing basic first-aid principles; and "don'ts" such as avoiding work during the hottest parts of the day.

Planned (or policy) adaption is undertaken by a government agency; in contrast, autonomous adaptation is undertaken by some combination of households, firms, and community organizations. The interaction of planned and autonomous adaptation is important but has received limited attention (Malik and Smith 2012). An important example is publicly sponsored training for "autonomous" behavioural responses that, once learned, do not need ongoing inputs from government (or at least may be scaled back). Indeed, awareness campaigns are of great potential importance for plans to promote and support autonomous adaptation to climate change; but little systematic research has been undertaken on this topic.

The chapter examines the awareness campaign in the eastern Indian state of Odisha on dos and don'ts during heat waves, under the Disaster Risk Management (DRM) Programme of the Government of India and United Nations Development Programme initiated in 2002.[1] This programme was implemented in 16 of the 30 districts of the state; the inclusion criteria for DRM programme districts were earthquake, flood, and cyclone occurrences, but not heat waves. Later, after these districts had been selected, a heat wave component was added to the programme. This provided a natural experiment to examine the impact of this intensive awareness campaign, taking these DRM districts as treatment units and the rest as controls. The heat wave index used was as defined by the Indian Meteorological Department (IMD); and temperature data of local weather stations were used to measure the number of heat wave and severe heat wave days in each district. The district-level death toll due to heat stroke for the period 1998–2010 was analysed using a panel data set and difference-in-difference (DID) estimation.

The results of the study provide evidence that districts included in the campaign had experienced reduction in deaths due to heat stroke during heat waves, which is attributable to this campaign, in comparison to other districts, as well as in comparison to non-heat wave periods.

# Literature Review and Analytical Framework

Studies analysing heat wave calamities have found various factors associated with increased death risk including low education (O'Neil, Zanobetti, and Schwartz 2003), lack of access to air-conditioning (Smoyer 1998), race, age, health problems, living alone, leaving home regularly, and other socio-economic factors (Gouveia, Hajat, and Armstrong 2003; Naughton et al. 2002; Semenza et al. 1996; O'Neil, Zanobetti, and Schwartz 2005, O'Neil et al. 2009). Studies examining heat-related deaths witnessed in Mexico City, Sao Paulo, and Santiago between 1998 and 2002 found same day and previous day temperatures and old age to be significantly related to deaths (Bell et al. 2008).

For the case of air pollution, there is some evidence that health education through mass media or public awareness campaigns on environmental quality brings substantial behavioural changes in people, though it seems to depend on the structure, timing as well as the soundness of the theoretical content of the campaign (Cutter and Neidell 2009; Hornik 2001, 435; Randolph and Viswanath 2004). Early warning has been found to be effective in saving lives during storms, and to be complimentary to other mortality reducing factors (Das and Vincent 2009). And there is some previous evidence that early heat wave warnings reduce deaths (Alberini, Mastrangelo, and Pitcher 2008; Ebi et al. 2004).

This chapter examines the effect of an awareness campaign in terms of reduced mortality from heat waves. Based on the previous literature, we model deaths due to heat wave as a reduced form as presented in Equation 1:

$$D = f\ (H,\ G,\ I,\ E,\ A) \tag{1}$$

In Equation 1, D denotes deaths, H is the extent of excessive heat, G represents other exogenous geographic factors, particularly forest cover and coastal location, I is income, E represents behavioural activity risks of hyperthermia, particularly through occupational exposure, and A is heat wave response awareness. The extent of excessive heat H must be represented by an appropriate index; we explore alternatives in the next section. Higher income I provides greater opportunities for adaptation, including use of motorized transportation and home air conditioning; and in general, better public goods are provided in higher income districts. Individuals may be particularly susceptible to heat if they work during the hottest periods of the day, E, either outside (including agricultural labourers and street workers) or in hot indoor environments (such as some factories). In addition to these factors, the impacts of heat waves will depend also on the extent of household awareness A about how to respond and adapt. We operationalize our general model in the following section.

## Methodology

This chapter uses difference-in-difference (DID) estimation and sample survey findings to measure the impact of awareness generation on mortality. DID estimation examines the treatment effect by comparing the treatment group after the treatment to both the treatment group before the treatment and an appropriate control group not receiving the treatment; this provides the counterfactual outcome (Card and Krueger 1994).[2] The DRM districts in Odisha are used as treatment groups and the non-DRM districts as control groups. The DRM districts, being more vulnerable to cyclone, flood, and earthquake compared to non-DRM districts, received intensive disaster management awareness and capacity building through print and electronic media use and additionally through grass-roots workers. Community-level efforts, including door-to-door outreach by volunteers, were limited to DRM districts. Media campaigns, however, reached non-DRM districts as well, and may have had effects depending on people's access to media, which varies with socio-economic characteristics; to this extent, our estimates may understate the impact of the programme on mortality reduction.

The DID specification used to derive the results is the following:

$$Y_{it} = \alpha_0 P_d + \alpha_1 G_d + \alpha_3 P_d^* G_d + \beta' Z_{it} + \varepsilon_{it} \tag{2}$$

where $Y_{it}$ is the outcome variable for the $i$th unit in the $t$th period, $P_d$ is the period dummy (=1 for post-treatment period and =0 for pre-treatment period), $G_d$ is the treatment unit dummy (=1 for treatment group and =0 for control group), $Z_{it}$ are the control variables for the $i$th unit at the $t$th period, and $\varepsilon$ is the error term. The estimated value of coefficient $\alpha$ shows the treatment effect.

In this chapter, the DID estimates are drawn from Das and Smith (2012); and survey results on awareness generation and media penetration in DRM areas are drawn from Das (2015). Das and Smith (2012) used panel data and a DID approach with controls, and estimated the following equation:

$$\begin{aligned}
Y_{it} = & \alpha_0 + \alpha_1 drm\_period + \alpha_2 drm\_district + \alpha_3 drm\_periodXdrm\_district + \alpha_4 T + \alpha_5 population_{it} \\
& + \alpha_6 DNDP_{it} + \alpha_7 PCI_{it} + \alpha_8 coastal\_dummy_i + \alpha_9 forest\_cov\ er_{it} + \alpha_{10} share\_agri\_labor_{jt} \\
& + \alpha_{11} share\_other\_wor\ ker_{it} + \alpha_{12} share\_m\ arg\ inal\_wor\ ker_{it} + \alpha_{13} HWD_{it} + \alpha_{14} SHWD_{it} \\
& + \alpha_{15} severity\_dummy_{it} + \alpha_{16}\ 40deg\ ree\_more_{it} + \varepsilon_{it}
\end{aligned} \tag{3}$$

The variables are defined as follows:

$Y_{it}$: Number of human deaths for the $i$th district (1, 2, ..., 30) in the $t$th year (1998, 1999, ..., 2010);

*Drm_period:* The treatment period dummy (=1 for 2003 and onwards for the 12 districts where DRM programme started in 2002 and =1 for 2004 and onwards for four districts where the programme started in 2003);[3]

*Drm_district:* The treatment group dummy (=1 for a DRM district if the entire district was covered by the programme; equalling the ratio of number of blocks covered by the programme to the total number of blocks of the district if only a subset of blocks has been covered by the programme, and = 0 for the rest of the districts in which no blocks are covered);

*T:* Time trend (to account for the physiological adaptation of human body to high temperature and other time variant changes);

*Population:* $i$th district population in the year $t$;

*DNDP:* $i$th district net domestic product in the year $t$ (account for growth as well as level of urbanization);

*PCI:* Per capita income of the $i$th district in year $t$;

*Coastal_dummy:* Dummy variable for the district adjoining the seacoast (controlling for the level of humidity and other factors). The state has seven such districts;

*Forest_cover:* Area (sq. km) of the district under forest cover (presence of vegetation is likely to reduce the heat impact);

*Share_agri_labour:* Percentage of population working as agricultural labour (poorer and likely to be more exposed);

*Share_other_worker:* Percentage of population working in occupations other than agriculture and household industries (including teachers, barbers, washermen, priests, and other industrial workers) likely to be better off, but jobs requiring going out of the house, leading to exposure);

*Share_marginal_workers:* Percentage of population not having any regular job (poorer people; chance to get a job depends on availability and may not be obtained during the peak heat period);

*HWD:* Number of heat wave days as defined by IMD;

*SHWD:* Number of severe heat wave days as defined by IMD;

*Excessive_hot_year:* Dummy variable for the year $t$ when the temperature deviation has been more than 10 °C (exceptionally hot years) in the $i$th district as per the temperature recorded by the nearest weather station or by the one falling in its agro-climatic zone;

*40degree_more:* Total number of days in the year $t$ when the temperature has crossed 40 °C in the $i$th district (too many days with marginally more than 40 °C temperature may not be captured by heat wave days, but may cause heat stress due to continuous high temperature);

ε: The error term.

Equation 3 is estimated with both fixed effects and random effects; a Poisson specification is used because of the count and non-negative nature of the dependent variable (Greene 2003 [sec. 21.9]). As mentioned earlier, the DRM programme was introduced in response to cyclone, earthquake, and flooding events; accordingly, the selection of DRM districts was plausibly random with respect to the heat wave occurrences. Further, estimation using DID addresses bias arising from differing initial conditions or ongoing time trends. Moreover, to allow for the possibility that other relevant variables differ and are important in district mortality outcomes, we also control for a set of relevant geographic and economic activity observables. The chapter uses alternative measures of heat waves in the general model to capture the impact on human body from heat stress for each of the districts. A limitation is that these methods cannot account for unobserved heterogeneity in treatment and control districts.

Income, wealth, and occupation may directly affect the ability of households to adapt. Moreover, if there were any non-random placement of the programme with respect to heat wave incidence, it would be correlated with the degree of affluence. We control for per capita income for these reasons. We further control for district-level net domestic product and population primarily to mop up its potential association with selection (income may also be correlated with other factors affecting capabilities to adapt). We also control for the percentage of three different types of workers who are likely to be more exposed to extreme heat as described earlier.

# Results

The panel data provides 13 years of observations on 30 districts, of which 16 districts are part of the DRM programme and the remaining 14 are not. Of the 13 years, five are pre-DRM and eight are post-DRM years. Table 13.1 presents the results. Our preferred estimates are based on the fixed effect estimator; we also present random effects estimates as a robustness check. Both fixed effect and random effect estimates give similar results on DRM programme impacts and confirm its positive and significant effect in reducing extreme health impact from heat waves. The interaction term, (DRM_period) X (DRM_district), that captures the programme effect has negative and significant coefficients in both the models.

Most of the other variables show coefficients along expected lines. All the different heat wave measures have positive and significant coefficients except the number of heat wave days (which is positive and insignificant). The excessive hot year dummy (years or areas when the temperature increase deviates from the normal temperature by 10 or more degrees) seems to be the biggest killer followed by the number of severe heat wave days. Insignificance of heat wave days suggests that heat stress mortality is observed only when the temperature goes beyond a certain threshold (mostly 44–45 °C for the state of Odisha); and the more the upward deviation from this threshold, the greater the impact on mortality. We note that heat stress may have significant negative impacts on human health even when it does not result in death; but this is beyond the scope of these results.[4]

Of the other variables, the ones with significant coefficients are time trend, forest cover, share of other workers in population, district net domestic product and, in some specifications, district net domestic product per capita (per capita income). The time trend has a negative and significant coefficient. This variable could also be capturing physiological adaptation (Davis et al. 2003) and the effects of other adaptive responses such as changing school and bus timing, opening *Jalchhatra* (state government free distribution of water), or newspaper reporting on deaths from heat wave leading to other precautionary behaviours that have helped reduce mortality. Results of forest cover is again on expected lines; the more the forest cover in a district, the less the deaths. In general, we may anticipate that richer districts would have better infrastructure and better capacity (both health and resources) to cope with heat waves; however, the district net domestic product has a positive and significant coefficient (and so is the district per capita income) implying that districts with higher economic activity are more vulnerable to heat stress, other things equal. In this regard, we note that data on per capita resources represent averages that do not account for inequality of distribution and other heterogeneity.

**Table 13.1**

*Random and fixed effect Poisson estimates to explain disaster risk management project impact on death from heat stroke*

| Explanatory variables | Random effect Poisson estimates | District fixed effect Poisson estimates |
|---|---|---|
| DRM_period | 2.015*** (0.165) | 1.842*** (0.178) |
| DRM_district | −1.091 (1.25) | − |
| DRM_periodXDRM_district | −0.683*** (0.117) | −0.536 ***(0.128) |
| Time_Trend | −0.590 ***(0.03) | −0.524*** (0.029) |
| Population | 0.104 **(0.055) | −0.111 (0.079) |
| DistrictNet Domestic Product | 0.152 ** (0.074) | 0.225 *** (0.083) |
| District Per Capita Income | 0.017* (0.009) | 0.012 (0.011) |
| Dummy_ Coastal Districts | −0.702 (1.5133) | − |
| Forest_cover | −0.002*** (0.0006) | −0.004*** (0.0005) |
| Population_share_agri_labor | −36.473(33.47) | 41.299 (118.05) |
| Population_share_other_worker | 51.408*** (14.669) | 61.911 ***(21.89) |
| Population_share_marginal_worker | 60.152 (40.542) | −46.441 (125.71) |
| Number_HeatWaveDays | 0.003 (0.007) | 0.001 (0.006) |
| Number_SevereHeatWaveDays | 0.057*** (0.007) | 0.067 *** (0.007) |
| Dummy_Excessive_Hot_Year | 0.712*** (0.065) | 0.716*** (0.065) |
| Days with more than 40degree temperature | 0.048*** (0.003) | 0.044*** (0.003) |
| Constant | −2.668 (2.193) | − |
| | | |
| /lnalpha | 1.034 (0.321) | − |
| Alpha | 2.814 (0904) | − |
| Wald Chi2 | Wald Chi2 (16)=5387.89, Pro>Chi2=0.00 | Wald Chi2 (14)=5373.24, Pro>Chi2=0.00 |
| Log likelihood | −1263.83 | −1066.72 |
| Loglikelihood ratio test of alpha=0 | Chibar2 (01)=1288.89, Pro>=chibar2=0.00 | − |
| Number of observations | 390 (groups=30, Observations per group=13) | 390 (groups=30, Observations per group=13) |

*Notes:*  1. Dependent variable—number of deaths in a district in a year due to heat stroke.

2. ***, **, and * imply the level of significance to be 1 per cent, 5 per cent, and 10 per cent, respectively.

3. Figures in parenthesis show standard errors.

Moreover, industrial and construction jobs are more common in urbanized areas, and may result in more heat exposure. Workers in construction and informal sector occupations may also have high head exposure. Supporting evidence for this interpretation is found in the positive and significant coefficient for the population percentage working as "other workers," who constitute workers mostly in services and industrial activities other than home industries. We note that the coefficient on marginal workers is statistically insignificant; while these are generally poorer people, their probability of receiving work is likely to be lower during heat wave periods when economic activity is reduced. Marginal worker status is also difficult to measure.

During April–May 2013, a sampling survey was conducted on poor urban workers in two cities, Bhubaneswar and Sambalpur, within DRM districts of Odisha. Workers covered were low-income self-employed urban workers who are mostly engaged in exposed manual activities including rickshaw pulling and porter services. When asked if they knew about the awareness programme, found it useful, and if they have taken the advice, a striking 99 per cent said they knew of the programme. Their sources of information were radio (63 per cent), newspapers (64 per cent), television (73 per cent), pamphlets (31 per cent), community volunteers (18 per cent), neighbours (14 per cent), and NGOs (12 per cent). Most had received the information from multiple sources; 83 per cent from at least three sources (either radio, or television, or newspaper, or pamphlets). Around 93 per cent of the respondents found the government campaign very helpful and 99 per cent reported to have changed some of their habits during heat waves because of the campaign. On average, it was found that during heat waves, 73 per cent of respondents drank water and 65 per cent ate cucumber and onion before leaving home; 63 per cent carried a water bottle; and 64 per cent carried an umbrella (Das 2015). These findings complement the results shown in Table 13.1 and add credibility to the argument that the underlying reason for the mortality-reducing effects identified in the regressions was that the awareness campaign leads to behavioural changes further leading to reduced health effects from heat waves.

## Concluding Remarks

Due to global climate change, heat wave occurrences have become more frequent, intense, and widespread in both developed and developing countries. Both long-term measures such as changing housing structure, town planning, and increasing green cover, and short-run adaptation measures such as warnings, health education, and advice on precautions are resorted to by policymakers to counter the impacts. However, there has been little research on the effectiveness of such strategies.

This chapter examined deaths due to heat waves in the eastern Indian state of Odisha and evaluated the impact of the DRM project of the Government of India and the United Nations Development Program, which was implemented by the Odisha State Disaster Management Authority in some of the districts of the state. Under the DRM programme, the most important strategy to control heat wave impacts was an awareness campaign of the dos and don'ts during heat wave periods. The results from DID estimation with appropriate controls show significant reduction in mortality in DRM districts compared to non-DRM districts; and this could have been because of the fact that the DRM districts had witnessed more intensive awareness generation than the non-DRM ones. We also report our sample survey findings from urban low-income workers in cities falling under DRM districts showing a high level of awareness on dos and don'ts during heat waves. While only indicative, results support the potential benefits of conducting further survey-based research on this topic.

During summer 2015, both Odisha and the neighbouring state of Andhra Pradesh witnessed severe heat waves. Although the population of these states is similar (about 42 million and 49 million people, respectively), the death toll was less than 100 in Odisha, whereas it reached more than 1,500 in Andhra Pradesh, where no such heat wave management activity or systematic awareness campaign was being undertaken. Although in itself this is only anecdotal evidence, it is consistent with our findings and underlines the priority of continued research in this promising area.

In particular, more research is needed to explore the effectiveness of awareness and role of different awareness media in changing peoples' behaviour. Research is needed to address whether there exist some limits to their compliance to dos and don'ts prescribed by the government because of financial, social, cultural, or other barriers. Research is also needed on programme effects on other health impacts that do not result in death. Moreover, high temperatures are associated with other negative development outcomes including lower incomes and greater violence. It is possible that awareness campaigns could address other effects of high heat described in the literature, such as conflict (Burke, Hsiang, and Miguel 2015; Smith 2015).

In addition, it will be valuable to consider not only fatality but also other health effects, such as heat exhaustion and non-fatal heat strokes, and symptoms such as vomiting and headaches; we did not have data on these variables and leave analysis of such effects for future research.

Heat waves are projected to worsen substantially with climate change, and policymakers all over the world are looking for effective and economical strategies to combat their health impacts. Although more research is needed, this chapter presents evidence that awareness campaigns could serve as a key adaptation strategy.

# Notes

1. The original UNDP-supported DRM programme ended in 2009; some programmes that it initiated (including heat wave awareness activities) are still ongoing.
2. We would not want to estimate impact only with differences across districts after programme implementation because these districts may have started with different levels of resilience; and we would not want to estimate impact only by comparing conditions before and after the programme in DRM districts alone because all districts may have improved during that period of time. DID is designed to address and account for these two sources of bias.
3. A one-year lag was used between the signing of the documents and actual implementation of the policy at the level of the public as per the suggestion of OSDMA officials. Moreover, information on the media campaign was available only from 2003.
4. Other health effects include heat exhaustion and non-fatal heat strokes, as well as symptoms such as vomiting and headaches. These can result in lost work days and other welfare costs. We did not have data on these variables and leave analysis of such effects for future research.

# References

Alberini, A., E. Mastrangelo, and H. Pitcher. 2008. "Climate Change and Human Health: Assessing the Effectiveness of Adaptation to Heat Waves." Mimeo, University of Maryland, Berkeley, CA, USA.

Bell, Michelle L., Marie S. O'Neill, Nalini Ranjit, Victor H. Borja-Aburto, Luis A. Cifuentes, and Nelson C. Gouveia. 2008. "Vulnerability to Heat-related Mortality in Latin America: A Case-crossover Study in São Paulo, Brazil, Santiago, Chile and Mexico City, Mexico." *International Journal of Epidemiology* 37 (4): 796–804. doi:10.1093/ije/dyn094

Burke, M., S.M. Hsiang, and E. Miguel. 2015. "Climate and Conflict." *Annual Review of Economics* 7: 577–617.

Card, D., and A.B. Krueger. 1994. "Minimum Wages and Employment: A Case Study of the Fast Food Industry in New Jersey and Pennsylvania." *American Economic Review* 84 (September): 772–93.

Cutter, W.B., and M. Neidell. 2009. "Voluntary Information Programs and Environmental Regulation: Evidence from 'Spare the Air'." *Journal of Environmental Economics and Management* 58 (3): 253–65.

Das, S. 2015. "Temperature Increase, Labour Supply and Cost of Adaptation in Developing Economies: Evidence on Urban Workers in Informal Sectors." *Climate Change Economics* 6 (2): 1550007. doi: 10.1142/S2010007815500074.

Das, S., and S.C. Smith. 2012. "Awareness as an Adaptation Strategy for Reducing Mortality from Heat Waves: Evidence from a Disaster Risk Management Program in India." *Climate Change Economics* 3 (2): 1250010. doi: 10.1142/S2010007812500108.

Das, S., and J.R. Vincent. 2009, 5 May. "Mangroves Protected Villages and Reduced Death Toll During Indian Super Cyclone." *Proceedings of the National Academy of Sciences, USA* 106 (18): 7357–60.

Davis, R., P.C. Knappenberger, P.J. Michaels, and W.M. Novicoff. 2003. "Changing Heat-related Mortality in the United States." *Environmental Health Perspectives* 111 (14): 1712–18.

Ebi, K.L., F.J. Teisberg, L.S. Kalkstein, L. Robinson, and R.F. Weiter. 2004. "Heat Watch/Warnings Systems Save Lives: Estimated Cost and Benefits for Philadelphia 1995–98." *Bulletin of the American Meteorological Society* 85 (3): 1067–68.

Gouveia, N., S. Hajat, and B. Armstrong. 2003. "Socio-economic Differentials in the Temperature–Mortality Relationship in Sao Paulo, Brazil." *International Journal of Epidemiology* 32 (3): 390–97.

Greene, W.H. 2003. *Econometric Analysis*, 5th ed. Upper Saddle River, NJ: Prentice Hall.

Hornik, R.C. 2001. *Public Health Communication: Evidence for Behavior Change*. New York: Lawrence Erlbaum Associates, Taylor and Francis group.

IPCC. 2007. "Summary for Policy Makers." In *Climate Change 2007: The Physical Science Basis. Contribution of Working Group 1 to the Forth Assessment Report of the Intergovernmental Panel on Climate Change*, S. Solomn, D. Qin, M. Manning, Z. Chen, M. Marquis, K.B. Averyt, M. Tignor, and H.L. Miller. Cambridge and New York, NY: Cambridge University Press.

Kunkel, K.E., P.D. Bromirski, H.E. Brooks, T. Cavazos, A.V. Douglas, D.R. Easterling, K.A. Emanuel, PYaGroisman, G.J. Holland, T.R. Knutson, J.P. Kossin, P.D. Komar, D.H. Levinson, and R.L. Smith. 2008. "Observed Changes in Weather and Climate Extremes in Weather and Climate Extremes in a Changing Climate." *Regions of Focus: North America, Hawaii, Caribbean, and U.S. Pacific Islands*, edited by T.R. Karl, G.A. Meehl, C.D. Miller, S.J. Hassol, A.M. Waple, and W.L. Murray. Washington, DC: U.S. Climate Change Science Program and the Subcommittee on Global Change Research.

Malik, A.S., and S.C. Smith. 2012. "Adaptation to Climate Change in Low-income Countries: Lessons from Current Research and Needs from Future Research." *Climate Change Economics* 3 (2).

Meehl, George A., and C. Tebaldi. 2004. "More Intense, More Frequent, and Longer Lasting Heat Waves in the 21st Century." *Science* 305 (5686): 994. doi:10.1126/science.1098704. PMID 15310900.

Mehnert P., J. Malchaire, B. Kampmann, A. Piette, B. Griefahn, and H. Gebhardt. 2000. "Prediction of the Average Skin Temperature in Warm and Hot Environments." *European Journal of Applied Physiology* 82: 52–60.

Menne, B., and K.L. Ebi (eds). 2006. *Climate Change and Adaptation Strategies for Human Health*. Darmstadt, Germany: Steinkopff-Verlag.

Naughton, M.P., A. Henderson, M.C. Mirabelli, R. Kaiser, J.L. Wilhelm, S.M. Kieszak, C.H. Rubin, and M.A. McGeehin. 2002. "Heat-related Mortality During a 1999 Heat Wave in Chicago." *American Journal of Preventive Medicine* 22 (4): 221–27.

O'Neill, M., R. Carter, J. Kish, C. Gronlund, J. White-Newsome, X. Manarolla, A. Zanobetti, and J. Schwartz. (2009, October 20). "Preventing Heat-related Morbidity and Mortality: New Approaches in a Changing Climate." *Maturitas* 64 (2): 98–103.

O'Neill, M.S., A. Zanobetti, and J. Schwartz. 2003. "Modifiers of Temperature and Mortality Association in Seven US Cities." *American Journal of Epidemiology* 157 (12): 1074–82.

———. 2005. "Disparities by Race in Heat Related Mortality in Four US Cities: The Role of Air Conditioning Prevalence." *Journal of Urban Health* 82 (2): 191–97.

Randolph, W., and K. Viswanath. 2004. "Lessons Learned from Public Health Mass Media Campaigns: Marketing Health in a Crowded Media World." *Annual Review of Public Health* 25: 419–37. doi: 10.1146/annurev. publhealth.25.101802.123046.

Semenza, J.C., C.H. Rubin, K.H. Falter, J.D. Selanikio, W.D. Flanders, H.L. Howe, J.L. Wilhelm. 1996. "Heat-related Deaths During the 1995 Heat Wave in Chicago." *New England Journal of Medicine* 335 (2): 84–90.

Sherwood, S.C., and M. Huber. 2010. "An Adaptability Limit to Climate Change due to Heat Stress." *Proceedings of the National Academy of Sciences* 107 (21): 9552–55. doi:10.1073/pnas.0913352107

Smith, S.C. 2015. "The Two Fragilities: Vulnerability to Conflict, Environmental Stress, and their Interactions as Challenges to Ending Poverty." In *The Last Mile in Ending Extreme Poverty*, edited by L. Chandy, H. Kato, and H. Kharas. Washington, DC: Brookings Institution Press.

Smoyer, K.E. 1998. "A Comparative Analysis of Heat Waves and Associated Mortality in St Louis, Missouri—1980–1995." *International Journal of Biometeorology* 42 (1): 44–50.

# 14

# Agricultural Vulnerability to Climate Change: Contribution of Socio-economic Factors

Amarnath Tripathi

## Introduction

In India, the agriculture sector is still the backbone of the economy—it contributes 14 per cent of the gross domestic product (GDP), 20 per cent of the total country's exports, and employs 59 per cent of the labour force. Over 70 per cent of the country's population reside in the rural areas and mainly depend on agriculture and its allied sectors (dairy, fisheries, and forestry). For the last two years, the agriculture sector in India has been in a distress situation mainly due to adverse weather conditions. In 2014, kharif (summer) crops were affected due to 12 per cent deficit rains, while rabi (winter) crops such as wheat and mustard got damaged due to unseasonal rains and hailstorm. This led to a decline in wheat production in 2014–15 by about 10 million tonnes, as against a record 95.85 million tonnes achieved in 2013–14 (GoI 2016). Similarly, rice production also declined to 105.48 million tonnes in 2014–15 from 106.65 million tonnes in 2013–14 (GoI 2016). Deficit monsoon rainfall[1] continued to 2015–16 and it again affected kharif crops severally. Similarly, rabi crops of this year have faced unexpected high temperatures. Again, lower production in both rice and wheat compared to the previous year is projected in the 4th advance estimates of food crops for the year 2015–16 (GoI 2016). These adverse weather situations are likely to increase in future because of climate change and, hence, more losses than the above-mentioned losses are expected in agriculture production, productivity, and farmer's income.

In India, climate change has become apparent for more than one decade—the climate data indicates a general warming trend and a decreasing monsoon precipitation trend (Jha and Tripathi 2011). It is also observed that possibility of the occurrence of extreme weather events (i.e., flood, drought, etc.) has increased. Some of recent extreme weather events such as Chennai flood in 2015, Kashmir flood in 2014, Uttarakhand flood in 2013, etc., are worthwhile here to recall. These abrupt changes in climate started affecting Indian agriculture adversely, as is noted in many recent studies (Auffhammer, Ramanathan, and Vincent 2011; Jha and Tripathi 2011). Indian agriculture is highly vulnerable to climate change because of its high sensitivity and low adaptive capacity to climate change (Tripathi 2016a). Low adaptive capacity of farmers in India stems from the fact that more than 80 per cent of Indian farmers are under the category of small and marginal. They are resource-poor and do not have enough income.

Against the above-mentioned background, this chapter attempts to ascertain factors affecting agricultural vulnerability to climate change by taking Uttar Pradesh (UP) (India) as a case study. To accomplish the above-mentioned objective, first some variables are selected using the review of literature on climate change vulnerability and considering experts' views, and then factor analysis is conducted to finalize significant factors affecting vulnerability to climate change. Findings of this chapter would be helpful in policy formulation to reduce vulnerability to climate change, which has become a major challenge. More importantly, it is being faced by almost each country across the world. Emission of anthropogenic gases is one of the main reasons of climate change. Hence, it is suggested to reduce emission of these gases to manage the problem of climate change (Stern 2007). But it requires global consensus because of interdependency. Let's assume that there are two nations and one of them controls emission of greenhouse gases while the other keeps emitting an increasing amount of greenhouse gases. The net level of emission of greenhouse gases will not be decreased because there is no boundary in the atmosphere between these two countries. Moreover, mitigation does not provide immediate relief. Its results are experienced after some time because of the presence of greenhouse gases already released in the atmosphere.

Highlighting its limitations discussed earlier does not mean that mitigation should not be focused on. Indeed, mitigation should be accompanied with emphasis on adaptation to climate change. Both mitigation and adaptation are complementary.

Adaptation to climate change depends on whether people perceive climate change and its associated risks or not. Perception is a cognitive process which involves receiving of sensory information and interpreting the received information. Interpretation of the received information relies on people's knowledge and experience. Next to perception in the adaptation process is people's response to perceived changes in climate. There are two types of responses; one refers to such responses that take place before impacts of climate change are observed and the second one denotes responses that take place after impacts of climate change have been observed. Any of these responses depends on people's adaptive capacity which is further determined by financial, human, social, physical, and natural capitals.

# Gaps in Literature

While climate change has become an important area of research in India, most studies[2] have focused either on the change in climatic variables or on the impact of climate change; few studies assess vulnerability to climate change. Of these, most assess vulnerability to natural hazards like cyclones for coastal regions or districts. Studies on the vulnerability of Indian coastal areas to cyclones have measured vulnerability either at the district level or for the coastal regions of the state as a whole and have considered factors such as cyclone frequency, population density, coast line length, some measures of cyclone damages witnessed, etc. (Jayanthi 1998; Kalsi et al. 2004; Kavi Kumar 2003; Patwardhan et al. 2003). These studies have been criticized because these did not consider natural systems variables and socio-economic factors, which significantly affect entities' vulnerability to climate change and variability. Das (2012) accepted these variables' importance and included these in her assessment of coastal vulnerability; she studied coastal villages of the Kendrapada district[3] and analysed the role of multiple factors on cyclone impacts.

Some studies have also attempted to examine agriculture's vulnerability to climate change and variability (Hiremath and Shiyani 2012; Malone and Brenkert 2008; O'Brien et al. 2004; Palanisami et al. 2009; Patnaik and Narayanan 2015). O'Brien et al. (2004) and Malone and Brenkert (2008) carried out a country-level assessment using district-level information, while Patnaik and Narayanan (2015), Palanisami et al. (2009), and Hiremath and Shiyani (2012) confined their study to a state or region. Like the previous studies, these studies also considered coastal states such as Tamil Nadu and Gujarat and ignored states such as UP where inland agriculture predominates and which also experiences climatic problems like droughts, although not as much as coastal states.

This study attempts to fill this gap in the literature by focusing on an inland state. The above-mentioned studies calculated the vulnerability index to identify most vulnerable regions in the country by aggregating several variables including both biophysical and socio-economic factors. This study endeavours to see whether socio-economic backwardness contributes to climate change vulnerability more than biophysical events.

## Concept of Climate Change Vulnerability

Vulnerability of a system depends on its biophysical and socio-economic characteristics. According to Intergovernmental Panel on Climate Change, vulnerability is "the degree to which a system is susceptible to, or unable to cope with, adverse effects of climate change, including climate variability and extremes" (McCarthy et al. 2001). This definition, further, suggests that vulnerability to climate change has three components—exposure, sensitivity, and adaptive capacity. Exposure refers to the character, magnitude, and the rate of climate change a system is or will be facing. Three elements are considered in exposure—one, objects of the system that can be affected by climate change, two, long- and short-term changes in climate and its variability itself, and three, drivers of climate change.

Sensitivity refers to the degree to which a system is affected by climate change and variability. It basically depends on biophysical characteristics of the system but it can be altered by socio-economic characteristics. We consider an example of soil fertility here to understand this better. Let's assume that there are two regions. "A," which has soil with high water-holding capacity and "B," which has low water-holding capacity. Further, we assume that both the mentioned regions are facing the problem of water deficit due to low rainfall. The region "A" would be lesser sensitive to low rainfall than the region "B" because "A" has better water-holding capacity than "B." High sensitivity of region "B" could be reduced by supplying water through irrigation.

Adaptive capacity refers to the ability or potential of a system to respond successfully to climate change and variability to avert their impact. Five types of capital assets can determine an entity's adaptive capacity: human, natural, financial, social, and physical (Scoones 1998). These capital assets are further classified into seven factors that influence adaptive capacity (Smit et al. 2001). These seven factors are: wealth, technology, education, institutions, information, infrastructure, and social capital.

Exposure and sensitivity together show the potential impact of climate change. Both exposure and sensitivity are positively related to vulnerability. However, adaptive capacity is inversely related to vulnerability. In other words, the greater the exposure or sensitivity, the greater is the vulnerability and likewise, the greater the adaptive capacity, the lesser is the vulnerability.

## Study Area

In the preceding sections, we have talked about gaps in literatures and elaborated the concept of vulnerability to climate change. Here, we make an attempt to fill the above-mentioned gap using the concept discussed earlier and selected UP for the purpose of the study. Although UP is poor in terms of per capita income, it is the leading state in terms of agriculture production in the country; its comparative advantage stems from a strong agriculture base with the most fertile land masses and a well-connected river network. This enables it to play a significant role in the country's food and nutrition security programme. UP is the largest producer of many food and non-food crops in India (Table 14.1). Notwithstanding, climate sensitivity to agriculture is very high in the state, and the recent changes observed in climate may be an obstacle to the economic development of the state (O'Brien et al. 2004). There is, therefore, an urgent need to make agriculture more resistant to climate change. It will help not only the state's economy but also the country.

Besides, UP, India's fifth largest state and its most populous, is diverse in geography and culture. A study based on a large and heterogeneous region always has a wider perspective because it provides a range of

**Table 14.1**

*Crop-wise largest producing states in India*

| Foodgrains | Rice | Wheat | Pulses |
|---|---|---|---|
| UP (19.80) | West Bengal (15.60) | UP (34.72) | Madhya Pradesh (27.33) |
| Punjab (12.36) | Andhra Pradesh (13.16) | Punjab (19.14) | Maharashtra (13.77) |
| Madhya Pradesh (7.34) | UP (12.70) | Haryana (13.20) | UP (13.34) |

| Sugarcane | Potato | | |
|---|---|---|---|
| UP (39.18) | UP (35.99) | | |
| Maharashtra (21.62) | West Bengal (24.63) | | |
| Tamil Nadu (10.83) | Bihar (14.65) | | |

*Source:* Author's own calculation based on data collected from Agriculture Statistics at a Glance (2014).
*Note:*    The value given in parentheses is state's share (in per cent) to all-India production.

outcomes, which can also be used for other parts of the country. UP was selected for this study keeping the above views in mind.

Located in the northern part of the country, UP is surrounded by Bihar in the east; Madhya Pradesh in the south; Rajasthan, Delhi, Himachal Pradesh, and Haryana in the west; and Uttaranchal in the north. Nepal touches its northern borders. It has 83 districts, 901 development blocks, and 112,804 inhabited villages. The state is divided into four economic regions: western, central, eastern, and Bundelkhand. The state is also divided into nine agro-climatic regions: central plain, south-western semi-arid, Bundelkhand, eastern plain, northeastern plain, Vindyan, Bhabhar and Tarai zone, western plain, and mid-western plain (Tripathi 2016a).

The western region is more developed than other regions. Its per capita income (₹17,273) at constant prices is significantly higher than the other three regions: central (₹13,940), Bundelkhand (₹12,737), and eastern (₹9,859) for year 2013–14. (Tripathi 2016b). Around 40 per cent of the state's population lives in the eastern region, but only 9.5 per cent lives in the Bundelkhand region, where the population density is also the lowest. Despite low population pressure, the region is socially and economically backward, because of its geographical and climatic conditions.

Moreover, the performance of agriculture varies greatly across regions in the state. The western region is agriculturally the most progressive; the largest chunk of the state's agriculture output comes from this region (around 50 per cent). The eastern region contributes around 28 per cent, next to the western region, of the total value of the state's agriculture output. Bundelkhand accounts for only 4 per cent of the state's gross value of the agricultural output. Agriculture in the Bundelkhand region is vastly rain-dependent, diverse, complex, under-invested, risky, and vulnerable. The average foodgrain yield in the western region is 2,577 kg per hectare—much higher than other regions, particularly the eastern (1,997 kg per ha) and Bundelkhand regions (1,067 kg per ha).

## Methods and Data

Vulnerability is a complex phenomenon, which has three components—exposure, sensitivity, and adaptive capacity. These components are themselves multifaceted. Hence, it is almost impossible to measure climate change vulnerability by a single variable. Each component is represented by a set of variables. In this paper, 23 indicators (four for exposure, eight for sensitivity and 11 for adaptive capacity) were selected to assess climate change vulnerability based on a review of literatures (Das 2013; O'Brien et al. 2004; Scoones 1998; Singh and Nair 2014; Smit et al. 2001; Tripathi 2016a; Yohe and Tol 2002). First, a list of possible variables of each component was prepared following the above literatures and then 23 indicating variables from the list were finalized based on experts' views and data availability. Table 14.2 presents all chosen variables, explains how each variable is quantified and their source of data, and includes the hypothetical relation of each indicating variable with vulnerability.

Factor analysis is a useful tool for investigating variable relationships for complex concepts such vulnerability and socio-economic status. This chapter uses factor analysis and calculates factor loadings that tell about strength and direction of relationship of each variable to the underlying factor. Four major steps are involved in the factor analysis. First, eigenvalue is generated for each factor. Number of factors is always equal to number of variables. For example, 23 variables are used in the factor analysis; hence, the number of factors will also be 23. Each factor captures a certain amount of the overall variance in the observed variables, and the factors are always listed in order of how much variation they explain, which is measured by eigenvalue. Before going to the next step, we decide how much factors are to be retained. It is generally decided based on the Kaiser criterion, which suggests to retain those factors that have eigenvalues equal to or higher than 1.

Second, after finalizing the number of factors to be retained, loading is estimated for each factor. It is commonly known as factor loading and its value and sign represent strength and direction of relationship between each variable and underlying factor, respectively. The higher the load, the more relevant it is in defining the factor's dimensionality. A negative value indicates an inverse impact on the factor. Third, to get a better interpretation and clear pattern of each factor, these factor loadings are rotated based on two different approaches—orthogonal and oblique. In orthogonal rotations, factors are not correlated with each other, while these are correlated with each other in oblique rotations. Finally, factor scores are estimated for each observation using factor loadings.

In this paper, the factor analysis is carried out using cross-section data of 70 districts of UP. There are 83 districts in the state, but data are available for 70 districts only. Hence, 70 districts were used for factor analysis in the paper. All data used are against either climatic variables or non-climatic or socio-economic variables. We collected information on climatic variables by district from the India Meteorology Department, Pune. Similarly, all non-climatic data by district were collected from the *Jila Sankhyikiya Patrika*. Climatic data were collected for the period from 1970 to 2010 to observe the frequency of extreme climate events and inter-annual variability over the past 40 years. We used a three-year moving average figure of each variable instead of taking a single-year figure to control seasonality effects in variables.

# Results and Discussions

In this paper, factor analysis was conducted twice—first, it was conducted on the 23 variables using oblique rotation (direct oblimin) and the value of Kaiser–Meyer–Olkin (KMO) statistic for each variable was calculated to determine the variables that were less important in explaining vulnerability. The results suggested that less important variables in describing vulnerability in UP were frequency of drought and flood, access to credit, and cropping intensity. The values of KMO for these variables were 0.4, which is below the limit of 0.5 (Field 2012). Hence, these variables were dropped and the factor analysis was again conducted on the remaining 20 variables. Estimates of the second round of factor analysis are presented here in detail. The value of KMO for the analysis is 0.68 which confirms that factor analysis is appropriate for the sample. All KMO values for each variable were greater than 0.53, which is above the limit of 0.5. A first analysis was conducted to generate eigenvalues for each component in the data using the principal component method. Four components had eigenvalues greater than 1, which is the Kaiser criterion for the extraction of factors. The scree plot validated the extraction of four factors. A scree plot displays the eigenvalues associated with a component or factor in a descending order versus the number of components or factors. It shows that four of those factors explain most of the variability because the line starts to straighten after factor 4 (Figure 14.1). The remaining factors explain a very small proportion of the variability and are likely to be unimportant.

**Table 14.2**
*Source of data against indicators to capture vulnerability*

| Determinants | Indicators | Variables | Unit of measurement | Hypothetical relationship | Data source |
|---|---|---|---|---|---|
| Exposure | Extreme climate events in last 40 years (from 1970 to 2010) | 1. Frequency of drought and flood | Number | Positive | IMD[1] |
| | | 2. Frequency of warming years (temperature above long-term average temperature) | Number | | |
| | Variability in climatic variables | 1. Inter-annual variation in rainfall | No unit | Positive | |
| | | 2. Variation in diurnal temperature | No unit | | |
| Sensitivity | Irrigated land | Irrigation ratio | % | Negative | JSP[2] |
| | Urbanization | Share of urban population | % | Positive | JSP |
| | Small and marginal farming | Percentage of small and marginal holdings in total holdings | % | Positive | JSP |
| | Crop diversification | Diversification index[3] | % | Negative | JSP |
| | Population | Rural population density | % | Positive | Census |
| | Agriculture share | Per cent of agriculture GDP | % | Positive | JSP |
| | Consumption of fertilizer | Total consumption of fertilizer | Kg | Negative | JSP |
| | Forestry | Per cent area under forest | % | Negative | JSP |
| Adaptive capacity | Social capital | Number of farmer members of primary cooperative societies | Number | Negative | JSP |
| | Natural capital | Groundwater level | mbgl[4] | Negative | JSP |
| | Human capital | Literacy rate | % | Negative | JSP |
| | | Sex-ratio | Number | Positive | JSP |
| | Financial capital | 1. Farm income | ₹ | Negative | JSP |
| | | 2. Per cent of people below poverty | % | Positive | JSP |
| | | 3. Average farm holding | Hectare | Negative | JSP |
| | | 4. Access to credit | ₹ | Negative | JSP |
| | | 5. Share of non-farm employment | % | Negative | JSP |
| | Physical capital | 1. Infrastructure index[5] | No unit | Negative | JSP |
| | | 2. Cropping intensity | % | Negative | JSP |

*Notes:*  1. India Meteorological Department, Ministry of Earth Sciences, Government of India, Pune, India.
2. *Jila Sankhyikiya Patrika* published from the Department of Economic and Statistics, Government of Uttar Pradesh, Lucknow, India.
3. Crop diversification index is calculated following the formula of simple crop diversity index.
4. Metres below ground level.
5. Here, infrastructure is a composite index of six infrastructure-related variables—number of primary agricultural societies per lakh rural population, number of regulated markets per lakh hectare of net sown area, percentage of electrified villages, total length of pucca road per thousand square kilometres, percentage of net irrigated area by canal and government tube wells, and storage capacity in kilogram per hectare net sown area.

**Figure 14.1**
*Scree plot of eigenvalues after factor*

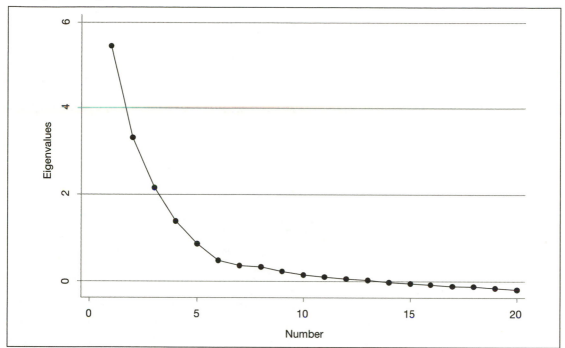

*Source:* Author's own calculation using information on variables mentioned in Table 14.2.

The four factors, which were extracted here, together explains 87 per cent of the variance. Table 14.3 shows the factor loading after rotation.

Following Stevens (2002), factor loadings of an absolute value greater than 0.3 were considered in the interpretation of the factors. There were factor loadings with both positive and negative coefficients in all extracted components. Except for a few cases, the signs of the coefficients were in line with our expectation. Results presented in Table 14.3 indicate that factor loadings of socio-economic factors are higher than those of biophysical factors. More importantly, it has been noted in each extracted component. The values of uniqueness suggest that forestry, extreme temperature event, rainfall variability, crop diversification, and access to credit are less relevant than other variables. The uniqueness values for the above variables were greater than 0.50. We find that greater the "uniqueness," the lower the relevance of the variable in the factor model. The values of both factor loading and uniqueness suggest that urbanization, share of non-farm employment, share of small and marginal landholdings, rural population density, and the average size of landholdings are the most important variables explaining agricultural vulnerability to climate change. The share of non-farm employment and the average size of landholdings were found adversely related with climate change vulnerability, while urbanization, share of small and marginal landholdings, and rural population density are positively associated with vulnerability.

## Conclusions and Policy Implications

This chapter has made an attempt to determine factors affecting agricultural vulnerability to climate change using factor analysis. It was carried out on 23 variables including both biophysical and socio-economic factors

**Table 14.3**
*Estimates of factor analysis*

| Variable | Factor1 | Factor2 | Factor3 | Factor4 | Uniqueness | KMO |
|---|---|---|---|---|---|---|
| Urbanization | 0.84 | | −0.40 | | 0.13 | 0.79 |
| Sex ratio | | −0.35 | 0.62 | | 0.44 | 0.61 |
| Share of non-farm employment | −0.99 | | | | 0.07 | 0.70 |
| Livestock | 0.40 | 0.38 | | | 0.50 | 0.80 |
| Forestry | | −0.32 | −0.34 | | 0.70 | 0.74 |
| Consumption of fertilizer | 0.43 | | 0.42 | | 0.41 | 0.89 |
| Extreme event in temperature | | −0.41 | | | 0.74 | 0.53 |
| Diurnal temperature | | | | 0.85 | 0.26 | 0.53 |
| Variance in rainfall | | −0.68 | | | 0.52 | 0.75 |
| Share of agriculture in GDP | −0.91 | 0.58 | | | 0.22 | 0.53 |
| Irrigation ratio | | 0.65 | 0.38 | | 0.28 | 0.69 |
| Share of small and marginal landholdings | | | 0.98 | | 0.07 | 0.57 |
| Crop diversification index | | | | −0.57 | 0.62 | 0.53 |
| Rural population density | 0.77 | | 0.31 | −0.30 | 0.18 | 0.78 |
| Rural poverty | −0.37 | −0.48 | | | 0.50 | 0.79 |
| Access to credit | 0.42 | | | | 0.84 | 0.63 |
| Farm income | | 0.86 | | | 0.33 | 0.69 |
| Literacy | 0.58 | | | 0.36 | 0.45 | 0.63 |
| Average land size | | | −0.98 | | 0.06 | 0.59 |
| Infrastructure index | | 0.50 | | 0.37 | 0.37 | 0.79 |
| Overall KMO | | | | | | 0.69 |
| Variance | 34 | 27 | 24 | 14 | | |

*Source:* Author's own calculation using factor analysis.
*Notes:*  1. KMO test is a measure of how used data are suited for factor analysis.
        2. Blanks represent abs (loading) < 0.3.

selected based on a review of literatures, experts' views, and data availability. UP was chosen for the above analysis because of its high sensitivity to climate change and low adaptive capacity. Findings of this paper suggest that socio-economic factors are more responsible for making agriculture highly vulnerable to climate change in developing regions than biophysical factors. It underlines the need of strengthening social and economic development of the state, for which investment in human, social, and financial capital would help.

Among socio-economic factors, urbanization, share of non-farm employment, share of small and marginal landholdings, rural population density, and average size of landholdings were found significant in explaining agriculture vulnerability to climate change in UP. In order to reduce climate change vulnerability in the state, specific actions targeting the contributing factors of high vulnerability would be required. In rural areas, increasing awareness and education, expanding rural non-farm sectors by providing credit, markets, and necessary skills, and improving the size of landholdings are some specific policy actions that could be fruitful here.

# Notes

1. The country received 14 per cent deficit rainfall during the monsoon of 2015–16.
2. For a list of studies, see Jha and Tripathi (2011), Jain and Kumar (2012), Dasgupta, Bhattacharjee, and Kumari. (2013), and Mall, Gupta, and Sonkar (2016).
3. Kendrapara is a highly cyclone-prone district of peninsular India.

# References

Auffhammer, M., V. Ramanathan, and J.R. Vincent. 2011. "Climate Change, the Monsoon, and Rice Yield in India." *Climatic Change* 111 (2): 411–24.

Das, S. 2012. "The Role of Natural Ecosystems and Socio-economic Factors in the Vulnerability of Coastal Villages to Cyclone and Storm Surge." *Natural Hazards* 64 (1): 531–46.

———. 2013. "Mapping the Regional Variation in Potential Vulnerability in Indian Agriculture to Climate Change—An Exercise Through Constructing Vulnerability Index." *African Journal of Environmental Science and Technology* 7 (4): 112–21.

Dasgupta, P., D. Bhattacharjee, and A. Kumari. 2013. "Socio-economic Analysis of Climate Change Impacts on Foodgrain Production in Indian States." *Environmental Development* 8 (1): 5–21.

Field, A.P. 2012. *Discovering Statistics Using SPSS: (and Sex and Drugs and Rock "n" Roll)*, 3rd ed. Los Angeles, CA: SAGE Publications.

GoI. 2016. *Second Advance Estimates of Production of Foodgrains for 2015–16*. New Delhi: Ministry of Agriculture and Farmers' Welfare, Government of India.

Hiremath, D.B., and R.L. Shiyani. 2012. "Evaluating Regional Vulnerability to Climate Change: A Case of Saurashtra." *Indian Journal of Agriculture Economics* 67 (3): 334–44.

Jain, S.K. and Vijay Kumar. 2012. "Trend Analysis of Rainfall and Temperature Data for India." *Current Science* 102 (1): 37–49.

Jayanthi, N. 1998. "Cyclone Hazard, Coastal Vulnerability and Disaster Risk Assessment Along the Indian Coasts." *Vayu Mandal* 28 (1–4): 115–19.

Jha, B., and A. Tripathi. 2011. "Isn't Climate Change Affecting Wheat Productivity in India." *Indian Journal of Agricultural Economics* 66 (3): 353–64.

Kalsi, S.R., N. Jayanthi, and S.K. Roy Bhowmik. 2004. *A Review of Different Storm Surge Models and Estimated Storm Surge Height in Respect of Orissa Super Cyclonic Storm of 29 October 1999*. New Delhi: Indian Meteorological Department, Government of India.

Kavi Kumar, K.S. 2003. *Vulnerability and Adaptation of Agriculture and Coastal Resources in India to Climate Change*. Mumbai: Indira Gandhi Institute of Development Research.

Mall, R.K., A. Gupta, and G. Sonkar. 2016. "Effect of Climate Change on Agricultural Crops." In *Current Developments in Biotechnology and Bioengineering: Crop Modification, Nutrition, and Food Production*, edited by S.K. Dubey, A. Pandey, and R.S. Sagwan, 23–39. Amsterdam, Netherland: Elsevier.

Malone, E.L., and A.L. Brenkert. 2008. "Uncertainty in Resilience to Climate Change in India and Indian States." *Climatic Change* 91 (3–4): 451–76.

McCarthy, J.J., O.F. Canziani, N.A. Leary, D.J. Dokken, and K.S. White. 2001. *Climate Change 2001: Impacts, Adaptation, Vulnerability*. Cambridge: Cambridge University Press.

O'Brien, K., R. Leichenko, U. Kelkar, H. Venema, G. Aandahl, H. Tompkins, A. Javed, S. Bhadwal, S. Barg, L. Nygaard, and J. West. 2004. "Mapping Vulnerability to Multiple Stressors: Climate Change and Globalization in India." *Global Environmental Change* 14 (4): 303–13.

Palanisami, K., C.R. Ranganathan, S. Senthilnathan, S. Govindraj, and S. Ajjan. 2009. *Assessment of Vulnerability to Climate Change for the Different Districts and Agro-climatic Zones of Tamil Nadu*. Coimbatore: Centre for Agriculture and Rural Development Studies.

Patnaik, U., and K. Narayanan. 2015, December 30. "Vulnerability and Climate Change: An Analysis of the Eastern Coastal Districts of India." Available at: https://mpra.ub.uni-muenchen.de/22062/ (accessed on 8 February 2017).

Patwardhan, A., K. Narayan, D. Pathasarathy, and U. Sharma. 2003. "Impacts of Climate Change on Coastal Zone." In *Climate Change and India: Vulnerability Assessment and Adaptation*, edited by P.R. Shukla, S.K. Sharma, N.H. Ravindranath, A. Garg, and S. Bhattacharga, 326–59. Hyderabad: University Press.

Scoones, I. 1998. *Sustainable Rural Livelihoods: A Framework for Analysis.* Brighton: Institute of Development Studies.

Singh, P.K., and A. Nair. 2014. "Livelihood Vulnerability Assessment to Climatic Variability and Change Using Fuzzy Cognitive Mapping Approach." *Climatic Change* 127 (3): 475491. doi: 10.1007/s10584-014-1275-0.

Smit, B., O. Pilifosova, I. Burton, B. Challenger, S. Huq, R.J.T. Klein, and G. Yohe. 2001. "Adaptation to Climate Change in the Context of Sustainable Development and Equity." In *Climate Change 2001: Impacts, Adaptation, Vulnerability*, edited by J.J. McCarthy, O.F. Canziani, N.A. Leary, D.J. Dokken, and K.S. White. Cambridge: Cambridge University Press.

Stern, N.H. 2007. *The Economics of Climate Change: The Stern Review.* Cambridge: Cambridge University Press.

Stevens, J.P. 2002. *Applied Multivariate Statistics for the Social Sciences.* New York, NY/London: Routledge.

Tripathi, A. 2016a. "Socioeconomic Backwardness and Vulnerability to Climate Change: Evidence from Uttar Pradesh State in India." *Journal of Environmental Planning and Management.* doi:10.1080/09640568.2016.1157059.

———. 2016b. "Agriculture is Still Engine of Economic Growth: Empirical Evidence from Uttar Pradesh, India." *Asian Journal of Agriculture and Development* 13 (1): 1–20.

Yohe, G., and R.S.J. Tol. 2002. "Indicators for Social and Economic Coping Capacity—Moving Toward a Working Definition of Adaptive Capacity." *Global Environmental Change* 12 (1): 25–40.

# 15

# Estimating the Economic Benefits of an Improved Aquatic Ecosystem and Watershed Management in the Tanguar Haor Wetland: An Application of Choice Modelling

Md Hafiz Iqbal

## Introduction

Bangladesh is a land of vast wetlands and abundant water. According to the definition enunciated in the Ramsar Convention, more than two-thirds landmass of this country has been classified as wetland (Ramsar Convention Secretariat 2010). Wetland ecosystem is of great importance to Bangladesh due to its extent and the critical economic and ecological roles that it plays in sustaining life and livelihoods in the country (Alam, Chowdhury, and Sobhan 2012). Tanguar Haor[1] is one of the most important wetlands of just not Bangladesh but also of South Asia (Bird Life International 2012). This unique wetland ecosystem has now gained international focus as well (IUCN 2011). The haven of biodiversity, place for migratory birds, and occurrence of wildlife are the most significant features that allowed this area to be designated as a Ramsar Site.

It is estimated that a total of 200 wetland plant species, 141 fish species under 35 families, 11 amphibians, 34 reptiles (6 turtles, 7 lizards, and 21 snakes), 206 birds, and 31 mammals are present in this haor (BNH 1997, 144; Gieson and Rashid 1997; IUCN 2011; Karim 1993; NERP 1993; Nishat 1993). Tanguar Haor is extremely rich in aquatic resources. The varied number of fish species is linked with a complex network of food web in the entire ecosystem; maintaining the integrity of the food web is a must for the ecological balance of the haor and to increase the fish production in Bangladesh. This place acts as a habitat for mother fish (they lay eggs here), as well as it is part of a larger haor basin across which the mother fishes travel. The estimated number of fish species in the Tanguar Haor is more than half of Bangladesh's total 260 freshwater fish species (DoZ 1997, 85–95; Nuruzzaman 1997). This haor is the largest source of animal protein used by the people of Bangladesh; across fiscal years, the government earned considerable revenue just from fisheries of this haor (IUCN 2011). In addition, it directly sustains the livelihoods of over 56,000 people from 88 surrounding villages and largely contributes to the country's food production, nutrition, food security, and tourism (Alam et al. 2012; IUCN 2011).

Aquatic ecosystem and watershed in the Tanguar Haor are now in a captious position due to overfishing and wetland degradation. Most of the fish stock are either fully or heavily exploited,[2] over-exploited,[3] and depleted[4] or are recovering[5] from overfishing very slowly. In addition, dewatering of certain key areas, repeated fish harvest every year, and leaving only a few fishes for breeding are the most unsustainable methods that have been associated with the fishing practices in this haor. Illegal fish catching by locals using the monofilament net and other illegal fishing *ghers*[6] depletes fish stock of this wetland. This has probably contributed to the disappearance of a large number of fishes in this natural pond which has led to genetic erosion and is a threat to indigenous fish species (GoB 2004). On the other hand, unsustainable use and destruction of swamp forests, and reed beds bring a negative effect to fishing resources as it provides shelter and food to the fish. Water pollution is another threat to floral and faunal species which frequently occurs. Thousands of boats continuously pollute the water through the use of fossil fuel which ultimately affects the fish population. In some places, due to sedimentation, navigation has faced difficulties, and soon it may be impossible to continue this important activity. Such sedimentation also fragments water bodies and disturbs the ecosystem by disrupting the routes for migration of fishes, preventing the completion of breeding cycles and resulting in depletion of fishes (Haider 2013).

From the political economy point of view, a legal basis for community co-management has yet to be adopted and recognized by the government without considering the preferences of the locals. Jalmahal (wetland) Leasing Policy, 2009, of the Ministry of Land, that prioritizes revenue-based wetland resource entitlements, guides not only the Ministry of Land itself but also the Ministry of Agriculture, Fisheries and Environment along with the Wetland Custodian District Administration. This policy does not have clear provisions for allowing or giving equal rights to manage wetland resources following a co-management approach. As a consequence, the dwellers around the Tanguar Haor have limited access to the resources in it which makes their livelihood vulnerable. In fact, just like anywhere else, there is no participation of the locals in the policy related to the maintenance or improvement of the haor, the base of their livelihood. Thus, it prompts them to explore alternative options for securing their livelihood, which ironically leads to further depletion of the aquatic ecosystem, wetland resources, water bodies, sanctuaries, and to loss of tourist attraction; illegal and over-harvesting of fish, trapping of birds, and destruction of swamp forests are a few pertinent examples.

In this context, the co-management approach can play an important role to enhance the livelihood condition of the locals. It was first introduced in haors of Bangladesh in 1998. It helps to protect and manage wetland resources with the participation of locals. The aims of co-management are to improve the governance of natural resources and strengthen legal and policy frameworks for collaborative management with communities (JDR 2015).

It follows that pursuing the co-management approach, for formulation of wetland policy, implementation of the associated regulation, and corresponding investment for sustainable utilization of resources of Tanguar Haor, the preference through the alternative choices of members of the society (especially of the fisherfolks as they are the key players to control the ecosystem of Tanguar Haor) must be taken into consideration. Such a possibility with respect to preferences has not been considered in the past.

This study intends to fill this important gap. It sets out the process of choice analysis in a logically consistent manner by determining the marginal willingness to pay (MWTP) and welfare effects associated with improvements to aquatic ecosystem and watershed management at household level. After all, improvements in aquatic ecosystem and watershed management of the Tanguar Haor require strong government intervention and commitment no doubt, but also in consideration of preferences of locals. Without the latter, conservation and prudent use of resources cannot be ensured.

The findings of this study provide a robust basis for policymakers, planners, researchers, government, and development partners for taking the required steps to ensure improved livelihood conditions for the fishing community. Empirical findings will also be helpful for implementing the aquatic ecosystem and associated watershed management projects. In addition, they can be useful to formulate and develop specified policies to lessen the vulnerability and build a resilient and sustainable aquatic ecosystem and watershed in Tanguar Haor. The findings can also be helpful for the management of similar wetlands.

The objective of this chapter is to explore the preferences of fisherfolks in consideration of different "scenario(s)" based on different attributes with respect to Tanguar Haor. The specific objective of this study is to measure the MWTP of an individual fisherperson against improved aquatic ecosystem and watershed management. Based on these estimates of economic benefits of improving the aquatic ecosystem, this chapter will offer a few recommendations for the sustainable management strategy of this haor. To generate empirically supported assessments fulfilling the research objectives, this study used the discrete choice experiment (CE) method.

## Materials and Methods

### Study Area

Tanguar Haor is located in Sunamgonj District under Sylhet Division in Northeastern Bangladesh adjacent to the Indian border. It has an area of 9,727 hectares of wetland with common property ownership (International Federation of Surveyors 2010). It is located between latitude from 25° 06″ to 25°1″ N and longitude from 91°01″ to 91°0″E (Chowdhury 2008). Approximately, one-third of area lay in Tahirpur Upazila[7] and the remaining in Dharmapasha Upazila. Patlai River, Hasmara River, Shib Bari Nadi, Ghashi Nadi, and Azrakhali Nadi are the main rivers of this haor and they control water flow around the year. The ecosystem of this haor is also influenced by Surma, Dhanu Baulai, and Jadukata Rivers. Meghalayan hills are in the north from which a number of hill streams flow through these rivers. This water flow also brings a huge amount of sediments to this haor. About 50 per cent of the area of this haor is water bodies and 31 per cent is crop land (IUCN 2015; Uddin et al. 2015). This haor consists of about 50 beels[8] of various sizes (*The Daily Star* 2008).

This haor is a large water-logged area between levees or banks of large river systems at the foothill of the Meghalayan-Jaintia Hill of Cherrapunji rainforest of India. Thus, this area remains under water for several months of each year which drains gradually during the winter. About 46 villages, home to 25,000 inhabitants depend on the natural resources of this haor. Majority of the local residents are involved in farming and fishing. 70 per cent heads of households are engaged in fishing while 20 per cent in agricultural activity, and the rest in daily labouring activities (Chowdhury 2008).

Climate of the Tanguar Haor is of sub-tropical monsoon nature with three dominating seasons: summer, monsoon, and winter. Summer is from April to June and temperature ranges from 30.9°C to 33.4°C. Humidity is 83 per cent in the wet season and 64 per cent in the dry season. Average annual rainfall is 8,000 mm. Evaporation enhances rainfall during the spring which causes flash flood in this haor (IUCN 2011). Water supply varies from 7,000 cubic meter/sec to 220 cubic meter/sec in July and February, respectively (Chowdhury 2008). Figure 15.1 shows the location of the Tanguar Haor.

The study used the stated preference approach, the CE framework which falls within the theories of consumer behaviour. It is well established that people cannot reveal their willingness to pay (WTP) for environmental goods and services which are not traded or closely related to any market goods and services. It follows that the stated preference is the appropriate valuation approach that enables estimation of the value of such goods and services. The most widely used approach of valuing ecosystem services under the stated preference are the conjoint analysis (CA), contingent valuation (CV), and CE. In CE, respondents are asked to make

**Figure 15.1**
*Study area (Tanguar Haor)*

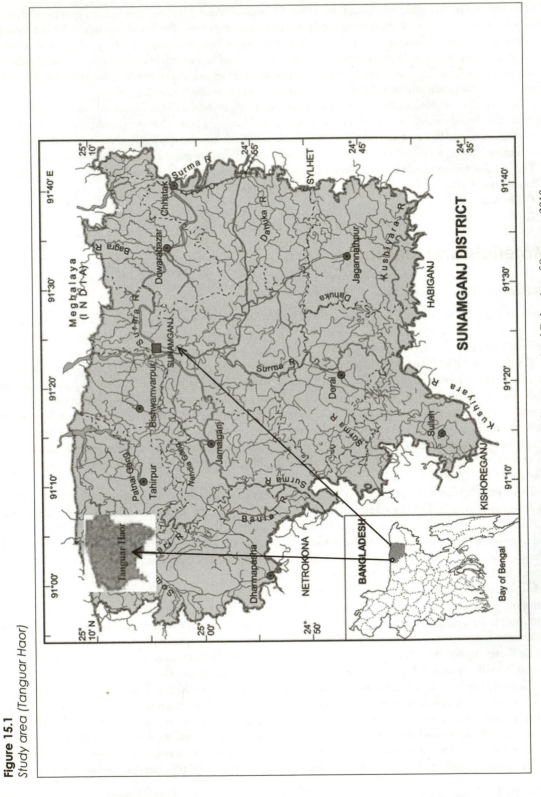

*Source:* Inset prepared by the author based on Google Map, 2015; Adapted from International Federation of Surveyors, 2010.
*Note:* This figure is not to scale. It does not represent any authentic national or international boundaries and is used for illustrative purposes only.

repeated hypothetical choices between alternatives described by varying levels of attributes. If a monetary (cost) attribute is included in CE, it is possible to estimate MWTP and the average WTP for a change in each of the other non-market attributes, and estimate the corresponding economic benefits (Nguyen et al. 2013).

Advantage of using CE is minimization of strategic bias due to the complexity of formulating strategic responses across multiple choices between different alternatives (Bennett and Blamey 2001). In general, CE applied to non-marketed goods assumes a specific continuous dimension as a part of the framework, in which a discrete choice is made (Alpizer et al. 2003). CE is argued to be a useful tool for valuing a multi-attribute public good or service, which includes wetlands and other natural resources, environmental goods, roads, highway, hospital, and so on (Hanley, Mourato, and Wright 2001).

CE is an economic valuation approach which enables taking some account of public preferences and also of economic efficiency (benefit-cost; Bergmann, Hanley, and Wright 2006). Estimation of the economic benefits of this study captures the total economic value of the improved aquatic ecosystem and watershed management of the Tanguar Haor. The benefits of improved aquatic ecosystem and watershed management include not only the expected increase in fish stock, reduction of poverty, and halting of destruction of wetlands but also increase/improvement in biodiversity, knowledge management, ecological balance, livelihood opportunities, and judicious use of resources for both present and future generations.

Inconsistency is a common feature of stated behaviour surveys. They are presumed to arise from observational difficulties of consumer behaviour (Agimass and Mekonnen 2011). Unobservable components, measurement error, heterogeneity of individuals' preferences, individual characteristics, omission of relevant attributes, and consideration of irrelevant attributes in the alternatives (of the CE) are usually held responsible for creation of observational difficulties. Use of two building blocks (random utility theory [RUT] and Lancasterian theory of value) of CE enable controlling for the observational difficulties in the utility-based stated behaviour surveys (Bergmann et al. 2006).

Lancasterian theory of value asserts that the utility derived from a good comes from the characteristics of that good, not from consumption of the good itself. Goods normally possess more than one characteristic and these characteristics or attributes will be shared with many other goods. The value of a good is then given by the sum of the value of its characteristics (Lancaster 1966).

RUT is very similar to the random service theory (RST). It states that not all of the determinants of the utility derived by individuals from their choices can be directly observable by the researcher and that an indirect determination of preferences is possible (Bergmann et al. 2006; McFadden 1974; Manski 1977).

If utility function of a representative individual is assumed to depend on a vector of environmental attributes and socio-economic factors, it could be formulated as (Agimass and Mekonnen 2011; Alpizer et al. 2003; Bennett and Blamey 2001; Birol, Karousakis, and Koundouri 2005):

$$U_{in} = V(Z_{in}, S_n) \tag{1}$$

where $U_{in}$ represents the unobservable (latent) utility from a given option $i$ of individual $n$; $Z_{in}$ is a vector of environmental attributes for option $i$ and individual $n$; and $S_n$ is a vector of socio-economic characteristics of individual $n$.

Incorporating the error term representing the random component as an additive term, the utility function could be explained by a deterministic (observable) portion and a random portion as follows (Agimass and Mekonnen 2011; Alpizer et al. 2003; Bennett and Blamey 2001; Birol et al. 2005):

$$U_{in} = V(Z_{in}, S_n) + \varepsilon_{in} \tag{2}$$

where $V(Z_{in}, S_n)$ represents the deterministic (observable) component and $\varepsilon_{in}$ represents the random component of the latent utility associated with alternative $i$ and individual $n$. We focus here on a probability function, defined over the alternatives which an individual faces, assuming that the individuals will try to maximize their economic benefit (Bennett and Blamey 2001; Louviere, Hensher, and Swait 2000). This probability is expressed as

$$P(i/C_n) = P\{(V_{in} + \varepsilon_{in}) > (V_{jn} + \varepsilon_{jn})\} \text{ for } i \neq j; j \in C \tag{3}$$

where $j$ is any option (other than $i$) provided to the individual in a given choice set and $C_n$ is the choice set provided to the individual.

Based on the above discussion about consumer behaviour and linear utility function for the improved programme with respect to respondents' characteristics and attitude, the following will be taken as respondent $j$'s utility against the improvement programme $i$:

$$U_i = \alpha + \beta Z_i + \gamma S_i + \varepsilon \tag{4}$$

where U indicates the indirect utility for programme $i$; $\alpha$ is a constant or alternative specific constant; Z is a vector of programme attributes; S is a vector of respondent's characteristics and attitude; and $\varepsilon$ is the stochastic unobserved component. The constant represents the average effect on choices over any variation that cannot be explained by the observed attributes or the respondent's characteristics and attitude. This study followed the structure of Equation 4 for it enables use of two econometric models specified for the analysis of the CE. The first model, the random parameter logit (PRL; basic) model, is designated to include proposed attributes of this study and the second one, the multinomial logit (MNL; extended) model, is designated to include proposed attributes and other relevant socio-economic-demographic (SED) variables interacting with intercept terms (vector alternative specific constant) of this study.

The alternative $i$ will be chosen over some other option $j$ if and only if $U_i > U_j$. Because of the unobserved component, the researcher can never expect to predict the choice perfectly, and this uncertainty is expressed in terms of choice probability like Equation 3. Because of the discrete nature of choices, logit econometric models are employed to estimate the concerned coefficients and assess their impacts on the probability of a choice of improvement programme.

The welfare changes from quality or quantity of environmental goods (attributes) could be given by the measure of compensating surplus (CS; Agimass and Mekonnen 2011; Alpizer et al. 2003; Bennett and Blamey 2001; Birol et al. 2005). CS is very helpful to generate estimates of the total WTP for an improvement programme that ensures the welfare in the society. The CS welfare measure is obtained by using the following formula (Hanemann 1982):

$$CS = -(1/\mu)\left[\ln \sum \exp(U_{0i}) - \ln \sum \exp(U_{1i})\right] \tag{5}$$

where $\mu$ is the marginal utility of income (generally represented by the coefficient for the monetary opportunity cost attribute in an experiment); and $U_{0i}$ $U_{1i}$ are the indirect utility functions before and after programme $i$ has been implemented. More specifically, $U_{0i}$ represents the indirect utility at the status quo in various scenarios and $U_{1i}$ is the indirect utility function associated with environmental changes in various scenarios.

The MWTP for an improvement in a single attribute can be represented as a ratio of coefficients, where Equation 5 reduces further to:

$$MWTP = -1\left(\frac{-\beta_{attribute}}{\beta_{cost\,attribute}}\right) \tag{6}$$

This part-worth formula effectively provides the marginal rate of substitution (MRS$_{ij}$) between the cost or payment attribute and the attribute in question.

## Data Collection and Survey Design

The pilot survey and focus group discussion (FGD) of this study were conducted from 27 September 2014 to 5 October 2014. They revealed that the ecosystem of Tanguar Haor has been degraded due to unplanned use of resources. The final survey design and variables selection were based on the findings of the pilot survey and FGD. Cross section data is used here to generate empirically supported assessments. Data was collected from the household of the fisherfolks of different villages of the Tanguar Haor through face-to-face interviews with the heads of households using questionnaires, from 27 January 2015 to 10 February 2015.

## Design of a Choice Experiment (CE)

CE survey design requires some steps to follow: definition and selection of attributes and their levels, experimental design, questionnaire development, and sampling strategy. Each is described further with some detail.

### Definition and Selection of Attributes and their Levels

The first step in undertaking a CE survey design is to identify the attributes and attribute levels which are to be included in the survey (Agimass and Mekonnen 2011). It is a critical component in a CE exercise. Selected attributes should be convenient, recognized, relevant, and understandable to the respondents. Moreover, the identified attributes should be consistent with policy instruments that are expected as outcomes from the alternatives provided and hence they should be relevant to the policymaking processes (Bennett and Blamey 2001).

Previous works revealed that the endemic, indigenous, and endangered fish species are needed for the protection of the ecological balance and biodiversity in Haor and also that some of them are facing possible extinction as the numbers are declining at an alarming rate due to over-exploitation, illegal fishing, and use of monofilament net to capture fishes, all of which warrant control (Agimass and Mekonnen 2011; de Graaf 2003). The FGD report of this study also suggested that fishing at the spawning grounds and spawning seasons should be controlled, restricted, and prohibited. Thus, fishing control during the breeding and spawning seasons is taken into consideration as one attribute of this study. This attribute consists of two levels: control during every other week between October and May and in every other month between June and September (monsoon season).

Swamp forests are beneficial for fish habitat. But it is noticed that the destruction of swamp forest is a rather common feature of the Tanguar Haor due to intense use of branches; sometimes the whole tree is used for construction of enclosures, called *khola* or *kathha* which entice fish for breeding within them and also for use as fuel by the local people. People in this region claimed that destruction of swamp forests and the consequent curtailment of the area under it is a major reason for the depletion of the aquatic ecosystem. However, plantation of wetland tree species such as Hijol (*Barringtonia acutangula*), Karoch (*Pongamia pinnata*), Barun (*Crataeva nurvala*), and Baladumur (*Ficus heterophylla*) can restore the swamp forests in the haor reed land. Thus, plantation in the haor reed land is another attribute of this study. This attribute has two levels: plantation with 25 m distance and plantation with 50 m distance.

Historically, during the winter months, residents of Tanguar Haor used to graze their cattle in fallow land of the haor. Local habitants still have the privilege of grazing their cows and goats there (Chowdhury 2008). But unlimited access to this valuable natural resource has created ecological imbalance. It is required to be kept under control in a planned manner which can contribute in restoring the biodiversity in future. Thus, license/right for grazing the cattle in the hoar is the third attribute of this study. It has three levels: 15 days, 30 days, and 45 days in the winter months.

Payment for any good or service can ensure the quality of that good or service and, hence, the level of social well-being. Thus, this study sets its fourth attribute as payment for fishing and grazing. Under the payment system, it is required for all fishermen to be registered for legal participation in fishing activities. Payment for the fishing permit attribute has three levels: Tk[9] 30,000, Tk 40,000, and Tk 45,000. Table 15.1 shows the different attributes with their respective levels.

**Table 15.1**
*Attributes and levels*

| *Attribute* | *Current levels* | *Improvement levels* |
| --- | --- | --- |
| Fishing control | No measures | Fishing control every other week between October and May, Fishing control every other month between June and September |
| Plantation at haor reed land | No measures | Plantation with 25 m distance, plantation with 50 m distance |
| Grazing permit for cattle | No measures | 15 days grazing, 30 days grazing, 45 days grazing |
| Payment for fishing and grazing | No measures | Tk 30,000, Tk 40,000, Tk 45,000 |

*Source:* Prepared by the author based on the findings of FGD, 2014.

**Table 15.2**
*An example of choice task*

| *Option example* | *Option A* | *Option B* | *Status quo* |
| --- | --- | --- | --- |
| Fishing control | Every other week | June to September | No change |
| Plantation at haor reed land | 50 m | 25 m | No change |
| Grazing permit for cattle | 30 days | 45 days | No change |
| Payment for fishing and grazing permit | 30,000 Tk. | 30,000 Tk. | No change |
| Your choice (please tick one only) | A ☐ | B ☐ | I would not want either A or B ☐ |

## Experimental Design

Experimental design is concerned with developing choice sets efficiently. In this study, four attributes have been used as stated above. A full factorial design, which includes all possible combinations of attributes and levels, resulted in 36 possible combinations. Software R was used for this purpose. According to the orthogonal design principle, by using fractional design, it has been randomly reduced to 16 for four versions of questionnaires and each version contains four combinations with three alternatives (options) including the status quo (for more details, see Table 15.2). Each respondent answered the choice cards twice.

## Questionnaire Development

This study followed the US National Oceanic and Atmospheric Administration (NOAA) and Food and Agriculture Organization (FAO) guidelines for the layout of its questionnaire. It was split into three parts. The first (warm up components) dealt with asking questions about the respondents' attitudes and observations about the state of Tanguar Haor and its natural resources, the second part focused on WTP through CE, and the last part included the SED data (e.g., income, age, educational attainment, kinds of captured fish per day in kg, and family size) of the respondents. CE, like the final version of questionnaire used in this study, followed the learnings from the pilot survey and FGD. The questionnaire was made in English but interviews were conducted in the local language, Bangla.

## Sampling Technique

To represent the population as a whole, a complete and accurate sample framework is necessary. In this study, households were the sample units and the sample frame was a set of fisherfolks. The economic agent "household" is taken into account for the decisions being taken at the household level. Usually a male member (father or eldest son) of household was interviewed after considering two distinct characteristics: He was the (solo or one of the) main earning members and he exercised substantial authority over family decisions. This study followed the purposive sampling technique. The purposive sampling method includes peoples' interest and excludes those who do not fulfil the research objectives. The advantage of purposive sampling is limitless. A researcher can eliminate the respondent who is not suitable for the survey and vice-versa. The surveys involved 452 households, of which 418 household representatives agreed to participate in the survey and respond to the questionnaire (response rate was 92%).

# Results and Discussion

## Definition of Variables

Definition of different attributes and SED variables used in the basic and extended models of this study are presented in Table 15.3.

## Estimation and Discussion of Results

To estimate the WTP for improved aquatic ecosystem and watershed management in the Tanguar Haor wetland and their attributes, the logit model with different forms was developed by using NLOGIT 4.0 software. Results for all 418 respondents from the logit models have two forms—random PRL (basic) model and MNL (extended) model, which are shown in Table 15.4.

### Random Parameter Logit or Basic Model

Basic model shows results only when the attributes of CE are included in the estimation involving econometrics. The coefficients are interpreted as the parameters of the indirect utility function, although the fact that they are confounded by a scale parameter means that one cannot directly interpret their numerical value. All attributes in the basic model are statistically significant except a few at conventional levels (at 1%, 5%, and 10% levels) with expected signs.

It is expected that the signs of fishing control and grazing permit for cattle should be negative because it affects the income and cattle food of the fishermen. But the results reveal exactly the opposite. At the time of pilot survey, FGD, and face-to-face interviews, most of the respondents and stakeholders had put more

**Table 15.3**

*Definition of attributes and variables*

| Attribute/Variable | Definition |
|---|---|
| ASC | Alternative specific constant (1: the alternative with changes and 0: the status quo) |
| fcr | Fishing control every other week during October to May, fishing control every other month during June to September |
| plt | Plantation at haor reed land with 25 m distance and with 50 m distance |
| gpc | Grazing permit for cattle 15 days grazing, 30 days grazing, 45 days grazing |
| pfg | Payment for fishing and grazing permit Tk 30,000, Tk 40,000, and Tk 45,000 |
| inc | Respondent's monthly income |
| age | Respondent's age |
| edu | Respondent's educational level (Illiterate: 0, Primary: 1, Secondary: 2, Higher secondary: 3, undergraduate or graduate: 4) |
| hhs | Respondent's household size (family size) |
| kcf | Kinds of captured fish per day in kg |

**Table 15.4**
Estimated models for the improved aquatic ecosystem and watershed management

| Model | Random PRL model | | | MNL model | | |
|---|---|---|---|---|---|---|
| Variables | Coefficient | Standard error | $P-Z>z$ | Coefficient | Standard error | $P-Z>z$ |
| ASC | 1.63400*** | 0.67031 | 0.0000 | −1.72139*** | 0.73062 | 0.0103 |
| fcr | 0.37131*** | 0.59123 | 0.0000 | 0.39316** | 0.60451 | 0.0351 |
| plt | 0.51101*** | 0.40934 | 0.0000 | 0.51270*** | 0.57971 | 0.0000 |
| gpc | 0.66079*** | 0.70935 | 0.0000 | 0.67127*** | 0.98903 | 0.0000 |
| pfg | −0.47034*** | 0.52319 | 0.0000 | −0.47377*** | 0.52361 | 0.0000 |
| inc | | | | 0.78412** | 0.40789 | 0.0446 |
| age | | | | 0.90185 | 0.41101 | 0.1790 |
| edu | | | | 0.61872* | 0.11402 | 0.1094 |
| hhs | | | | 0.78094*** | 0.14795 | 0.0001 |
| kcf | | | | 0.09401* | 0.60985 | 0.0609 |
| Log-likelihood | −377.0980 | | | −341.6288 | | |
| Pseudo R-squared | | 0.565853 | | | 0.230911 | |
| Akaike info criteria (AIC) | | 0.636552 | | | 0.507791 | |
| No. of observation (n) | | 418 | | | 418 | |

Income: Mean = 153911; Standard deviation = 121.589; Min. value: 30000; Max. value: 700000.

Age: Mean = 40.85650; Standard deviation = 9.088471; Min. value: 20; Max. value: 70.

Education level: Mean = 1.17225; Standard deviation = 1.40424; Min. value: 0; Max. value: 4.

Family size: Mean = 5.13397; Standard deviation = 1.52591; Min. value: 2; Max. value: 8.

Captured fish (kg/day): Mean = 17.29457; Standard deviation = 7.90410; Min. value: 1; Max. value: 177.

*Note:* ***Significant at 1% (0.01), **Significant 5% (0.05), and *Significant 10% (0.10).

emphasis on control of fishing and grazing permits. In particular, they argued that practice of uncontrolled fish harvest and grazing at the breeding and spawning seasons and pre-monsoon season is harmful for the aquatic ecosystem of the Tanguar Haor. Given this, positive signs of fishing control and grazing permit in the basic model are to be expected. Positive signs of the coefficients of fishing control and plantation at Haor reed land imply that the probability of choosing an alternative scenario with changes in attribute improvements will increase for the levels of these attributes increasing and vice-versa. The probability of choosing an alternative increases either as the levels of desirable attributes in that alternative rise or the levels of undesirable attributes fall relative to the levels of the attributes in other alternatives (Bennett and Blamey 2001). The negative sign of the coefficients of the grazing permit of cattle and payment for fishing permit indicates that higher payment and utility are negatively correlated. The value of Pseudo R-squared (goodness of fit) of 0.565853 implies that 56.6 per cent of the total variation in the outcome variable (respondent utility) can be explained by the variation of attributes of this model.

## Multinomial Parameter Logit or Extended Model

In many cases, heterogeneity in preferences within the population is expected. The MNL model allows more flexibility and continuous form of preference heterogeneity. In addition, this model overcomes the independence of the irrelevant alternative (IIA) assumption. A large number of SED variables were proposed to be included in the extended model based on the standard consumer theory. Like the basic model, all variables are significant except a few at the 1 per cent, 5 per cent, and 10 per cent levels. The coefficients of an alternative specific constant along with monthly income, educational level, and captured fish indicate it. The coefficients of an alternative specific constant along with family size are significant at different levels. This indicates that SED characteristics are the important determinants of the choice of alternative scenario of improvements. A positive coefficient of monthly household income indicates that as household income increases, the probability of choice improvement scenario option also increases and vice-versa. Educational level and captured fish also hold the same characteristics like household income. On the other hand, a negative coefficient of family size indicates that the family size and the probability of choice improvement scenario move in the opposite directions. But we cannot say anything about the age as it is not significant at either levels.

The result of the MNL model is better than the random PRL model. But, the MNL model has lower pseudo R-squared value (0.230911) which does not seem to fit well for a discrete choice model. But it has been argued that pseudo R-squared between 0.2 and 0.4 is adequate and does not give scope to reject the estimated results (Agimass and Mekonnen 2011; Birol et al. 2005). The pseudo R-squared of the random PRL model is 0.230911 and this is considered as a well-fitted model. The value Pseudo R-squared (goodness of fit) of 0.230911 implies that 23.1 per cent of the total variation in outcome variable (respondent utility) can be explained by the variation of attributes and other SED variables of this model.

## Marginal Willingness to Pay

Due to the higher value of goodness of fit, this study depended upon the random PRL to estimate the MWTP and economic welfare. When the attribute being sacrificed is a monetary one, the trade-off estimated is known as implicit price or MWTP for the attribute in question (Bennett and Blamey 2001). It indicates the amount of money respondents are willing to pay for an improvement in the environmental attribute (Agimass and Mekonnen 2011). MWTP expresses the amount of money respondents are willing to pay for an improvement in the environmental attribute. MWTP has a significant role for policymaking (Agimass and Mekonnen 2011). MWTP for three attributes of per household for improvement aquatic ecosystem and watershed management in the Tanguar Haor is estimated using Equation 6. The estimated results are presented in Table 15.5.

## Estimation of Welfare Effects

The main purpose of a CE is to estimate the welfare effects of change in the attributes (Alpizer, Carlsson, and Martisson 2001). Economic welfare management involves an investigation into the difference between

**Table 15.5**
Marginal willingness to pay for the attribute

| Attribute | Coefficient | Standard error | P\|−Z\|>z |
|---|---|---|---|
| Plantation | 1.086469363 | 1.1300 | 0.0000 |
| Fishing control | 0.789450185 | 0.7823 | 0.0000 |
| Grazing permit for cattle | 1.404919845 | 1.3558 | 0.0000 |

the utilities of the individual that could be achieved under the status quo and alternatives scenarios (Agimass and Mekonnen 2011; Bennett and Blamey 2001). In order to undertake an analysis of this nature, this study assumed a simple utility function by imposing a constant marginal utility of income. However, it depends upon purely discrete choices. For example, in the case of fishing control or grazing permit experiment of Tanguar Haor, the welfare measures were dependent on what has been included in the survey.

This study used a few alternative scenarios in its CE. The lower scenario includes the following: fishing control every other month during June to September; plantation at haor reed land with 25 m distance; and 15 days grazing permit for cattle. On the other hand, the upper scenario includes the following: fishing control every other week during October to May; plantation at haor reed land with 50 m distance; and 45 days grazing permit for cattle (for more details, see Table 15.1). The reported WTP for the scenario indicate the amount that respondents are willing to pay in order to experience an improvement in their utility (which results from a movement from the status quo to the changed alternative scenarios). The total WTP was estimated for two improvement scenarios presented as

- Moderate (improvement): Fishing control every other week during October to May; Plantation with 25 m distance; and 30 days grazing permit.
- Upper (improvement): Fishing control every other month during June to September; Plantation with 50 m distance; and 45 days grazing permit.

Using Equation 5, the estimated result of welfare effects is shown in Table 15.6.

## Summary and Conclusions

Wetland conservation is typical of many environmental issues where non-use value may be highly significant. The lack of recognition of non-use and other components of value by markets and other decision-making processes is a major cause of degradation or depletion of wetlands like Tanguar Haor. To determine the values of wetlands (for making a case for its protection), CE is one non-market valuation approach. In this chapter, it was applied to estimate the value of the aquatic ecosystem and other resources of the Tanguar Haor wetland. Preferences of fisherfolks were examined by focusing on three environmental attributes—fishing control,

**Table 15.6**
Estimation of welfare effects (economic surplus)

| Alternative improvement scenario | WTP for the scenario |
|---|---|
| Moderate scenario | Tk 63783.64587 |
| Upper scenario | Tk 95675.46881 |

plantation at haor reed land, and grazing permit for cattle. Furthermore, a monetary attribute, payment, for fishing and grazing was also included in the CE. The study limited the number of alternatives and attributes which helped in reducing the task complexity (Agimass and Mekonnen 2011). The result indicated that a grazing permit for cattle was highly valued as compared to plantation. It was also found that a number of SED attributes have a positive impact on the probability of opting for one of the improvement scenarios.

The results make a clear case for the government to take immediate action against harvesting of mother fish during the breeding season, as well as to ensure more plantation that are helpful for fish, reptile, amphibians, mammals, birds, and other endangered species, apart from controlling grazing through permits. For sustainable utilization of the fish stock, sound and effective management needs to be given more priority. In that perspective, co-management is perhaps the only possible and, therefore, the suggested approach to alleviate the decline of the fish stock. Lastly, it is necessary to revise the existing National Wetland Policy of Bangladesh to protect the ecosystem of Tanguar Haor in both quantitative and qualitative terms, which is a necessary condition for ensuring livelihood sustainability of the fisherfolks of this haor.

## Notes

1. Haors are bowl-shaped depressions of considerable aerial extent lying between the natural levees of rivers or high lands of the northeast region of Bangladesh. In most cases, haors have formed as a result of peripheral faulting leading to the depression of haor areas. During the wet season, the haors are full of water, but during the dry season, they dry up (Bangladesh Haor and Wetland Development Board 2012).
2. The fishery is operating at or close to an optimal yield level, with no expected room for further expansion (FAO 2005).
3. The fishery is being exploited at above a level which is believed to be sustainable in the long term, with no potential room for further expansion and a higher risk of stock depletion/collapse (FAO 2005).
4. Catches are well below historical levels, irrespective of the amount of fishing effort exerted (FAO 2005).
5. Catches are again increasing after having been depleted (FAO 2005).
6. Local name of fish farm in Bangladesh is *gher*.
7. *Upazila* is a small administrative unit of Bangladesh (sub-district).
8. Beels are shallow lakes or lake-like wetland with static water. Sometimes these are perennial but more often seasonal. The water surfaces are contiguous with the groundwater table and are sustained from groundwater to a large extent. Lake-like wetland is popularly known as Beel in eastern Indian states of West Bengal, Assam, and Bangladesh.
9. Tk. is stands for Taka (Currency of Bangladesh).

## References

Agimass, F., and A. Mekonnen. 2011. "Low-income Fishermen's Willingness-to-Pay for Fisheries and Watershed Management: An Application of Choice Experiment to Lake Tana, Ethiopia." *Ecological Economics* 71 (2011): 162–70.

Alam, A.B.M.S., M.S.M. Chowdhury, and I. Sobhan. 2012. *Biodiversity of Tanguar Haor: A Ramsar Site of Bangladesh*: Vol. I. *Wildlife*. Dhaka: IUCN.

Alpizer, F., F. Carlsson, and P. Martisson. 2001. "Using Choice Experiments for Non-market Valuation." Working Papers in Economics No. 52, Gothenburg University, Gothenburg.

———. 2003. "Using Choice Experiments for Non-market Valuation." *Economic Issues* 8(1): 83–110.

Bangladesh Haor and Wetland Development Board. 2012. *Master Plan of Haor Areas*: Vol. 2. *Main Report*. Dhaka: Ministry of Water Resources, Government of the People's Republic of Bangladesh.

Bennett, J., and R. Blamey. 2001. "The Choice Modeling Approach to Environmental Valuation." In *New Horizons in Environmental Economics,* edited by J. Bennett, R. Blamey, E.O. Wallace, and F. Henk. Cheltenham, UK: Edward Elgar Publishing Limited.

Bergmann, A., N. Hanley, and R. Wright. 2006. "Valuing the Attributes of Renewable Energy Investments." *Energy Policy* 34 (9): 1004–14.

Bird Life International. 2012. "Important Bird Areas Factsheet: Tanguar Haor and Panabeel." Available at: www.bird-life.org (accessed on 27 April 2017).

Birol, E., K. Karousakis, and P. Koundouri. 2005. "Using a Choice Experiment to Estimate the Non-use Values of Wetlands: The Case of Cheimaditida Wetland in Grace." Environmental Economy and Policy Research Discussion Paper Series, Department of Land Economy, University of Cambridge, UK.

BNH. 1997. "Survey of Flora." In *Draft Final Report: Tanguar Haor and Narikel Jinjira*, Vol. 1. Dhaka: Bangladesh National Herbarium, National Conservation Strategy Implementation Project 1, Ministry of Environment and Forest, GoB.

Chowdhury, A.H. 2008 "The State of Community Based Sustainable Management of Tanguar Haor, What Measures Are to Be Taken?"

De Graaf, M. 2003. "Lake Tana Piscivorous Burbus (Cyprinidae, Ethiopia): Ecology, Evolution, and Exploitation." Doctorol Thesis, Experimental Zoology, Wageningen University, The Netherlands. Available at: http://library.wur.nl/WebQuery/wurpubs/fulltext/121409

DoZ. 1997. *Final Report (Draft) on Survey of Fauna (Narikel Jinjira and Tanguar Haor)*. Vol. 1. Dhaka: National Conservation Strategy Implementation Project 1, Department of Zoology, University of Dhaka, Ministry of Environment and Forest, GoB.

FAO. 2005 "Review of the State of World Marine Fisheries Resources." Available at: ftp://ftp.fao.org/docrep/fao/007/y5852e/Y5852E23.pdf (accessed on 27 April 2017).

Gieson, W., and S.M.A. Rashid. 1997. "Management Plan for Tanguar Haor, Bangladesh." *NCSIP-1*. Dhaka: Ministry of Environment and Forests.

GoB. 2004. *Tanguar Haor Wetland, Biodiversity Conservation Project*. Dhaka: Ministry of Environment and Forests, Government of the People's Republic of Bangladesh.

Haider, M.S. 2013 "Impact of Community-based Natural Resources Management and Co-management on the Livelihoods of People in the Hakaluki Haor Area." Available at: http://ewcbookstore.org/fox/2013connectingcommunities11hakalukihaor.pdf (accessed on 27 April 2017).

Hanemann, W.M. 1982. "For Marginal Welfare Measures Discrete Choice Models." *Economics Letters* 13 (2–3): 129–36.

Hanley, N., S. Mourato, and R.E. Wright. 2001. "Choice Modeling Approaches: A Superior Alternative for Environmental Valuation." *Journal of Economic Surveys* 15 (3): 435–62.

International Federation of Surveyors. 2010. *Spatial Planning in Coastal Regions: Facing the Impact of Climate Change*. Edited by I. Boateng. Copenhagen, Denmark: International Federation of Surveyors. Available at: www.fig.net/resources/publication/figpub/pub55/figpub55.asp (accessed on 13 February 2015).

IUCN. 2011. *Biodiversity of Tanguar Haor: A Ramsar Site of Bangladesh*: Vol. I. *Wildlife (Amphibians, Reptiles, Birds and Mammals)*. Available at: www.iucn.org/bangladesh (accessed on 27 April 2017).

———. 2015. "Tanguar Haor Management Plan Framework and Guidelines." Dhaka, Bangladesh. Available at: portals.iucn.org/liberary/fiels/documents/2015-052.pdf

JDR. 2015. "Action Research for Policy Reforms to Enable Improved Community Co-management of Wetlands in Bangladesh." Available at: https://www.winrock.org/wp-content/uploads/2016/05/Call-for-JDR-3RD-Wetland-Policy-Research-Proposals-3.pdf (accessed on 27 March 2015).

Karim, A. 1993. "Plant Diversity and Their Conservation in Freshwater Wetlands." In *Freshwater Wetlands in Bangladesh: Issues and Approaches for Management,* edited by A. Nishat, Z. Husain, M.K. Roy, and A. Karim, 75–103. Gland, Switzerland: The World Conservation Union.

Lancaster, K. 1966. "A New Approach to Consumer Theory." *Journal of Political Economy* 74 (2): 132–57.

Louviere, J.J., D. Hensher, and J. Swait. 2000. *Stated Choice Methods: Analysis and Application*. Cambridge: University Press.

Manski, C. 1977. "The Structure of Random Utility Models." *Theory and Decision* 8 (3): 229–54.

McFadden, D. 1974. "Conditional Logit Analysis of Qualitative Choice Behavior." In *Frontiers in Econometrics*, edited by P. Zarembka. New York: Academic Press.

NERP (Northeast Regional Water Management Project/FAP6). 1993. *Wetland Resources Specialist Study (Final draft)*. Dhaka: Canadian International Development Agency (CIDA).

Nguyen, T.C., J. Robinson, S. Kaneko, and S. Komatsu. 2013. "Estimating the Value of Economic Benefits Associated with Adaptation to Climate Change in a Developing Country: A Case Study of Improvements in Tropical Cyclone Warning Services." *Ecological Economics* 86: 117–28.

Nishat, A. 1993. "Freshwater Wetlands in Bangladesh: Status and Issues." In *Freshwater Wetlands in Bangladesh: Issues and Approaches for Management*, edited by Ainun Nishat, Z. Hussain, M.K. Roy, and A. Karim, 9–21. Gland: IUCN–The World Conservation Union.

Nuruzzaman, A.K.M. 1997. "Towards Sustainable Development: The National Conservation Strategy of Bangladesh." *NCS Implementation Project 1* (Draft Final Report). Dhaka: Ministry of Environment and Forest.

Ramsar Convention Secretariat (RCS). 2010. "Wise Use of Wetlands: Concepts and Approaches for the Wise use of Wetlands." *Ramsar Handbooks for the Wise Use of Wetlands*. 4th ed., Vol. 1. Gland: Ramsar Convention Secretariat.

*The Daily Star*. (2008, December 27). "A Sample Matter of the Environment." *The Daily Star*, 16, Dhaka, Bangladesh.

Uddin, M.R., M.G.U. Miah, M.S.I. Afrad, H. Meraj, and M.S.H. Mandal. 2015. "Land Use Change and Its Impact on Ecosystem Services, Livelihood in Tanguar Haor Wetland of Bangladesh." *Scientia* 12 (2): 78–88.

# 16

# Impact of Land Use and Land Cover Changes on Physical Space for Fishers in Kanyakumari Coast, India*

Priya Parasuram, Rajakumari S., and Ramachandra Bhatta**

## Introduction

Coastal population in India is around 300 million, accounting for one-fourth of the total population of the country. Population in coastal areas of India is growing at the rate of 2.0 per cent, much higher than the average annual population growth rate of 1.5 per cent during 2001–2011. The 73 coastal districts (out of a total of 593 districts of the country) have a share of 20 per cent of the national population living within 50 km of the coastline. The coast also includes 77 cities and towns, including some of the largest and most dense urban agglomerations—Mumbai, Kolkata, Chennai, Kochi, and Visakhapatnam. There are 13 major ports and 187 minor ports in addition to 2 more planned along India's 7,516-km coastline (including island territories). India is the sixth largest producer of fish with an annual potential yield of 3.92 million tonnes FRAD, CMFRI 2016. An estimated 200,000 traditional crafts carry out traditional fishing, and there are about 35,000 mechanized fishing boats that are enhancing their fishing capacity annually (ibid.).

Meyer and Turner (1992) show that the human impact on environment is a product of not only the number of people but also the level at which they consume and the character of material and energy flows in production and consumption. The role of human activities in altering the coastal ecosystem services and its impact on human well-being is the main focus of this chapter. Improved understanding of problems related

* This chapter is based on the research carried out as part of the in-house research study of the National Centre for Sustainable Coastal Management (NCSCM) under the World-Bank-aided Integrated Coastal Zone Management (ICZM) Project of the Ministry of Environment, Forests and Climate change, Govt. of India.

** The authors thank Ramesh Ramachndran, Director, NCSCM, for providing the facilities to carry out the research. The authors also thank Purvaja Ramachandran, Division Incharge (ISE Division), NCSCM, to extend all the support to publish this work, and Ahana Laxmi, NCSCM, for providing valuable suggestions for the improvement of an earlier draft of the chapter. We thank NCSCM project staff Mahalakshmi, Sundari, Karthi, Kumaran, Arun Bharath, Arumugam, and Rosy Siji for their help in developing and delineating the village maps and data analysis. However, all mistakes remain our own.

to coastal land management within the coastal regulation zone (CRZ) provides the foundation for evaluating the alternative options for decision-making (Bhat and Bhatta 2004). This chapter contributes to the understanding of how human activities affect coastal ecosystem in spite of the existence of a governing system. The land use changes and, hence, coastal ecosystem services are linked to broader demographic, economic, social, and political forces (Tobar 2012). The coastal land management decisions may result in trade-offs in the delivery of different ecosystem services. It is important to understand the consequences of such land use changes on the capacity of different ecosystems to provide services to poor coastal communities.

Coastal resources are increasingly being used for promoting economic growth and also as a sink for land-based pollutants. The dependence of coastal communities on diverse coastal ecosystems is acute in most of the developing countries, and erosion of the capacity of these resources would setback the prospects of tackling poverty. The Millennium Ecosystem Assessment (2005) pointed out that degradation of coastal ecosystems could have uneven impacts on poor communities. As per the 2010 Marine Census, it was estimated that 47 per cent of 4.0 million fishers in India live below the poverty line and most of them are traditional fishers (CMFRI 2010). Thus, any decline in the share of fish produced would lead to loss of income to the coastal community.

The social well-being approach for developing coastal management plan involves three main components, namely meeting basic human needs, freedom, and quality of life. The significant increase in coastal population, infrastructure development attracting settlements along the shoreline, rising fishing assets, fishing intensity, and income and tourism development are some of the factors of concern owing to their likely impact on coastal ecosystem goods and services. Therefore, it is important for coastal planners to consider differential impact on different stakeholder groups while preparing the management plan. This chapter focuses on the changes in the physical availability of space for occupation-related activities of the traditional fishing communities.

National environmental policy of government of India (Ministry of Environment, Forest and Climate Change 2006) has emphasized that

> [T]raditionally, village commons water sources, grazing grounds, local forests, fisheries, etc., have been protected by local communities from over-exploitation through various norms, which may include penalties for disallowed behaviour. M.S. Swaminathan Committee (2009) on Policy and legal framework for Integrated Coastal Zone Management (ICZM) has emphasized that the immediate need in conservation of the coastal areas is to protect the habitats of fishing communities. These communities are in double danger as well—ironically, from conservation and from development. On one hand, these communities are marginalized and even alienated from their lands because of the need for conservation in marine parks or forested islands and on the other, they are in jeopardy because of large development projects which displace them and take over their lands and livelihoods. Their land is today prized for tourism and high-end housing projects. Future policies for coastal area management must reverse these trends and find approaches to conserve and protect vulnerable ecosystems and secure livelihoods and habitats of its people.

The state is also promoting different types of development projects to cater to the needs of the increasing coastal population and also projects to provide infrastructure services. These developments are shrinking the space available for traditional activities and have increased vulnerability of the communities (Rodrigues 2010). Increasingly, the beach spaces traditionally used by fishing communities are leased out to private organizations for providing tourism services and maintenance of sanitation, which were hitherto maintained by the local self-governments.

## Methodology

Spatially explicit data on land cover and land use exist for most of the coast. Contiguous areas of a given land cover type can be delineated. It was decided to select a few villages within 500 m and a few outside 500 m from the high tide line (HTL) to understand the physical and socio-economic changes with regulatory institutions governing the coastal space allocation. The CRZ 1991 and 2011 imposes restrictions on buildings and constructions within 500 m, and hence it is expected that the fishers should be able to enjoy better physical space availability for their dwelling and traditional fishery-related activities within 500 m. The study utilizes the population census data for the coastal villages from 1991, 2001, and 2011 to delineate the temporal and spatial changes in the demographic, physical, and socio-economic changes in the coastal areas that are predominantly inhabited by fishers and other traditional coastal communities. In addition to the population census data for 1991, 2001, and 2011, Marine Census data for two successive periods, 2005 and 2010, were used to capture the socio-economic and demographic changes in the coastal fishing communities. The availability of per capita fishing space was estimated by dividing the fishers' population with unspoilt spaces such as landing centres, open spaces, and sandy beaches, presuming that they would be available for all traditional activities of fishers.

## Study Area

Located in the southern fringe of the Indian coast, the transition zone between the east and west coast, the Kanyakumari coast constitutes as an essential part of the coastal ecosystem for its fish, tourism, and services sector. Some of the villages in this region have undergone changes during the tsunami disaster in 2004 and economic growth thereafter. A set of fishing villages in Kanyakumari which are located within 500 m from the HTL and just outside 500 m (1 km from the HTL) are selected for a detailed study. Kanyakumari is a densely populated coastal district with the fishing community (all Catholic, mostly Mukkavars) living on a very thin strip of coast near the sea. In the present study, we selected 12 fishing villages for an in-depth analysis of shrinking fishing space for traditional fishing activities. The villages that were listed as fishing villages in the Marine Census report (CMFRI 2010) were selected. The fishing villages are densely populated and houses are often right near the HTL or bang on the seawall. The increasing population in fishing villages (and the prosperity of some sections) is resulting in some fishing families buying land in the nearby areas and moving out. According to the local fishers' association, in some parts, there is spill-over of the fishing villages into the neighbouring agrarian areas creating a new zone of mixed communities. However, in other areas, there is informal ban on fishing communities buying land in neighbouring agrarian villages. Fishing families face no problem in terms of housing permits on account of the CRZ, but there is a general shortage of land and severe congestion. As in other districts described earlier, here also the gaps on the coast between fishing villages are outside the control of the fishing community, and it is in these areas that sand mining and other non-permitted activities take place. The panchayats are seen as external bodies and fishing communities generally do not strongly identify with them. Table 16.1 provides the names of the fishing villages, area, total population, and population density in the 11 selected villages of Kanyakumari. Figure 16.1 provides a diagrammatical representation of the selected villages along the Kanyakumari coast for the present study.

## Results and Discussion

Understanding the relationship between population growth and land use/land cover changes, taking into account the historical rights of coastal communities, is the main focus of the present analysis. The study considers two decadal changes in the coastal village population density and land use/land cover changes for 11 coastal fishing villages of Kanyakumari, Tamil Nadu. The following section presents the results of the data analysis. The district has 22 coastal villages of sizes in the range of 4.55–22.22 sq. km.

**Table 16.1**

*Total population in Kanyakumari coastal villages*

| S. no. | Villages | Area (sq. km) | Total population (no.) | | Population density (no/sq. km) | |
|---|---|---|---|---|---|---|
| | | | *2001* | *2011* | *2001* | *2011* |
| 1. | Agasteeswaram | 9.68 | 4,632 | 7,638 | 478 | 789 |
| 2. | Dharmapuram | 13.98 | 19,684 | 6,196 | 1,408 | 443 |
| 3. | Ezhudeesam | 12.06 | 18,776 | 16,478 | 1,556 | 1,366 |
| 4. | Kadiapatnam | 21.22 | 16,428 | 26,589 | 774 | 1,253 |
| 5. | Kanyakumari | 11.88 | 8,228 | 9,773 | 692 | 822 |
| 6. | Keezhkulam | 14.61 | 12,403 | 13,097 | 848 | 896 |
| 7. | Kolachel | 4.69 | 10,176 | 9,836 | 2,169 | 2,097 |
| 8. | Madhusoodhanapuram | 15.8 | 14,842 | 5,928 | 939 | 375 |
| 9. | Manavalakuruchi | 12.54 | 10,412 | 10,969 | 830 | 874 |
| 10. | Tamaraikulam | 11.89 | 10,749 | 11,776 | 904 | 990 |
| 11. | Thengamputhur | 13.76 | 3,733 | 91 | 271 | 6.61 |
| | Average | 12.91 | 11,823.91 | 10,761 | 988 | 901 |

*Source:* National census data 2001 and 2011.

Kanyakumari is the second most densely populated district in Tamil Nadu. The high population density is one of the indicators of urbanization that is going on in this tourism area. Table 16.1 presents the details of the 11 selected fishing villages of Kanyakumari with the population and area of each of the selected village. The results show that the density has marginally declined from 988 to 901 during 2001–11. The shoreline change data (see the appendix) of all the selected villages clearly mentions that sea erosion/accretion could be the main reason for the reduction of the population (which would lead to migration to nearby places); this data shows a wide gap between 2001 and 2011 statistics at least in some villages.

The changes in the overall employment pattern of coastal villages of Kanyakumari reflect in the current macro-level changes that are happening in India. During the decade 2001–11, there was a marginal decline (0.62%) in the rural population of the coastal Kanyakumari indicating migration from rural to urban areas. Table 16.2 shows that the total number of people dependent on agriculture and allied activities have declined from 11 to 3 per cent during the period of two decades (1991–2011), whereas the percentage of population dependent on services (tourism) has doubled from 14 to 31 per cent indicating the growth of service sector as a potential source of employment with higher income opportunities. It is due to the scope of getting more income with less investment in a short span of time. With declining space and resources for crop activities and small-scale fishing, the local communities are experiencing loss of profitability in these occupations and are moving and opting for small-service-sector occupations. However, sustainability of such tourism services with increasing erosion and cultural crisis with large influx of tourists is not clearly identified.

During the last 10 years, the fishers' population (Marine Census CMFRI 2005 and 2010) in coastal villages have also increased in absolute terms, although in some of the villages there was decline in the fishing population. The villages located within 500 m have shown an average increase in the fishing population by 34 per cent and outside 500 m have shown an increase of 5 per cent. Thus, the tendency to move closer to the coast by fishers is very high in spite of restrictions imposed on construction activities by CRZ notifications. The

**Figure 16.1**
*Coastal villages of Kanyakumari district*

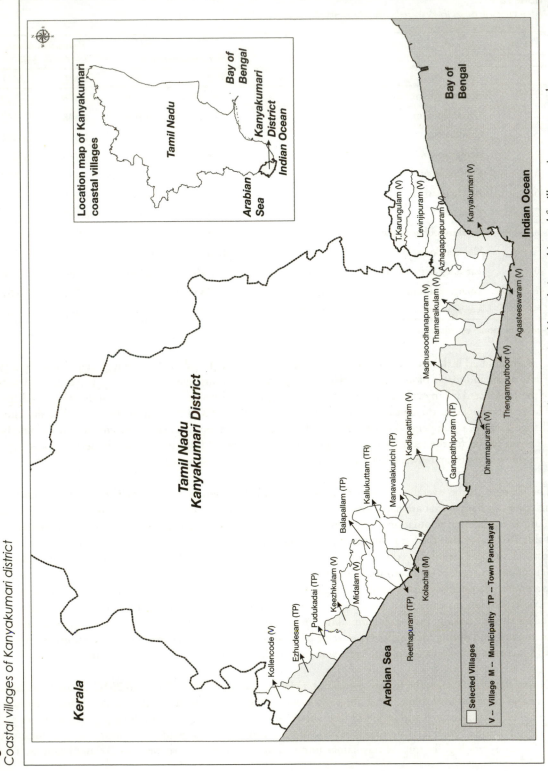

*Note:* This figure is not to scale. It does not represent any authentic national or international boundaries and is used for illustrative purposes only.

**Table 16.2**
*Structural changes in the employment*

| Year | 1991 | 2001 | 2011 |
|---|---|---|---|
| Total population | 80,307 | 130,063 (0.61) | 118,371 (–0.62) |
| Percentage of population engaged in agriculture and allied activities | 11.43 | 4.42 (–0.37) | 2.95 (–0.39) |
| Percentage of population engaged in Industrial workers | 2.88 | 1.81 (0.017) | 1.82 (–0.08) |
| Percentage of population engaged in services | 14.10 | 25.75 (1.95) | 30.67 (0.08) |
| Others (including non-workers) | 71.57 | 68.01 | 64.54 |
| Overall | | (–0.005) | (–0.13) |

*Source:* Population census data 1991, 2001, and 2011 and CMFRI census 2010.

effectiveness of controlling the movement of population towards the coast to reduce development pressure through CRZ and other regulations have not yielded desired results in Kanyakumari.

The areas of each village within and outside 500 m selected for the analysis are presented in Table 16.3. It indicates that although each village boundary and/or the size are different, the total area is same since the area was obtained exactly by dividing the total 1 km distance from the shoreline. From the table, it is very much directed that the villages within 500 m show a 17.77 per cent of change in the total population in 2010 compared to 2005, whereas in villages beyond 500 m, the growth rate is comparatively less. Since tourism activities are increasing in coastal villages and areas near to the shore, people are more focused on tourism as an allied activity than the primary sector. Further, this leads to more pollution and other environmental issues with no adequate waste management and sustainable techniques present. Moreover, it is very evident that the land use pattern has changed and the land area is utilized more for temporary development activities than for sustainable livelihood activities.

Table 16.4 presents the percentage changes in the land use/land cover in the selected villages of the district. The share of land under settlements, industries, and commercially and socially built-up area has increased significantly both in less than and greater than the 500 m zone. On the other hand, the share of vegetation, open spaces, water bodies, and other suitable spaces for fishery-related activities have declined during 2001–13. Further, the rate of shrinkage in the total available area for fishery-related activities is significantly high during 2005–13. The stakeholders were more concerned about the soil erosion and related issues in the coastal areas, as represented in the appendix and Figure 16.2, as it may lead to scarcity of working space for fishers in the coastal areas, which will definitely affect the productivity and efficiency of the fishing population.

The increase in the share of commercially built-up area is almost same for less than and greater than the 500 m zone (Table 16.5). It indicates that the regulatory measures, such as the CRZ, could not reduce the developmental activities. The changes in the per capita open area available for the overall population are presented in Table 16.6. There has been significant decline in the area available per person during the two decadal periods due to enormous increase in the built-up area. The declined rate of per capita open area representing that the common ecosystem services has declined significantly.

**Table 16.3**

*Changes in fisher's population in the fishing villages*

| Taluk | Distance from sea shore (m) | Fisher population | | |
|-------|------|------|------|------|
| | | 2005 (nos) | 2010 | % |
| Kanyakumari | <500 | 7,942 | 7,770 | –2.17 |
| Kesavanputhenthurai | <500 | 1,743 | 1,655 | –5 |
| Kovalam | <500 | 3,807 | 3,820 | 0.34 |
| Pallam | <500 | 2,582 | 2,429 | –5.9 |
| Periyakkadu | <500 | 898 | 886 | –1.3 |
| Pillaithoppu | <500 | 1,368 | 1,800 | 31.6 |
| Puthenthurai | <500 | 1,253 | 1,350 | 7.74 |
| Rajakkamangalamthurai | >500 | 3,998 | 4,367 | 9.23 |
| Kolachel | >500 | 8,136 | 9,947 | 22.3 |
| Kurumpannai | <500 | 3,121 | 4,272 | 36.9 |
| Melakadiyapattinam | <500 | 3,627 | 4,730 | 30.4 |
| Periyavillai | >500 | 1,695 | 2,877 | 69.7 |
| Inayam | <500 | 4,465 | 4,362 | –2.3 |
| Enayamchinnathurai | <500 | 1,115 | 5,128 | 360 |
| Ezhudesamchinnathurai | >500 | 5,129 | 1,031 | –80 |
| Keezhamidalam | <500 | 1,473 | 1,905 | 29.3 |
| Marthandanthurai | <500 | 4,985 | 6,374 | 27.9 |
| Melmidalam | <500 | 1,956 | 2,041 | 4.35 |
| Poothurai | <500 | 4,410 | 4,178 | –5.3 |
| Overall | <500 | 2,983 | 3,513.33 | 17.77 |
| Overall | >500 | 4739.5 | 4555.5 | –3.88 |

*Source:* Marine census data CMFRI (2010), ICAR (2005 and 2011). Growth rate has been calculated by using the formula (present population – past population)/past population × 100.

*Note:* The extreme values such as 360 per cent in Enayamchinnathurai have been excluded as outliers.

The average per capita open area for all the selected coastal villages has declined from 526.09 sq. m in 1991 per person to 80.94 sq. m in 2011, indicating a decline by 6–7 times.

The per capita area availability of open area per individual fisher has been estimated separately for less than 500 m from the HTL and greater than 500 m from the HTL and presented in Tables 16.7 and 16.8. Based on the data available on fishers' population and total open spaces (open spaces and sandy beaches) per capita area available for fishers' activities have been obtained by dividing the total open area by the total fishing population. The average per capita area available for an individual fisherman within 500 m of the HTL has declined from 5584.67 sq. m in 2001 to 1092.65 sq. m representing a decline by five times. On the other hand, the decline in the per capita availability in beyond 500 m from the HTL declined from 3399.36 sq. m to 445.15 sq. m representing a decline by eight times and is half of the area available compared to the CRZ area. Thus, the regulatory measures, such as the CRZ, has resulted in reduced intensity of development within the 500 m zone from the HTL compared to the area outside the CRZ (>500 m–1 km).

**Figure 16.2**
*Shoreline status of Kanyakumari coast*

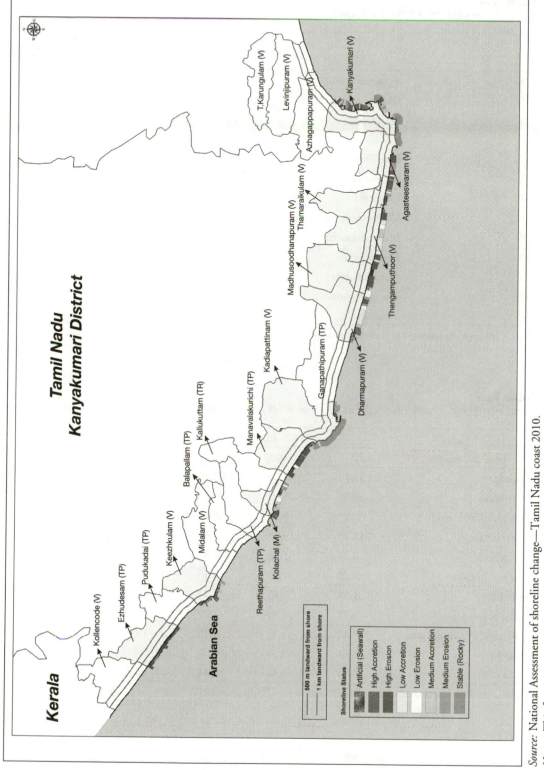

Tamil Nadu
*Kanyakumari District*

Kerala

**Arabian Sea**

Kollencode (V)
Ezhudesam (TP)
Pudukadai (TP)
Keezhkulam (V)
Midalam (V)
Balapallam (TP)
Kallukuttam (TR)
Manavalakurichi (TP)
Kadiapattinam (V)
Reethapuram (TP)
Kolachal (M)
Ganapathipuram (TP)
Dharmapuram (V)
Madhusoodhanapuram (V)
Thamaraikulam (V)
Thengamputhoor (V)
Agasteeswaram (V)
T.Karungulam (V)
Levinjipuram (V)
Azhagappapuram (V)
Kanyakumari (V)

500 m landward from shore
1 km landward from shore

**Shoreline Status**

Artificial (Seawall)
High Accretion
High Erosion
Low Accretion
Low Erosion
Medium Accretion
Medium Erosion
Stable (Rocky)

*Source:* National Assessment of shoreline change—Tamil Nadu coast 2010.

*Note:* This figure is not to scale. It does not represent any authentic national or international boundaries and is used for illustrative purposes only.

**Table 16.4**
Area of the selected fishing villages

| S. no. | Villages | Area (sq. km) | |
|--------|----------|---------------|-------------|
| | | <500 m | 500 m–1 km |
| 1. | Agasteeswaram | 1.81 | 1.87 |
| 2. | Dharmapuram | 197 | 2.04 |
| 3. | Ezhudeesam | 2.08 | 2.11 |
| 4. | Kadiapatnam | 1.60 | 1.46 |
| 5. | Kanyakumari | 3.09 | 2.92 |
| 6. | Keezhkulam | 1.46 | 1.56 |
| 7. | Kolachel | 1.42 | 1.22 |
| 8. | Madhusoodhanapuram | 0.88 | 0.94 |
| 9. | Manavalakuruchi | 1.71 | 1.78 |
| 10. | Reethapuram | 1.15 | 1.26 |
| 11. | Tamaraikulam | 1.14 | 1.04 |
| 12. | Thengamputhur | 2.15 | 2.26 |
| | Total Area | 20.46 | 20.46 |

*Source:* National Assessment of shoreline change—Tamil Nadu coast 2010.

**Table 16.5**
Land use/Land cover changes in the selected fishing villages (figures in percentages)

| Year/Land use area (%) | <500 m (20.46 sq. km) | | | >500 m (20.46 sq. km) | | |
|------------------------|------|------|------|------|------|------|
| | 2001 | 2005 | 2013 | 2001 | 2005 | 2013 |
| Settlements | 37.39 | 48.25 | 62.49 | 34.87 | 46.86 | 67.67 |
| Vegetation | 36.58 | 26.06 | 11.85 | 48.86 | 38.74 | 13.88 |
| Open land with scrub | 9.11 | 6.20 | 3.14 | 11.65 | 8.91 | 5.41 |
| Sandy area | 10.20 | 9.13 | 7.62 | – | – | – |
| Water body | 2.24 | 1.86 | 1.34 | 2.25 | 1.91 | 1.45 |
| Port and harbours | 1.29 | 1.50 | 2.30 | – | – | – |
| Industries | 1.00 | 1.75 | 2.93 | 0.50 | 1.15 | 2.10 |
| Social built-up area | 0.27 | 0.50 | 1.29 | 0.67 | 1.22 | 2.35 |
| Commercial built-up area | 1.88 | 3.35 | 5.40 | 1.81 | 3.26 | 5.66 |
| Quarries | 0.64 | 0.56 | 0.50 | 0.35 | 0.29 | 0.25 |
| Aquaculture | 0.69 | 1.38 | 1.84 | 0.67 | 1.09 | 1.49 |

*Source:* National Assessment of shoreline change—Tamil Nadu coast 2010.

**Table 16.6**

*Per capita open area in the selected villages for the overall population*

| Villages | Total open area available (sq. km) | | | Total population (nos.) | | | Per capita space available (in sq. m) | | |
|---|---|---|---|---|---|---|---|---|---|
| | 1991 | 2001 | 2011 | 1991 | 2001 | 2011 | 1991 | 2001 | 2011 |
| Agasteeswaram | 2.55 | 1.93 | 0.98 | 6,190 | 4,632 | 7,638 | 404.69 | 404.69 | 121.41 |
| Dharmapuram | 3.29 | 2.67 | 1.20 | 3,915 | 19,684 | 6,196 | 849.84 | 121.41 | 202.34 |
| Ezhudeesam | 3.06 | 1.82 | 0.94 | 17,803 | 18,776 | 16,478 | 161.87 | 80.94 | 40.47 |
| Kadiapatnam | 2.34 | 1.65 | 0.93 | 109,93 | 16,428 | 26,589 | 202.34 | 80.94 | 40.47 |
| Kanyakumari | 4.31 | 3.59 | 2.09 | 2,454 | 8,228 | 9,773 | 1740.15 | 445.15 | 202.34 |
| Keezhkulam | 2.42 | 1.97 | 0.91 | 13,490 | 12,403 | 13,097 | 161.87 | 161.87 | 80.94 |
| Kolachel | 0.43 | 0.40 | 0.40 | 4,640 | 10,176 | 9,836 | 80.94 | 40.47 | 40.47 |
| Madhusoodhanapuram | 1.11 | 0.80 | 0.38 | 1,550 | 14,842 | 5,928 | 728.43 | 40.47 | 80.94 |
| Manavalakuruchi | 2.95 | 2.56 | 1.64 | 10,643 | 10,412 | 10,969 | 283.28 | 242.81 | 161.87 |
| Tamaraikulam | 1.70 | 1.33 | 0.94 | 3,327 | 10,749 | 11,776 | 526.09 | 121.41 | 80.94 |
| Thengamputhur | 3.78 | 3.14 | 1.95 | 5,302 | 3,733 | – | 728.43 | 849.84 | – |
| Average | 2.54 | 1.99 | 1.12 | 7,300 | 11,823 | 11,828 | 526.09 | 242.81 | 80.94 |

*Source:* National Census data 2001 and 2011, CMFRI Census 2010.

**Table 16.7**

*Per capita availability of area/fisherman (Area<500 m from HTL)*

| Name of villages | Population (nos.)* | | | | Area available** | | | |
|---|---|---|---|---|---|---|---|---|
| | Total | | Fishing and allied | | Total area (in sq. km) | | Per capita space available (in sq. m) | |
| | 2001 | 2011 | 2001 | 2011 | 2001 | 2011 | 2001 | 2011 |
| Ezhudesam | 18,776 | 16,478 | 94 | 128 | 0.08 | 0.04 | 890.31 | 364.22 |
| Keezhkulam | 12,403 | 13,097 | 20 | 63 | 0.17 | 0.11 | 8,296.06 | 1,659.21 |
| Kolachel | 10,176 | 9,836 | 460 | 24 | 0.08 | 0.08 | 202.34 | 3,197.02 |
| Kadiapattinam | 16,428 | 26,589 | 505 | 847 | 0.37 | 0.20 | 728.43 | 242.81 |
| Dharmapuram | 19,684 | 6,196 | 1,387 | 191 | 0.48 | 0.31 | 364.22 | 1618.74 |
| Madusudhanapuram | 14,842 | 5,928 | 850 | 451 | 0.11 | 0.05 | 121.41 | 121.41 |
| Thengamputhoor | 3,733 | 91 | 16 | 1 | 0.74 | 0.59 | 46,134.20 | – |
| Thamaraikulam | 10,749 | 11,776 | 1,068 | 612 | 0.28 | 0.22 | 242.81 | 364.22 |
| Agasteeswaram | 4,632 | 7,638 | 99 | 45 | 0.29 | 0.10 | 2,954.21 | 2,266.24 |
| Kanniyakumari | 8,228 | 9,773 | 1,064 | 830 | 0.70 | 0.47 | 647.50 | 566.54 |
| Manavalakurichi | 10,412 | 10,969 | 189 | 310 | 0.21 | 0.15 | 1,092.65 | 485.62 |
| Average | 130,063 | 11,8371 | 5,752 | 3,502 | 0.32 | 0.21 | 5,584.67 | 1,092.65 |

*Sources:* *National census data 2001 and 2011.

      ** Shoreline change data, NCSCM 2010.

*Note:* For the purpose of arriving at the per capita available only area under open spaces and beaches have been included.

**Table 16.8**

*Per capita availability of area/fisherman (Area > 500 m–1 km)*

| Name of villages | Population (nos) | | | | Area available | | | |
| | Total | | Fishing and allied activities | | Total area (in sq. km) | | Per capita space available (in sq. m) | |
| | 2001 | 2011 | 2001 | 2011 | 2001 | 2011 | 2001 | 2011 |
|---|---|---|---|---|---|---|---|---|
| Ezhudesam | 18,776 | 16,478 | 94 | 128 | 0.06 | 0.04 | 687.97 | 364.22 |
| Keezhkulam | 12,403 | 13,097 | 20 | 63 | 0.08 | 0.05 | 3,844.52 | 849.84 |
| Kolachel | 10,176 | 9,836 | 460 | 24 | 0.04 | 0.02 | 80.94 | 849.84 |
| Kadiapattinam | 16,428 | 26,589 | 505 | 847 | 0.27 | 0.15 | 526.09 | 161.87 |
| Dharmapuram | 19,684 | 6,196 | 1,387 | 191 | 0.17 | 0.08 | 121.41 | 404.69 |
| Madusudhanapuram | 14,842 | 5,928 | 850 | 451 | 0.08 | 0.06 | 80.94 | 121.41 |
| Thengamputhoor | 3,733 | 91 | 16 | 1 | 0.48 | 0.30 | 29,865.83 | – |
| Thamaraikulam | 10,749 | 11,776 | 1,068 | 612 | 0.13 | 0.06 | 121.41 | 80.94 |
| Agasteeswaram | 4,632 | 7,638 | 99 | 45 | 0.11 | 0.05 | 1,133.12 | 1,092.65 |
| Kanyakumari | 8,228 | 9,773 | 1,064 | 830 | 0.34 | 0.24 | 323.75 | 283.28 |
| Manavalakurichi | 10,412 | 10,969 | 189 | 310 | 0.15 | 0.08 | 768.90 | 242.81 |
| Overall | 130,063 | 118,371 | 5.752 | 3,502 | 0.17 | 0.10 | 3,399.36 | 445.15 |

*Source:* National Census 2001 and 2011.

In the Kanyakumari coast, the number of non-mechanized units (families owning) located within 500 m has declined from 1,720 units in 2005 to 631 units in 2010 indicating the non-viability or inability to maintain and recover its potentialities. There has been a general decline in the number of non-mechanized fishing units in the country due to a decline in fish availability within the territorial waters. This may be due to overuse of mechanized boats in some villages which leads to exploitation of the available fish resources.

The changes in the location of fishing units (within and outside 500 m) and fishing intensity expressed in terms of different category of fishing (mechanized, motorized, and non-motorized) show the increasing need for accessing the coastal resources for their occupation. Most of the mechanized fishers who were hitherto outside the CRZ area have moved into the CRZ area, which is reflected in the data presented in Table 16.9. The number of mechanized units declined by 75 outside the CRZ, and the same increased by 40 units within the CRZ area. The data indicates that many of the small-scale fishers might have converted themselves into mechanized fishers and/or moved out of the fishing occupation due to a decline in the profitability and less availability of resources. The outboard engine fishing boats have increased by more than twofold outside the CRZ and by a small percentage within the CRZ. The results presented in Table 16.9 clearly show that there has been a drastic decline in traditional fishing units indicating a decline in the catch rate and, hence, indicating inclination towards outboard engine boats to enable going for fishing into longer distance and for longer duration.

## Conclusion

Land use/land cover changes modified by humans in response to specific development needs are the common reasons affecting the availability of coastal space for fishers' activities. Such changes also affect the coastal fish production, biodiversity, water availability, and other ecosystem services. This article presents an approach to

**Table 16.9**

*Distribution of fishing units in coastal zone of Kanyakumari*

| Within CRZ (<500 m) | 2005 | 2010 | % change |
|---|---|---|---|
| Mechanized | 141 | 181 | 28.37 |
| Outboard | 1,085 | 1,227 | 13.09 |
| Non-mechanized | 1,720 | 631 | −63.31 |
| Outside CRZ (>500 m–1 km) | 2005 | 2010 | % change |
| Mechanized | 112 | 38 | −66.07 |
| Outboard | 110 | 279 | 153.63 |
| Non-mechanized | 529 | 387 | −26.84 |

*Source:* Marine Census Report, CMFRI 2005 and 2010.

know the changes in coastal physical space availability for fishers. The macro-level change in physical space availability has been delineated through secondary and spatial data analysis. The results clearly indicate the declining availability of per capita physical space over the last 10 years in spite of decline in the number of traditional fishers due to growth of commercially built-up areas and decline in open spaces and vegetation. There has been a significant decline in the per capita availability of physical space both within and outside 500 m, although the rate of decline in less than 500 m-zone from the HTL was relatively less compared to that in the area in greater than 500 m. The analysis suggests that the rate of decline was accelerated in recent years indicating the vulnerability of coastal fishers to reduced space and declining benefits such as provisioning (fish, sand, and horticulture produce), regulating (controlling erosion, floods, and groundwater salinization), supporting (marine fish nursery grounds and biodiversity conservation), and cultural services (tourism, spiritual attachment to fishing as an occupation) provided by coastal and marine ecosystems to the coastal commons. It also indicates the decline in the reduction of provisioning and supporting services of the coastal ecosystem. A detailed assessment of the real status at the ground level and the factors affecting the accessibility and governance (social, economic, and religious) would be required to develop appropriate strategies to protect the livelihood opportunities of the coastal fishers. The literature suggests that the coastal ecosystem provides maximum number of services listed by the Millennium Ecosystem Assessment (UNEP 2006). Hence, efforts need to be initiated by authorities to reduce congestion of human activities along the coast in order to protect the flow of ecosystem services on a sustainable basis.

# Appendix

**Table A16.1**

*Shoreline status in the selected villages*

| S. no | Villages | Area (sq. km) | Total population (no.) 2001 | 2011 | Population density (no/sq. km) 2001 | 2011 | Shoreline status (between 2000 and 2010, in meters) | Avg. rate of change of shoreline |
|---|---|---|---|---|---|---|---|---|
| 1. | Agasteeswaram | 9.68 | 4,632 | 7,638 | 478 | 789 | Erosion, 29 m–62 m | Erosion, 3 m/yr–6 m/yr |
| 2. | Dharmapuram | 13.98 | 19,684 | 6,196 | 1,408 | 443 | Mostly Erosion, 26 m–83 m Patches of accretion, 17 m–119 m | Erosion, 3 m/yr–8 m/yr Accretion, 2 m/yr–12 m/yr |

(Table A16.1 *continued*)

(Table A16.1 continued)

| S. no | Villages | Area (sq. km) | Total population (no.) | | Population density (no/sq. km) | | Shoreline status (between 2000 and 2010, in meters) | Avg. rate of change of shoreline |
|---|---|---|---|---|---|---|---|---|
| | | | 2001 | 2011 | 2001 | 2011 | | |
| 3. | Ezhudeesam | 12.06 | 18,776 | 16,478 | 1,556 | 1,366 | Erosion, 60 m–112 m | |
| 4. | Kadiapatnam | 21.22 | 16,428 | 26,589 | 774 | 1,253 | Mostly rocky coast Patches of accretion on the southern end, 12 m–27 m patches of erosion on the northern side, 23 m–78 m | Accretion, 1 m/yr–3 m/yr Erosion, 2 m/yr–8 m/yr |
| 5. | Kanyakumari | 11.88 | 8,228 | 9,773 | 692 | 822 | Mostly erosion, 15 m–196 m patches of accretion, 12 m–53 m | Erosion, 2 m/yr–20 m/yr Accretion, 1 m/yr–5 m/yr |
| 6. | Keezhkulam | 14.61 | 12,403 | 13,097 | 848 | 896 | Mostly accretion besides seawalls, 18 m–135 m Patches of erosion, 12 m–17 m | Accretion, 2 m/yr–14 m/yr Erosion, 1 m/yr–2 m/yr |
| 7. | Kolachel | 4.69 | 10,176 | 9,836 | 2,169 | 2,097 | Mostly erosion, 16 m–138 m Patches of accretion, 15 m–21 m | Erosion, 2 m/yr–14 m/yr Accretion, 1.5 m/yr–2 m/yr |
| 8. | Madhusoodhanapuram | 15.8 | 14,842 | 5,928 | 939 | 375 | Erosion, 19 m–68 m | Erosion, 2 m/yr–7 m/yr |
| 9. | Manavalakuruchi | 12.54 | 10,412 | 10,969 | 830 | 874 | Erosion, 31 m–108 m | Erosion, 3 m/yr–11 m/yr |
| 10. | Tamaraikulam | 11.89 | 10,749 | 11,776 | 904 | 990 | Erosion, 17 m–38 m | Erosion, 2 m/yr–4 m/yr |
| 11. | Thengamputhur | 13.76 | 3,733 | 91 | 271 | 6.61 | Mostly erosion, 22 m–54 m Patches of marginal accretion, 15 m–37 m | Erosion, 2 m/yr–5 m/yr Accretion, 2 m/yr–4 m/yr |

*Source:* National Assessment of shoreline change—Tamil Nadu coast 2010.

*Classification*

Less than –5.0 m— High erosion

–5.0 m to –2.0 m—Medium erosion

–2.0 m to –0.5 m—Low erosion

–0.5 m to 0.5 m—Stable coast (or rocky)

0.5 m to 2.0 m—Low accretion

2.0 m to 5.0 m—Medium accretion

More than 5.0 m—High accretion

# References

Bhatt, Mahadev, and Ramachandra Bhatta. 2004. "Considering Aquacultural Externality in Coastal Land Allocation Decisions in India." *Environmental and Resource Economics* 29 (1).

CMFRI (Central Marine Fisheries Research Institute). 2010. *Annual Report.* Cochin: CMFRI.

Government of Tamil Nadu. "Coastal Erosion in Kaniyakumari District." Available at: http://www.kanyakumari.nic.in/seaerosion.html (accessed on 20 August 2013).

FRAD, CMFRI. 2016. "Marine Fish Landings in India," 2015, Technical Report, CMFRI, Kochi.

Meyer, William B., and Billie L. Turner. 1992. "Human Population Growth and Global Land Use/Cover Change." *Annual Review of Ecology and Systematics* 23 (1): 39–61.

Millennium Ecosystem Assessment. 2005. *Ecosystems and Human Well-being: Biodiversity Synthesis.* Washington, D.C.: World Resources Institute.

Ministry of Environment, Forest and Climate Change. 2006. *National Environment Policy.* New Delhi: Government of India.

———. 2009. *Report of the Expert Committee on Coastal Management Zone.* New Delhi: Government of India.

———. 2011. *Coastal Regulation Zone Notification.* New Delhi: Government of India.

Rodriguez, S. 2010. *Claims of Survival: Coastal Land Rights of Fishing Communities.* Bengaluru: Dakshin Foundation.

Tobar, Ingrid M. 2012. "Geo Statistical Analysis of Land Use Land Cover Changes and Population Growth Trends in the Komadugu—Yobe River Basin in Nigeria." PhD Thesis, University of Missouri, Kansas City.

UNEP (United Nations Environment Programme). 2006. "Marine and Coastal Ecosystems and Human Well Being. A Synthesis Report Based on the Findings of Millennium Ecosystem Assessment." Synthesis Report, UNEP, Washington, D.C.

# 17

# Adoption and Diffusion of Micro-irrigation Technologies in Gujarat, Western India: Do Institutions and Policies Matter?*

Chandra Sekhar Bahinipati and P.K. Viswanathan**

## Introduction

The state of Gujarat in western India, consisting of seven agro-climatic zones, is mostly covered by arid and semi-arid regions. While the state receives rainfall in a range of minimum 18 days (north-west arid region) to maximum 63 days (southern hills) in a year, almost 90 per cent of the total rainfall occurs during the monsoon season (Mehta 2013; Varshneya et al. 2009). High variability in temperature and rainfall is observed across the agro-climatic regions in the state (Hiremath and Shiyani 2012; Mehta 2013; Ray, Mohanty and Chincholokar 2009). As a result, the state has been experiencing frequent droughts over the years (Kishore 2013). Hiremath and Shiyani (2013), for instance, report that the state had 12 drought years between 1978 and 2008—a drought year at least once in every three years (Cenacchi 2014).

Despite the drought conditions along with looming water scarcity across regions, farmers had continued with intensive irrigation practices overtime. For example, the state had achieved an overall irrigation ratio (irrigated area as percentage of the gross cropped area) of 40 per cent by 2011–12, while it was hardly 7 per cent in the early 1960s (Government of Gujarat, hereafter, GoG 2008, 2013). Given the high inequality in the distribution of surface water across the state,[1] around 80–85 per cent of the total area was irrigated through groundwater sources (Kishore 2013; Shah 2009; Viswanathan and Pathak 2014). Since groundwater is a "common pool resource" with unregulated withdrawal as well as absence of marginal pricing for water, over-extraction

* This chapter forms part of a research study supported by South Asian Network for Development and Environmental Economics (SANDEE), Nepal.
** The authors would like to thank Professor Suresh Kumar, Tamil Nadu Agricultural University, for comments and suggestions on the earlier version. The earlier versions of the chapter were presented at the national seminar on "Role of public policy in development process: Emerging economic/social scenarios in the Indian economy," SPISER, Ahmedabad, India, and 12th Annual International Water Resource Economics Consortium Meeting, Washington, D.C. Earlier version of this manuscript is published in a working paper series of Gujarat Institute of Development Research, Ahmedabad, India. All views, interpretations, conclusions, and recommendations made in this chapter are those of the authors and not of those of the supporting and presently affiliated institutions. Usual disclaimers apply.

and inefficient allocation are quite widely observed in the state (Kishore 2013), thus reflecting Hardin's (1968) paradox of "tragedy of commons." As of 2011, the stage of groundwater development (SGWD)[2] in the state was around 67 per cent against 41 per cent in 2004, with four districts falling in over-exploited (critical) category and five districts falling under grey/semi-critical category (Bahinipati and Viswanathan 2016). Over the past several years, various studies have pointed about depletion of groundwater in many parts of western India, particularly in Gujarat (Kumar 2005; Narula et al. 2011). The impending water crisis, along with the emerging challenges of adverse environmental and climatic uncertainties, underscores the imperatives for adopting the water-saving technologies, while also maintaining high levels of farm production. Micro-irrigation system (MIS) is one of the interventions widely promoted by the state government in the recent years as part of the various water and energy supply and demand management measures[3] undertaken.

Micro-irrigation (MI), consisting of drip and sprinkler irrigation, is considered to be the pillar of "sustainable intensification" of farming (Fishman, Gulati and Li 2014). This is highly acceptable in regions experiencing water scarcity and over-exploitation of groundwater (Caswell and Zilberman 1985; Palanisami et al. 2011). Empirical evidences around the world suggest that MIS saves water up to 40 per cent to 80 per cent and enhances water use efficiency[4] (Palanisami et al. 2011; Saleth and Amarasinghe 2010). Apart from this, a large number of other benefits are also reported: reduced tillage requirement, energy use, labour cost, reduction in cost of well deepening and incidence of well failures, and increase in crop yields and fertilizer-use efficiency (Bahinipati and Viswanathan 2016; Fishman et al. 2014; Kumar and Palanisami 2011; Kumar and van Dam 2013; Kumar 2007, 2013; Kumar et al. 2004; Narayanamoorthy 2001, 2004, 2005; Palanisami, Palanichamy, and Shanmugam 2002; Verma, Tsephal, and Jose 2004; Viswanathan and Bahinipati 2015).

Given the positive externalities of adopting MI, the Government of India (GoI) has promoted it since the early 1980s[5] (see Bhamoriya and Mathew 2014). However, a significant trend in adoption was not achieved yet. For instance, only around 9 per cent of the total potential area was brought under MI as of 2010 (Palanisami et al. 2011), which had increased to 14 per cent in 2013 (Palanisami 2015). Based on the recommendation of the task force on MI set up in 2004, the GoI launched a centrally sponsored scheme on MI in 2006, and this was further revised in 2010 with the announcement of the "National Mission on Micro Irrigation (NMMI)." In particular, the task force recommended subsidizing farmers' capital cost and also suggested to provide greater flexibility to states in terms of designing institutions and subsidy disbursement (Pullabhotla, Kumar and Verma 2012).

In Gujarat, the state government had set up a special purpose vehicle (SPV), called the Gujarat Green Revolution Company (GGRC) limited in 2004–05, which acts as a nodal agency to promote MI across the state. In addition, the state government has evolved a differential subsidy policy such that amount of financial subsidy differs with respect to social groups (Schedule Caste [SC]/Schedule Tribe [ST]), geographical location, and marginal landholdings.

In this backdrop, this chapter aims to examine the role of institutional innovations and subsidy policy interventions in the diffusion of MI across the state in the recent years. It has larger policy implications as it investigates the effectiveness of NMMI's recommendations in terms of enhancing adoption of MI in the state. Rest of the chapter is organized as follows. In the next section, we present an overview of the policy and institutional interventions with respect to MI in Gujarat. It is followed by a section that includes a detailed analysis of adoption and diffusion of MI in the state. The chapter concludes with key findings and some policy recommendations.

# Micro-irrigation: Institutional Innovations and Subsidy Policy

As noted, the adoption of MI has been promoted by the GoI as part of the water demand management programme, especially in the water-starved states, namely, Gujarat, Rajasthan, Maharashtra, and Andhra Pradesh. The government has set up a three-tier system at the national, state, and district levels for the effective implementation of MI. Three committees were constituted at the national level to look into different tasks, namely, National Committee on Plasticulture Applications in Horticulture (NCPAH), executive committee on MI scheme, and the technical support group (TSG). The NCPAH is the central body responsible for enhancing adoption of MI across India. While the executive committee looks into overall activities of diffusion of MI, the TSG committee, consisting of experts from different disciplines, provides guidance in the technical matters (GoI 2014).

At the state level, State Micro Irrigation Committee (SMIC) was constituted under either the agriculture or the horticulture department. Some states also set up SPV to enhance adoption of MI. The main duty of this committee is to conduct baseline and feasibility studies and ensure smooth allocation of funds across the districts (GoI 2014). Under SMIC, District Micro Irrigation Committee (DMIC) is formed in each district. Like the SMIC, the activities of DMIC include reviewing district action plan, mobilizing credit requirement of the prospective MI adopters, monitoring and reviewing the physical and financial progress of the MI system, and reviewing the submission of utilization certificate by the implementing agency (GoI 2014). However, the modalities for promoting MI scheme are not the same across the states (Bassi 2013). While states such as Gujarat and Andhra Pradesh have their own SPV to promote MI (e.g., GGRC in case of Gujarat and Andhra Pradesh Micro Irrigation Project [APMIP] in Andhra Pradesh), either the state agriculture or the horticulture department is responsible for implementing the scheme in other states (Bhamoriya and Mathew 2014). Further, the subsidy scheme also varies across the states with regard to social groups, landholdings, and geographical location (Institute for Resource Analysis and Policy 2012). In the following, we provide a brief review of the institutional intervention and policies for the promotion of MI in Gujarat.

In Gujarat, the SPV, that is, the GGRC was formed in 2004–05 by the state government to promote adoption and diffusion of MI in the state—it is a joint initiative of the Gujarat State Fertilizer and Chemicals Ltd, Gujarat Narmada Valley Fertilizers Company Ltd, and the Gujarat Agro Industries Corporation Ltd. Figure 17.1 shows the processes of implementing MI scheme. As per the GGRC norms, farmers have to approach first to a recognized MI installation company, and after that, the respective company does a survey at the farm and estimates the total cost of installing the system. Also, the MI installation company takes the administrative responsibility and generates awareness—this reduces transaction cost to both government and consumer (Pullabhotla et al. 2012). Along with the survey record and cost estimates, the farmer makes an application to the GGRC, with the payment of remaining cost (i.e., beneficiary share) excluding the eligible subsidy amount. After verification of the documents, the GGRC places a work order to the concerned MI company with releasing 15 per cent of the total cost. There is third-party verification after the installation of MI and after that, 75 per cent of the total cost is released. The remaining 10 per cent is paid after 5 years—this is to make sure that the company provides the necessary "after installation" service for smooth working of the system (Bassi 2013).

Instead of implementing Pigouvian tax to control overuse of common pool resources, the governments, mostly in the developing nations including India, find it easy to provide subsidy for adoption of resource-efficient technologies, especially for water and energy, in order to reduce pressure on these resources (Fishman et al. 2014). Both the national and state governments provide subsidy on capital cost, which varies from ₹19,700 to ₹1,27,700/ha depending on the crops and the specific devices and gadgets installed.[6] It is reported that on an average, the cost of MI system installation incurred by the beneficiaries ranged between ₹54,457 and ₹72,086/ha for drip system and ₹20,481 to ₹28,171/ha for sprinkler system, depending on the cropping patterns, crop spacing, etc. (GoI, 2014). Figure 17.2 outlines the various subsidy programmes adopted by the government. All the farmers, irrespective of social group status, landholding, crops, and geographical location, are entitled to get subsidy of 50 per cent of capital cost of MI or ₹60,000/ha, whichever is lower,[7] of which, 40 per cent is provided by the national government, and the state government bears the remaining 10 per cent. Moreover, the farmers in the 54 notified dark-zone[8] talukas (defined as per GoG norms)[9] get additional 10 per cent subsidy for any crops since April 2012, that is, 60 per cent of capital cost or ₹60,000/ha, whichever is lower (Figure 17.2). To promote adoption of MI in dark-zone talukas, the government has withdrawn the restriction of electricity connection[10] for agriculture since 2012—it was made mandatory that the farmers adopt MI in order to get new electricity connection.[11] Given their poor

**Figure 17.1**

*Process of implementation of MIS under GGRC*

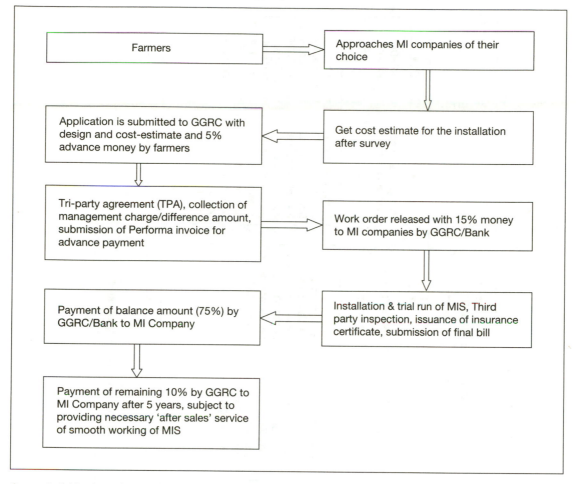

*Sources:* Pullabhotla et al. (2012); Bassi (2013).

socio-economic status, the tribal farmers in the 43 tribal talukas are entitled to get a subsidy of 75 per cent of capital cost of installing MI or ₹90,000/ha, whichever is lower since 2008.[12]

From January 2015, the GoG announced that all the SC and ST farmers in the state are eligible to avail 75 per cent of capital cost of MI or ₹90,000//ha, whichever is lower.[13] Though various studies have found credit constraint as one of the major determinants of MI adoption (Namara, Nagar and Upadhyay 2007; Palanisami et al., 2011), there were no separate financial incentives for small and marginal farmers. This has been a major reason for the lower adoption of MI in Gujarat in particular. Hence, an additional subsidy was announced since March 2015 for small and marginal farmers. But, still the subsidy is different between dark-zone and non-dark-zone talukas.[14] For instance, the small and marginal farmers in the non-dark-zone talukas are entitled to get subsidy of 60 per cent of installation cost of MI or ₹70,000, whichever is lower. Whereas, the farmers in the dark-zone talukas are entitled for a subsidy of 70 per cent of total capital cost of installing MI or ₹70,000, whichever is lower (see Figure 17.2).

In addition, the Gujarat Water Resource Development Corporation (GWRDC) also promotes installation of MI on the public tube wells owned by them, mostly in the north Gujarat districts of Banaskantha,

**Figure 17.2**
*Details of subsidy provided by Government of Gujarat and GGRC*

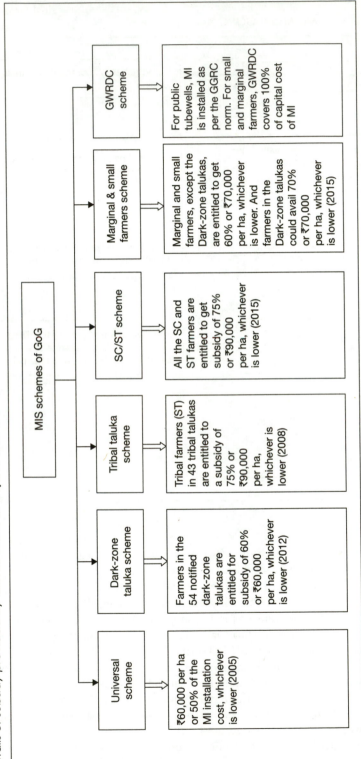

*Source:* Authors' figure based on various government orders (GOs) of GoG.

*Note:* Parenthetic figures indicate that the year in which the subsidy policy has been implemented.

Gandhinagar, Mehsana, Patan, and Sabarkantha. Under this scheme, small and marginal farmers were entitled to avail 75 per cent of total capital cost or ₹90,000, whichever is lower (Viswanathan and Bahinipati 2015), and currently, it is reported that the GoG subsidizes 100 per cent of cost of capital of pressurized irrigation network system (PINS) and MI installation on public tube wells (GWRDC, personal communication). Further, the GoG provides additional support for promoting MI scheme in the state. For instance, Gujarat Urja Vikas Nigam Limited (GUVNL) provides electricity connection on priority basis to the farmers adopting MI. To enhance adoption of MI in the command areas of surface irrigation schemes, the government supports for installation of PINS in the canal commands of Sardar Sarovar Project (SSP)—the entire cost of PINS installation is reported to be borne by the Sardar Sarovar Narmada Nigam Ltd. (SSNNL) and the capital cost of MI shared by both the government and the beneficiary farmers as per the GGRC norms (see Figure 17.2).

In the following sections, we analyse the status and trends in adoption of the different subsidy programmes for promoting MI across regions in the state under various institutional arrangements.

# Trends and Patterns of Diffusion and Adoption of MIS in Gujarat

## Micro-irrigation Adoption: Overall Scenario

It is reported that about 4.94 million ha area was covered under MI in India as of 2010, of which, 1.9 million ha was under drip irrigation (i.e., 38% of the total area) and 3 million ha under sprinkler irrigation (i.e., 62%; see Table 17.1). Among the states, Maharashtra occupied first position with a coverage of 0.9 million ha, accounting for 18 per cent of the total area under MI (see Table 17.1 and Figure 17.3).

The states Rajasthan and Andhra Pradesh occupied second and third positions, respectively. The total area reported under the MI in Gujarat was 0.41 million ha, and the state occupies sixth position in India. The area irrigated under drip systems was the highest, that is, 0.23 million ha accounting for 56 per cent of the total area under MI, which is much above the national average (38%) and similar to the patterns in the states such as Tamil Nadu, Maharashtra, and Andhra Pradesh. In terms of the total reported area under MI as proportion

**Table 17.1**

*Area under micro-irrigation in major states in India, 2010*

| Name of State | Drip irrigation ('000 ha) | (%) share | Sprinkler irrigation ('000 ha) | (%) share | Total MI ('000 ha) | % of total area under MIS |
|---|---|---|---|---|---|---|
| Andhra Pradesh | 505.21 | 66.29 | 256.91 | 33.71 | 762.12 (3) | 15.42 |
| Chhattisgarh | 6.36 | 6.23 | 95.74 | 93.77 | 102.10 (10) | 2.07 |
| Gujarat | 226.77 | 55.66 | 180.67 | 44.34 | 407.45 (6) | 8.24 |
| Haryana | 11.35 | 2.08 | 533.74 | 97.92 | 545.09 (5) | 11.03 |
| Karnataka | 209.47 | 35.20 | 385.58 | 64.80 | 595.05 (4) | 12.04 |
| Madhya Pradesh | 51.71 | 26.53 | 143.23 | 73.47 | 194.95 (7) | 3.94 |
| Maharashtra | 604.44 | 67.17 | 295.38 | 32.83 | 899.82 (1) | 18.21 |
| Rajasthan | 30.05 | 3.35 | 866.59 | 96.65 | 896.64 (2) | 18.14 |
| Tamil Nadu | 153.44 | 84.65 | 27.83 | 15.35 | 181.27 (8) | 3.67 |
| West Bengal | 0.25 | 0.16 | 150.20 | 99.84 | 150.44 (9) | 3.04 |
| India | 1897.28 | 38.39 | 3044.94 | 61.61 | 4942.22 | – |

*Source:* Sankaranarayanan et al. (2011).

*Note:* The figures in the parentheses indicate rank of the respective state.

**Figure 17.3**
*Share (%) of major states in area under MIS (2010)*

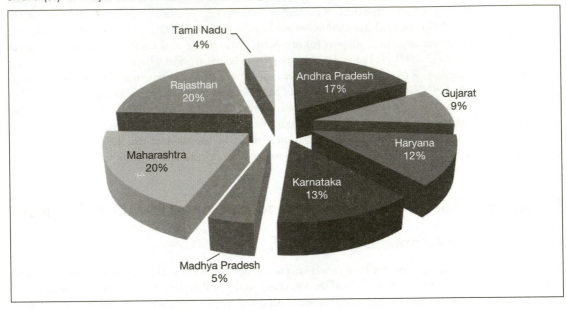

*Source:* Table 17.1.

of the potential area, it is observed that Gujarat has a lower share achieved so far, that is, around 9 per cent of the total potential area (Palanisami et al. 2011), which is notably lower as compared to other major states. As of 2014–15, Gujarat roughly covered around 20 per cent of the total net sown area. This is despite the state having taken various initiatives in terms of designing institutions and several ongoing schemes for promotion of MI within the state. Moreover, it should be noted that GGRC model performs better in the context of promoting MI in the state as compared to the various models adopted by the other states (Palanisami 2015).

Based on the discussion in the foregoing and some literature (Caswell and Zilberman 1985; Palanisami et al. 2011), we propose a hypothesis that there could be a higher probability of adopting MI in a region where water is a scarce resource and/or a high dependency on groundwater for irrigation. Since state's agro-ecological conditions satisfy both, an increasing trend was found with respect to the number of farmers adopting MI and the area under MI[15] (Table 17.2 and Figure 17.4). The figures report the year-wise adoption scenario.[16] For instance, 12.96 thousand farmers had adopted MI by the year 2006–07, and this number increased more than 10 times in the recent years, that is, 140.1 thousand and 123.78 thousand farmers in 2013–14 and 2014–15, respectively.

Likewise, 25.7 thousand ha land was under MI during 2006–07, which had increased by around 9 times to 224.95 thousand ha during 2013–14 and 200.55 thousand ha during 2014–15. Indeed, both the number of MI-adopting farmers and the corresponding area had significantly increased after 2009–10 (Figure 17.4).

From Figure 17.5, it may be seen that around 81 per cent of the farmers (and the area) have adopted MI between 2010–11 and 2014–15. This reveals that the MI technology was popularly adopted in Gujarat within a shorter span of less than 5 years.

## MI Adoption: Size Class-wise Pattern

When we examine the adoption patterns across land size classes, it is found that currently, medium farmers (2–10 ha) are the dominant adopters of MI in Gujarat, who accounted for 60 per cent of the total number of

**Table 17.2**

Year-wise trends in the adoption of micro-irrigation in Gujarat (2005–06 to 2014–15)

| Year | Total | | Achievement under Tribal Scheme | | Crop groups-wise area coverage under MIS (in '000 ha) | | Category of farmers (in '000) covered under MIS | | | | Grant from GoG & GoI under MIS (₹ in million) |
|---|---|---|---|---|---|---|---|---|---|---|---|
| | No. of farmers adopted MI (in '000) | Area under MI ('000 ha) | No. of farmers adopted MI (in '000) | Area under MI ('000 ha) | Agriculture crops | Horticulture | Marginal | Small | Medium | Large | |
| 2005–06 | 7.22 | 15.89 | – | – | 10.49 | 5.40 | 1.04 | 3.38 | 1.86 | 0.93 | 230 |
| 2006–07 | 12.96 | 25.70 | – | – | 19.60 | 7.63 | 1.56 | 7.86 | 3.09 | 1.29 | 1,110 |
| 2007–08 | 31.89 | 48.97 | 1.99 | 3.31 | 36.67 | 13.59 | 1.39 | 7.56 | 13.94 | 9.61 | 1,100 |
| 2008–09 | 38.90 | 56.76 | 2.53 | 3.74 | 42.10 | 15.63 | 2.51 | 12.88 | 22.92 | 1.13 | 1,610 |
| 2009–10 | 38.13 | 62.06 | 9.94 | 14.14 | 56.68 | 14.14 | 2.90 | 12.81 | 26.49 | 1.33 | 1,390 |
| 2010–11 | 66.56 | 103.53 | 25.97 | 33.41 | 91.32 | 11.17 | 4.32 | 19.13 | 39.99 | 2.16 | 2,560 |
| 2011–12 | 90.65 | 149.26 | 24.12 | 34.62 | 137.29 | 13.19 | 6.91 | 27.47 | 54.36 | 2.65 | 4,300 |
| 2012–13 | 131.02 | 209.88 | 32.19 | 42.12 | 188.72 | 16.48 | 10.98 | 35.44 | 77.58 | 4.25 | 5,820 |
| 2013–14 | 140.10 | 224.95 | 20.97 | 28.21 | 202.00 | 23.26 | 15.11 | 39.42 | 81.64 | 4.04 | 6,670 |
| 2014–15 | 123.78 | 200.55 | 27.64 | 38.71 | 170.99 | 29.56 | 13.34 | 33.09 | 73.09 | 4.26 | 5,310 |
| Total (2005–15) | 681.21 (14.38) | 1097.55 (11.00) | 145.35 | 198.26 | – | – | 60.06 (3.44) | 199.04 (14.42) | 394.96 (25.68) | 31.65 (43.96) | 30,100 |

*Source:* Authors' table based on data collected from GGRC.

*Note:* The figures in the parentheses indicate the percentage figure out of the total famers and area in Gujarat.

**Figure 17.4**
Trends in no. of MI adopted farmers and area under MI (2005–06 to 2014–15)

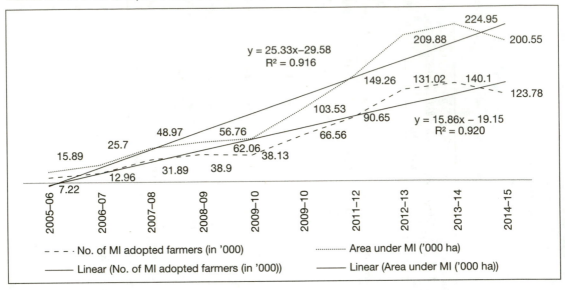

Source: Table 17.2.

**Figure 17.5**
Year-wise percentage of total MI adopted farmers and area under MI

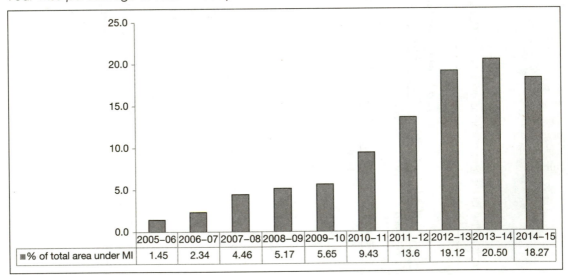

| | 2005–06 | 2006–07 | 2007–08 | 2008–09 | 2009–10 | 2010–11 | 2011–12 | 2012–13 | 2013–14 | 2014–15 |
|---|---|---|---|---|---|---|---|---|---|---|
| ▦% of total area under MI | 1.45 | 2.34 | 4.46 | 5.17 | 5.65 | 9.43 | 13.6 | 19.12 | 20.50 | 18.27 |

Source: Table 17.2.

**Figure 17.6**

*Year-wise percentage of farmers and area under MI by land size classes (2005–06 to 2014–15)*

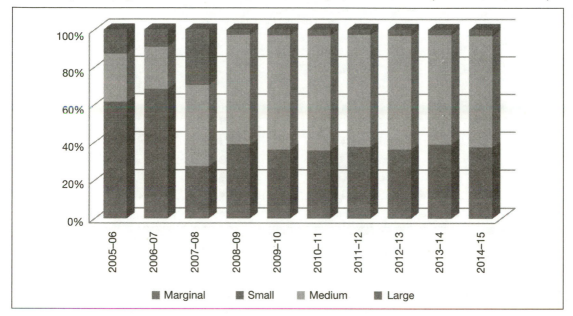

*Source:* Table 17.2.

MI farmers during 2014–15 (Figure 17.6). The combined share of small (1–2 ha) and marginal (<1 ha) farmers was 37 per cent during the same period. It is also important to note that in the initial years of launching of the MI scheme, the small and marginal farmers were the largest adopters, whose combined share was 61 per cent during 2005–06, which had increased to 68 per cent in the next year (2006–07).

The latter years saw an increasing trend in adoption by the medium farmers with the share of large farmers remaining stable at about 3 per cent since 2008–09. While looking at Figure 17.7, it is found that around 44 per cent of the total large farmers and 26 per cent of the total medium farmers have adopted MI; it is very low in the case of marginal and small farmers, that is, 3 per cent and 14 per cent, respectively. This reveals that the MI is mostly adopted by medium and large farmers, while 66 per cent of the total farmers are small and marginal. Overall scenario suggests that there is still a potential for increasing MI adoption particularly among the small and marginal farmers. This also raises a question needing further probing as to why a large percentage of small and marginal farmers do not adopt MI. In fact, the state government, as outlined above, has recently initiated a separate subsidy policy for small and marginal farmers (see Figure 17.2) and hopefully, this will motivate these farmers to adopt MI in the near future.

## Micro-irrigation Adoption Across Agro-climatic Regions

The agro-climatic region-wise status of MI adoption in the state is presented in Tables 17.3 and 17.4, respectively. It is observed that both the indicators (i.e., total number of MI-adopting farmers and total area under MI) have seen an increasing trend over the years across agro-climatic regions.

For instance, the compound annual growth rate (CAGR) of number of MI-adopting farmers across regions was 34.7 per cent (Table 17.3), and it was 31 per cent in case of area under MI between 2006–07 and 2013–14 (Table 17.4). This, in other words, signifies that the proactive state policy of providing subsidy in the range of 50–75 per cent would have motivated a large number of farmers to adopt MI over the years, in addition to the anticipated economic, physical, and environmental benefits of MI.

**Figure 17.7**

*Percentage of total farmers by land size classes (2005–06 to 2014–15)*

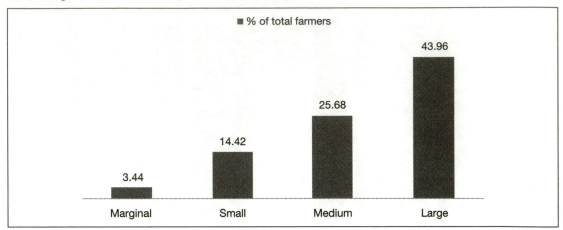

*Source:* Table 17.2.

**Table 17.3**

*Agro-climatic zone-wise number of farmers adopting MIS in Gujarat (2006–07 to 2013–14)*

| Agro-climatic region | 2006–07 | 2007–08 | 2008–09 | 2009–10 | 2010–11 | 2011–12 | 2012–13 | 2013–14 | Total | CAGR (%) |
|---|---|---|---|---|---|---|---|---|---|---|
| North-west Arid | 0.59 (4.5) | 0.75 (2.4) | 0.76 (1.9) | 0.81 (2.1) | 1.26 (1.9) | 0.80 (0.9) | 4.84 (3.7) | 5.82 (4.2) | 15.62 (2.8) | 33.27 |
| North Gujarat | 2.43 (18.8) | 6.6 (20.7) | 6.35 (16.3) | 13.89 (36.4) | 21.46 (32.3) | 25.90 (28.6) | 44.22 (33.7) | 47.65 (34.0) | 168.51 (30.6) | 45.04 |
| Middle Gujarat | 1.05 (8.1) | 1.62 (5.1) | 2.15 (5.5) | 3.32 (8.7) | 7.83 (11.8) | 15.58 (17.2) | 17.08 (13.0) | 13.39 (9.5) | 62.02 (11.3) | 37.55 |
| North Saurashtra | 2.73 (21.1) | 9.95 (31.2) | 18.78 (48.3) | 12.22 (32.1) | 13.67 (20.5) | 27.67 (30.5) | 30.96 (23.6) | 37.52 (26.8) | 153.50 (27.9) | 38.75 |
| South Gujarat | 1.69 (13.0) | 2.11 (6.6) | 2.13 (5.5) | 1.81 (4.7) | 10.62 (15.9) | 7.29 (8.0) | 10.94 (8.3) | 8.00 (5.7) | 44.60 (8.1) | 21.47 |
| Southern Hills | 0.86 (6.6) | 0.94 (2.9) | 1.17 (3.0) | 0 (0) | 4.78 (7.2) | 3.62 (3.9) | 5.53 (4.2) | 3.65 (2.6) | 20.55 (3.7) | 19.75 |
| South Saurashtra | 3.61 (27.9) | 9.91 (31.1) | 7.56 (19.4) | 6.06 (15.9) | 6.93 (10.4) | 9.80 (10.8) | 17.46 (13.3) | 24.08 (17.2) | 85.42 (15.5) | 26.75 |
| Gujarat | 12.96 | 31.89 | 38.90 | 38.13 | 66.56 | 90.65 | 131.02 | 140.10 | 550.21 | 34.66 |

*Source:* Adopted from Bahinipati and Viswanathan (2016).

*Note:*    The reported figures are in '000; Figures in parentheses indicate percentage; CAGR.

Further, disaggregation across the agro-climatic regions reveals that a majority of farmers adopted MI in the three agro-climatic regions, namely, north Gujarat, north Saurashtra, and south Saurashtra, as these regions are reportedly experiencing severe water scarcity and high levels of groundwater extraction. While the north Gujarat has been reported as critical and over-exploited (SGWD>85%), the other two regions (i.e., north Saurashtra and south Saurashtra) fall under dark category (SGWD is in between 65–85%; see GoI 2014). Together, these three regions cover around 74 per cent of the total MI-adopting farmers and 75 per cent of the

**Table 17.4**

Agro-climatic zone-wise area under MIS in Gujarat (2006–07 to 2013–14)

| Agro-climatic region | 2006–07 | 2007–08 | 2008–09 | 2009–10 | 2010–11 | 2011–12 | 2012–13 | 2013–14 | Total | CAGR (%) |
|---|---|---|---|---|---|---|---|---|---|---|
| North-west Arid | 2.11 | 2.46 | 2.30 | 2.40 | 3.50 | 2.19 | 9.68 | 12.06 | 36.70 | 24.37 |
| | (8.2) | (5.0) | (4.1) | (3.9) | (3.4) | (1.5) | (4.6) | (5.4) | (4.2) | |
| North Gujarat | 5.98 | 12.78 | 13.08 | 24.38 | 34.08 | 48.64 | 75.92 | 78.68 | 293.53 | 38.02 |
| | (23.3) | (26.1) | (23.0) | (39.3) | (32.9) | (32.6) | (36.2) | (34.9) | (33.3) | |
| Middle Gujarat | 2.27 | 3.00 | 3.67 | 6.04 | 13.74 | 24.88 | 23.55 | 17.52 | 94.68 | 29.09 |
| | (8.8) | (6.1) | (6.5) | (9.7) | (13.3) | (16.7) | (11.2) | (7.8) | (10.7) | |
| North Saurashtra | 4.62 | 13.01 | 22.06 | 17.16 | 21.81 | 43.41 | 52.21 | 63.98 | 238.26 | 38.91 |
| | (17.9) | (26.6) | (38.9) | (27.7) | (21.1) | (29.1) | (24.9) | (28.4) | (27.0) | |
| South Gujarat | 3.92 | 3.49 | 3.54 | 3.04 | 13.73 | 10.55 | 15.55 | 12.27 | 66.09 | 15.32 |
| | (15.3) | (7.1) | (6.2) | (4.9) | (13.3) | (7.1) | (7.4) | (5.5) | (7.5) | |
| Southern Hills | 1.56 | 1.59 | 1.81 | 0 | 6.36 | 5.05 | 6.62 | 4.35 | 27.34 | 13.64 |
| | (6.1) | (3.3) | (3.9) | (0) | (6.1) | (3.4) | (3.2) | (1.9) | (3.1) | |
| South Saurashtra | 5.25 | 12.63 | 10.31 | 9.04 | 10.32 | 14.53 | 26.34 | 36.09 | 124.52 | 27.26 |
| | (20.4) | (25.8) | (18.2) | (14.6) | (9.9) | (9.7) | (12.6) | (16.1) | (14.1) | |
| Gujarat | 25.70 | 48.97 | 56.76 | 62.06 | 103.53 | 149.26 | 209.88 | 224.95 | 881.11 | 31.15 |

*Source*: Adopted from Bahinipati and Viswanathan (2016).

*Notes*: The reported figures are in '000 ha; Figures in parentheses indicate percentage; CAGR.

total area under MI in the state. Among them, north Gujarat occupies the first position in terms of number of farmers adopting MI (i.e., 168.51 thousand farmers, i.e., around 31% of total farmers) and total area under MI (i.e., 293.53 thousand ha, i.e., around 33% of total area) in the state. This reveals that hydrological scenario also acts as a major determinant in the adoption of MI in the state.

## Micro-irrigation Adoption Scenario in Dark-zone and Tribal Talukas

It has been noted that the subsidy amount varies with respect to socio-economic group and geographical location in Gujarat under the new policy frame (see Figure 17.2). In this subsection, we examine the possible impact of extra subsidy provided to dark-zone and tribal talukas on the diffusion and adoption of MI. Table 17.5 presents the year-wise number of farmers adopting MI and area under MI by dark-zone and tribal talukas in the Gujarat state. Figures 17.8 and 17.9 show year-wise farmers and area under MI in the dark-zone and tribal talukas, respectively.

As noted, the state government announced extra 10 per cent subsidy since 2012 in the case of dark-zone talukas, mainly to reduce the over-exploitation of groundwater as observed under the conventional irrigation system. Notably, an increasing trend was observed in the case of farmers and area under MI in dark-zone talukas (see Figure 17.8). Certainly, this sharp increase in adoption of MI could have happened due to the extra subsidy given to the farmers in the dark-zone talukas, which also coincided with the lifting of the ban on water extraction and the release of agricultural power connections. Moreover, in order to identify the specific impact of the treatment (additional subsidy), one needs to apply various methods of impact evaluation (e.g., difference-in-difference, regression discontinuity design approach, etc.)—this is future area of research. In the meantime, Fishman et al. (2014) find an evidence of additional subsidies enhancing adoption of MI in Gujarat state, that is, drip irrigation by 32 per cent, the area installed with drips by 30 per cent and the probability of having at least one purchase by 11 per cent. In fact, there is no such study so far which mainly focused on the dark-zone talukas, which signifies the relevance of this analysis.

The state government has provided additional subsidy to the tribal farmers in the tribal talukas since 2008. An increasing adoption trend was also observed in the case of number of tribal farmers adopting MI

**Table 17.5**

*Trends in adoption of MI in the dark-zone and tribal talukas*

| Year | Dark-zone* | | | | Tribal talukas | | | |
|---|---|---|---|---|---|---|---|---|
| | No. of farmers adopting MI | | Total area under MI | | No. of farmers adopting MI | | Total area under MI | |
| | No. (in '000) | % | in '000 ha | % | No. (in '000) | % | in '000 ha | % |
| 2006–07 | 3.4 | 2.1 | 6.8 | 2.4 | 1.9 | 1.6 | 4.22 | 2.6 |
| 2007–08 | 7.9 | 4.9 | 13.8 | 4.9 | 3.08 | 2.6 | 4.84 | 2.9 |
| 2008–09 | 7.4 | 4.6 | 14.5 | 5.1 | 3.82 | 3.2 | 6 | 3.6 |
| 2009–10 | 14.8 | 9.2 | 25.9 | 9.2 | 6.88 | 5.8 | 9.67 | 5.9 |
| 2010–11 | 13.4 | 8.3 | 24 | 8.5 | 28.34 | 23.9 | 36.91 | 22.4 |
| 2011–12 | 20.7 | 12.9 | 38.8 | 13.7 | 24.9 | 21.0 | 36 | 21.9 |
| 2012–13 | 39 | 24.2 | 69.1 | 24.5 | 26.9 | 22.7 | 35.87 | 21.8 |
| 2013–14 | 54.3 | 33.7 | 89.3 | 31.6 | 22.8 | 19.2 | 31.02 | 18.9 |
| Total (2006–14) | 160.9 | 100 | 282.2 | 100 | 118.62 | 100 | 164.53 | 100 |

*Source:* Authors' compilation based on data collected from GGRC.

*Note:*    * The figures reported excludes tribal talukas.

**Figure 17.8**
*Year-wise farmers and area under MI in the dark-zone talukas (2006–07 to 2013–14)*

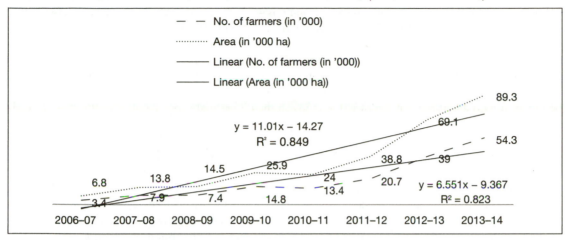

*Source:* Table 17.5.

**Figure 17.9**
*Year-wise trends in number of farmers and area under MI in tribal talukas (2006–07 to 2013–14)*

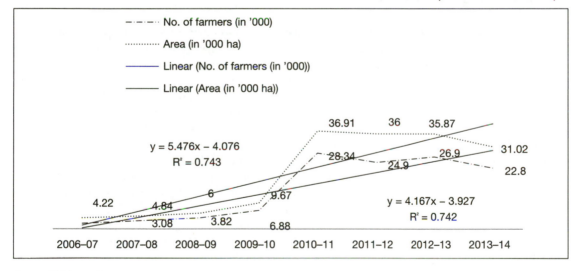

*Source:* Table 17.5.

until 2012–13 as evident from Figure 17.9. For instance, around 1.99 thousand tribal farmers had adopted MI in 2007–08 with an area of 3.31 thousand ha, and this number and area had increased to 32.19 thousand farmers and 42.12 thousand ha, respectively by 2012–13 (Table 17.5). However, a declining trend was observed in the last two years as compared to the previous three years. The reported adoption of MI during the latest two years was 20.97 thousand farmers and 27.64 thousand farmers, respectively. This may be explained in terms of the point that by 2014–15, all potential farmers with access to groundwater irrigation sources would have adopted the MIS and further adoption would call for development of new groundwater sources on which MIS could be implemented. Nevertheless, this point needs further empirical validation.

In the case of tribal talukas, it may be seen that there was a sudden rise in the number of farmers and area under MI in the 2010–11 as compared to 2009–10. For instance, around 3.82 thousand farmers adopted MI in the year 2008–09 with 6 thousand ha area, and this was increased to 6.88 thousand farmers (with 9.67 thousand ha area) in 2009–10 and 28.34 thousand farmers (with 36.91 thousand ha area) in 2010–11. After that, these figures remained more or less same as that of the previous year. It may be surmised that the substantial increase in the number of farmers adopting MI in the tribal talukas certainly reflects on the immediate response towards the new policy of incremental (differential) subsidy for MIS in the tribal talukas.

On the whole, the major reasons for this increased adoption in the dark-zone and tribal talukas could be the awareness about the benefits of MI along with the differential subsidy policy of the state, providing higher rate of subsidies to farmers in the tribal and dark-zone talukas as well as the suitability of the system for various agricultural crops, etc. As a cumulative outcome, the total amount of subsidy provided by the government had increased by more than sixfold over the 10-year period from ₹1,110 million during 2006–07 to ₹6,710 million during 2013–14 and ₹5,310 million in 2014–15 (Table 17.2). In contrast to the existing findings that MI is suitable mostly for horticultural and high valued commercial crops, for majority of Indian states (Palanisami et al. 2011), it is found that a large percentage of MI-adopted area in Gujarat is under conventional agricultural crops (see Table 17.2). This contrast may be explained in terms of the prevalence of different state-sponsored subsidy schemes for promotion of MI in Gujarat, unlike other states.

## Concluding Remarks

This chapter makes a comprehensive review of the state policy and intervention for the promotion of MIS in Gujarat during the last decade. While the promotion of MI in Gujarat corresponds with the NMMI, an unequivocal dynamism was observed in the expansion of MI in the state as compared to other states. This dynamism in the promotion of the MI can be attributed to the specific policies and interventions that the state had vigorously adopted and followed in terms of provision of differential subsidies targeted towards the farmers segregated by their socio-economic status as well as the physical and economic water scarcity of the agro-ecological regions. In this regard, the chapter provides a detailed analysis of the trends in the status of adoption of MIS in Gujarat under the various subsidy policy and institutional innovations.

By and large, the analysis reveals that the rate of adoption of the MI has been quite significant across farm size classes, agro-climatic regions, water-stressed talukas as well as tribal farmers. However, it is important to note that the initial responses towards adoption of the MI as evinced by the farmers and regions may have been exceptionally influenced by the specific subsidy policies and institutional interventions. While the initial enthusiasm in the adoption of a frontier water-saving technology as MI is quite contextual and commendable, it needs to be further explored that: "how far the MI technological interventions make a significant and sustainable impact on the agrarian performance of the regional economies and the rejuvenation of the heavily depleted groundwater aquifers in the state."

Further, though the adoption of MI had been significant, the aggregate level of adoption in the state is still low in terms of total farmers and coverage of area under MI, that is, only around 14 per cent of the total farmers have undertaken MI with 11 per cent of the total potential area between 2005 and 2015. This indicates that the diffusion of MI is still low across the state, even though the state has launched differential interventions and subsidy policies to enhance the adoption rate. It may be quite interesting to find out "why a large number of farmers still do not adopt to such water-saving technologies while there are favourable policies and differential subsidy programmes?" Further, it is also important to investigate the impact of various government incentives, including subsidy policies, on diffusion of MI as well as the changing cropping pattern across the state.

# Appendix

## Table A17.1

*District-wise number of farmers adopting MIS in Gujarat, 2006–07 to 2015–16*

| District Name | 2006–07 | 2007–08 | 2008–09 | 2009–10 | 2010–11 | 2011–12 | 2012–13 | 2013–14 | 2014–15 | 2015–16 | Total |
|---|---|---|---|---|---|---|---|---|---|---|---|
| Ahmedabad | 0.05 | 0.13 | 0.29 | 0.42 | 0.32 | 1.06 | 1.62 | 2.39 | 0.99 | 1.27 | 8.54 |
| Amreli | 0.47 | 2.65 | 4.54 | 2.60 | 2.81 | 6.47 | 5.34 | 7.86 | 4.42 | 6.25 | 43.40 |
| Anand | 0.21 | 0.21 | 0.19 | 0.22 | 0.24 | 0.38 | 0.36 | 0.43 | 0.31 | 0.30 | 2.84 |
| Arvalli* | – | – | – | – | – | – | – | – | 6.87 | 4.47 | 11.34 |
| Banaskantha | 0.97 | 3.84 | 3.59 | 6.52 | 10.66 | 13.80 | 24.41 | 25.40 | 29.19 | 30.34 | 148.72 |
| Bharuch | 0.71 | 0.74 | 0.66 | 0.76 | 0.91 | 1.15 | 1.96 | 2.49 | 1.33 | 1.06 | 11.77 |
| Bhavnagar | 0.47 | 2.63 | 3.45 | 2.71 | 4.91 | 6.86 | 9.08 | 8.36 | 4.98 | 6.95 | 50.40 |
| Botad* | – | – | – | – | – | – | – | – | 2.16 | 4.90 | 7.07 |
| Chhota Udaipur* | – | – | – | – | – | – | – | – | 4.75 | 3.22 | 7.97 |
| Dahod | 0.01 | 0.02 | 0.16 | 0.50 | 1.85 | 3.43 | 5.68 | 3.28 | 4.23 | 2.44 | 21.60 |
| Devbhumi Dwarka* | – | – | – | – | – | – | – | – | 1.94 | 2.58 | 4.53 |
| Gandhinagar | 0.14 | 0.20 | 0.14 | 0.17 | 0.40 | 0.50 | 1.36 | 1.71 | 1.31 | 1.43 | 7.37 |
| Gir Somnath* | – | – | – | – | – | – | – | – | 4.45 | 5.30 | 9.75 |
| Jamnagar | 0.54 | 1.64 | 3.99 | 2.59 | 1.33 | 4.24 | 3.15 | 5.61 | 2.15 | 2.90 | 28.14 |
| Junagadh | 3.23 | 7.72 | 6.04 | 5.23 | 6.14 | 8.73 | 15.76 | 21.77 | 9.60 | 10.14 | 94.36 |
| Kheda | 0.17 | 0.22 | 0.18 | 0.28 | 0.36 | 0.65 | 1.32 | 2.55 | 2.01 | 2.01 | 9.75 |
| Kutch | 0.59 | 0.75 | 0.76 | 0.81 | 1.26 | 1.73 | 4.84 | 5.82 | 5.00 | 3.61 | 25.16 |
| Mahisagar* | – | – | – | – | – | – | – | – | 0.82 | 1.02 | 1.83 |
| Mehsana | 0.20 | 0.28 | 0.35 | 0.38 | 0.59 | 0.89 | 2.56 | 4.71 | 2.80 | 2.48 | 15.24 |
| Morbi* | – | – | – | – | – | – | – | – | 1.78 | 2.13 | 3.91 |
| Narmada | 0.19 | 0.50 | 0.64 | 1.06 | 3.05 | 1.63 | 1.96 | 1.83 | 1.97 | 1.81 | 14.64 |
| Navsari | 0.63 | 0.66 | 0.47 | 0.00 | 1.67 | 1.58 | 2.01 | 1.58 | 1.58 | 1.23 | 11.42 |
| Panchmahal | 0.03 | 0.11 | 0.20 | 0.61 | 1.26 | 2.98 | 2.09 | 1.09 | 1.33 | 1.10 | 10.81 |

(Table A17.1 *continued*)

(Table A17.1 continued)

| District Name | 2006–07 | 2007–08 | 2008–09 | 2009–10 | 2010–11 | 2011–12 | 2012–13 | 2013–14 | 2014–15 | 2015–16 | Total |
|---|---|---|---|---|---|---|---|---|---|---|---|
| Patan | 0.09 | 0.21 | 0.16 | 0.38 | 0.32 | 0.48 | 1.87 | 2.20 | 2.23 | 2.24 | 10.18 |
| Porbandar | 0.39 | 2.19 | 1.52 | 0.83 | 0.80 | 1.07 | 1.70 | 2.31 | 2.05 | 2.27 | 15.13 |
| Rajkot | 0.82 | 2.28 | 5.81 | 3.14 | 2.70 | 7.31 | 7.00 | 11.33 | 5.15 | 7.36 | 52.90 |
| Sabarkantha | 0.98 | 1.95 | 1.83 | 6.03 | 9.17 | 8.23 | 12.40 | 11.25 | 5.00 | 5.86 | 62.69 |
| Surat | 0.49 | 0.61 | 0.55 | 0.00 | 1.42 | 1.65 | 2.00 | 2.00 | 2.05 | 1.45 | 12.22 |
| Surendranagar | 0.44 | 0.75 | 0.99 | 1.18 | 1.91 | 2.79 | 6.39 | 4.36 | 2.99 | 4.62 | 26.42 |
| Tapi | 0.29 | 0.26 | 0.29 | 0.00 | 5.24 | 2.87 | 5.03 | 1.68 | 3.16 | 2.34 | 21.16 |
| The Dangs | 0.00 | 0.00 | 0.08 | 0.00 | 1.29 | 0.39 | 1.25 | 0.51 | 0.78 | 0.50 | 4.80 |
| Vadodara | 0.63 | 1.07 | 1.42 | 1.72 | 4.12 | 8.13 | 7.62 | 6.05 | 0.83 | 0.88 | 32.47 |
| Valsad | 0.23 | 0.27 | 0.63 | 0.00 | 1.82 | 1.66 | 2.28 | 1.55 | 1.97 | 1.53 | 11.94 |
| Gujarat | 12.96 | 31.89 | 38.90 | 38.13 | 66.56 | 90.65 | 131.02 | 140.10 | 122.17 | 127.98 | 800.37 |

*Source:* Authors' compilation based on data collected from GGRC and http://111.90.173.51/GGRCWEBAPS/Page/FrmRptDstTalukaSumm.aspx; accessed on 11 November 2016.

*Note:* The reported figures are in '000; '–' means not available and * New district.

**Table A17.2**
*District-wise area under MIS in Gujarat, 2006–07 to 2015–16*

| District Name | 2006–07 | 2007–08 | 2008–09 | 2009–10 | 2010–11 | 2011–12 | 2012–13 | 2013–14 | 2014–15 | 2015–16 | Total |
|---|---|---|---|---|---|---|---|---|---|---|---|
| Ahmedabad | 0.16 | 0.33 | 0.79 | 1.47 | 1.04 | 3.13 | 3.91 | 4.95 | 2.67 | 3.03 | 21.48 |
| Amreli | 0.65 | 3.10 | 5.05 | 3.46 | 4.06 | 9.84 | 8.93 | 13.74 | 7.74 | 9.94 | 66.51 |
| Anand | 0.39 | 0.31 | 0.29 | 0.27 | 0.28 | 0.48 | 0.38 | 0.47 | 0.36 | 0.29 | 3.53 |
| Arvalli* | – | – | – | – | – | – | – | – | 10.45 | 7.45 | 17.90 |
| Banaskantha | 1.99 | 7.07 | 7.54 | 11.70 | 17.34 | 26.50 | 43.26 | 44.68 | 50.36 | 49.73 | 260.17 |
| Bharuch | 1.86 | 1.35 | 1.26 | 1.48 | 1.71 | 2.01 | 3.07 | 3.85 | 2.21 | 1.66 | 20.46 |
| Bhavnagar | 0.63 | 3.05 | 3.53 | 3.46 | 7.15 | 10.27 | 13.73 | 12.64 | 7.04 | 9.33 | 70.83 |
| Botad* | – | – | – | – | – | – | – | – | 3.99 | 7.89 | 11.88 |
| Chhota Udaipur* | – | – | – | – | – | – | – | – | 5.74 | 3.73 | 9.47 |

| District Name | 2006–07 | 2007–08 | 2008–09 | 2009–10 | 2010–11 | 2011–12 | 2012–13 | 2013–14 | 2014–15 | 2015–16 | Total |
|---|---|---|---|---|---|---|---|---|---|---|---|
| Dahod | 0.03 | 0.07 | 0.23 | 0.85 | 3.29 | 5.72 | 7.56 | 4.36 | 5.80 | 3.43 | 31.33 |
| Devbhumi Dwarka* | – | – | – | – | – | – | – | – | 4.21 | 5.93 | 10.14 |
| Gandhinagar | 0.43 | 0.44 | 0.29 | 0.31 | 0.60 | 1.06 | 1.95 | 2.44 | 1.79 | 1.93 | 11.24 |
| Gir Somnath* | – | – | – | – | – | – | – | – | 5.46 | 6.21 | 11.67 |
| Jamnagar | 0.87 | 2.20 | 4.80 | 3.66 | 2.32 | 6.80 | 5.51 | 10.52 | 3.94 | 5.03 | 45.65 |
| Junagadh | 4.63 | 9.65 | 7.77 | 7.58 | 8.93 | 12.75 | 23.23 | 31.45 | 14.06 | 13.47 | 133.52 |
| Kheda | 0.51 | 0.54 | 0.48 | 0.64 | 0.95 | 1.36 | 2.06 | 3.26 | 2.80 | 2.58 | 15.19 |
| Kutch | 2.11 | 2.46 | 2.30 | 2.40 | 3.50 | 4.32 | 9.68 | 12.06 | 10.56 | 7.88 | 57.28 |
| Mahisagar* | – | – | – | – | – | – | – | – | 1.02 | 1.67 | 2.69 |
| Mehsana | 0.51 | 0.51 | 0.56 | 0.70 | 0.99 | 1.45 | 3.28 | 5.44 | 3.62 | 3.13 | 20.18 |
| Morbi* | – | – | – | – | – | – | – | – | 2.84 | 3.04 | 5.88 |
| Narmada | 0.32 | 0.66 | 0.85 | 1.56 | 3.56 | 2.08 | 2.69 | 2.60 | 3.12 | 2.72 | 20.16 |
| Navsari | 1.06 | 1.03 | 0.69 | 0.00 | 2.44 | 2.30 | 2.70 | 2.13 | 2.04 | 1.47 | 15.85 |
| Panchmahal | 0.06 | 0.16 | 0.31 | 1.04 | 1.98 | 5.11 | 2.96 | 1.59 | 1.98 | 1.65 | 16.83 |
| Patan | 0.24 | 0.56 | 0.48 | 0.99 | 0.77 | 0.76 | 4.85 | 4.74 | 4.89 | 5.81 | 24.09 |
| Porbandar | 0.61 | 2.98 | 2.55 | 1.46 | 1.39 | 1.79 | 3.11 | 4.64 | 3.95 | 3.76 | 26.24 |
| Rajkot | 1.19 | 2.88 | 6.46 | 3.99 | 3.83 | 10.54 | 10.80 | 17.85 | 8.65 | 11.34 | 77.53 |
| Sabarkantha | 2.66 | 3.86 | 3.41 | 9.21 | 13.33 | 13.61 | 18.67 | 16.44 | 7.37 | 8.73 | 97.29 |
| Surat | 1.09 | 1.06 | 0.93 | 0.00 | 2.14 | 2.60 | 3.36 | 3.25 | 3.53 | 2.20 | 20.16 |
| Surendranagar | 1.28 | 1.77 | 2.21 | 2.60 | 4.44 | 5.96 | 13.26 | 9.23 | 6.67 | 10.59 | 58.01 |
| Tapi | 0.65 | 0.42 | 0.50 | 0.00 | 6.32 | 3.86 | 6.42 | 2.57 | 4.75 | 3.45 | 28.94 |
| The Dangs | 0.00 | 0.00 | 0.10 | 0.00 | 1.30 | 0.40 | 1.25 | 0.52 | 0.75 | 0.48 | 4.80 |
| Vadodara | 1.29 | 1.92 | 2.37 | 3.23 | 7.23 | 12.22 | 10.59 | 7.84 | 1.42 | 1.46 | 49.56 |
| Valsad | 0.51 | 0.56 | 1.02 | 0.00 | 2.62 | 2.35 | 2.67 | 1.70 | 2.10 | 1.62 | 15.15 |
| Gujarat | 25.70 | 48.97 | 56.76 | 62.06 | 103.53 | 149.26 | 209.88 | 224.95 | 197.90 | 202.61 | 1281.62 |

*Source:* Authors' compilation based on data collected from GGRC and http://111.90.173.51/GGRCWEBAPS/Page/FrmRptDstTalukaSumm.aspx; accessed on 11 November, 2016.

*Note:* The reported figures are in '000 ha'; '–' means not available and * New district.

## Notes

1. Almost 70 per cent of the freshwater resources are concentrated in the south and central regions, while 75 per cent of the agricultural lands are spread across North, Saurashtra, and Kutch regions (Viswanathan and Pathak 2014).
2. It is the ratio of annual groundwater draft and net annual groundwater availability in percentage.
3. The other measures are as follows: Sardar Sarovar Project, river lining and inter-basin transfer of water, Sardar Patel Participatory Water Conservation Scheme, and the Jyotigram Yojana (Kishore 2013).
4. It is the ratio of water used in plant metabolism to water lost by the plant through transpiration.
5. The GoI introduced a central scheme during 1982–83 (i.e., sixth plan) for MI under Ministry of Water Resources (minor irrigation division). Under this, the GoI provides subsidy of 50 per cent to farmers with the matching contribution from the state government. Out of the total subsidy amount, 75 per cent was allocated for small and marginal farmers and the rest (25%) for other group of farmers. Since it was not well received in the seventh plan, the GoI modified the scheme, that is, the subsidy amount limited to 50 per cent of total cost or ₹15,000/ha, whichever is lower (Narayanamoorthy 2006).
6. The rate of subsidy provided by the national government (under the NMMI) is fixed uniformly for different categories of farmers with a limit of 5 hectares. However, the rate of subsidy provided under the state schemes range from 50 per cent to 80 per cent of the total capital costs in case of general farmers and 50 per cent to 100 per cent of capital costs in case of small and marginal and tribal farmers (GoI 2014).
7. Earlier the limit was ₹50,000/ha (see Government Resolution No. PRCH-102005-497-N dated 09.05.2005), and based on Government Resolution (GR) No. TAP/122008/79/B of GoG taken on 10/7/2008, this was enhanced to ₹60,000/ha.
8. Region where there is an over-extraction of groundwater with the extent of groundwater reaching critical levels.
9. As per GR No. GWR-2003-14.J1 (Narmada, Water Resources, Water Supply and Kalpsar Department) dated 16/12/2003, 57 talukas of the state were notified as dark-zone talukas. As of now, there are only 54 talukas; because, two talukas mentioned in this GR such as Bhildi and Panthawada were no more named as taluka (based on personal communication with department officials), and Vagdod taluka of Patan district was merged in Patan taluka (Census 2011).
10. As per the GR dated 19/9/2001, the groundwater levels were very low in certain areas, and therefore, the GoG had decided not to permit water extraction by tube wells in the interest of geo-hydrology of the regions and the public at large (see http://deshgujarat.com/2012/02/28/gujarat-govt-to-give-power-connection-to-57-talukas-under-dark-zone/ accessed on 12th May 2015).
11. See GR No: PRCH-102005-497(38) dated 3/4/2012.
12. See GR No: VKY-2007-345-DSeg date 6/10/2008.
13. See GR No: PRCH/102005/497(38)/Part-2/N dated 3/1/2015.
14. See GR No: PRCH/102005/497(38)/Part-4/N dated 19/3/2015.
15. The information presented in this study were collected from GGRC and pertains to the period from 2006–07 to 2014–15. Some farmers could have adopted MI before GGRC intervened and some may have adopted without support of GGRC (e.g., farmers under the GWRDC scheme)—such information is not included in the analysis in this section.
16. Tables A17.1 and A17.2 report district-wise adoption of MIS and area under MIS in Gujarat.

## References

Bahinipati, C.S., and P.K. Viswanathan. 2016. "Determinants of Adopting and Accessing Benefits of Water Saving Technologies: A Study of Public Tube Wells with MI Systems in North Gujarat." In *Micro Irrigation Systems in India: Emergence, Status and Impacts in Select Major States*, edited by P.K. Viswanathan, M. Dinesh Kumar, and A. Narayanamoorthy. Singapore: Springer.

Bassi, N. 2013. "Institutional Intervention in Promotion of Micro-irrigation Systems in India: Inter-state Comparison." Training Compendium on "Managing Agricultural Water Demand in India: Applying Integrated Approaches," organized by Gujarat Institute of Development Research, Ahmedabad, 21–25 October.

Bhamoriya, V., and S. Mathew. 2014. "An Analysis of Resource Conservation Technology: A Case of Micro-irrigation System (Drip Irrigation)." Final Report of Centre for Management in Agriculture, Indian Institute of Management, Ahmedabad.

Caswell, M., and D. Zilberman. 1985. "The Choices of Irrigation Technologies in California." *American Journal of Agricultural Economics* 67 (2): 224–33.

Cenacchi, N. 2014. "Drought Risk Reduction in Agriculture: A Review of Adaptive Strategies in East Africa and the Indo-Gangetic Plain of South Asia." IFPRI Discussion Paper 01372, IFPRI, Washington, DC.

Fishman, R., S. Gulati, and S. Li. 2014. "Should Resource Efficient Technologies Be Subsidized? Evidence from the Diffusion of Drip Irrigation in Gujarat." Paper presented at the ISI, Delhi.

GoG. 2008. *Socio-economic Review 2007–08: Gujarat State.* Gandhinagar: Directorate of Economics and Statistics, Government of Gujarat.

———. 2013. *Socio-economic Review 2012–13: Gujarat State.* Gandhinagar: Directorate of Economics and Statistics, Government of Gujarat.

GoI. 2014, June. "National Mission on Micro Irrigation (NMMI): Impact Evaluation Study." Report submitted by Global Agri-system to the Government of India, Ministry of Agriculture, Department of Agriculture and Cooperation, New Delhi.

Hardin, G. 1968. "The Tragedy of the Commons." *Science* 162 (3859): 1243–48.

Hiremath, D.B., and R.L. Shiyani. 2012. "Adapting Gujarat to Climatic Vulnerabilities: The Road Ahead." *Research Journal of Recent Sciences* 1 (5): 38–45.

———. 2013. "Analysis of Vulnerability Indices in Various Agro-climatic Zones of Gujarat." *Indian Journal of Agricultural Economics* 68 (1): 122–37.

Institute for Resource Analysis and Policy. 2012. "Micro Irrigation Business in India: Potential, Challenges and Prospects." Report submitted to Infrastructure Finance Company Ltd., Mumbai.

Kishore, A. 2013. "Supply- and Demand-side Management of Water in Gujarat, India: What Can We Learn?" *Water Policy* 15 (3): 496–514.

Kumar, M.D. 2005. "Impact of Electricity Prices and Volumetric Water Allocation on Energy and Groundwater Demand Management: Analysis from Western India." *Energy Policy* 33 (1): 39–51.

———. 2007. "Groundwater Management in India: Physical, Institutional and Policy Alternatives." New Delhi: SAGE Publications.

———. 2013. "Water Saving and Yield Enhancing Micro Irrigation Technologies in India: Theory and Practice." Background Paper submitted to GIDR for developing the joint proposal for submission to the ICSSR, New Delhi.

Kumar, S.D., and K. Palanisami. 2011. "Can Drip Irrigation Technology Be Socially Beneficial? Evidence from Southern India." *Water Policy* 13 (4): 571–87.

Kumar, M.D., K. Singh, O.P. Singh., and R.L. Shiyani. 2004. "Impacts of Water Saving and Energy Saving Irrigation Technologies in Gujarat." Research Report 2, Natural Resources Economics and Management Foundation, Anand, India.

Kumar, M.D., and J.C. van Dam. 2013. "Drivers of Change in Agricultural Water Productivity and Its Improvement at Basin Scale in Developing Economies." *Water International.* doi:10.1080/02508060.2013.793572

Mehta, N. 2013. "An Investigation into Growth, Instability and Role of Weather in Gujarat Agriculture: 1981–2011." *Agricultural Economics Research Review* 26 (Conference Issue): 43–55.

Namara, R.E., R.K. Nagar, and B. Upadhyay. 2007. "Economics, Adoption Determinants and Impacts of Micro-irrigation Technologies: Empirical Results from India." *Irrigation Science* 25 (3): 283–97.

Narayanamoorthy, A. 2001. *Impact of Drip Irrigation on Sugarcane Cultivation in Maharashtra.* Pune: Agro-Economic Research Centre, Gokhale Institute of Politics and Economics.

———. 2004. "Drip Irrigation in India: Can It Solve Water Scarcity?" *Water Policy* 6 (2): 117–30.

———. 2005. "Efficiency of Irrigation: A Case of Drip Irrigation." Occasional Paper 45, Department of Economic Analysis and Research, National Bank for Agriculture and Rural Development, Mumbai, India.

———. 2006. "Potential for Drip and Sprinkler Irrigation in India." Draft prepared for the IWMI-CPWF project on "Strategic Analysis of National River Linking Project in India." Available at: http://s3.amazonaws.com/zanran_storage/nrlp.iwmi.org/ContentPages/44110729.pdf

Narula, K., R. Fishman, V. Modi, and L. Polycarpou. 2011. "Addressing the Water Crisis in Gujarat, India." Columbia Water Center White Paper, Columbia Water Center, New York.

Palanisami, K. 2015. "Micro-irrigation Neglected." *Economic and Political Weekly* 50 (51): 5.

Palanisami, K., K. Mohan, K.R. Kakumanu, and S. Raman. 2011. "Spread and Economics of Micro-irrigation in India: Evidence from Nine States." *Economic and Political Weekly* 46 (26 and 27): 81–86.

Palanichamy, N., K.V. Palanisamy, and T.R. Shanmugam. 2002. "Economic Performance of Drip Irrigation in Coconut Farmers in Coimbatore." *Agricultural Economics Research Review* (Conference Issue): 40–48.

Pullabhotla, H.K., C. Kumar, and S. Verma. 2012. "Micro-irrigation Subsidies in Gujarat and Andhra Pradesh Implications for Market Dynamics and Growth." Water Policy Research Highlight 43, IWMI-TATA Water Policy Program, Anand, India. Available at: http://www.iwmi.cgiar.org/iwmi-tata/PDFs/2012_Highlight-43.pdf

Ray, K., M. Mohanty, and J.R. Chincholokar. 2009. "Climate Variability Over Gujarat, India." ISPRS Archives XXXVIII-8/W3 Workshop Proceedings: Impact of Climate Change on Agriculture. Available at: http://www.isprs.org/proceedings/xxxviii/8-W3/B1/3-81.pdf (accessed on 15 November 2013).

Saleth, R.M., and U.A. Amarasinghe. 2010. "Promoting Irrigation Demand Management in India: Options, Linkages and Strategy." *Water Policy* 12 (6): 832–50.

Sankaranarayanan, K., P. Nalayani, M. Sabesh, S. Usharani, R.P. Nachane, and N. Gopalakrishnan. 2011. "Low Cost Drip: Low Cost and Precision Irrigation Tool in Bt Cotton." Technical Bulletin No. 1/2011, Central Research Institute for Cotton, Coimbatore Station, Coimbatore.

Shah, Tushaar. 2009. "Climate Change and Groundwater: India's Opportunities for Mitigation and Adaptation." *Environment Research Letter* 4 (3): 1–13.

Varshneya, M.C., V.B. Vaidya, V. Pandey, L.D. Chimote, K.S. Damle, A.M. Shekh, and B.I. Karande. 2009. "Forecasting of Rainfall for Gujarat Based on Astro-meteorology." *Asian Agri-History* 13 (1): 25–37.

Verma, S., S. Tsephal, and T. Jose. 2004. "Pepsee Systems: Grass Root Innovation Under Groundwater Stress." *Water Policy* 6 (4): 1–16.

Viswanathan, P.K., and C.S. Bahinipati. 2015. "Exploring the Socio-economic Impacts of Micro-irrigation Systems (MIS): A Case Study of Public Tube Wells in Gujarat, Western India." *South Asia Water Studies Journal* 1 (1): 1–25.

Viswanathan, P.K., and J. Pathak. 2014. "Economic Growth and the State of Natural Resources and the Environment in Gujarat: A Critical Assessment." In *Growth or Development: Which Way is Gujarat Going*, edited by Indira Hirway, Amita Shah, and Ghanshyam Shah, 380–432. New Delhi: Oxford University Press.

# 18

# Gender Differences in Social Capital and Collective Action: Does Social Identity Matter in Joint Forest Management?

Biswajit Ray, Promita Mukherjee, and Rabindra N. Bhattacharya*

## Introduction

Community-based natural resource management (CBNRM) is fundamentally premised on collective action. Over the past few decades, CBNRM, along with promotion of sustainable livelihood, has become a popular conservation and development strategy. However, one of the limitations of this conservation model is the biases ingrained in community norms and expectations that exclude certain groups of people such as women, poor, and the lower caste people, who usually confront multiple constraints in their attempts to participate in collective action.[1] To reduce women's marginalization, emphasis is now on understanding the factors affecting gender differences in co-management–related collective action. Some of the discourses towards this end such as group-based studies (e.g., Adkins 2005; Agarwal 2000) and social capital literature (e.g., Molyneux 2002; Westermann, Ashby, and Pretty 2005) argue that gender differences in participation and collective management arise because social networks are themselves gendered. The women, environment, and development literature, by contrast, suggest that sexual division of labour creates gender differences in collective action (e.g., Jackson 1998). Jackson (ibid.) and Agarwal (1992) consider women as inherently closer to nature since women often play an active role in the protection efforts, keeping an informal lookout, or forming patrol groups parallel to men due to their greater dependence on local commons (Agarwal 2000). So women should be the "most appropriate participants" in co-management of natural resources. However, these studies do not explain what accounts for gender differences in social capital and collective action; rather, they build on the assumption that inclusion of women in commons

* We thank the reviewer, Asimina Christoforou, Helena Lopes, and the participants of 7th Biennial Conference of the Indian Society for Ecological Economics, 2013, for their helpful comments. We also thank Department Research Support (DRS)-I at the Department of Economics, University of Calcutta, for funding the study.

management would promote collective action and gender relations in resource-dependent societies, which are mostly patriarchal (Agarwal 2001). However, this assumption was questioned in many studies (e.g., Molyneux 2002).

Furthermore, our knowledge about the implications of gender differences in social capital and, therefore, how to shape programmes to build social capital is incomplete (Krishna 2000). While Westermann et al. (2005) and Molyneux (2002) show that gender differences may lead to differences in creating social capital, Gotschi, Njuki, and Delve (2009) confirm that distribution of social capital benefits is even more gender-sensitive. From the literature, it remains unclear, however, whether an actor's identity impinges on gender differences in community resource management. Since social capital is broadly understood as a social resource based on which people follow different livelihood strategies requiring coordination and collective action (Scoones 1998, 8), integrating an identity perspective in the analysis of gender differences in collective action is imperative. Most importantly, development policies and programmes are identity-driven; policymakers often assume, a priori, that the marginalized groups will want to participate in collective action because such programmes meet their needs, and a better understanding of women's and men's motivations for joining such groups would help policymakers assess the success of their programmes. Moreover, gender may also act as an organizing principle for collective action around which women (or men) may organize in response to constraints within the household and the broader social environment (Pandolfelli, Meinzen-Dick, and Dohrn 2008).

Given this importance of identity in development, this chapter draws on the social identity theory (SIT), which identifies two types of social identity of an actor—natural identity such as gender and caste or group-based identity such as collective or individual identity. An actor is said to be collective (individual) when shared (self-)interests shape his/her behaviours (Araral 2009). The shared interests define and strengthen the actions of the members who act for the collective. Thus, social identity can be considered as a precursor that promotes or impedes collective action in community resource conservation (Polletta and Jasper 2001). Based on this theory, we examine whether gender differences in natural resource management are nested in the differences in actors' identities. Specifically, the chapter seeks to understand how actor's gender as an identity and collectivism/individualism influence the stock and usage of social capital, and, above all, collective action in joint forest management in India.

The rest of the chapter is organized as follows. The theory of social identity is detailed in the section "Social Identity Theory: A Brief Overview." In the section "Gender Differences in Social Capital and Collective Action: Social Identity Hypotheses," we present the link between social identity and collective action and the related hypotheses. Multidisciplinary views on gender and social capital are presented in the section titled "Social Capital and Joint Forest Management in India." Methods of data collection and measurement of the study variables are described in "Data Collection and Methods." Section "Results and Discussions" follows. The final section concludes.

# Social Identity Theory: A Brief Overview

SIT defines a person's social identity as her sense of identifying with others in a social group (Tajfel and Turner 1986). When we belong to a group, we often derive some sense of identity from that group. So social identity is also called group identity. Although developed in sociology, the concept is being increasingly used in economics, starting with Akerlof and Kranton (2000), to understand social capital formation and cooperation (e.g., Chen and Li 2009; Christoforou 2012), conflict resolution, gender discrimination, and even sustainable forest governance (Ray and Bhattacharya 2013; Ray, Mukherjee, and Bhattacharya 2014).

Social identity has three major components: categorization, identification, and comparison. Through categorization we put people, including ourselves, into categories, while identification helps us to associate ourselves with certain groups. Finally, we compare our groups with other groups. The simplest measure of social identity is therefore group membership, where membership criteria may range from art preferences (e.g., Chen and Li 2009) to social attributes such as caste and gender (Ray and Bhattacharya 2013).

The theory asserts that behaviour of actors including individuals and households, in a group is based on the degree of common fate (implicit interdependence among group members). When interdependence is high, then group membership becomes highly relevant and, accordingly, individuals respond as members of the group, seek shared interests, and thus hold a collective identity. Otherwise, they hold an individual identity. Further, SIT conveys that status and identity are correlated and that the high-status individuals/households such as rich perceive that success is linked more to their unique individual identity element such as their capability (Sell 1997). So, the element of common fate is less strong among them and, consequently, high-status people act less as a collective. By contrast, the low-status people believe that the status category is an important determinant of outcomes and low-status people remain as a collective to minimize the risk arising out of conflict and discrimination. Evidence on community-based conservation suggests that women, especially in South Asia are more marginalized and interdependent than men (Agarwal 2001); one implication of SIT is that women participate in conservation activities more collectively than men. However, women's collectivism may vary across contexts and culture.

In short, the theory suggests that in social dilemma like CBNRM: (a) people are biased towards own group; (b) low-status actors like women are more likely to hold collective identity, while high-status actors like men tend to hold individual identity; and (c) people with collective identity tend to cooperate more than those holding individual identities to achieve the goals of the group they belong to (Ray and Bhattacharya 2013; Sell 1997).

# Gender Differences in Social Capital and Collective Action: Social Identity Hypotheses

## Gender Identity and Social Capital

Social capital reflects the access to social resources that are embedded in networks and may provide various benefits, such as information, influence, and control. Putnam (1993) argues that social capital seems to be far from homogenous. Accordingly, social networks may allocate resources differently and, thus, may result in different outcomes for social groups.

Two approaches explain gender differences in the creation of social capital. Gender socialization literature, closely related with social identity literature, attributes gender differences in social capital to gender identity. Gender identity, the literature argues, gets activated due to gender-specific socialization experiences. The literature asserts that the masculine role endorses more instrumental qualities and the feminine role endorses more communal and socio-emotional traits (Bem 1974). These tend to make women's networks more socio-emotional, based on an informal social support network of their everyday interpersonal relationships of trust and cooperation (More 1990). Consequently, their networks may be limited with opportunities to mobilize valued resources compared to the formal networks of men (van Emmerik 2006).

The gender and forest co-management literature, on the other hand, deals with the nature of women's works and conveys that in many societies, the social norms that define gender roles place certain types of networks more within women's domain. For example, women are often the main actors in complex gift exchanges, and in some communities also in forging marriage alliances (Sharma 1980). Further, in the absence of substantial assets or financial resources in their control, "friendships among women are... often cemented by small acts of cooperation and mutual aid" (ibid., 190). This involves more commonly non-monetary help, such as sharing surplus home produce, helping to cook for guests during weddings and birth ceremonies, and so on. This everyday accumulation of social capital falls especially in the domain of women unlike men in market-related activities (Agarwal 2000). These arguments lead to the following hypothesis:

*Hypothesis 1.* Women are more likely to be connected in informal networks, while men's networks are more likely to be formal.

## Social Identity and Social Capital

The social identity approach treats social capital as a collective resource and suggests that the conditions under which members of a collective engage in creating and sustaining the reservoir of social capital depend on the nature and context of the members' network. For example, within a network of villagers working at night to protect the local forest from illegal tree-cutters, the reservoir of social capital depends upon the members' willingness to help maintain an informal communication system alerting other villagers to risks from timber mafias and attacks by stray animals. Unless individuals identify themselves with others, such networks may not be built. However, this feature of social capital is not free from the free rider problem (Putnam 2000).

Given these features, the problem of how to create social capital can be solved by the proper identification of the actor (Granovetter 1985). Two distinct forms of identification are relevant for understanding an individual's willingness to contribute to the creation of social capital within a particular organization (Kramer 2006). These are the individuals' personal identities within the organization and their collective identities. Individuals' personal identities correspond to how they think of themselves as unique, separate members. For example, the leader of a forest management organization might consider himself unique because he may be the only person with the leadership quality. By contrast, individuals' collective identities correspond to the largest relevant organizational aggregate. Accordingly, individuals construe the available social capital in terms of the individual/personal social capital their investments generate and the bonding (within-group) or bridging (between-group) social capital. Given this identity-based notion of social capital, social identity affects social capital creation through cognitive, motivational, and hedonic transformations of human behaviour (Kramer 2006). Cognitive transformations occur through self-categorization and social categorization (Turner 1987). Women, for example, often categorize themselves in terms of collective identities compared to men because they usually think in terms of characteristics such as emotions and solidarity that they have in common with the collective as a whole. These are often the characteristics of informal networks. Motivational orientation refers to the subjective utility that individuals assign to their outcomes versus the outcomes afforded to others in situations of outcome interdependence (Kramer 2006). In the context of hedonic transformation, individuals with collective identities will anticipate that socially defecting choices on their part lead to negative hedonic outcomes (e.g., feelings of guilt or shame, or the fear of being labelled a free rider and of social sanction) as collective identities can engender a form of moralistic trust—trust construed as a duty or obligation on the part of individuals to engage in trustworthy actions (Rotter 1980). Moralistic trust is stronger in individuals with collective identity (Kramer 2006). Such trust is identity-based and so facilitates collective behaviour because it is conferred simply on the basis of recognition of individuals based on their shared interests in a group. We here postulate the following hypothesis:

*Hypothesis 2.* Actors with collective identity are more likely to create bonding (within-group) and bridging (between-group) social capital more in terms of informal networks, whereas actors with individual identities derive benefits from any form of networks by means of their influence and power, irrespective of their investment in social capital.

## Social Identity and Gender Differences in Collective Action

The influence of social identity on collective action manifests through its moderating the effect of group size (Kramer and Brewer 1984) and redefining self-interest (Coleman 1961). Olson (1965, 65) argued that "the larger a group is, the farther it will fall short of providing an optimal supply of any collective good...

in short, the larger the group, the less it will further common interests." While theorizing the detrimental effects of group size on collective outcomes, researchers of common pool resource (CPR) management implicitly assume that the individual decision-maker is the basic unit of interest. Thus, group size is defined in terms of the number of individuals in the organization/group. SIT (e.g., Tajfel and Turner 1986), however, demonstrates that self-interest may not always be defined at the individual level. Coleman (1961) noted that:

> Classic economic theory always assumes that the individual will act in "his" interest; but it never examined carefully the entity to which "his" refers… in many situations men act as if the "his" refers to some entity larger than themselves. That is, they appear to act in terms, not of their own interest, but in the interests of a collectivity (p. 24).

Brewer and Silver (2000) argue that collective identity may create a common social boundary that acts to reduce the social distance among group members. Thus, whether individuals respond pro-socially to a social dilemma may depend on whether they think of themselves as single and autonomous individuals or as part of a larger aggregate or social unit. Thus, social identity is a "group resource that is critical to the ability of the group to mobilize collective action…." (Brewer and Silver 2000, 154).

In community-based forestry, this implies that when a group has a strong collective identity, group size does not matter in cooperation. Moreover, men tend to be involved in those conservation activities that maintain their individual identity and, thus, exclude women from decision-making (Ray et al. 2014). This makes women more marginalized. Moreover, women's forest dependency is greater, everyday, and more immediate (Agarwal 2000). So women tend to be more collective (ibid.) and their proportional strength as decision-makers matters in forest co-management (Agarwal 2010). Hence, we hypothesize the following:

*Hypothesis 3.* Men's and women's participation in collective actions in community-based forest management are driven by their identity.

*Hypothesis 4.* Collective identity rather than individual identity and women's proportional strength in the decision-making committee of a forest management group promote collective action and maturity of the group irrespective of its size.

However, the above-discussed literatures remain silent about the distributive equity of social capital benefits. Moreover, it may be difficult to understand who benefits more from social networks—men or women, because women's networks may be inherently distinct from men's networks because of women's nature of work (Agarwal 2000). Nevertheless, these approaches hold a consensus that because men and women generally hold different identities; distribution of social capital benefits should also be gendered. In sum, we anticipate that in forest co-management, gender differences in social capital and collective action are nested in actor's identity differences. To test this main hypothesis, we examine the validity of the above four hypotheses embedded in it based on household surveys in the forest areas of West Bengal, India.

## Social Capital and Joint Forest Management in India

In the context of India's joint forest management, those activities that a particular culture considers best undertaken collectively and those that are more likely to create shared identity have created social capital (Krishna 2004). Homogeneous social structures such as tribal villages in rural India have developed social cohesion and community identity, which often form mutual trust for collective action for joint forestry (D'Silva and Pai 2003). Complimentary relationship between forest officers and the locals have also created social capital (Ray and Bhattacharya 2011). Krishna (2004) noticed a number of sources of social capital and shared identity in India like labour groups. Because they have a history of self-help movements by local people to preserve forests, some states such as Orissa and Uttaranchal have successfully built social networks.

Moreover, a village may possess a high level of solidarity if it can collectively tackle issues such as crop disease and natural calamity that require immediate help from the locals as well as government.

In West Bengal, our study area, the most common forms of social capital include: (a) the existence of systems of mutual assistance, gift exchange, marriage alliance, and respect for reciprocal norms in women's everyday work (Agrawal 2000), (b) rotating silvicultural work schemes based on reciprocity, (c) labour groups, and (d) NGO-led informal cooperation through various activities such as vegetation monitoring and a number of development projects and additional support activities to bolster the participatory social capital. Informal cooperation in rural communities of West Bengal typically reflects the norms of solidarity and reciprocity that have built a social safety net to address human–animal conflicts, and chronic or seasonal shortages in labour and food. On the other hand, illegal poaching and other timber-harvesting activities represent lack of stocks of cognitive social capital like conservation-friendly attitudes of a community. Significantly, social capital in rural West Bengal is often found to be related to productivity, equity, and sustainability of CBNRM (Mukherjee 2005).

# Data Collection and Methods

## Selection of Forestry Organizations and Households

The analysis draws on a field study conducted in the forest areas managed by seven Joint Forest Management Committees (JFMCs) located in West Midnapore and Jalpaiguri (now Alipurduar) districts of West Bengal, India during June–December 2010. The choice of the two districts does not undermine the problems of forest management in the other districts/regions. Moreover, the sheer magnitude of the problem and extent of national and international interventions for co-management in West Midnapore and Jalpaiguri also prompted the choice of the study areas. At the same time, as the two districts vary considerably in terms of biophysical and socio-economic characteristics, the selection of the study sites was considered likely to yield more information on co-management.

The focus of the fieldwork was to evaluate the significance of natural identities (e.g., gender) and collectivism/individualism of the forest dependent households in explaining the gender differences, if any, in the stock and usage of social capital and the associated implications on the maturity of the local forest management organizations. Seven JFMCs were selected from the two districts based on, among other factors, their variations in the following criteria relevant to this study: (a) apparent degree of success in forest management in terms of forest conditions and forest benefits/access; (b) degree of women's participation; (c) household-level diversity reflecting different identities; (d) group size (number of members of the JFMCs); (e) size of the forests, and (f) existence of various forms of social networks, which are considered as associational social capital. Panialguri, Kalkut-Cheko, and Poro-Basti JFMCs are located in the Northern part of West Bengal. They manage moist deciduous sal and teak forests. By contrast, Salbani, Chharadhan, Mahuldanga, and Bansachati JFMCs situated in the West Midnapore district of the southern part of West Bengal manage dry deciduous sal forests.

We confined the surveys to the heads of sample households and interviewed every third household of the relatively large JFMCs (with more than 50 member households); otherwise, we selected every second household. Pre-tested questionnaires were used to elicit information from the respondents on various forms of social identity like gender and organizational identity in terms of their organizational commitment (OC), informal and formal social networks they are connected with, their investment in and benefit from such networks, and collective forest conservation activities. We adopted a quantitative–qualitative triangulation method for data collection (Creswell 2002) and collected data on only the forms of networks which the local stakeholders considered to have significant impacts on collective action; and hence did not collect data on personal social capital as it is supposed to be linked more to individual's gains than co-management. We also extracted some qualitative information through interviews and chats with the experts and the key informants and also consulted several documents to understand the local conservation and development issues more precisely. Altogether, 383 household were interviewed and the final analysis rests on 341 questionnaires as 42 questionnaires were incomplete.

## Study Variables: Description and Measurement

### Organizational Commitment and Collective Identity of JFMCs

We measure respondents' collective identity by extracting information on their OC because it is generally defined as the relative strength of an individual's identification with and involvement in a particular organization (Mowday, Porter, and Steers 1982, 27). We used a set of statements to measure OC of respondents (Table A18.1) adopted from the popular OC Questionnaire (Balfour and Wechsler 1996; Mowday, Steers, and Porter 1979), while the other statements were constructed using participatory rural appraisal (PRA) method in the study areas. We considered those statements that emphasize a member's likelihood to expend extra effort, take pride in her organizational membership, and experience overall affection for the organization.

In line with the OC literature, we use a five-point Likert scale for each statement ranging from strongly agree (5) to strongly disagree (1). We then standardized and summed the statement scores to arrive at an average OC score. Respondents with above average (below average) score were defined as having high (low) OC. At the organization level, a JFMC is defined to have a *high* (*low*) collective identity if at least 75 per cent of its members are found to have *high* (*low*) commitment. If this figure is in between 50 and less than 75 per cent, then the collective identity of the JFMC is referred to as *moderate*.

To check the consistency of the commitment scale, we calculated Cronbach's alpha (Cronbach 1951). It is defined as the proportion of true score variance to observed score variance. Here true scores reflect the respondents' true commitment, while stated scores represent their stated commitment. Conventionally, if alpha exceeds 0.70 for a scale (implying that 70% of the responses captured via the scale are true), then we treat the respondents' responses as reliable. The OC scale used here appeared reliable (Cronbahc's Alpha = 0.85). Regarding the validity of the scale, we found that the average commitment scores of the top and the bottom 25 per cent of the respondents (reflecting high and low commitments) vary significantly ($t = 3.27$, $p = 0.01$). Also, the commitment scores of the households of Garam Basti, a non-study village located near the Panialguri JFMCs appeared highly correlated with those of the surveyed villagers (Pearson's Correlation coefficient ($r$) = 0.78). These two findings suggest that the commitment scale used in this research was valid.

### Women's Presence

We measure women's presence in co-management through their participation in the Executive Committee (EC) meetings of the JFMC following the typology of participation developed by Agarwal (2001, 2010) ranging from *nominal* to *interactive* (*empowering*). When women are just the members of the EC and do not participate in any other activities, their participation is defined as *nominal*. When the EC women are "informed of the decision *ex post facto;* or attending meetings and listening in on decision-making, without speaking up," they have a *passive participation*. *Consultative participation* occurs when an EC women is "asked an opinion in specific matters without guarantee of influencing decisions." Despite this, they may also have an *activity-specific participation* describing a situation of "being asked to (or volunteering to) undertake specific tasks." If one "expresses opinions, whether or not solicited, or takes initiatives of other sorts," she is assigned to have an *active participation*. *Interactive (empowering) participation* takes place when one has "voice or influence in the group's decisions, holding positions as office bearers" (ibid.).

### Stock and Usage of Social Capital

Social capital creation is an outcome of continuous investment of time and resources by households (Narayan 1998). Accordingly, following Gotschi et al. (2009), we construct an index of social capital investment by summing: the number of times a household has helped others and given credit, made in-kind contribution like giving others surplus home produce as seen in women's networks (Agarwal 2000), involved in forging marriage alliances, number of friends a household has and the number of times it has invited others, number of influential contacts it has established with key local actors such as governmental leaders, traditional leaders, NGO/projects-related personnel etc., and number of times it has contributed to conflict resolution.

The benefits of the above networks include access to help-in-need (food, sickness, labour, counselling etc.), credit, institutions (local self-government, market, agricultural input/tools, etc.), source of information (family, community members, other communities, local market etc.), cross-cultural access (receiving invitations from people of other culture), and more importantly, number of problems faced (due to differences in social status, gender, religion, culture, and other problems like those between JFMC and forest department). A household earns for each type of benefit a score of 1 if it has access to that benefit and 0 otherwise. The scoring pattern was reversed in the case of number of problems because it represents lack of social capital. The index of social capital benefits of a household is the sum of these access scores less the problem scores.

A high value of the investment index reveals that a household possesses a high stock of social capital while a high value of the benefit index signals a greater usage of social capital by the individual. At the JFMC level, these indices represent the stock and usage of social capital of the organization. We anticipate that a JFMC with high stock and/or greater usage of social capital achieve high collective action.

## Collective Action

Measurement and types of collective action vary across studies. For example, Varughese and Ostrom (2001) construct a qualitative index of collective action applying their subjective judgement on community forestry in Nepal. Somanathan, Prabhakar, and Mehta (2007) consider the number of forest council meetings held and hiring of watchmen for forest management as the measures of collective action in northern India. We consider the following aspects and scoring rule of collective action to construct a quantitative index of collective action based on Mukherjee (2011).

## Scoring Rules

*Rule compliance:*

(i)   Award 10 points to the JFMC where more than 60 per cent of the JFMC members are well aware of the CPR rules and abide by them accordingly;

(ii)  Award 0 points to the JFMC, where majority users (>60%) do not know and follow operational rules of the JFMC;

(iii) Award 5 points to the JFMC where the situation is intermediate of (i) and (ii).

*Rule infractions:*

(iv)  Award 10 points to the JFMC where rules infractions are, on average, less than once every year in the last five years and the defectors have to pay fines within stipulated time/date in the event of non-compliance.

(v)   Award 0 point to the JFMC where rules infractions are, on average, more than twice every year in the last five years and defectors are not penalized oftentimes or the JFMC let them go unnoticed.

(vi)  Award 5 points to the JFMCs where situations are intermediate of (v) and (vi).

*Participation:*

(vii) Award 10 points to the JFMCs where more than 60 per cent of the members attend every conservation-related (General Body) meeting in the last five years.

(viii)  Award 0 point to the JFMCs where more than 60 per cent of the members do not attend the JFMC meeting in the last five years.

(ix)  Award 5 points to the JFMCs where meeting attendance is intermediate of (vii) and (viii).

*Awareness about the Joint Forest Management:*

(x)  Award 10 points to the JFMCs where more than 60 per cent of the members are aware of the objectives and benefits of joint forest management;

(xi)  Award 0 point if more than 60 per cent of the JFMC members do not this much knowledge about JFM;

(xii)  Award 5 points if the situation of the JFMCs is intermediate of (xi) and (xii).

Following this scheme, a JFMC can obtain 0–40 points. The Oscoring method appeared robust since the scores under our scheme of awarding points and that of Ray and Bhattacharya (2011) were highly correlated (Pearson's correlation coefficient of absolute scores of different JFMCs = 0.93 [$p < 0.01$]) and the rank correlation (Kendall's Tau) = 0.81 ($p < 0.02$). Therefore, in the two schemes, the absolute and the relative positions of the JFMCs remain unchanged.

## Group Maturity

Group maturity is defined as a group's potential for self-defining and self-sustaining activity (Pretty and Ward 2001, 209). Scholars explain the stages through which groups/organizations progress towards maturity in different ways. Mooney and Reiley (1931) consider five stages of group life cycles, including emergence, growth, maturity, decline, and death. While Handy (1985) conceptualizes group maturity as organizational learning through the stages of forming to performing of groups, Pretty (1995) sees this closely related with members' participation. Further, group maturity is also linked with the nature of the wider development process through co-management among other stages (Pretty and Ward 2001). These models convey that the organizations in the later stages are capable of resisting shocks and stresses, and are also likely to innovate more, and hence have lower probability of decline.

In commons management, Pretty and Ward (2001, 218) have operationalized the concept based on some criteria which can be found at three stages of organizational development termed reactive dependence, realization independence, and awareness interdependence.[2] Westermann et al. (2005, 1787) consider the following seven criteria to measure group maturity: (a) group objectives concerning natural resource management which reflect whether the group is reactive, regenerative, or innovative; (b) the group's views on change (whether the group avoids change, adjusts to change, or creates new opportunities); (c) whether the group monitors and evaluates its own progress; (d) the degree of external dependence to solve problems; (e) collective or individual planning and testing; (f) the importance of external aid for group formation; and (g) resilience of the group (capacity to survive external disturbances that tend to break up the group). Following this literature, we capture group maturity for the sampled JFMCs using 10 criteria (Table A18.2). We award a JFMC a score of 1–3 for each criterion if it is in the stage 1–3 under that criterion. Thus, the maturity score varies from 10 to 30. The higher score of a JFMC reflects greater maturity of the organization.

# Results and Discussion

## Gender Differences in Social Networks

Table 18.1 reports different forms of social networks in the study villages—the first four constitute informal networks and the rest are formal or market-linked. Further, Table 18.1 shows a number of observations

**Table 18.1**

Gendered differences in social networks differentiated by social identity

| Actors' identity | Obs. | Forms of social network[a] | | | | | | |
|---|---|---|---|---|---|---|---|---|
| | | Gift-exchange | Mutual aid | Marriage alliance | Kinship/Friendship | Formal membership (non-forestry) | Connection with local power structure | Connections with market |
| Male | 182 | 14.29 | 14.29 | 8.24 | 12.09 | 36.81 | 48.90 | 71.43 |
| Female | 159 | 67.30 | 67.30 | 44.03 | 60.38 | 37.11 | 16.35 | 16.35 |
| Individual | 177 | 23.16 | 19.21 | 13.56 | 11.30 | 24.86 | 42.37 | 51.98 |
| Collective | 164 | 59.76 | 65.24 | 40.24 | 65.24 | 52.44 | 22.56 | 37.20 |
| Male individual | 122 | 8.20 | 5.74 | 5.74 | 2.46 | 28.69 | 51.64 | 68.85 |
| Male collective | 60 | 28.33 | 35.00 | 13.33 | 35.00 | 56.67 | 43.33 | 78.33 |
| Female individual | 55 | 52.73 | 47.27 | 29.09 | 29.09 | 18.18 | 23.64 | 18.18 |
| Female collective | 104 | 76.92 | 80.77 | 53.85 | 80.77 | 50.00 | 11.54 | 15.38 |
| EC males | 18 | 22.22 | 22.22 | 11.11 | 22.22 | 55.56 | 22.22 | 22.22 |
| EC females | 10 | 90.00 | 60.00 | 60.00 | 60.00 | 40.00 | 40.00 | 40.00 |
| Total | 341 | 39.00 | 39.00 | 24.93 | 34.90 | 36.95 | 33.72 | 45.45 |

*Source:* Author Survey.

*Notes:* [a] Figures are in percentages. Male: male head of the household; Female: female head of the household; Individual: households with individual identity; Collective: households with collective identity; Male individual: males with individual identity; Likewise, the other terms in Table 18.1 can be explained.

pertinent to the queries posed above. First, participants with collective identity are connected more with informal networks, mainly through gift exchange, mutual aid, and friendship/kinship. By contrast, participants with individual identity are connected in formal networks, especially with the local power structure and market. Second, while women are involved mostly in gift exchange and mutual aid, connection with markets is the most dominant form of men's network. Thus, both genders as a natural identity and participants' collective identity matter in social network. Besides, the high-status females like those in the ECs of the JFMCs (denoted by *EC females*) are more connected with the local market and in the local power structure than the general female members. Most importantly, gender differences in social networks have increased significantly between males with individual identity (denoted by *male individual*) and females with collective identity (denoted by *female collective*). This suggests that identity differences between men and women may make gender differences in social networks more distinct.

The findings reinforce empirical evidence on gender differences in social network from a social identity perspective. Agarwal (2000) and Westermann et al. (2005) posit that women and men depend on different types of social networks based on their everyday forms of collaboration. Women usually collect fuel wood, fetch water, and bring up a child. Such informal networks provide women with access to household resources such as water and firewood. By contrast, men are often engaged in more formal networks, like community councils that improve access to economic resources and decision-making (or power; Agrawal 2000). At the same time, women usually reveal more relational and altruistic behaviour due to their role and responsibility for reproduction (Folbre 1994; Sharma 1980), while men are more individualistic and more engaged in formal collaboration, decision-making, and organized power structures. The implication is that women and men may value collaboration differently based not only on reciprocal relationships and a higher dependence on social relations as stated by Cleaver (1998) and Agrawal (2000) but also on their identity differences. Here we extend the existing literature and suggest that differences in identity leads to more obvious gender differences in the creation of social capital.

## Distribution of Social Capital Benefits

Table 18.2 shows the distributive equity in social capital benefits across the different groups. Here social capital benefits include increasing the likelihood to receive support in case of need, access to information, and so on using one's supportive social networks. The table demonstrates that men or male-headed households as compared to women are more successful in obtaining credit and helps in need and accessing different institutions or information. Similarly, men have reported experiencing and suffering from problems significantly less often than women or female-headed households. They also have greater cross-cultural access such as having friends and attending invitations parties of another culture, communities, and religions.

It emerged that women in leadership positions (i.e., EC females) can improve their social capital benefits, as they do partly catch up with males in terms of accessing institutions and help, but it remains more likely for male members than female leaders to obtain credit. Although all the female leaders derive benefits from their access to help in need, they lag behind male leaders (EC males) in tapping other benefits. In short, the distribution of social capital benefits is highly male-biased including both leaders and non-leaders.

In contrast, households with individual identity build up formal networks (Table 18.1) and enjoy greater access to credit, institutions, and influential persons, and, consequently, a majority of them report fewer problems than those with collective identity (Table 18.2). Interestingly, males with individual identity capture social capital benefits significantly more than females with collective identity. These findings raise some serious concerns about co-management. First, although co-management aims to achieve conservation with community development, we find that low-identifying stakeholders like females invest more in the creation of social networks (Table 18.1) but do not ultimately get significant benefits in return. Rather, women confront more problems than men do (Table 18.2). Second, since social capital benefits are identity-determined (Christoforou 2012), actors' identity differences create inequitable distribution of these benefits.

**Table 18.2**

*Gendered differences in social capital benefits differentiated by social identity*

| Participants | Credit | Help-in-need | Institutions | Access to social capital benefits | | | | |
| | | | | Influential persons | Source of information | Number of problems | Cross-cultural access | Number of invitation |
|---|---|---|---|---|---|---|---|---|
| Male | 73.63 | 71.43 | 63.19 | 71.43 | 65.38 | 66.48 | 71.43 | 73.63 |
| Female | 39.62 | 55.97 | 41.51 | 27.67 | 37.11 | 76.73 | 65.41 | 65.41 |
| Individual | 87.01 | 84.75 | 72.32 | 70.06 | 57.63 | 55.93 | 72.32 | 72.32 |
| Collective | 45.12 | 62.80 | 50.00 | 47.56 | 50.00 | 65.24 | 52.44 | 54.88 |
| Male individual | 63.11 | 63.11 | 59.84 | 54.10 | 59.84 | 59.84 | 59.84 | 68.85 |
| Male collective | 55.00 | 71.67 | 50.00 | 75.00 | 61.67 | 31.67 | 83.33 | 66.67 |
| Female individual | 21.82 | 58.18 | 23.64 | 47.27 | 52.73 | 30.91 | 36.36 | 40.00 |
| Female collective | 34.62 | 61.54 | 46.15 | 34.62 | 42.31 | 19.23 | 34.62 | 38.46 |
| EC males | 83.33 | 83.33 | 77.78 | 88.89 | 83.33 | 83.33 | 61.11 | 72.22 |
| EC females | 60.00 | 100.00 | 60.00 | 40.00 | 30.00 | 40.00 | 40.00 | 40.00 |
| Total | 57.77 | 64.22 | 53.08 | 51.03 | 52.20 | 75.07 | 68.62 | 69.79 |

*Source:* Author Survey.

For example, in the study areas, households with individual identity, who hold mostly high status, are deriving all kinds of social capital benefits and confronting fewer problems than people with collective identity (Table 18.2). This casts doubt on whether co-management has meaningfully served the resource dependent community.

The practical implication is that both of the differences in gender's identity and the differences in group identity often lead to distinct social networks of men and women that reproduce power relations and determine access to various institutions. Patterns of power relations between men and women at the household level get translated into gendered group relations. For instance, the fact that men represent the household and women have to ask their permission to engage in extra-household activities often results in dominance of men talking in group discussions and restricts women from expressing their opinions. This reveals that the creation of all women groups only addresses a part of the "gender problem" (Gotschi et al. 2009) because sometimes mixed groups are more cooperative in natural resource co-management (Agarwal 2010). Though mixed groups perpetuate female subordination and restrict female participation in leadership positions, women in mixed groups may enter masculine social spaces and establish contacts and capture some of the male resources that help them to access information and help in need than the all-women groups (Gotschi et al. 2009). This may reduce gender differences in the stock and usage of social capital and encourage high collective action.

## Men's and Women's Identity and Participation in Collective Action

Table 18.3 presents significant gender differences in collective action. We divide the collective activities into identity-preserving activities such as decision-making and implementation, and general activities like forest patrolling. Clearly, there exist significant gender differences in collective activities. Moreover, when stakeholder identity interacts with gender, these gender differences become more distinct. Thus, Table 18.3 suggests that high-identifying stakeholders like men tend to be interested and involved more in identity-preserving collective actions such as decision-making, monitoring etc. to exercise command and control over others that in turn help them to maintain their status in the village society.

**Table 18.3**
Men's and women's identity and gender differences in collective action

| Actors | Identity-preserving activities (column a–d) | | | | General activities (column e–h) | | | |
|---|---|---|---|---|---|---|---|---|
| | Office bearing (a) | Monitoring (b) | Decision-making and implementation (c) | Conflict resolution (d) | Information collection and sharing (e) | Nominal attendance at meetings (f) | Forest patrolling and regeneration (g) | Does not participate in any activities (h) |
| Men | 7.3 | 48.6 | 70.9 | 79.9 | 15.1 | 19.6 | 11.7 | 24.6 |
| Women | 1.2 | 10.5 | 1.2 | 0.0 | 79.0 | 75.3 | 85.8 | 35.2 |
| Male individual | 8.5 | 67.5 | 81.7 | 82 | 18.2 | 10 | 12.62 | 7.1 |
| Female Collective | 1.2 | 13 | 1.2 | 0 | 82 | 68.50 | 90.20 | 20.88 |

*Source:* Author Survey.
*Note:* Sum of percentage across each row may exceed 100 per cent, as people of each group may be involved in more than one collective activity.

**Table 18.4**
Linking collective identity and women's presence with group maturity

| Forest Management Committees | Identity of the JFMCs | % of women as decision-makers in the executive committee | Women's participation | Stock of social capital (average score) | Social capital benefits (average score) | Group size (no of members in the JFMC) | Group maturity index | Collective action score |
|---|---|---|---|---|---|---|---|---|
| Chharadhan | collective | 33 | activity-specific | 55 | 60 | 31 | 23 | 40 |
| Panialguri | collective | 33 | Active | 60 | 70 | 381 | 23 | 35 |
| Salbani | moderately collective | 33 | Active | 62 | 55 | 96 | 21 | 30 |
| Kalkut-Cheko | moderately collective | 0 | Passive | 55 | 30 | 119 | 17 | 25 |
| Mahuldanga | moderately collective | 33 | activity-specific | 45 | 55 | 75 | 19 | 20 |
| Poro-Basti | individual | 0 | Nominal | 50 | 20 | 184 | 15 | 15 |
| Banschati | individual | 0 | Nominal | 35 | 10 | 52 | 11 | 10 |

*Source:* Author Survey.

## Collective Identity, Proportion of Women as Decision-makers and Maturity of the Forestry Organizations

Table 18.4 reports the possible link between identity of the local forestry organizations and their maturity. Clearly, Chharadhan and Panialguri are the only two out of the seven JFMCs that hold collective identities with more committed members, and this commitment surprisingly does not depend on their group size (Pearson's correlation coefficient between group size and collective identity of the JFMCs=0.30, $p=0.51$; Table A18.3). Although Chharadhan and Panialguri are the smallest and largest organizations in the study sites, both have obtained the highest score of group maturity. This indicates that they have already reached the stage of *awareness interdependence* with greater resilience. Thus, collective identity in the form of OC if activated within a group moderates the negative effect of group size on collective action. This may be attributable to higher stock and usage of social capital (Pretty and Ward 2001) or women's greater active participation as decision-makers in these JFMCs (Agarwal 2000) or both.

However, Poteete and Ostrom (2004) suggest the most interesting explanation of identity-induced collective action. They reason that income effect may explain this unexpected phenomenon. When a forest resource is a non-rival and normal collective good, and group size is small (e.g., Banschati), a higher per capita contribution by the members is required to conserve a forest. This may discourage the members from cooperating as a collective. Therefore, the transaction costs of cooperation become higher. The converse experience (e.g., Panialguri JFMC) is also true. Olson (1965) emphasizes the influence of group size on the costs of collective provision; transaction costs increase with group size and raise the costs of initiating collective action. Larger groups are expected to bear higher transaction costs due to heterogeneous choices and constraints of the stakeholders in resource conservation. However, the present study shows that the largest JFMC (Panialguri) is successful in progressing towards maturity. We note that in Panialguri, the local people value the local forest significantly for its environmental and climatic benefits, in-situ features, and sustained flow of resource benefits meeting local subsistence needs. This might imply that they treat the local forest as a normal good. Whenever their contributions to forest management, which Poteete and Ostrom (2004) consider as incomes, increase due to their collective identity, they claim more of such benefits from the local forest that might further make the locals more collective.

By contrast, in organizations such as Poro-Basti and Banschati JFMC, where individual identity outweighs collective identity, free-riding ruins trust among actors and therefore prevents them from progressing towards maturity (Pretty and Ward 2001). These organizations confront various sociocultural obstacles to development such as the nominal representation of women in the decision-making body due to strong patriarchy. Also, the benefits of social networks in these organizations do not percolate down to all households, who invest in building social networks. This is manifested in the low scores of social capital benefits of Poro-Basti and Banschati (Table 18.4). As a result, both JFMCs have higher transaction costs and poor maturity (Ray and Bhattacharya 2011). These organizations are likely to be at an early stage of *reactive dependence* (Pretty and Ward 2001).

Gotschi et al. (2009) contend that despite having high social capital, a system may not achieve sustainable cooperation if social capital benefits are low or some individuals reap most of these benefits. We confront a similar situation in the study areas when we compare Kalkut-Cheko and Mahuldanga JFMCs.

Most importantly, women's presence as decision-makers does matter in promoting group maturity and collective action. Table 18.4 shows that where women's proportional strength and hence the level of participation are greater, collective action is also higher. This finding is supported elsewhere (Agarwal 2015). Moreover, evidence from Mahuldanga and Salbani JMFCs implies that moderately collective organizations may also achieve high group maturity if their female members participate actively in various co-management activities. However, some small organizations (e.g., Banschati) do not significantly progress towards maturity because women's participation in these organizations is either nominal or passive and members are also less collective.

Although joint forest management is being practiced in the study areas over the past two decades, we observe that women in all the seven JFMCs are yet to be fully empowered. This leaves room for improving gender relation and maturity of these organizations. From a social identity perspective, we suggest that because women tend to hold collective identity, community organizations should ensure women's interactive participation in development programmes for successful management of community resources.

# Conclusions

This chapter builds on the social identity perspective of the different and complementary roles of women and men in the analysis of social capital formation and the potential consequences of such differences for natural resource management groups. We are guided by the main proposition that gender differences in social capital formation and collective action are more identity-based; and that the organizations with better representation of women would achieve greater progress towards maturity. Generally, women report more commitment to their organizations than men (Mathieu and Zajac 1990) because women have to overcome more barriers and hence make an extra effort to gain empowerment in an organization (Grusky 1966). This extra effort may be reflected in a higher commitment by females.

This chapter has established a number of hypotheses. On the one hand, the hypotheses relating to gender differences in social capital are valid because women tend to have a more collective identity than men and such identity relates them with informal networks. Another set of hypotheses relates women's presence with collective action through identity. Overall finding is that maturity and collective action of a co-management organization improve with a higher degree of women's participation because women's participation as decision-makers enhances people's overall conservation-related attitudes (Ray, Mukherjee, and Bhattacharya forthcoming). A related finding is that organizations, where actors are not collective, may have less progress towards maturity. Such proposition is not surprising because social relations are often identity-driven (Kramer 2006), and collectivism rather than group size of an organization matters more in sustaining cooperation.

In summary, perhaps norms of reciprocity operate in groups where women are actively present in decision-making and that this may be the result of women's tendency to remain as a collective that sustains their frequent collaboration through informal social networks. Consequently, we recommend that interventions to improve collective action for natural resource management should directly address the gender and identity composition of the members of a co-management organization because women tend to be more collective than men, and, in particular, the groups' relational and instrumental social capital, and any norms, rules, or networks that exclude women from participation and decision-making. Women should also be able to comprehend their patterns of interdependence so as to influence and facilitate gender relations and dynamics in collective action groups. Most importantly, the meaning of participation and common fate to women and men should be assessed to better understand the dynamics and processes of how they use collective action resources in gender-differentiated groups.

# Appendix

## Table A18.1
*Statements used to measure organizational commitment*

| *Organization commitment scale used in the study* |
| --- |
| There's not much to be gained by sticking with this organization indefinitely (reversed). (Mowday et al. 1979). |
| I treat any failure of the local JFMC/group as my own (PRA). |
| My livelihood is dependent on how we, as the members of the local JFMC, perform (PRA). |
| I stand by any member of my JFMC when there is any conflict with other JFMCs for whatever the reason (PRA). |
| If not allowed to speak up in a group meeting, I, as a member, still adhere to the group decision (PRA). |
| I find that my values and the organization's values are very similar (Mowday et al. 1979) |
| I am willing to put in a great deal of effort beyond that normally expected in order to help this organization to be successful (Mowday et al. 1979). |
| Had I not been a member of the local JFMC, I would not be able to extract forest resources as sustainably as I do it now (PRA). |
| I feel a strong sense of belonging to this organization (Balfour and Wechsler 1996). |
| I feel like "part of the family" at this organization (Balfour and Wechsler 1996). |
| I am proud to tell others that I am part of this organization (Mowday et al. 1979). |
| I really care about the fate of this organization (Mowday et al. 1979). |
| To know that my own work had made a contribution to the good of the organization would please me (Cook and Wall 1980, 51). |

*Note:*   Organization in the statements implies JFMCs in the study areas.

## Table A18.2
*Three-stage model of group maturity*

| Criteria | *Stage 1*<br>*Reactive dependence* | *Stage 2*<br>*Realization independence* | *Stage 3*<br>*Awareness interdependence* |
| --- | --- | --- | --- |
| Group formation | Initiated by external agency or emerging | Because one or more of its members took the initiative and there was external agency support to help it form | Because one of more of the members took the initiative to form the group without external support |
| Group objective | To conserve resources from further degradation, or to restore resources to a previous state, defensive | To adjust to new realities and regenerate forest resources, reactive | To create new opportunities in managing a natural-resources-integrating conservation with livelihood development |
| Rules and norms | Externally imposed or derived | Development of own rules and norms | Evolution and strengthening of rules and norms |
| Attitudes | No significant change in attitudes, beliefs and values—backward-looking group-making sense of old realities | Realization of new capacities—inward-looking group-making sense of new reality | Conceptualization of new insights—forward-looking group—shaping reality |

| Criteria | Stage 1 Reactive dependence | Stage 2 Realization independence | Stage 3 Awareness interdependence |
|---|---|---|---|
| Views of change | Fear of change | Adjusting to change in a reactive way | Creating change for new opportunities in proactive manner |
| Management and learning | Eco-efficiency—reducing costs and damage | Collective planning for experimentation—Regeneration—adoption of regenerative technology for sustainable use of natural capital | Redesign according to basic ecological principles—innovation for developing new system of management |
| External links and networks | Few or no links with other groups, link from above to below | Links with other groups—send information upward or realizes information can flow upward | Capable of promoting spread and initiating new groups—strong link with external agencies |
| Collective activities | Relies on external facilitators to sustain group activities | Tries to self-promote collective action before seeking external help for conflict resolution | Facilitators no longer needed |
| Recognition of group value | Some recognition that group has value to achieve something new | Members increasingly willing to invest in group itself | Group likely to express social value of group |
| Resilience | Breakdown possible before achieving group objectives | Breakdown possible after achievement of initial goals | Unlikely to breakdown—passed a threshold—objectives redefined after achieving initial goals |

**Table A18.3**

Correlation matrix on different attributes of forest management organizations

| | Collective action score | Identity of JFMC | % of women as decision-makers in the executive committee | Women's participation | Group size (no of members in the JFMC) | Stock of Social capital | Usage of social capital | Group maturity index |
|---|---|---|---|---|---|---|---|---|
| Collective action score | 1 | | | | | | | |
| Identity of JFMC | 0.945*** | 1 | | | | | | |
| % of women as decision-makers in the executive committee | 0.722 | 0.764 | 1 | | | | | |
| Women's participation | 0.783** | 0.806** | 0.955*** | 1 | | | | |
| Group size | 0.227 | 0.300 | 0.122 | 0.263 | 1 | | | |
| Stock of social capital | 0.801** | 0.656* | 0.506 | 0.677* | 0.440 | 1 | | |
| Usage of social capital | 0.850*** | 0.899*** | 0.942*** | 0.961*** | 0.338 | 0.684* | 1 | |
| Group maturity index | 0.941*** | 0.922*** | 0.865*** | 0.904*** | 0.310 | 0.809** | 0.964*** | 1 |

*Note:* *, **, and *** represent level of significance at 10, 5, and 1 per cent, respectively (one-tailed).

## Notes

1. For example, women, poor, and the lower caste people face constraints that arise out of shortages of time and labour, general adverse perceptions and low expectations of other stakeholders about their contributions to resource management (Mukherjee, Ray, and Bhattacharya [forthcoming]), and rules made by the influential people (Agarwal 2001).
2. According to Pretty and Ward (2001, 219–20), *reactive dependence* refers to the first stage of organizational development when a group reacts to external threats or crises and tends to look for external facilitators. *Realization independence* is the second stage where an already formed group develops new capabilities to become independent to tackle disturbances. With this realization, such independent groups progress towards the stage of *awareness–interdependence*. At this stage, groups are engaged in shaping their own development path.

## References

Adkins, L. 2005. "Social Capital: The Anatomy of a Troubled Concept." *Feminist Theory* 6 (2): 195–211.

Agarwal, B. 1992. "The Gender and Environment Debate: Lessons from India." *Feminist Studies* 18 (1): 119–58.

———. 2000. "Conceptualising Environmental Collective Action: Why Gender Matters." *Cambridge Journal of Economics* 24 (3): 283–310.

———. 2001. "Participatory Exclusions, Community Forestry, and Gender: An Analysis for South Asia and a Conceptual Framework." *World Development* 29 (10): 1623–48.

———. 2010. "Does Women's Proportional Strength Affect Their Participation? Governing Local Forests in South Asia." *World Development* 38 (1): 98–112.

———. 2015. "Power of Numbers in Gender Dynamics: Illustrations from Community Forestry Groups." *The Journal of Peasant Studies* 42 (1): 1–20.

Akerlof, G., and R. Kranton. 2000. "Economics and Identity." *Quarterly Journal of Economics* 115 (3): 715–53.

Araral, E., Jr. 2009. "What Explains Collective Actions in the Commons? Theory and Evidence from the Philippines." *World Development* 37 (3): 687–97.

Balfour, D.L., and B. Wechsler. 1996. "Organizational Commitment: Antecedents and Outcomes in Public Organizations." *Public Productivity and Management Review* 19 (3): 256–77.

Bem, S.L. 1974. "The Measurement of Psychological Androgyny." *Journal of Consulting and Clinical Psychology* 42 (3): 155–62.

Brewer, M.B., and M.D. Silver. 2000. "Group Distinctiveness, Social Identification, and Collective Mobilization." In *Self, Identity and Social Movements*, edited by S. Stryker, T.J. Owens, and R.W. White, 153–71. University of Minnesota Press.

Chen, Y., and S.X. Li. 2009. "Group Identity and Social Preferences." *American Economic Review* 99 (1): 431–57.

Christoforou, A. 2012. "On the Identity of Social Capital and the Social Capital of Identity." *Cambridge Journal of Economics* 37 (40): 719–36.

Cleaver, F. 1998. "Choice, Complexity, and Change: Gendered Livelihoods and the Management of Water." *Agriculture and Human Values* 15 (4): 293–99.

Coleman, J. 1961. *Papers on Non-market Decision-making*. New York: Vantage.

Cook, J., and T. Wall. 1980. "New Work Attitude Measures of Trust, Organizational Commitment and Personal Need Non-fulfillment." *Journal of Occupational Psychology* 53 (1): 39–52.

Creswell, J.W. 2002. *Research Design: Qualitative, Quantitative, and Mixed Methods Approaches*. Thousands Oak, CA: SAGE Publications.

Cronbach, L.J. 1951. "Coefficient Alpha and the Internal Structure of Tests." *Psychometrika* 16 (3): 297–334.

D'Silva, E., and S. Pai. 2003. "Social Capital and Collective Action: Development Outcomes in Forest Protection and Watershed Development." *Economic and Political Weekly* 38 (14): 1404–15.

Folbre, N. 1994. *Who Pays for the Kids: Gender and the Structures of Constraint*. London: Routledge.

Gotschi, E.J. Njuki, and R. Delve. 2009. "Equal Numbers, Equal Chances? A Case Study of Gender Differences in the Distribution of Social Capital in Smallholder Farmer Groups in Bu´zi District, Mozambique." *European Journal of Development Research* 21(2): 264–82.

Granovetter, M. 1985. "Economic Action and Social Structure: The Problem of Embeddedness." *American Journal of Sociology* 91(3): 481–510.

Grusky, O. 1966. "Career Mobility and Organizational Commitment." *Administrative Science Quarterly* 10 (4): 488–503.

Handy, C. 1985. *Understanding Organisations*. Harmondsworth: Penguin Books.

Jackson, C. 1998. "Gender, Irrigation and Environment: Arguing for Agency." *Agriculture and Human Values* 15 (4): 313–24.

Kramer, R.M. 2006. "Social Identity and Social Capital: The Collective Self at Work." *International Public Management Journal* 9 (1): 25–45.

Kramer, R.M., and M.B. Brewer. 1984. "Effects of Group Identity on Resource Use in a Simulated Commons Dilemma." *Journal of Personality and Social Psychology* 46 (5): 1044–57.

Krishna, A. 2000. "Creating and Harnessing *Social Capital. In Social Capital: A Multifaceted Perspective,* edited by P. Dasgupta and I. Serageldin, 71–93. Washington, D.C.: The World Bank.

———. 2004. "Understanding, Measuring and Utilizing Social Capital: Clarifying Concepts and Presenting a Field Application from India." *Agricultural Systems* 82 (3): 291–305.

Mathieu, J.E., and D.M. Zajac. 1990. "A Review and Meta-analysis of the Antecedents, Correlates, and Consequences of Organizational Commitment." *Psychological Bulletin* 108 (2): 171–94.

Molyneux, M. 2002. "Gender and the Silence of Social Capital: Lessons from Latin America." *Development and Change* 33 (2): 167–88.

Mooney, J.D., and A.C. Reiley. 1931. *Onward Industry*. New York: Harper.

More, G. 1990. "Structural Determinants of Men's and Women's Personal Networks." *American Sociological Review* 55 (5): 726–35.

Mowday, R., R. Steers, and L.W. Porter. 1979. "The Measurement of Organizational Commitment." *Journal of Vocational Behavior* 14 (1): 224–27.

Mowday, R.T., L.W. Porter, and R.M. Steers. 1982. *Employee–Organization Linkages: The Psychology of Commitment, Absenteeism, and Turnover*. New York: Academic Press.

Mukherjee, N. 2005. "Measuring Social Capital: Forest Protection Committees in West Bengal." *Economic and Political Weekly* 37 (29): 2994–97.

Mukherjee, P. 2011. "Attitudes, Institution and Cooperation: Does Gender Matter in Joint Forest Management in West Bengal, India?" MPhil Dissertation, Department of Economics, Rabindra Bharati University, India.

Mukherjee, P., B. Ray, and R.N. Bhattacharya. Forthcoming. "Status Differences in Collective Action and Forest Benefits: Evidence from Joint Forest Management in India." *Environment Development and Sustainability*. Available at: https://link.springer.com/article/10.1007/s10668-016-9830-7 (accessed on 28 August 2017).

Narayan, D. 1998. "Global Social Capital Survey." PREM, Republic of Uganda. Available at: www.mapl.com.au/pdf/uguest.pdf (accessed on 27 April 2017).

Olson, M. 1965. *The Logic of Collective Action*. Cambridge: Harvard University Press.

Pandolfelli L., R. Meinzen-Dick, and S. Dohrn. 2008. "Gender and Collective Action: Motivations, Effectiveness and Impact." *Journal of International Development* 20 (1): 1–11.

Polletta, F., and J.M. Jasper. 2001. "Collective Identity and Social Movements." *Annual Review of Sociology* 27: 283–305.

Poteete, A.R., and E. Ostrom. 2004. "Heterogeneity, Group Size and Collective Action: The Role of Institutions in Forest Management." *Development and Change* 35 (3): 168–81.

Pretty, J. 1995. *Regenerating Agriculture: Policies and Practice for Sustainability and Self-reliance*. London: Earthscan Publications.

Pretty, J., and H. Ward. 2001. "Social Capital and the Environment." *World Development* 29 (2): 209–27.

Putnam, R. 1993. "The Prosperous Community: Social Capital and Public Life." *American Prospect* 4 (4): 35–42.

———. 2000. *Bowling Alone: The Collapse and Revival of American Community*. New York: Simon & Schuster.

Ray, B., and R.N. Bhattacharya. 2011. "Transaction Costs, Collective Action and Survival of Heterogeneous Co-management Institutions: Case Study of Forest Management Organizations in West Bengal, India." *Journal of Development Studies* 47 (2): 253–73.

———. 2013. "Stakeholder Attitudes and Conservation of Natural Resources: Exploring Alternative Approaches." In *Development and Sustainability: India in a Global Perspective*, edited by S. Banerjee and A. Chakrabarti, 463–95. New Delhi: Springer.

Ray, B., P. Mukherjee, and R.N. Bhattacharya. 2014. "Does Social Identity Matter in Gender Differences in Cooperation and Decision-making? An Experimental Study of Community-based Resource Management." Paper presented at the 17th World Congress of International Economic Association, 6–10 June, Dead Sea, Jordan.

———. Forthcoming. "Attitudes and Cooperation: Does Gender Matter in Community-based Forest Management?" *Environment and Development Economics*. Available at: https://doi.org/10.1017/S1355770X16000358 (accessed on 28 August 2017).

Rotter, J.B. 1980. "Interpersonal Trust, Trustworthiness, and Gullibility." *American Psychologist* 35 (1): 1–7.

Scoones, I. 1998. *Sustainable Rural Livelihoods: A Framework for Analysis*. Brighton: Institute for Development Studies.

Sell, J. 1997. "Gender, Strategies, and Contributions to Public Goods." *Social Psychology Quarterly* 60 (3): 252–65.

Sharma, U. 1980. *Women, Work and Property in North-west India*. London: Tavistock.

Somanathan, E., R. Prabhakar, and B.S. Mehta. 2007. "Collective Action for Forest Conservation: Does Heterogeneity Matter?" In *Inequality, Cooperation and Environmental Sustainability*, edited by J.M. Baland, P. Bardhan, and S. Bowles, 234–73. New Delhi: Oxford University Press.

Tajfel, H., and J.C. Turner. 1986. *The Social Identity Theory of Intergroup Behaviors*. In *Psychology of Intergroup Relations*, edited by S. Worchel and W. Austin, 7–24. Chicago, IL: Nelson-Hall.

Turner, J.C. 1987. *Rediscovering the Social Group: A Self-categorization Theory*. Oxford: Basil Blackwell.

van Emmerik, I.J. Hetty. 2006. "Gender Differences in the Creation of Different Types of Social Capital: A Multilevel Study." *Social Networks* 28 (1): 24–37.

Varughese, G., and E. Ostrom. 2001. "The Contested Role of Heterogeneity in Collective Action: Some Evidence from Community Forestry in Nepal." *World Development* 29 (5): 747–65.

Westermann, O., J. Ashby, and J. Pretty. 2005. "Gender and Social Capital: The Importance of Gender Differences for the Maturity and Effectiveness of Natural Resource Management Groups." *World Development* 33 (11): 1783–99.

# 19

# Economy–environment Impact Intensity Assessment in an Integrated Framework Analysis to the Rat-hole Coal Mining in Jaintia Hills District, India*

Lekha Mukhopadhyay

## Introduction

Economic growth leads to biogeophysical and chemical changes to the environment, affecting sensitivity, adaptive capacity, and vulnerability of the ecosystem and thus livelihood patterns in the society. In environment–economy–society interface the diagnosis of the problem and assessment of overall impact on livelihood patterns, being a part of environmental planning, is a challenging task. It calls forth building up of an analytical framework which can characterize the genesis of the problem and assess the impact intensity in an integrated way. This obviously needs to cross various disciplinary boundaries and work in the multiple paradigms.

Pure economic analysis-based models consider environmental management through managing natural and man-made resources satisfying weak sustainability criterion. It is principally capital theoretic and analyses various resource development scenarios with the potential of alternative investment possibilities. Thus, a switchover from one resource mix to another with gradual substitution of natural non-renewable capital by manufactured capital through technological progress are the keys to control anthropogenic biogeochemical

* This chapter is a part of the research work funded under Fulbright-Nehru Environmental Leadership Program, 2012–13 (Grant number: 1676/FNELP/2012) and done in collaboration with Stockholm Environment Institute (SEI), US organization; Davis, CA, USA. A version of this chapter has been presented in International Conference on Inequality and Sustainability, 9–10 November 2012, Tufts University, Medford, MA, and also in the Theory Colloquia in the Department of Economics, University of California, Riverside, on 9 January 2013. For estimation methodology in case of increase in surface run-off, the author is thankful to Vishal Mehta, senior scientist, SEI, Davis, CA. The author is also grateful to Chris Swartz, senior scientist, SEI, Boston, MA, for his active guidance while choosing the water quality parameter. The valuable interaction with and academic support from David Purkey (SEI, Davis, CA), Eric Kemp Benedict (SEI, Bangkok, Thailand) and A. Colin Cameron (Department of Economics, UC Davis) helped the author to enrich this work.

changes in environment. In Dasgupta–Heal–Solow (Dasgupta and Heal 1974) framework to make the sub-stitution of natural resources by manufactured capital, natural resource needs to be essential only in a "weak" sense. For that, the elasticity of substitution between manufactured capital and natural non-renewable capital must be greater than one. And in case, elasticity is equal to one, the share of manufactured capital in the output must be greater than the share of the natural capital in the output. To ensure constant sustain-able consumption and intergenerational equity, according to Hartwick's rule, investment in other forms of capital must exceed the monetary value of depleted natural resources that contribute to the production of marketed goods (Howarth 2007). In a pure economic-based analysis, the link between growth and envi-ronmental degradation (like pollution) is captured mostly in terms of the Environmental Kuznets curve. It argues that pollution can rise with economic growth and the resources can be expended to reduce pollution (Beckerman 1992). As a consequence, in this theoretical construct, the appropriate policy targets minimizing the environmental cost of development, where cost is expressed in terms of market price or shadow price. In the ideal situation, however, as exhaustible resources become scarce, market price is expected to rise, which may prevent exhaustion of resources and thereby encouraging substitution by technological progress. In real-ity, if price mechanism is institutionally dysfunctional and does not reflect the scarcity of resources, it makes environmental management and planning more difficult.

Economic analytical approach is quantitative and functions in a single paradigm delimited by economic boundaries. The decision analysis and system analysis-based plan models, on the other hand, are policy ori-ented. They analyse various policy alternatives and structural interrelationship between the relevant variables to forecast their implications vis-à-vis environment. These models are mostly simulation based and interdis-ciplinary in character. In these categories, one is the Multiple-criteria Decision Analysis (MCDA) method that is often used in environmental planning. It employs the linear average algorithm to prioritize among various decision parameters that function across various environmental economic paradigms.[1] Analytical Hierarchy Process models (Golden, Wasil and Harker 1989; Harker and Vargas 1987; Harker 1986, 1987; Saaty and Vargas 1987; Saaty 1990a, 1990b), and Life Cycle Analysis (Baumann and Tillman 2004; Rex and Baumann 2008) provide the instruments of decision theoretic environmental planning for assessment of environmental impact. Water Evaluation and Planning (WEAP) of SEI (Loon, Mathijssen, and Droogers 2007; Sánchez et al. 2011), Soil Water Assessment Tool (SWAT) of USDA and Texas A&M University (Einheuser et al. 2014), various biophysical models at a global scale like GLOBIOM (Global Biosphere Management Model) (focusing on land use between agriculture, bioenergy, and forestry) and GEPIC (GIS [Geographical Information System]-based EPIC [Environmental Policy Integrated Climate] model), and BeWhere of International Institute for Applied System Analysis (IIASA) have made exemplary contribution in environmental planning in an integrated framework.

Capital theoretic economic models are competent enough to characterize the path of economic develop-ment of a particular society to explain whether it is sustainable (or not) in the long run. For environmental impact assessment where a typical path of economic growth or development is the root cause of environ-mental problems, economic diagnosis is rather important. The objective of environmental planning and impact assessment, namely, sustainable development is well articulated into the analytical structure of capi-tal theoretic model itself. But it has a major weakness as it can neither cross the economic boundaries nor encompass various biogeophysical–chemical environmental components that function in an interactive way with economic components in the path of development, which is required to be transmitted into the plan dialogue. Decision theoretic and system analysis-based environmental plan models and impact assessment methods, on the other hand, although working in an integrated framework, cannot properly take care of the trend of economic growth of a particular society, which in most of cases is the root cause of environmental problem. Since those plan models are dominated by the researchers with background in engineering and natural sciences, their approach and solution are essentially technocratic (Korhonen et al. 2004) with no or less involvement of social sciences. As development occurs in the environment–economy–society interface, both at a temporal and at a spatial scale, environmental scientists and policymakers need to encompass vari-ous environmental (biogeochemical and ecological) and socio-economic components at a time that function temporally and spatially in an interactive way. In due course of time, although various reductionist methodologies have evolved, still we are bereft of the ideas on how to formulate the interlinkage between various components of human activities and natural world to derive the effective policy outcomes.

The analytical framework and methodology discussed in this chapter intends to minimize the existing knowledge gap. Rapid expansion of rat-hole coal mining driven by export demand from Bangladesh, leading to various biogeochemical changes in environment is negatively impacting the rice and fish seed productions—the two chosen components of agricultural livelihood in Jaintia Hills District, Meghalaya, India. Within the chain of causality, the statistically significant linkages between the various economic and environmental components are used to indicate the kind of management packages (including soil quality, hydrology, water quality, mining, etc.) that would be required to address the negative impact on rice and fish seed production.

## Framework, Method, and Data Sources

The method in this chapter takes the essence of capital approach to sustainable development in the combined Driver-Pressure-State-Impact-Response (DPSIR), RIVM (1995; UNEP/RIVM 1994), and Sustainable Livelihood (SL) frameworks (DFID 1997, 2000; Figures 19.1 and 19.2). First, it purports to describe analytically how in the chain of causality economic drivers, creating pressures on biogeochemical environment with a given state or condition on environment can impact the SL outcome of the society. Second, it devises a methodology to measure the impact intensity, which can be used in economic–environmental planning for prioritizing among the alternative management scenarios. The schematic representation of the analytical framework is shown in Figure 19.3. The hypothetical context here is similar to the one studied in this chapter described in the following section. Here demand from industry and market are assumed to be the driving forces for the rapid mineral extraction that change hydrology, water quality, and soil nutrient (for example) which in turn affect cultivation and income. With the objective of planning for sustainable development, substitution of mined resources by manufactured capital needs a specific type of industrialization with switchover of investment from mining to the industrial sector with low (or no) dependence of inputs from the mined resources. The single-headed straight arrows in Figure 19.3 indicate the impact, say, of industrial demand and other market demand on cultivation and income directly, or the one indirectly mediated by mining and mining-induced changes in hydrology, water quality, and soil nutrients. This integrated framework is applied in an empirical context, namely, in Jaintia Hills District in Northeast India where market-driven artisanal "rat-hole" coal mining with its consequent negative impact on environment has caused the shift of livelihood from an

**Figure 19.1**
*DPSIR framework*

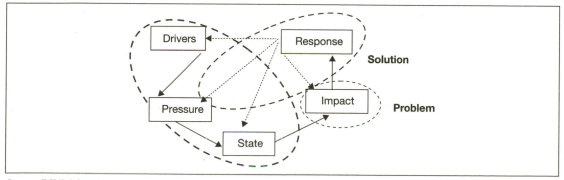

*Source:* RIVM (1995).

**Figure 19.2**
*Sustainable livelihood framework*

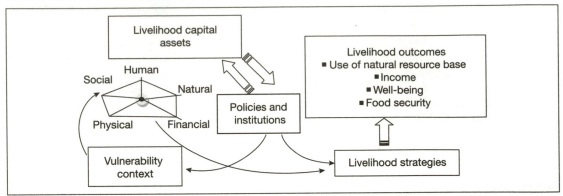

*Source:* DFID (2000).

**Figure 19.3**
*Schematic representation of the proposed analytical framework*

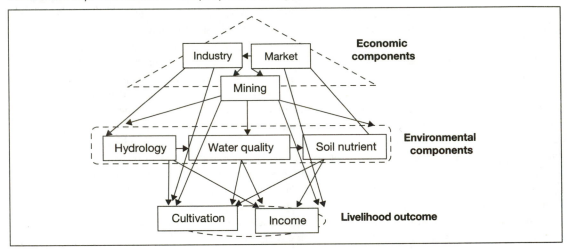

agro-based to a mine-based one. The causality model has been tested by the statistical path coefficient analysis using time series data, collected from various government reports and research works across disciplines.

# Empirical Context: Rat-hole Coal Mining in Jaintia Hills District, Meghalaya, India

Jaintia Hills District lying between 25°5′ N–25°4′ N in latitudes and 91°51′ E–92°45′ E in longitudes, covering an area of 3,819 km² is one of the seven districts of the state of Meghalaya. It has an international boundary in the south with Bangladesh (Figure 19.4). The population of the district is 392,852 (2011 Census) of which 96 per cent is tribal. According to the Geological Survey of India in 1974, the total coal reserve in the district was 39 million tons. Sutnga, Lakadong, Musiang Lamare, Khilehriat, Loksi, Lad Rymbai, Rymbai, Byrwai, Chyrmang, Bapung, Jarain, Shkentalang, Lumshnong, Sakynphor, etc., are the main coal-bearing

**Figure 19.4**
*Coal mining area of Jaintia Hills district of Meghalaya, India*

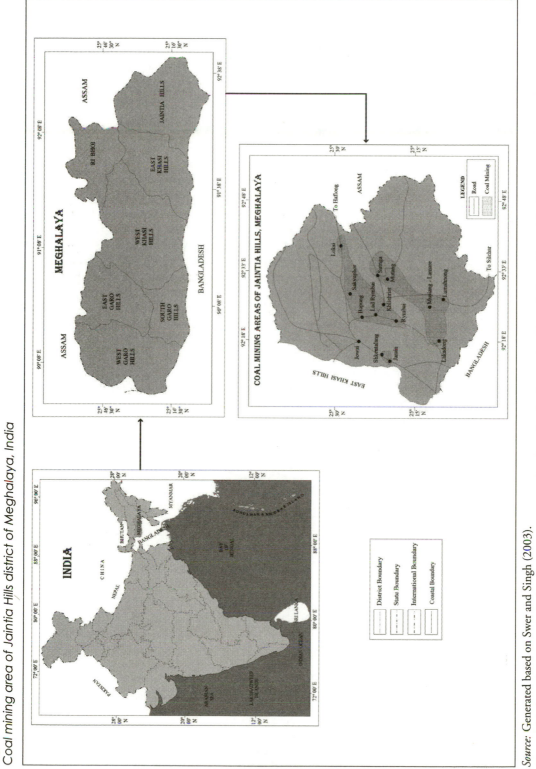

*Source:* Generated based on Swer and Singh (2003).

*Note:* This figure is not to scale. It does not represent any authentic national or international boundaries and is used for illustrative purposes only.

areas of the district that altogether cover 57.9 km² (Sahu and Goel 2004). Jaintia Hills District although constitutes only 7.48 per cent of the total coal reserve of the state, it contributes 75 per cent of the total coal production (Sarma 2005). After the independence of Bangladesh in 1971 and after Jaintia was granted its district autonomy in 1972, coal extraction in Jaintia District has been rapidly rising (Figure 19.5). From 1975 till 2007, coal production has increased by 161 per cent (generated from the Directorate of Economics and Statistics, Meghalaya). There are at least five possible reasons for this rapid unregulated depletion of coal resources. First, there is a rising demand for coal export to Bangladesh, and second, the rising demand in Meghalaya and other states in India for coal as fuel in industrial production. Jaintia coal is sub-bituminous with high sulphur (principally organic) content (more than 5%; Behra 2007). It is mostly used as fuel in the small- and medium-scale industries such as cement, bricks, tea, fertilizer, etc., in Bangladesh and in India. It is neither used by power plants nor is it useful for manufacturing industries because of its high sulphur content. Demand for coal as input for cement and brick production, that is, in construction industry in Meghalaya may be taken as an indicator of industrialization and infrastructural development in the state, while coal extraction in response to the rising export demand is purely a market-driven phenomenon.

Increasing demand for Meghalaya coal in Bangladesh is evident by the export trend over the time (Figure 19.6). Dawki–Tamabil road that crosses the border of Bangladesh with land customs station at Dawki in Jaintia District plays a significant role in coal-exporting activities. During 2005–06, for example, 70 per cent of the total royalty from coal export to Bangladesh enjoyed by Meghalaya was contributed by Jaintia District itself (Rout 2006).

Third reason for rapid coal extraction in the district is an (undercurrent) apprehension of nationalization of the coal extraction. Given the typical constitutional right of land ownership enjoyed by tribal community that follows the Sixth Schedule of the Constitution of India, government of Meghalaya cannot and does not intervene into artisanal private mining in tribal land. But there is every possibility that any day government can take over the ownership of the coal mines by amending the Constitution. The state government drafted a Mining and Mineral Policy in 2004 (Government of Meghalaya 2012, 96) as per the directives from the Supreme Court but kept it in abeyance to enact the corresponding laws in the Parliament under pressure from powerful mining lobbies as reported in *The Statesman* (Mukhim 2012).

Fourth driving force for rampant coal mining is poverty. Wherever the landowner needs some emergency cash and expects that there may be coal beneath, forest is cleared and a shaft of diameter varying from 3 m to 10 m is sunk. Hole is dug into coal seam and goes deeper and deeper for several kilometres following the seam.

**Figure 19.5**
*Coal extraction—Jaintia Hills district (1974–75 to 2009–10)*

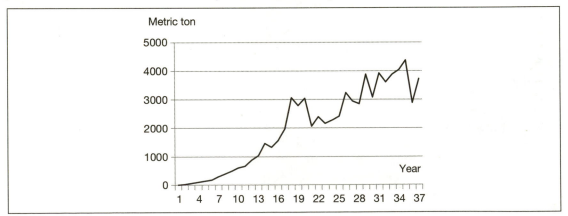

*Source:* Data for the figure taken from Directorate of Mineral Resources, Government of Meghalaya, *Statistical Handbook* (1976), *District-level Key Statistics* (multiple series from 1977 to 2010), Shillong.

**Figure 19.6**

*Coal export to Bangladesh from Meghalaya (1989–90 to 2005–06)*

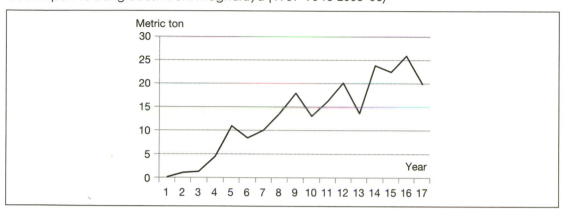

*Source:* Data for the figure taken from Commissioner Customs, Government of Meghalaya, *Meghalaya State Development Report (2008–09): Trade and Industrial Development,* Shilong; Rout (2006).

These burrows or holes are big enough to accommodate just one person to crawl in with tools and basket or wheeled cart to carry out coal to the depots located near the main road. This is known as "rat-hole mining" as it is similar to the burrow making by the rats. There are approximately 5,000 coal mines in this district. In total, 99 per cent of the workers in the mines are migrants from Indian states of Assam, Bihar, and Jharkhand besides Bangladesh and Nepal.[2] Daily wage rate for mineworkers (particularly for digging and cutting the coal with maximum life risk) is much higher than the agricultural wages (Lamin 1995). The coal bed and seams in this particular area are horizontal to the ground and few meters deep in the form of thin seam (30 to 212 cm in thickness; Guha Roy 1992) lying along the bedding planes of the host rock. Due to this peculiar geological characteristic of the coal beds in this area, large-scale mining is not economically profitable.

Fifth important reason for rapid extraction is the undefined property rights to the underground coal in the land under the possession of the tribals. Reaping the immediate benefit from mining (McDuie-Ra 2007) without getting concerned with the long-term consequences may have been the reason for rapid exhaustion of coal. When the landowner starts digging burrow, it is within the jurisdiction of his or her private land but as he or she enters underground, there is no private property demarcation; like groundwater, coal becomes a common pool resource under open-access regime. As he or she cannot restrain his or her competitive neighbour to encroach upon coal resource in "his" or "her" region, he or she wants to extract rapidly as much as he or she can. All these factors led to rampant unscientific coal mining in this area. Although it is completely illegal and unscientific, government collects huge revenue in the form of royalty and transport tax from mine owners (Blahwar 2010).

The rampant unscientific archaic rat-hole coal mining, along with the absence of post-mining treatment and management of mined areas, is making the fragile ecosystems of the area more vulnerable to environmental degradation. Mining-induced deforestation leads to the increasing surface run-off and thus washing off the soil nutrients. Mine spoils or overburden create extremely rigid substrata for the plant growth. Continued soil acidification due to acid mine drainage (AMD) and toxic elements of coal spoils such as Al, Fe, Mn, Cu have caused enormous damage to the plant biodiversity in this area (Sarma 2005). Due to mining-induced changes in land-use pattern and soil pollution, area of fallow land has steadily increased (Figure 19.7). Between 1975 and 2007, there has been decrease in forest area (Figure 19.8) by 12.5 per cent while area under mining has increased threefold (Sarma, Tripathi, and Kushwaha 2010). The cultivable wasteland in Jaintia District is found to be the highest (31%) in the state of Meghalaya (generated from the data from Directorate of Economics and Statistics, Meghalaya).

AMD in the surface water bodies, in the river streams from the active coal mines,[3] coal dumps, and abandoned mines, is a common phenomenon in Jaintia District. It is indicated by low pH (between 2 and 3),

**Figure 19.7**

*Area of fallow land (in hectare) in Jaintia Hills district (1990–91 to 2007–08)*

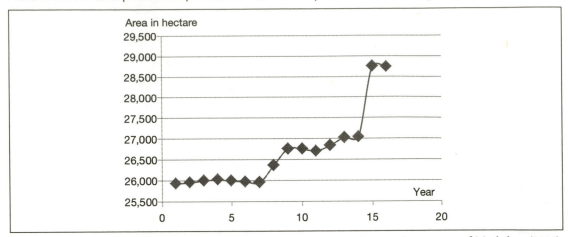

*Sources:* Data for the figure taken from Directorate of Economics and Statistics in Government of Meghalaya (2009), Statistical Abstract of Meghalaya, Shillong.

**Figure 19.8**

*Dense forest area (log sq. km): 1975–2007*

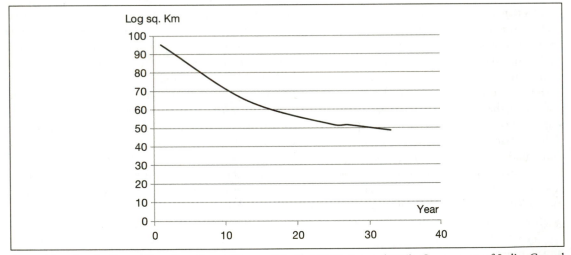

*Sources:* Data for the figure taken from Forest Survey of India (2003); Sarma (2005); Government of India, Central Statistical Organization (2008), *Environmental Accounting of Natural Resources;* CES, NEHU Shillong.

high conductivity, high concentration of sulphates, iron and toxic heavy metals, low dissolved oxygen (DO), and high Biochemical Oxygen Demand (BOD) in the river stream water (Blahwar 2010; Swer and Singh 2004) in the coal belt area. Pyrite from surrounding coal gets quickly hydrolyzed in slightly acidic water, releases protons and sulphate further adding acidity and increasing sulphate concentration. pH values (annually on an average) in stream Kyrukhla in Khilehriat coalfield area since 1994–95 till 2007–08 has been observed to be steadily declining (Figure 19.9). AMD has been injurious to aquatic biota, including fish, amphibians, aquatic plants, and insects (Swer and Singh 2004).

AMD has also created a major constraint to the availability of potable water (Dkhar 2010). Rice productivity on an average in the coalfield area is observed to be 860 kg/ha (where soil pH on an average is 3.54)

**Figure 19.9**

*Average pH value of water in Kyrukhla stream in pre- and post-monsoon period (1994–2003)*

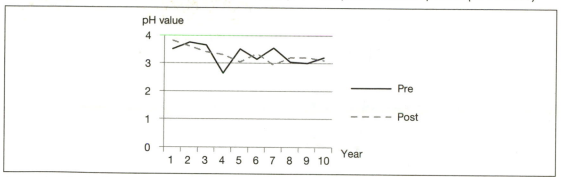

*Source:* Data for the figure taken from Meghalaya State Pollution Control Board, Government of Meghalaya, *Annual Report* (multiple series from 1994–95 to 2003–04).

compared to 1926 kg/ha in non-mined area (where soil pH is 4.35 on an average) and 1123 kg/ha in the abandoned mining sites. Rice crop shoot in the coal-mined area is 2.75 gram per pot compared to 7.90 gram per pot in non-mined area (Choudhury et al. 2010).[4]

Along with rapid expansion of rat-hole coal mining in Jaintia, there has been an increase in income and employment of a section of people associated with mining activities. The disparities in wage rates (Sahu and Goel 2004) have also increased. The local people usually do not sell their labour in the mines and most of the time they lease out their land to the coal traders and exporters. The area under agricultural land has been steadily declining for diversion to coal mining. The overall socio-economic impact is the undergoing shift from agro-based livelihood to coal-based livelihood. With this ground reality at the backdrop and economic theoretical propositions of sustainable development, the key premise of this chapter is that the ongoing shift of livelihood from agro-based to coal-based is not sustainable. While characterizing the development path, it identifies the factor(s) that are playing a significant role (impacting) to make the existing development path economically and environmentally (un)sustainable. Further, it looks at the policy implications.

## Statistical Path Coefficient Analysis

In this chapter, the integrated analytical framework in Jaintia context, developed from DPSIR and SL frameworks, has been fitted into the statistical path coefficient modelling. In Meghalaya, after food processing, the second largest investment (more than 3.6 million Rupees) has been made in cement industry. Coal is significantly used as an input in cement production. As demand for cement is associated with infrastructural development, production in cement industry in Meghalaya is considered as a potential indicator for alternative form of industrialization. It is an alternative form because here industrialization occurs through investment priority in Social Overhead Capital (SOC) and not through the investment in Direct Productive Activity (DPA; Hirschman 1958). And further, coal export is an indicator of outflow of capital from indigenous production to the export markets in Bangladesh. The cement production and coal extraction in the present analysis have been proposed to be tested as the driving forces to rapid coal extraction that lead to the pressure on environment indicated by increase in surface run-off (associated with mining-induced deforestation), fallow land and AMD indicated by pH, and sulphate concentration in the stream flow in the coal belt area. These mining-induced pressures and impacts are changing the livelihood strategies from agro-based to mine-based. This change is reflected in per capita decline in rice production and fish production over time (Figures 19.10 and 19.11)—the two key indicators of agro-based livelihood. This integrated framework by a stylized chain of causality not only explains the impact generating process at various levels in economy–environment–society

**Figure 19.10**
Per capita rice production (1990–91 to 2006–07)

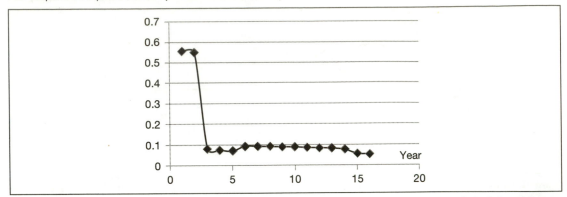

*Sources:* Data for the figure taken from Directorate of Economics and Statistics, Government of Meghalaya, *District-level Key Statistics* (multiple series from 1990 to 2007), Shillong; Census of India, 1991, 2001; National Health Mission, Jaintia Hills in Government of Meghalaya (2010), *National Health Mission: District Action Plan (2010–11): Jaintia Hills.*

**Figure 19.11**
Fish seed production (1991–92 to 2006–07)

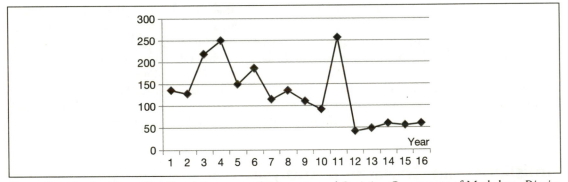

*Sources:* Data for the figure taken from Directorate of Economics and Statistics, Government of Meghalaya, *District-level Key Statistics* (multiple series from 1990 to 2007), Shillong; Census of India, 1991, 2001; National Health Mission, Jaintia Hills, Government of Meghalaya (2010), *National Health Mission: District Action Plan (2010–11): Jaintia Hills.*

nexus but also characterizes the path of development of the society. The methodology has been devised to assess how, directly and indirectly, various driving economic, hydrological, hydrogeochemical, and land diversification forces, in an interactive way, are impacting the trend in the change in rice and fish production over time. In the proposed models (a) demand for coal export and (b) cement production are found to act as economic drivers. The surface run-off acts as hydrological driver. The two water quality indicators of acid mine drainage viz., (a) pH value and (b) concentration of sulphate in a particular stream water in coal belt area, function as hydro-geochemical driver. Since the study is based on the secondary data, the choice of the scenario framework is partially dependent on the availability of such data. Due to paucity of data, the declining trends of rice production and fish production have been studied separately in two distinct path models.

The rice-coal extraction and fish-coal extraction paths are studied with time series data of 18 years (1990–2007) and 10 years (from 1994–95 to 2003–04), respectively. Data corresponding to each year has been considered as one observation; thus, we have two sets with 18 and 10 observations. Since agricultural production in Jaintia District is principally rain fed, mining-induced change in water quality in river stream does not affect rice production; water quality index (WQI) value is not chosen in rice-coal path model. AMD affects the soil quality and thus the agriculture. Since time series data for soil quality (like total metal load via chemical extraction/digestion of the sediments [Gilchrist et al. 1994], or bio-availability of that load [Keon et al. 2001; Swartz et al. 2004] are not consistently available, area of fallow land (Falnd as a proxy of degraded soil) instead is taken into account. Shrinkage of forest area reduces the landscape's capacity to intercept, retain, and transpire precipitation. As deforested areas become sources of surface water run-off, it moves much faster than subsurface flows. It is the reason for generating data for mining-induced increase in surface run-off (IncSrf) by the following equation:

$$IncSrf_t = (P_t - ET_{Ref}) * Frstlost_t$$

where $P$: rainfall precipitation, $ET$: evapotranspiration, $Frslost$: area of loss of forest estimated from percentage change of area from dense forest area to coal mine area from satellite imagery data of 1975, 1987, 1999, 2001, and 2007 (Sarma et. al 2010). For ET, we have taken the average of the values of crop-ET in Jaintia based on the data from 1901 to 2001 (ARGHYAM 2012).

For water quality analysis, we have considered 10 (from 1994–95 to 2003–04) years' pH and sulphate concentration data of the water in Kyrhukhla stream, at Khliehriat, flowing at the heart of coal belt area. Low pH value and high sulphate concentration are the indicators of AMD. The formula we used for constructing index is the following: (pH score + Sulphate score)$^2$/100. The pH score and sulphate score we used here are taken from Modified Acid Mine Drainage Index (MAMDI) from Kuma, Younger, and Buah (2011).[5] We have chosen one particular river stream as a representative of all AMD affected streams in Jaintia.[6] In the class of structural equation modelling, statistical path analysis that we have used purports to fit the proposed structural model against the null model that assumes that there is no relation between the variables proposed in the model. It is recursive. Each variable enters stage by stage to explain the variable followed in the next stage. This shows the potential causal dependencies between the variables. Each of the rice-coal and fish-coal path models consists of four observed exogenous, two observed endogenous, and four unobserved exogenous or latent variables (as described in Table A19.1). Using AMOS (Analysis of a Moment Structure) (of IBM SPSS 20), we have generated path diagrams for rice-coal and fish-coal path modelling (Figures 19.12a and 19.12b).

**Figure 19.12a**
*Rice-coal path diagram*

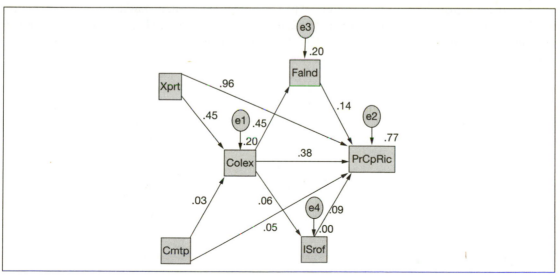

**Figure 19.12b**
*Fish-coal path diagram*

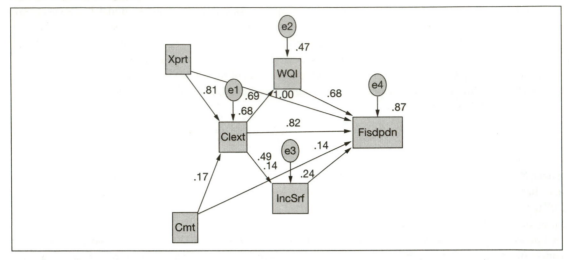

At stage one, coal export in Bangladesh (Xprt) and cement production (Cmt or Cmtp) enter to explain rapid coal extraction (Colex or clext) and at stage two, Colex or clext enters to explain increase in surface run-off (ISrof) and area of fallow land (Falnd) for rice-coal path model and (IncSrf) and WQI for fish-coal path model. Finally, ISrof and Falnd enter to explain the per capita rice production (PrCpRic) and IncSrf and WQI to explain fish seed production (Fisdpdn).

Path coefficients estimated from layered multiple regression analysis show the size effect of each of the observed component, and they are displayed against their respective single-headed arrows in the path diagram. Effects are direct and indirect. Indirect effects or impacts are those that are mediated by others. Maximum Likelihood method of estimation is used and thus it does not assume uncorrelated error terms. The path coefficients we considered here are standardized coefficients based on standardized data. They thus show the relative importance of each of the proposed independent variables. Although these are regression coefficients, this type of structural equation modelling is more general than regression models themselves. Any particular variable can act as a dependent variable at one layer and as an independent one at another.

So far the examination of "fit" of an estimated path model is concerned, it considers how well it models the data. It thus tests the "fit" against the "null" model that presumes no correlation between the observed variables. Thus, rejection of "null" model in the path analysis implies goodness of fit. There are varying fit indices found in the literature (Bentler 1990; Kline 2011) categorized under Absolute Fit Index (AFI) and Relative Fit Index (RFI). Absolute indices are computed using formulae that include discrepancies (matrix of residuals) and degrees of freedom (df) and sample size. It is absolute in the sense that it does not compare the estimated model with any other. Formulae for relative indices consider discrepancies of the estimated model from a "null" model. Roughly, for AFI and RFI, values above 0.9 are considered to be adequate. Among AFIs, the most common used measure is Chi-square ($\chi^2$). Relative $\chi^2$, Comparative Fit Index (CFI), Tucker Lewis Index (TLI) belong to the RFIs.

Relative $\beta = \dfrac{\chi^2}{df}$  CFI $= 1 - \dfrac{\hat{\delta}_M}{\hat{\delta}_B}$ where, $\hat{\delta}_M = \max(\chi_M^2 - df_M, 0)$ where $\delta$ measures the degree of mis-specification of the model. Subscript $M$ and $B$ indicate estimated and base or null models, respectively. The

formula for TLI $= 1 - \dfrac{\frac{\chi_M^2}{df_M}}{\frac{\chi_B^2}{df_B}}$.

The indices based on residuals that look at discrepancies between observed and predicted covariances include Root Mean Square Residual (RMR), Root Mean Square Error of Approximation, etc.

Among the various fit indices criteria, we found that proposed rice-coal path model has satisfied the acceptable threshold levels of relative $\chi^2$ and RMR. The fish-coal path model on the other hand satisfies $\chi^2$ fit and relative $\chi^2$ (Table A19.1).

## Results of the Statistical Path Analysis

The results of the statistical path analysis (Tables A19.2, A19.3a, A19.3b, and A19.4) establish that export of coal in Bangladesh has the largest size effect (in terms of direct, indirect, and overall effects with statistical significance) to explain the variability in per capita rice production. And in all the cases, the effect is negative. Due to the direct (unmediated) effect of xprt on PrCpRic, when xprt goes up by 1 standard deviation, PrCpRic goes down by 0.958 standard deviations. This is in addition to the indirect (mediated) effect that xprt has on PrCpRic. And in terms of indirect (mediated) effect also, export has the largest effect on per capita rice production. So far as the fish seed production is concerned, the direct effect of export (negative) is the largest and the effect (positive) of water quality (AMD) index is the second largest (Tables A19.5, A19.6a, A19.6b, and A19.7). Pearson correlation coefficient between WQI and fish seed production (Fisdpdn) is the largest among all others.

## Conclusion

From the results of the statistical analysis, we can reach some important conclusions on the coal-based economic development in Jaintia District. Rising coal export from Meghalaya to Bangladesh acts as the major driving force to rapid coal extraction. This indicates that there is flight of (natural) capital from coal mining through the export market without any corresponding augmentation of human-made capital through industrialization in the district.

Thus, the basic premise of Heal–Solow–Dasgupta–Hartwick approach to sustainable development, that is, substitution of natural capital by manufactured capital does not occur. Hence, we may conclude that the shift of livelihood from agro-based to coal-based along the existing development path in Jaintia District is unsustainable because export is the major driver to the coal extraction. After coal reserve is exhausted, this development path will no longer be sustained. Rising demand for coal export (Xprt) leading to a rise in coal extraction (Colex), leading to the increase in the area of fallow land (Flnd), was statistically significant in explaining the declining trend of per capita rice production in Jaintia District. Both rising demand for coal export (Xprt) leading to a rise in coal extraction (Colex) leading to the increase in surface run-off (Isrof) and rising demand for coal export (Xprt) leading to a rise in coal extraction (Colex) leading to the rise in AMD in (WQI) paths were found to be significant in explaining the declining trend of fish seed production. The first diagnostic result shows the chain of causality between coal export, coal mining, mining-induced degradation of soil quality, and rice production. Thus, to redirect the growth path towards economy–environment–sustainability, it indicates that the regulated coal mining, with soil quality management, is required in case of rice production. In the case of fish production, on the other hand, two significant chains of causality are detected, namely, (a) coal export, coal mining with surface run-off due to mining-induced deforestation and (b) coal export, coal mining with AMD. The second set of results, on the other hand, indicates the priority of coal mining—hydrology and water quality management—packages to resolve the problem of fish seed production. In both cases, however, all hydrogeological, hydrogeochemical, and land diversification management packages must be tied up with coal export market regulations.

# Appendix: Statistical Tables

**Table A19.1**

*Rice-coal and fish-coal path models and model fit indices*

| Fit index | Acceptable threshold levels | Rice-coal path model | Fish-coal path model |
|---|---|---|---|
| Chi sq (absolute fit) | Low chi-sq to d.f with an insignificant p value; p 0.05 | | |
| 0.02 | 0.05 | | |
| Relative chi-square (Chi-sq/df) | 2.1 (Tabachnick and Fidell 2007); 3.1 (Kline 2011) | 3.46 | 2.12 |
| RMR (root mean square residual) | Good models have small (RMR<0.10) | 0.05 | 0.16 |

**Table A19.2**

*Pearson correlation matrix in case of rice-coal path analysis*

| | | cmt | Xprt | Colex | isrf | Falnd | PrCpRic |
|---|---|---|---|---|---|---|---|
| cmt | Pearson correlation | 1 | | | | | |
| | Sig. (2-tailed) | | | | | | |
| | N | 18 | | | | | |
| xprt | Pearson correlation | −0.001 | 1 | | | | |
| | Sig. (2-tailed) | 0.996 | | | | | |
| | N | 18 | 18 | | | | |
| Colex | Pearson correlation | 0.033 | 0.446 | 1 | | | |
| | Sig. (2-tailed) | 0.895 | 0.063 | | | | |
| | N | 18 | 18 | 18 | | | |
| isrf | Pearson correlation | 0.595** | 0.036 | 0.059 | 1 | | |
| | Sig. (2-tailed) | 0.009 | 0.888 | 0.816 | | | |
| | N | 18 | 18 | 18 | 18 | | |
| Falnd | Pearson correlation | −0.138 | 0.776** | 0.449 | −0.035 | 1 | |
| | Sig. (2-tailed) | 0.585 | 0.000 | 0.062 | 0.890 | | |
| | N | 18 | 18 | 18 | 18 | 18 | |
| PrCpRic | Pearson correlation | 0.126 | −0.829** | −0.097 | 0.105 | −0.670** | 1 |
| | Sig. (2-tailed) | 0.619 | 0.000 | 0.701 | 0.678 | 0.002 | |
| | N | 18 | 18 | 18 | 18 | 18 | 18 |

*Notes:* * Significantly different from zero at the 0.05 level (two-tailed).

** Correlation is significant at the 0.01 level (two-tailed).

**Table A19.3a**
*Standardized indirect effects in case of rice-coal path*

| Dependent variable ('Depvar') | | Independent variable ('Indepvar') | Estimate |
|---|---|---|---|
| Colex | <--- | xprt | 0.446* |
| Colex | <--- | cmt | 0.034 |
| Isrf | <--- | Colex | 0.059 |
| Falnd | <--- | Colex | 0.449* |
| PrCpRic | <--- | Colex | 0.377* |
| PrCpRic | <--- | xprt | −0.958** |
| PrCpRic | <--- | Falnd | 0.137 |
| PrCpRic | <--- | isrf | 0.092 |
| PrCpRic | <--- | cmt | 0.048 |

*Notes:* * Significantly different from zero at the 0.05 level (two-tailed).
** Significantly different from zero at the 0.001 level (two-tailed).

**Table A19.3b**
*Standardized indirect effects in case of rice-coal path*

| Variable | cmt | Xprt | Colex | Falnd | isrf |
|---|---|---|---|---|---|
| Colex | 0 | 0 | 0 | 0 | 0 |
| Falnd | 0.015 | 0.2 | 0 | 0 | 0 |
| Isrf | 0.002 | 0.026 | 0 | 0 | 0 |
| PrCpRic | 0.011 | 0.143 | −0.056 | 0 | 0 |

**Table A19.4**
*Ranking of size effect on per capita rice production*

| | cmt | xprt | Colex | Falnd | Isrf |
|---|---|---|---|---|---|
| Direct effect | 5 | 1 (−)* | 2 (+)* | 3 (−) | 4 (+) |
| Indirect effect | 3 | 1 | 2 | NIL | NIL |

**Table A19.5**
*Pearson correlation matrix in case of fish-coal path*

| | | Cmt | Xprt | Clext | IncSrf | WQI | Fisdpdn |
|---|---|---|---|---|---|---|---|
| Cmt | Pearson correlation | 1 | | | | | |
| | sig. (two-tailed) | | | | | | |
| | N | 10 | | | | | |
| Xprt | Pearson correlation | −0.734* | 1 | | | | |
| | sig.(two-tailed) | 0.016 | | | | | |
| | N | 10 | 10 | | | | |
| Clext | Pearson correlation | −0.470 | 0.762* | 1 | | | |

(Table A17.1 *continued*)

(Table A17.1 *continued*)

|  |  | Cmt | Xprt | Clext | IncSrf | WQI | Fisdpdn |
|---|---|---|---|---|---|---|---|
|  | sig. (two-tailed) | 0.170 | 0.010 |  |  |  |  |
|  | N | 10 | 10 | 10 |  |  |  |
| IncSrf | Pearson correlation | −0.211 | 0.500 | 0.451 | 1 |  |  |
|  | sig. (two-tailed) | 0.558 | 0.141 | 0.191 |  |  |  |
|  | N | 10 | 10 | 10 | 10 |  |  |
| WQI | Pearson correlation | 0.620 | −0.800** | −0.647* | −0.397 | 1 |  |
|  | sig. (two-tailed) | 0.056 | 0.005 | 0.043 | 0.255 |  |  |
|  | N | 10 | 10 | 10 | 10 | 10 |  |
| Fisdpdn | Pearson correlation | 0.614 | −0.784** | −0.345 | −0.272 | 0.809** | 1 |
|  | sig. (two-tailed) | 0.059 | 0.007 | 0.329 | 0.448 | 0.005 |  |
|  | N | 10 | 10 | 10 | 10 | 10 | 10 |

*Notes:* * Correlation is significant at the 0.05 level (two-tailed).
     ** Correlation is significant at the 0.01 level (two-tailed).

**Table A19.6a**
*Standardized direct effects in case of fish-coal path*

| Dependent variable ('Depvar') |  | Independent variable ('Indepvar') | Estimate |
|---|---|---|---|
| Clext | <--- | Xprt | 0.807** |
| Clext | <--- | Cmt | 0.173 |
| WQI | <--- | clext | −0.689* |
| IncSrf | <--- | clext | 0.493 |
| Fisdpdn | <--- | IncSrf | 0.14 |
| Fisdpdn | <--- | WQI | 0.68** |
| Fisdpdn | <--- | clext | 0.823** |
| Fisdpdn | <--- | Xprt | −1.086** |
| Fisdpdn | <--- | Cmt | −0.141 |

*Notes:* * Significantly different from zero at the 0.05 level (two-tailed).
     ** Significantly different from zero at the 0.001 level (two-tailed).

**Table A19.6b**
*Standardized indirect effects in case of fish-coal path*

| Standardized indirect effects |  |  |  |  |  |
|---|---|---|---|---|---|
|  | Cmt | Xprt | clext | IncSrf | WQI |
| Clext | 0 | 0 | 0 | 0 | 0 |
| IncSrf | 0.085 | 0.398 | 0 | 0 | 0 |
| WQI | −0.119 | −0.556 | 0 | 0 | 0 |
| Fisdpdn | 0.073 | 0.342 | −0.399 | 0 | 0 |

*Notes:* * Significantly different from zero at the 0.05 level (two-tailed).
     ** Significantly different from zero at the 0.001 level (two-tailed).

**Table A19.7**

*Ranking of size effect on fish seed production*

|  | *Cmt1* | *Xprt1* | *Colex1* | *ISrof1* | *WQI* |
|---|---|---|---|---|---|
| Direct effect | 4 (–) | 1 (–) | 2 (+)* | 4 (+) | 3 (+)* |
| Indirect effect | 3 (+) | 2 (+) | 1 (–) | NIL | *NIL* |

*Note:*    * Significantly different from zero at the 0.05 level (two-tailed).

**Table A19.8**

*Description of variables in rice-coal path model and fish-coal path model in Jaintia context*

| *Types of variables* | *Rice-coal path model* | *Fish-coal path model* |
|---|---|---|
| Observed endogenous variables | (i)   Colex (coal extraction)<br>(ii)  ISrof (increase in surface runoff),<br>(iii) Falnd (fallow land),<br>(iv)  PrCpRic (per capita rice production) | (i)   Clext (coal extraction),<br>(ii)  IncSrf (increase in surface runoff),<br>(iii) WQI (water quality index),<br>(iv)  Fisdpdn (fish seed production) |
| Observed exogenous variables | (i)   Xprt (coal export to Bangladesh),<br>(ii)  Cmt (cement production) | (i)   Xprt (coal export to Bangladesh),<br>(ii)  Cmtp (cement production) |
| Unobserved exogenous variables (latent variables) | e1. e2. e3. e4 | e1. e2. e3. e4 |

# Notes

1. For instance, in designing the land use pattern there may be available a number of options: $(O_1, O_2, ........, O_n)$ of using a parcel of land such as use for agriculture, use for mining, or use as a forest reserve, and so on. These options can be assessed according to various criteria, $(C_1, C_2, ........, C_m)$ like ecological criteria, for example, protecting biodiversity or maintaining intact landscapes, or creating recreation opportunities, and so on. The decision-makers have to assign a "score" or weight for each option $(O_1, O_2, ........, O_n)$ against each criterion $(C_1, C_2, ........, C_m)$ either in cardinal or in ordinal terms. Multi-criteria methods are employed to combine the criteria scores obtained for each option into an overall preference ranking or choice of option and thus provide with various algorithm for aggregation like Aggregated Integrated Randomization Method, Analytical Hierarchy Process (AHP) method, Data Envelope Analysis (DEA), and so on.

2. According to an estimate from an NGO, 70,000 (50,000 from a different source of information and there is a debate about the exact number!) children in the age between 7 and 17 are working in these private mines as the casual labour under private contractors without any security to their lives and livelihood (Impulse 2011).

3. AMD occurs while dewatering the mines in the post-monsoon period to start mining in the dry winter period (Blahwar 2010).

4. Soil pH in the dumping site of the coalfield area is around 2.42 and 2.56 in the paddy field nearby (Barua and Khare 2010). Representative soil samples from different land uses (namely, non-mined, coal-mined, and mining sites abandoned from 4 years) of the three major coal belts, namely, Bapung, Sutnga, and Khliehriat in Jaintia Hills District show that coal mining has caused the decrease in the soil pH by about one unit compared to the soil free from mining activity where pH is 4.35.

5. In constructing the AMD Index, we have followed the basic premise of Gray and Kuma on MAMDI (Gray 1996; Kuma et al. 2011). Due to the non-availability of data following, we have re-normalized the scoring system for these two constituents—pH and sulphate and reconstructed MAMDI (constrained by data, our index is not much rigorous one and cannot capture some of the toxic elements of AMD, particularly metallic ones). Following Kuma et al. (2011) and considering the fact that pH may have more of an effect on the benthic community in the river than sulphate, DO levels on fish health, greater weight has been put (0.55) on pH and lesser (0.45) on sulphate.

6. The choice of Kyrhukhla stream as a representative stream affected by coal mine-induced AMD is quite justifiable. We compared the water quality data from this stream with different data sets used in various studies on AMD in different time periods in different locations in Jaintia District as referred in our article. Blahwar (2010) took water samples from 36 locations along the Umiurem–Umtarang watershed area in central Jaintia District during 2009. Study by Sahoo et al. (2012) was based on water samples from 12 locations of mine discharges, 32 locations in the stream water, and 13 locations for dug well water during 2007. Das and Ramanujam (2011) on the other hand were concerned with the sample water data from (a) streams receiving mine wastes, (b) streams receiving acid water through seepage from coal storage, and (c) streams in the abandoned mine (5–7 years) sites in four seasons during 2008–09. There are no significant differences in those data with the secondary time series data we considered in Kyrhukhla stream water.

# References

ARGHYAM. 2012. "India Waterportal, Bangalore, India." Available at: http://www.indiawaterportal.org/data (accessed on 1 November 2012).

Baruah, B.P., and P. Khare. 2010. "Mobility of Trace and Potentially Harmful Elements in the Environment from High Sulfur Indian Coal Mines." *Applied Geochemistry* 25 (11): 1621–31.

Baumann, H., and A.M. Tillman. 2004. *The Hitch Hiker's Guide to LCA*. Lund, Sweden: Studentlitteratur.

Beckerman, W. 1992. "Economic Growth and the Environment: Whose Growth? Whose Environment?" *World Development* 20 (4): 481–96.

Behra, P. 2007. "Volatile Displacement of Meghalaya Coal—A Pointer to Explore Low Sulphur Coal." *Journal of Earth System Science* 116 (2): 137–42.

Bentler, P.M. 1990. "Comparative Fit Indexes in Structural Models." *Psychological Bulletin* 107 (2): 238–46.

Blahwar, B. 2010. *Identification of the Extent of Artisanal Coal Mining and Related Acid Mine Water Hazards Using Remote Sensing and Field Sampling: A Case Study in Jaiñta Hills of North-eastern India*. Enschede, The Netherlands: Applied Earth Sciences University of Twente. Available at: http://www.itc.nl/Pub/Home/library/Academic_output/AcademicOutput.html?p=8&y=10&l=20 (accessed on 9 May 2012).

Choudhury, B.U., A. Malang, R. Webster, K.P. Mohapatra, B.C. Verma, M. Kumar, A. Das, M. Islam, and S. Hazarika. 2017. "Acid Drainage from Coal Mining: Effect on Paddy Soil and Productivity of Rice." *Science of the Total Environment* 583: 344–51.

Das, M., and P. Ramanujam. 2011. "Metal Content in Water and Filamentous Algae Microspora Quadrata Hazen from Coal Mine Impacted Streams of Jaintia Hills District, Meghalaya, India." *International Journal of Botany* 7 (2): 170–76.

Dasgupta, P., and G. Heal. 1974. "The Optimal Depletion of Exhaustible Resources." *Review of Economic Studies* 42: 3–28.

Department for International Development (DFID). 2000. "Sustainable Livelihoods Guidance Sheets." Available at: www.livelihood.org/info/info_guidancesheets.htm (accessed on 15 October 2012).

DFID (Department for International Development). 2000. "Sustainable Livelihoods Guidance Sheets." DFID document. Available at: www.livelihood.org/info/info_guidancesheets.htm (accessed on 15 October 2012).

Dkhar, S.G. 2010. "Water Merchants of Jaintia Hills." A Report, 25 May 2010. Available at: (http://www.countercurrents.org/dkhar250510.htm accessed on 15 December 2012).

Dutch National Institute for Public Health and the Environment (RIVM). 1995. *A General Strategy for Integrated Environmental Assessment at the European Environment Agency*. Copenhagen: European Environment Agency.

Einheuser, M.D., A.P. Nejadhashemi, L. Wang, S.P. Sowa, and S.A. Woznicki. 2014. "Linking Biological Integrity and Watershed Models to Assess the Impacts of Historical Land Use and Climate Changes on Stream Health." *Environmental Management* 51 (6): 1147–63.

Esqueda, G.S., J.E. Ospina-Norena, C. Gay-Garcia, and C. Conde. 2011. "Vulnerability of Water Resources to Climate Change Scenarios. Impacts on the Irrigation Districts in the Guayalejo-Tamesí River Basin, Tamaulipas, México." *Atmósfera* 24 (1): 141–55.

Gilchrist, S., A. Gates, Z. Szabo, and P.J. Lamothe. 2009. "Impact of AMD on Water Quality in Critical Watershed in the Hudson River Drainage Basin: Phillips Mine, Hudson Highlands, New York." *Environmental Geology* 57: 397–409.

Golden, B., E. Wasil, and P. Harker, eds. 1989. *The Analytic Hierarchy Process: Applications and Studies*. Berlin/New York: Springer.

Government of Meghalaya, Mining and Geology Department. 2012. *The Gazette of Meghalaya*. Shillong: Government of Meghalaya, Mining and Geology Department.

Gray, N.F. 1996. "The Use of an Objective Index for the Assessment of the Contamination of Surface Water and Ground Water by Acid Mine Drainage." *Water and Environment Journal* 10 (5): 332–40.

Guha Roy, P.K. 1992. "Coal Mining in Meghalaya and its Impact of Environment." *Environment Conservation and Wasteland Development in Meghalaya*. Shillong: Meghalaya Science Society.

Harker, P.T., ed. 1986. "The Analytic Hierarchy Process." *Socio-economic Planning Science* 20 (6).

———. 1987. "Alternative Modes of Questioning in the Analytic Hierarchy Process." *Mathematical Modelling* 9 (3-5): 353–60.

Harker, P.T., and L.G. Vargas. 1987. "The Theory of Ratio Scale Estimation: Saaty's Analytic Hierarchy Process." *Management Science* 33 (11): 1383–403.

Hirschman, Albert O. 1958. *The Strategy of Economic Development*. New Haven, CT: Yale University Press.

Howarth, R.B. 2007. "Towards an Operational Sustainability Criterion." *Ecological Economics* 63 (4): 656–63.

Impulse. 2011. "An Exploratory Study of Children Engaged in Rat Hole Mining in the Coal Mines of Jaintia Hills District, Meghalaya." Available at: hrn.or.jp/activity/2011/02/08/201102_Meghalaya.pdf (accessed on 3 August 2012).

Keon, N.E., C.H. Swartz, D.J. Barbander, C. Harvey, and H.F. Hemond. 2001. "Validation of an Arsenic Sequential Extraction Method for Evaluating Mobility in Sediments." *Environmental Science and Technology* 35 (13): 2778–84.

Kline, R.B. 2011. *Principles and Practice of Structural Equation Modelling*. 3rd ed. New York: The Guilford Press.

Korhonen, J., F. von Malmborg, P.A. Strachan, and J.R. Ehrenfeld. 2004. "Editorial Management and Policy Aspects of Industrial Ecology: An Emerging Research Agenda." *Business Strategy and the Environment* 13: 289–305.

Kuma, J.S., P.L. Younger, and W.K. Buah. 2011. "Numerical Indices of the Severity of Acidic Mine Drainage: Broadening the Applicability of the Gray Acid Mine Drainage Index." *Mine Water Environment* 30 (1): 67–74.

Lamin, H. 1995. *Economy and Society in Meghalaya*. New Delhi: Har-Anand Publication.

Loon, A. Van, H. Mathijssen, and P. Droogers. 2007. "Water Evaluation and Planning System Gediz Basin—Turkey." WatManSup project. Available at: http://www.futurewater.nl/downloads/2007_VanLoon_FW65.pdf (accessed on 16 February 2013).

McDuie-Ra, D. 2007. "Anti-development or Identity Crisis? Misreading Civil Society in Meghalaya, India." *Asian Ethnicity* 8 (1): 43–59.

Mukhim, P. 2012. "Mining, Damming, Extracting and What Else…?" A report in *The Statesman*, 13 May 2012. Available at: http://www.thestatesman.com/northeast/meghalaya (accessed on 5 September 2012).

Rex, E., and H. Baumann. 2008. "Implications of an Interpretive Understanding of LCA Practice." *Business Strategy and the Environment* 17: 420–30.

Rout, L. 2006. "Impact of Coal Mining and Trading on the Economy of Meghalaya: A Case Study Jaintia Hills District." PhD Dissertation, North Eastern Hill University, Shillong.

Saaty, T.L. 1990a. "An Exposition of the AHP in Reply to the Paper Remarks on the Analytic Hierarchy Process." *Management Science* 36 (3): 259–68.

———. 1990b. "How to Make a Decision: The Analytic Hierarchy Process." *European Journal of Operation Research* 48: 9–26.

Saaty, T.L., and L.G. Vargas, eds. 1987. "The Analytic Hierarchy Process: Theoretic Developments and Some Applications." *Mathematical Modelling* 9(3-5).

Sahoo, P.K., S. Tripathy, Sk. Md. Equeenuddin, and M.K. Panigrahi. 2012. "Geochemical Characteristics of Coal Mine Discharge vis-à-vis Behavior of Rare Earth Elements at Jaintia Hills Coalfield, Northeastern India." *Journal of Geochemical Exploration* 112: 235–43.

Sahu, B.P., and N.P. Goel. 2004. "Social and Environmental Impact Assessment of Opencast Mining in Meghalaya: A Case Study of Jaintia Hills." In *Environment and Development: Development of Geoenergy Resources and its Impact on Environment and Man of North East India*, edited by Z. Husain and S.K. Barik, 273–89. New Delhi: Regency Publications.

Sánchez, G.T. Esqueda, J.E. Ospina, C. Gay-Garcia, and A.C. Conde. 2011. "A Vulnerability of Water Resources to Climate Change Scenarios: Impacts on the Irrigation Districts in the Guayalejo-Tamesí River Basin, Tamaulipas, México." *Atmósfera* 24 (1): 141–55.

Sarma, K. 2005. "Impact of Coal Mining on Vegetation: A Case Study in Jaintia District of Meghalaya, India. Available at: http://environmentportal.in/files/coal%20mining-jaintia%20hills.pdf (accessed on 12 December 2012).

Sarma, K., R.S. Tripathi, and S.P.S. Kushwaha. 2010. "Land Use/Land Cover Change Analysis in Coal Mine Affected Areas in Jaintia Hills District of Meghalaya, Northeast India Using Remote Sensing and GIS Technique." *Indian Journal of Tropical Biodiversity* 16 (1): 43–50.

Swartz, C.H., N.E. Keon, B. Badruzzman, A. Ali, D. Barbander, J. Jay, J. Besancon, S. Islam, H.F. Hemond, and C. Harvey. 2004. "Mobility of Arsenic in a Bangladesh Aquifer: Inferences from Geochemical Profiles, Leaching Data, and Mineralogical Characterization." *Geochimica et Cosmochimica Acta* 68 (22): 4539–57.

Swer, S., and O.P. Singh. 2003. "Coal Mining Impacting Water Quality and Aquatic Diversity in Jaintia Hills District of Meghalaya." *ENVIS Bulletin Himalayan Ecology* 11 (2): 26–33.

Tabachnick, B.G. and L.S. Fidell. 2007. Using Multivariate Statistics (5th ed.). New York: Allyn and Bacon.

UNEP (United Nations Environment Program)/RIVM (Rijksinstituut voor Volksgezondheid en Milieu in Dutch). 1994. "An Overview of Environmental Indicators: State of the Art and Perspectives." UNEP Environment Assessment: Technical Report 94-01, Nairobi, Kenya.

# 20

# Measuring Welfare of Forest Dependent Communities in a Mine-spoiled Degraded Ecosystem

Narendra Nath Dalei and Yamini Gupt*

## Introduction

The livelihoods of indigenous people depend upon the stock of resources available in the forest. In a natural state of forest ecosystem, resources are abundant and enough to support the livelihoods. But once human intervention like mining degrades the ecosystem, the natural growth rate declines and remains much lower than extraction rate of resources, undermining the livelihood base. Faced with resource scarcity, people start migrating to other areas in search of jobs and alternative sources of livelihood.

The Purnapani area of the Indian state of Odisha is an example of the above scenario where the livelihood of forest dependent communities was largely affected by a degraded forest, the ecosystem of which was changed due to mining activities. The Purnapani Limestone and Dolomite Quarry (PL&DQ) was started initially as a captive manual mine of the Rourkela Steel Plant (RSP). Manual mining operation of PL&DQ was started in September 1958 and the mechanized mining in 1965. The total land contributed by Purnapani villagers for mining, township, and railway line construction was 569.64 acres. In 2003, there was a closure of the operation of mines and about 2,000 workers, working in the mines as well as other forest dependent communities,[1] lost their livelihood.

In this chapter, we explore how the community welfare of indigenous and forest dependent communities in the Purnapani area changed over time with degradation in ecosystem services. A resource extraction model is formulated for this purpose. Next, a survey of literature on resource extraction and linkages between ecosystem and economy is offered, followed by a discussion of methodology. Later, the study area and primary survey are discussed, followed by the result and discussion. The chapter ends offering some policy recommendations.

* The authors greatly acknowledge the Department of Biotechnology, Government of India, for financial support to carry out this study through the project entitled, "Environmental Biotechnology Restoration Ecology" sanctioned to the Centre for Environmental Management of Degraded Ecosystem (CEMDE), University of Delhi. The authors are thankful for the support provided by CEMDE for research and analysis and the logistic support provided by Purnapani Limestone and Dolomite Quarry (PL&DQ), Steel Authority of India (SAIL), to carry out the primary surveys.

# Review of Literature

There is no doubt that forest dependent communities are an integral part of forest ecosystems. The overarching questions that motivated us to survey the literature are: What kinds of resource extraction models exist? Is there any linkage between ecosystem and economy in this regard? Is there any impact of degraded forest ecosystem services on resource extraction? Do degraded forest ecosystems services impact the livelihood of local people? The following survey will answer these questions in order to identify the gap in the literature.

## Resource Extraction

Forest dependent people extract resources such as timber, fuel wood, fruits etc. from forests. Keeping in mind resource availability, time, and distance to the forest, they take household level decisions regarding when and from where to extract resources. Based on this premise, sophisticated household level resource extraction models were developed by many scholars; few of them are described here. Amacher, Hyde, and Kanel (1996) modelled household utility as a function of fuelwood, leisure, and other goods while Bluffstone (1995) modelled household utility as a function of cooked food. The extraction model of Bluffstone (1995), being a model of household agro-forestry system under open access with a perfect off-farm labour market, focused on the sum of the present discounted values of consumption of cooked food and the sum of purchased and home-produced food grains. Dayal (2006), while developing a model of household utility function, found that village location, ownership of biogas, and caste are correct explanatory variables for forest biomass extraction. Lopez-Feldman and Wilen (2008) have modelled resources of marketable non-timber forest products (NTFP) taking space in a single dimension and they find that extraction takes place in day trips and the only variable input that extractors control is the allocation of their time. Bardhan et al. (2001) tried to analyse the role of different determinants of deforestation by using household data concerning collection of firewood and did not find any evidence in support of the leading hypothesis of extraction leading to environmental degradation. Assuming the stock of resource and the annual flow of products and services to be given within the framework of a one-period labour allocation model, Chopra and Dasgupta (2008) found that households typically divide time between collections from commons, working for a wage income and leisure. Robinson et al. (2008), while designing a resource extraction model, found that when the location of resource implies a distance cost to extraction, the spatial pattern of extraction varied period by period leading to a multi-period and cyclical steady state.

## Ecosystem and Economy Linkages

Degraded forest ecosystem in many cases is a result of economic development, urbanization, and industrial advancement. Millennium Ecosystem Assessment (2005) also indicates that over the past 50 years, humans have changed ecosystems more rapidly and extensively than in any comparable period of time in human history, largely to meet the rapidly growing demands for food, freshwater, timber, fibre, and fuel. Population pressure and economic activity beyond the carrying capacity of the natural environment threatens the earth's ecosystems by over-utilization of resources (Arrow et al. 1995). Economic activity is putting a stress on the biological resources and jeopardizing the ecosystem services to the point where production processes and consumer well-being are being negatively impacted (Arrow et al. 1995; Eichner and Tschirhart 2007; Norgaard 1994). Human activities are impairing the flow of ecosystem services on a large scale, and many of the human activities that modify or destroy natural ecosystems may cause deterioration of ecological services whose value, in the long term, dwarfs the short-term economic benefits that the society gains from those activities (Daily 1997). Human economies and natural ecosystems are inextricably linked: common economic variables such as incomes and prices affect and are affected by common ecosystem variables such as resilience and species populations (Tschirhart 2000). Models of economies and ecosystems largely disregard one another though the biological underpinnings are encompassed in the phrase ecosystem services, which refers to a wide range of conditions and processes through which natural ecosystems, and the species that are part of them, help sustain and fulfil human life (Daily 1997). Bioeconomic models that merge economic and ecosystem concepts tend to address isolated markets and very few species. They do not address the myriad ways in which changes in an economy influence ecosystem functions, and in turn how changes in ecosystem functions send a feedback to the economy (Tschirhart 2000).

The ecological approach for biodiversity measurement is based on species richness and abundance, and emphasizes the fact that abundant species must contribute more than rare species (Olfa and Pierre 2004). Economists take into account the contribution of each species to biodiversity measurement, and economic approach is based, mostly, on the work of Weitzman (1992, 1993, and 1998) who developed an axiomatic analysis to measure biodiversity using a distance function based on pair-wise dissimilarity between species according to their attributes. Nehring and Puppe (2002) extend this idea to consider many attributes. The intuition behind the dissimilarity approach is "more diversity is better than less." Olfa and Pierre (2004) have observed that the natural (virgin) state of biodiversity, as an important issue, is not considered in ecological and economic approaches. They explore that all measures miss out an important element of biodiversity valuation that is the reference value of biodiversity relative to each ecosystem. Constructing a biodiversity measure, they find that the closer the biodiversity is to its natural state the higher is its value. According to Eichner and Tschirhart (2007), if natural biodiversity is associated with resiliency of ecosystems and relatively stable populations, then the natural state potentially may provide the greatest flow of ecosystem services.

In each of the resource extraction models, priority has been given only to resource extraction as a means of livelihood and the decision regarding efficient allocation of time and effort for generating livelihood. A survey of available literature related to resource extraction reveals little evidence regarding impact of degraded forest ecosystem services (consequence of human intervention like mining, urbanization, industrialization, etc.) on resource extraction and livelihood. Thus, this study fills an important gap in the literature, which focuses on resource extraction behaviour of forest dependent communities and shows how the welfare of the communities declined due to mining activities.

## Methodology

In this section, we first formulate a resource extraction model and then develop a Net Present Value (NPV) criterion to see how welfare has changed over a period of time for the community.

The community welfare function for the indigenous and other forest dependent communities for $n$ discrete time periods can be written as:

$$W = W(U_t) \text{ for } t = 0,1,...n \tag{1}$$

where, $W$ is social welfare function of the communities for the time period, $t = 0$ to $n$ with utility being $U$. Considering the time preference of the communities, the community welfare function in its discounted utility form can be written as:

$$W = U_0 + \frac{U_1}{1+\rho} + \frac{U_2}{(1+\rho)^2} + \cdots + \frac{U_n}{(1+\rho)^n} \tag{2}$$

However, utilities are unobservable. Therefore, by replacing sum of discounted utilities with sum of discounted Net Economic Benefit (NEB), we can obtain the NPV for the communities in place of community welfare function as:

$$NPV = \pi_0 + \frac{\pi_1}{1+\rho} + \frac{\pi_2}{(1+\rho)^2} + \cdots + \frac{\pi_n}{(1+\rho)^n} \qquad (3)$$

where, $\pi$: Net Economic Benefit
$\rho$: Social Discount Rate
$NPV$: Net Present Value

The indigenous households extract forest resources and get the NEB, which is functionally related to stock of forest resource and extraction level at time $t$.

Hence,
$$\pi_t = \pi(F_t, R_t) \qquad (4)$$

Where $F_t$ is the forest resource stock and $R_t$ is the extraction level.

The level of extraction, which is affected by unsustainable mining activities, can be compared for different time periods. The mining activities impacted the resource extraction level over a period of time by directly degrading forest ecosystem services, which led to a different time path for the forest resource stock $F_t$. Suppose that $R_{it}$ denotes the extraction level that results in stock of forest resource $F_{it}$ for $i^{th}$ state of ecosystem. Here we calculate the NPV of benefit from resource extraction in different states of the ecosystem over the time horizon, $t=0, 1, \ldots, n$. Assuming a constant time invariant social discount rate $\rho$, the discount factor can be written as:

$$D = \frac{1}{1+\rho} \qquad (5)$$

The present value comparison of benefit from resource extraction in $i^{th}$ state of ecosystem for the $t^{th}$ time period is presented in Table 20.1.

For the initial time period (pre-mining period in present case), we calculate discounted NPV of the extracted resources $R_{0t}$ and the resulting resource stock $F_{0t}$ in the natural state of the ecosystem. Then this discounted sum can be compared with discounted NPV of extraction level for the other states of ecosystem during the respective time periods. In each time period, the discounted NPV will also be different for different households depending upon their resource utilization pattern. The state of ecosystem that maximizes the present value of net benefit or NPV out of extracted resources will be preferred (as it provides the greatest flow of benefit to the communities).

Thus, the NPV that we obtain can be classified into various categories depending upon the optimum allocation of time for the household members for different economic activities and forest resource utilization

**Table 20.1**
*The present value comparison*

| State of ecosystem: $i=0$ | State of ecosystem: $i=1$ | $\ldots$ | State of ecosystem: $i=n$ |
|---|---|---|---|
| $\sum_{t=0}^{n} D^0 \pi(F_{0t}, R_{0t})$ | $\sum_{t=0}^{n} D^1 \pi(F_{1t}, R_{1t})$ | $\ldots$ | $\sum_{t=0}^{n} D^n \pi(F_{nt}, R_{nt})$ |

*Source:* Author's formulation.

patterns. Hence, the NPVs can be classified as $NPV_1, NPV_2, ..., NPV_n$, depending upon the types of ecosystem prevalent during different time periods.

The sum of discounted NEB derived from extraction of forest resources can be modelled as:

$$NPV_{it} = f(X_1, X_2, ..., X_k) \qquad (6)$$

Where,

NPV: Net Present Value of extracted forest resources of $i^{th}$ state of ecosystem and $t^{th}$ time period.

$X_1, X_2, ..., X_k$: various determinants of NPV.

The NPV for the time period $t = i$ to $n$ will be a continuous variable which can be estimated using ordinary least squares (OLS) method. But in the present case, the state of ecosystem for more than one time period remains the same because its characteristics are determined by biophysical elements of nature, which remain same for a long period. Therefore, NPV will remain more or less the same for a particular state of ecosystem though the time period varies. Thus, for one state of ecosystem, we can consider NPV as one category (see Tables 20.2 and 20.3, where NPV is different for each state of ecosystem). Similarly, for other states of ecosystem, the NPV will be of a different category. Thus, the dependent variable (NPV) in our model will be an unordered categorical which can be estimated using multinomial logistic regression (MNLR) model.

There are several advantages of MNLR model: (a) the response variable is an unordered categorical; (b) multiple predictors can be taken into account; (c) it is heteroscedasticity consistent (Aldrich and Nelson 1984; Mahapatra and Kant 2005); and (d) results of this model are found to be more informative and robust compared to the results of dichotomous logistic and OLS regression methods, and it always provides more

**Table 20.2**

*Time period and state of forest ecosystem*

| Period | State of forest ecosystem |
|---|---|
| Pre-mining (before 1955) | natural state |
| Transition (1955–60) | transition state |
| Mining (1961–2003) | degraded state |
| Post-mining (2003–05) | degraded state |

*Source:* Author's formulation based upon primary survey.

**Table 20.3**

*Frequency distribution of available replicates*

| Period | NPV ($\rho = 4.3$) (in ₹) | State of ecosystem | $NPV_{it}$ (category of NPV) | Freq. |
|---|---|---|---|---|
| Pre-mining (before 1955) | 270,477 | natural state | $NPV_0$ | 78 |
| Transition (1955–60) | 50,876 | transition state | $NPV_1$ | 78 |
| Mining (1961–2003) | 7,661 | degraded state | $NPV_2$ | 78 |
| Post-mining (After 2003) | 1,380 | degraded state | $NPV_3$ | 78 |
| Total | | | | 312 |

*Source:* Authors' computation and formulation.

accurate results than the multinomial probit regression model (Hilbe 2009). The MNLR model with $j$ categories of response variable can be written as:

$$\ln\left[\frac{p(Y_i)}{p(Y_j)}\right] = \alpha_{i0} + \alpha_{i1}X_1 + \alpha_{i2}X_2 + \cdots + \alpha_{ik}X_k + \dot{\varepsilon}_i \tag{7}$$

Where, $Y_j$ is the NPV of $j^{th}$ category in $i^{th}$ state of ecosystem; $Y_i = NPV_1, NPV_2, \ldots, NPV_n$; and $X_1$ to $X_k$ are explanatory variables.

## Study Area and Primary Survey

We have selected Purnapani area (latitudes 22° 24′ 38″ and 22° 24′ 52″ north and longitudes 84° 51′ 42″ and 84° 54′ 23″ east) of Sundergarh district of the state of Odisha (see Figure 20.1) where, the PL&DQ is situated between latitudes of 22°24′50″ and 22°24′00″ and longitudes 84°51′40″ and 84°53′25″.

The area[2] consists of four villages, namely, Purnapani, Gattitangar, Bhojpur, and Karkatnasa; one abandoned mine; and one reserved forest.[3] The total geographical area of the study site is 1,552 hectares along with 10.77 hectares of forest and 230.53 hectares of mine-spoiled area. The study area consists of total cultivated area of 1,310.7 hectares with a population size of 7,743 persons as per the 2001 Census. The inhabitants of Purnapani area were dependent on the forest for their livelihood, as there existed a reserved forest inside the area. Therefore, these inhabitants were an integral part of the local forest ecosystem. The

**Figure 20.1**
*Location map of Purnapani area inside the Sundergarh district*

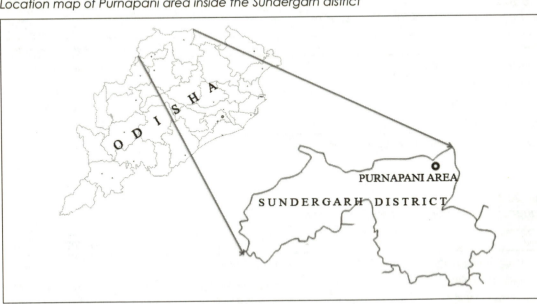

*Source:* Dalei and Gupt (2014).

*Note:* This figure is not to scale. It does not represent any authentic national or international boundaries and is used for illustrative purposes only.

local reserved forest is now in a degraded state due to the mining activities (for details on study area, please see Dalei and Gupt 2014).

Taking into account the mining activities in Purnapani area, the time period is divided into four sub-periods—pre-mining, transition, mining, and post-mining.

The forest ecosystem during the pre-mining period (before 1955) was in a natural state. Considering that the mining activity was based on manual and mechanized operations and their environmental impacts, the period from 1955 to 1960 is considered as a transition period—the period when the local economy was moving from forest dependent to a mining dependent one. Consequently, the ecosystem was moving from its natural state to a degraded state due to mining activities. Therefore, the state of ecosystem between natural and degraded state is considered as a transition state of ecosystem. The period from 1960 to 2003 is considered as the "mining period" when the mining operation was active with heavy population pressure leading to severe deforestation. The period between 2003 and 2005 is considered as "post-mining period" when the mining operation was inactive but its impact could be felt in terms of abandoned mines, overburdened dump, and degraded forest. Therefore, during mining and post-mining period, the state of forest ecosystem was degraded (for details on state of ecosystem, see Dalei and Gupt 2014; also see, Table 20.2).

In order to collect data for our study, we conducted a primary survey of 315 households selected from a population of 1,052 households following the circular systematic random sampling method during March to August 2009. The data so gathered were cross-sectional waves of information from each respondent selected based upon their age for each particular state of ecosystem (for detail sampling design, please see Dalei and Gupt 2014).

# Results and Discussion

In this section, we compare and estimate the NPV for all the time periods based on its determinants.

## Comparison of NPV

Computation of NPV was undertaken from the real gross economic benefit (GEB) derived from the forest resources at 2008 prices by following the market price approach.[4] Subsequently, we computed total extraction cost (TEC) of forest resources by multiplying time devoted by the household members for extraction of resources into its real opportunity cost.[5] The NEB was followed from this and was calculated as:

$$NEB = GEB - TEC \qquad (8)$$

The NEB presented in Equation 8 was computed for each household for all the four time periods. Then in order to know the level of welfare derived from forest resources by the communities, we discounted the sum of household level NEB for each time period by considering the discount rate ($\rho$) as 4.3.[6] Further, we computed corresponding values of NPV for four states of ecosystem for each time period as shown in Table 20.3. Based upon the level of welfare derived by the communities in terms of NPV, we categorized it into four categories, namely, $NPV_0$, $NPV_1$, $NPV_2$, and $NPV_3$ for pre-mining, transition, mining, and post-mining periods, respectively. We observed from Table 20.3 and Figure 20.2 that the level of welfare in terms of NPV derived from extraction of forest resources declined exponentially since the pre-mining period due to degradation of ecosystem services which is a result of unsustainable mining activities.

**Figure 20.2**

*Trend of NPV in Purnapani area*

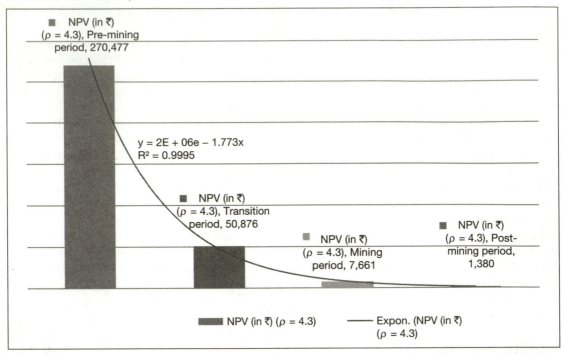

*Source:* Drawn by authors using Table 20.3.

In this analysis, $NPV_0$ is taken as the referent group with which other replicates of the *NPVs* were compared. The natural state of ecosystem produces adequate amount of resources relative to demand conditions. NPV of communities for this time period is computed as ₹270 thousands.

The state of ecosystem in the transition state is neither in a natural state nor in a fully degraded state. The amount of collectable resources available in the forest is just equal to the demand for it by the indigenous and other forest dependent people. So in the transition state, the sum of discounted NEB of the communities is categorized as $NPV_1$, which has been declined by around 81 per cent as compared to *NPV* of pre-mining period (see Table 20.3 and Figure 20.2).

During the mining and post-mining periods, the state of ecosystem was so degraded that it was not possible to produce adequate amount of natural resources relative to demand conditions of the indigenous and other forest dependent communities. In fact, people had to spend more time inside the forest for extraction of required amount of resources. So in the degraded state, the sum of discounted NEB of the communities derived from forest being categorized as $NPV_2$ and $NPV_3$ for mining and post-mining period declined by around 97 and 99 per cent as compared to *NPV* of pre-mining period, respectively.

## Analysis of Determinants of NPV

The descriptive statistics of determinants of NPV are presented in Table 20.4 and explained in the following subsections.

### Number of Working Members (NWM)

NWM in Purnapani area includes members of the households who are working either to earn wages or are involved in self-employment activities. These members after their regular work extract resources from the

**Table 20.4**

*Mean values of predictor variables (Mean±SD)*

| Explanatory variables | Pre-mining period (before 1955) | Transition period (1955–60) | Mining period (1961–2003) | Post-mining period (after 2003) |
|---|---|---|---|---|
| NWM | 3.5±1.97 | 4.32±2.37 | 2.53±1.58 | 2.51±1.51 |
| ANC | 15.82±23.78 | 2.36±6.85 | 1.71±3.31 | 7.14±13.60 |
| LOH | 3.82±4.81 | 3.47±4.89 | 2.02±2.95 | 2.77±5.37 |
| ATW | 6.96±2.63 | 7.18±2.44 | 5.54±3.72 | 5.79±3.6 |
| ATS | 5.01±5.17 | 4.53±4.10 | 4.13±3.61 | 3.62±3.29 |
| DFF | 0.26±0.44 | 0.28±0.45 | 0.26±0.44 | 0.26±0.44 |
| DFF–1 (Freq.) | 20 | 22 | 20 | 20 |
| DFF–0 (Freq.) | 58 | 56 | 58 | 58 |
| PFL | 0.14±0.35 | 0.17±0.38 | 0.22±0.42 | 0.22±0.42 |
| PFL–1 (Freq.) | 11 | 13 | 17 | 17 |
| PFL–0 (Freq.) | 67 | 65 | 61 | 61 |

*Source:* Primary survey by author.

forest to supplement their livelihood. During the pre-mining period, the average NWM per household was 3.5, which increased by 23 per cent during transition period and declined by 28 per cent during mining and post-mining periods relative to pre-mining period, respectively.

## Amount of Nuts Collected from the Forest (ANC)

Nuts such as *char*, cashew nut, *kusum nut*, and other wild nuts are collected by the forest dependent communities from the forest in Purnapani area. During pre-mining period, the average ANC by the households was 15.82 kilogram per annum, which declined by 85 per cent during transition period, 89 per cent during mining, and 55 per cent during post-mining period relative to pre-mining period. This declining trend of nuts in Purnapani area is because of degraded forest ecosystem due to mining activities.

## Land Owned by the Households (LOH)

LOH in Purnapani area consisted of high, medium, and low land for agricultural purposes only. During pre-mining period, the average amount of LOH was 3.82 acres, which declined by 9 per cent during transition period, 47 per cent during mining, and 27 per cent during post-mining period relative to pre-mining period. This declining trend in Purnapani area was because of diversion of land for mining activities by the households.

## Average Time Spend for Earning Wages (ATW)

ATW varies depending upon the amount of time devoted for extracting resources from the forest. During the pre-mining period, the ATW was 6.96 hours per day, which increased by 3 per cent during transition period and declined by 20 per cent and 17 per cent during both mining and post-mining period, respectively, relative to pre-mining period. During mining and post-mining period, the ATW declined because more time was devoted for extracting resources from the forest relative to pre-mining and transition period. This is because during the latter two periods, resource scarcity occurred due to degraded forest ecosystems and mining activities.

## Average Time Spent in Self-Employment Activities (ATS)

Similarly, ATS varies depending upon the amount of time devoted for extracting resources from the forest.

During the pre-mining period, the ATS was 5.01 hours per day, which declined by 10 per cent during the transition period, 18 per cent during mining, and 28 per cent during post-mining period relative to pre-mining period.

The declining trend of ATS is because of resource scarcity due to degraded forest ecosystems and mining activities.

### Distance of the Households from Forest (DFF)

Forest resources are more accessible for those households who are staying inside the forest than those who are staying outside the forest area. During the transition period, out of 78 households, 28 per cent were staying inside the forest and some 72 per cent were staying outside the forest area. However, during pre-mining, mining, and post-mining periods, 26 per cent households were staying inside the forest and some 74 per cent were staying outside the forest area.

### Possession of Forestland by the Household (PFL)

In Purnapani area, households cleared forestland for cultivation purpose. During pre-mining and transition period, 14 per cent of households and 17 per cent of households, respectively, had possessed some amount of forestland whereas the remaining households had not possessed any amount of forestland. However, during both mining and post-mining periods, 22 per cent of households had possessed some forestland. During the latter two periods, number of households possessing forestland increased due to mining activities undertaken on their own land.

## Econometric Analysis and Estimation of NPV

The results of the MNLR model are given in Table 20.5. The coefficient of predictor variables of the MNLR model represents the change in log odds associated with one unit change in the predictor variable. A positive coefficient of the variable increases the log odds, while a negative coefficient decreases it when other predictors are held constant. However, it is easy to interpret Relative Risk Ratio (RRR) rather than log odds. The base of natural log raised to the power equal to the magnitude of the coefficient denotes the factor by which the RRR change when the explanatory variable increases by one unit. For example, the RRR of the NWM suggests that *ceteris paribus* with an increase in one working member, the relative risk of NPV derived from forest during transition period relative to pre-mining period, is likely to increase significantly by 130 per cent. However, during post-mining period, the relative risk of NPV had declined relative to NPV of pre-mining period by 80 per cent with increase in one working member. However, the NWM does not significantly affect (*p*-value=0.170) NPV during mining period relative to pre-mining period.

The NWM is a significant predictor of NPV because the households of the community with more NWM will access forestland more for extracting forest resources during transition period relative to pre-mining period. More access of forestland for extracting resources during transition period relative to pre-mining period will bring higher level of community welfare through greater attainment of NPV. This is due to the fact that during the transition period, the forest was not degraded enough, and forest ecosystems were producing adequate amount of resources required by the local communities. However, during post-mining period, forest degradation and degradation of ecosystem services due to abandoned mines and overburdened dumping led to scarcity of forest resources. So community welfare in terms of NPV is likely to decrease significantly during the post-mining period relative to pre-mining period with a one-unit increase in working members of the households of the communities.

The ANC is also a significant predictor of NPV derived from the forest by the communities. The RRR of ANC from the forest suggests that with an increase in collection of one more kilogram of nuts, the relative risk of NPV derived from the forest during transition, mining, and post-mining period relative to pre-mining period is likely to decrease significantly by 91 per cent, 89 per cent, and 97 per cent, respectively, keeping all other things constant. This is because during transition, mining, and post-mining period,

**Table 20.5**

*Result of multinomial logistic regression (N=312)*

| Equations | Variables | Coef. | Std. Err. | RRR | Sig. |
|---|---|---|---|---|---|
| $NPV_1/NPV_0$ | NWM | 0.2636072 | 0.1280726 | 1.301617 | *** |
| | ANC | −0.0988711 | 0.0199126 | 0.9058595 | *** |
| | DFF | 0.228598 | 0.5898655 | 1.256837 | |
| | LOH | −0.0466606 | 0.0394183 | 0.9544113 | |
| | PFL | 0.851138 | 1.194561 | 2.342311 | * |
| | ATW | −0.05731 | 0.0708113 | 0.9443013 | |
| | ATS | −0.0451046 | 0.0493016 | 0.9558975 | |
| $NPV_2/NPV_0$ | NWM | −0.1684638 | 0.1037504 | 0.8449619 | |
| | ANC | −0.1185045 | 0.0243107 | 0.8882478 | *** |
| | DFF | 0.8156886 | 1.109945 | 2.260732 | * |
| | LOH | −0.1697529 | 0.049775 | 0.8438733 | *** |
| | PFL | 1.032421 | 1.424252 | 2.807855 | ** |
| | ATW | −0.1771924 | 0.0583338 | 0.8376186 | ** |
| | ATS | −0.0057946 | 0.0540849 | 0.9942222 | |
| $NPV_3/NPV_0$ | NWM | −0.2261545 | 0.093528 | 0.7975949 | * |
| | ANC | −0.031478 | 0.0115185 | 0.9690123 | *** |
| | DFF | 0.7874738 | 1.037456 | 2.197837 | * |
| | LOH | −0.0642497 | 0.0382294 | 0.9377708 | |
| | PFL | 0.7656221 | 1.019852 | 2.150332 | * |
| | ATW | −0.1617158 | 0.0564632 | 0.8506829 | ** |
| | ATS | −0.0899027 | 0.0474214 | 0.9140201 | * |

*Source:* Author's own analysis from primary survey data.

*Notes:* *** indicates significance at 10 per cent, ** indicates significance at 5 per cent, and * indicates significance at 1 per cent level. Out of total sample size (household) of 312, STATA 11 considered only 311 household as valid observation and ignored remaining 1 household because of existence of missing values.

degradation of forest ecosystem services due to unsustainable mining activities and its abandonment leads to resource scarcity. Thus, collection of resources like nuts from the forest during these periods was taking more time and effort so that its collection cost was comparatively higher leading to decline in NPV in relation to pre-mining period.

DFF does not affect NPV significantly during the transition period relative to the pre-mining period. However, other things being given, DFF is a significant predictor of NPV of the communities during mining and post-mining period relative to NPV of the communities during pre-mining period. The RRRs of DFF suggest that community welfare in terms of NPV is likely to be increased more significantly by 226 per cent during mining period and 219 per cent during post-mining period relative to pre-mining period, respectively, for those households of the communities who were residing inside the forest relative to for those who were residing far away from the forest.

LOH does not affect NPV significantly during transition and post-mining period relative to pre-mining period. However, other things being given, LOH is a significant predictor of NPV of the communities during mining period relative to NPV of the communities during pre-mining period. The RRRs of LOH suggest that community welfare in terms of NPV is likely to be decreased more significantly by 84 per cent during mining period relative to pre-mining period if a household owns one more acre of land. Because, in order to own one more acre of land for agriculture,[7] the household will have to clear one acre of forestland, which is leading to deforestation and further degradation of ecosystem services. Thus, NPV is likely to decline significantly during the mining period relative to pre-mining period due to degradation of ecosystem services leading to resource scarcity.

The PFL is a significant predictor of NPV derived from the forest by the communities. The RRR of PFL suggests that NPV derived from the forest during the transition, mining, and post-mining periods relative to pre-mining period is likely to be increased significantly by 234 per cent, 281 per cent, and 215 per cent, respectively, for those households who have possessed some amount of forestland relative to those who have not possessed any amount of forestland, keeping all other things constant. This is because those households who have possessed some amount of forestland are more likely to access forest resources as it is available closer to their land relative to those who do not possess it.

ATW does not affect NPV significantly during the transition period relative to pre-mining period. However, other things being given, ATW is a significant predictor of NPV of the communities during mining and post-mining period relative to NPV of the communities during pre-mining period. The RRRs of ATW suggest that community welfare in terms of NPV is likely to decline more significantly by 84 per cent during mining period and 85 per cent during post-mining period relative to pre-mining period, respectively, if the members of the household spend one more hour for earning wages. Because more hours spent for earning wages lead to less availability of time for extracting resources from forest during mining and post-mining period relative to pre-mining period. Thus, NPV decreases during these periods relative to the pre-mining period.

ATS does not predict NPV significantly during the transition and mining period relative to pre-mining period. However, ATS is a significant determinant of NPV during post-mining period relative to pre-mining period. The RRR of ATS revealed that with one additional hour of ATS, the NPV is more likely to decline significantly by 91 per cent during post-mining period relative to pre-mining period, other things being given. This is due to the fact that more hours spent in self-employment activities lead to less availability of time for extracting resources from forest during post-mining period relative to pre-mining period. Thus, NPV decreases during this period relative to pre-mining period due to less amount of resource extraction from the forest.

## Conclusion and Policy Recommendations

We measured the welfare of Purnapani forest dependent communities in terms of discounted NPV, which declined exponentially in Purnapani area since pre-mining period. The results of the MNLR model also indicate that the welfare of the forest dependent communities had been affected by most of its determinants in a statistically significant manner. In fact, our analysis found that the community welfare declined significantly during the post-mining period relative to pre-mining period with increase in NWM in the family. During the post-mining period, unsustainable mining activities, overburdened dump, and degraded state of ecosystem services were leading to scarcity of resources in the forest.

Other things being given, the community welfare was likely to decrease more significantly during the mining and post-mining period relative to pre-mining period due to unsustainable mining activities.

In Purnapani area, the communities were more vulnerable during mining and post-mining period due to mine-spoiled degraded ecosystems. However, this kind of vulnerability of the communities can be corrected through a policy change towards adoption of drastic and large-scale ecological restoration in the mine-spoiled degraded site. Without large-scale ecological restoration, it would be very difficult to make the livelihood of forest dependent communities sustainable in Purnapani area. Being an integral part of the forest ecosystem, these people become endangered species of the human genus. Through our research and analyses, we suggest that the entire degraded land of Purnapani area should be restored back ecologically in order to bring the entire local forest ecosystem to a natural or close to a natural state. Though ecological restoration has already been initiated in many parts of the country including in Odisha, we suggest that all mine-spoiled areas throughout the country need to be identified and large-scale ecological restoration needs to be undertaken to bring back degraded forest ecosystem to a natural or close to a natural state.

## Notes

1. These communities were depending on forest directly and on mining activities indirectly for their livelihood. However, at the end due to closure of mining operation and degradation of forest they lost their livelihood.
2. Purnapani is the name of a village and Purnapani area is defined by the authors in the name of Purnapani village.
3. As per the Wildlife Protection Act, 1972, "reserve forest" means the forest declared to be reserved by the state government under sec. 20 of the Indian Forest Act, 1927 (16 of 1927). As per the Indian Forest Act, 1927, the state government may constitute any forestland or wasteland, which is the property of government, or over which the government has proprietary rights, or to the whole or any part of the forest produce of which the government is entitled, a reserved forest in the manner hereinafter provided.
4. In order to derive GEB, we followed only market price approach. We ignored other non-market valuation techniques due to resource and time constraints. In order to compute real GEB, we considered a set of constant prices (2008 as the base year) of forest resources extracted by the households. These prices were collected from the local market of Purnapani area during primary survey.
5. We assume real wage rate (wage rate at 2008 prices = ₹40/-) as the opportunity cost of time devoted to extract resources from the forest.
6. We considered real rate of interest of the year 2008 as the discount rate (World Bank).
7. No sample household have purchased agricultural land from others.

## References

Aldrich, J.H., and F.E. Nelson. 1984. *Linear Probability, Logit and Probit Models: Sage University Paper Series on Quantitative Applications in the Social Sciences*. Beverly Hills, CA: SAGE Publication.

Amacher, G.S., W.F. Hyde, and K.R. Kanel. 1996. "Household Fuelwood Demand and Supply in Nepal's Tarai and Mid-Hills: Choice Between Cash Outlays and Labor Opportunity." *World Development* 24 (11): 1725–36.

Arrow, K., B. Bolin, R. Costanza, P. Dasgupta, C. Folke, C.S. Holling, B.-O. Jansson, S. Levin, K.-G. Maeler, C. Perrings, and D. Pimentel. 1995. "Economic Growth, Carrying Capacity and the Environment." *Science* 268 (5210): 520–21.

Bardhan, P., J. Baland, S. Das, D. Mookherjee, and R. Sarkar. 2001. "Household Firewood Collection in Rural Nepal: The Role of Poverty, Collective Action and Modernization." Working Paper, University of California, Berkeley, CA.

Bluffstone, R.A. 1995. "The Effect of Labor Market Performance on Deforestation in Developing Countries Under Open Access: An Example from Nepal." *Journal of Environmental Economics and Management* 29 (1): 42–63.

Chopra, K., and Dasgupta, P. 2008. "Nature of Household Dependence on Common Pool Resources: An Empirical Study." *Economic and Political Weekly* 43(08): 58–66.

Daily, G.C., ed. 1997. *Nature's Services*. Washington, DC: Island Press.

Dalei, N., and Y. Gupt. 2014. "Livelihood Sustainability of Forest Dependent Communities in a Mine-spoiled Area." *International Journal of Ecological Economics and Statistics* 35 (4): 30–47.

Dayal, V. 2006. "A Microeconometric Analysis of Household Extraction of Forest Biomass Goods in Ranthambhore National Park, India." *Journal of Forest Economics* 12 (2): 145–63.

Eichner, T., and J. Tschirhart. 2007. "Efficient Ecosystem Services and Naturalness in an Ecological/Economic Model." *Environmental and Resource Economics* 37 (2007): 733–55.

Hilbe, J.M. 2009. *Logistic Regression Models: Texts in Statistical Science Series*. Boca Raton, Florida: Chapman & Hall, CRC Press.

Lopez-Feldman, A., and J.E. Wilen. 2008. *Poverty and Spatial Dimensions of Non-timber Forest Extraction*. Cambridge: Cambridge University Press.

Mahapatra, K., and S. Kant. 2005. "Tropical Deforestation: A Multinomial Logistic Model and Some Country-specific Policy Prescriptions." *Forest Policy and Economics* 7 (2005): 1–24.

Millennium Ecosystem Assessment. 2005. *Ecosystems and Human Well-being: Synthesis*. Washington, DC: Island Press.

Nehring, K., and C. Puppe. 2002. "A Theory of Diversity." *Econometrica* 70 (3): 1155–98.

Norgaard, R.B. 1994. *Development Betrayed: The End of Progress and a Coevolutionary Revisioning of the Future*. New York: Routledge.

Olfa, K., and L. Pierre. 2004. "The Natural State as a Basis for Biodiversity Measurement." Working Paper, Université de Québec À Montréal, Montréal.

Robinson, E.J.Z. H.J. Albers, and J.C. Williams. 2008. "Spatial and Temporal Modeling of Community Non-timber Forest Extraction." *Journal of Environmental Economics and Management* 56 (3): 234–45.

Tschirhart, J. 2000. "General Equilibrium of an Ecosystem." *Journal of Theoretical Biology* 203 (1): 13–32.

Weitzman, Martin L. 1992. "On Diversity." *The Quarterly Journal of Economics* 107 (2): 363–405.

———. 1993. "What to Preserve? An Application of Diversity Theory to Crane Conservation." *The Quarterly Journal of Economics* 108 (1): 157–83.

———. 1998. "The Noah's Ark Problem." *Econometrica* 66 (6): 1279–98.

World Bank. 2008. World Developed Indicator (WDI). Available at: http://data.worldbank.org/indicator/FR.INR.RIN R?end=2016&locations=IN&start=2008&view=chart (accessed on 10 April 2011).

# About the Editors and Contributors

## Editors

**Pranab Mukhopadhyay** is with the Department of Economics, Goa University. He studied at Presidency College (now Presidency University), Kolkata, and Jawaharlal Nehru University, New Delhi, and is a Fellow of the South Asian Network for Development and Environmental Economics (SANDEE). His current research interest has been ecosystem services, institutions, and development.

**Nandan Nawn** is an Associate Professor and the Head of Department of Policy Studies, TERI University, New Delhi, where he teaches various courses in the interface of environment, development, and economics. He is an economist by disciplinary training with a doctoral degree from Jawaharlal Nehru University. His research interests lie in ecological economics, agrarian studies, and environment and development. His works have been published in various journals including *Journal of Agrarian Change, Economic and Political Weekly,* and *Journal of Human Development and Capabilities.* Recently, he has co-edited *Economic Challenges for the Contemporary World: Essays in Honour of Prabhat Patnaik.* Presently, he is a co-editor of the "Review of Environment and Development" in *Economic and Political Weekly* and the Secretary of the Indian Society for Ecological Economics (INSEE).

**Kalyan Das** is with OKD Institute of Social Change and Development, Guwahati. He obtained his PhD from Jawaharlal Nehru University. His present research interests are industry, environment, labour market, and livelihood issues, and he is involved in a number of research projects on Northeast India.

## Contributors

**Ramachandra Bhatta** is ICAR Emeritus Scientist (economics) and was with National Centre for Sustainable Coastal Management. Earlier, he was associated with Erasmus Mundus Program of the European Union at Belgium and also a SANDEE Fellow/Consultant at Maldives during 2008–09.

**Rabindra N. Bhattacharya** is currently Honorary Adjunct Professor, School of Oceanographic Studies, Jadavpur University, Kolkata. Areas of his research interests include environmental economics and development economics. He has published in almost all the leading journals on environmental and development economics and supervised many PhD scholars.

**Chandra Sekhar Bahinipati** obtained his PhD in economics from Madras Institute of Development Studies, Chennai. Currently he is with Gujarat Institute of Development Research, Ahmedabad. He will be joining Department of Humanities and Social Sciences, Indian Institute of Technology Tirupati in September 2017. His research interests include climate change economics, economics of adaptation, loss and damage, natural resource management, impact evaluation, environmental economics, and development economics. He has published several research papers in the peer reviewed journals such as *Climate and Development, Regional*

*Environmental Change*, *Water Policy*, *Current Science*, *International Journal of Disaster Risk Reduction*, and *Global Business Review*.

**Kanchan Chopra** was Director and Professor, Institute of Economic Growth, New Delhi, till 2009. She has published extensively and her latest book is titled *Development and Environmental Policy in India: The Last Few Decades*. She is a Fellow of the Beijer Institute of Ecological Economics, Stockholm, and of SANDEE. In 2011, she was elected Fellow of the Third World Academy of Sciences. In 2016, she received the Boulding Award conferred by the International Society for Ecological Economics.

**Narendra Nath Dalei** is presently with the Department of Economics and International Business in University of Petroleum and Energy Studies (UPES), Dehradun. He is a recipient of certified reviewer award (2014) and outstanding reviewer award (2015) from *Energy Policy*. His current areas of research are on degraded ecosystems, mining activities, and livelihood patterns; climate change and agricultural ecosystems; and energy and environmental interactions. He has published several research papers in national and international journals of repute.

**Saudamini Das** is NABARD Chair Professor at the Institute of Economic Growth. She is presently a Fellow of SANDEE and has been a Maler Scholar at Beijer Institute of Ecological Economics. She works on environmental and climate change issues, including extreme events. Her works have been published in journals such as *Proceedings of National Academy of Sciences* and *World Development*, besides as book chapters.

**Vikram Dayal** works at the Institute of Economic Growth. He is the author of the book titled *The Environment in Economics and Development: Pluralist Extensions of Core Economic Models*, Springer Briefs in Economics series in 2014. In 2009, he co-edited the *Oxford Handbook of Environmental Economics in India* with Kanchan Chopra.

**Utpal Kumar De** is currently Head, Department of Economics, the North Eastern Hill University, Shillong. His research interests are agricultural economics, issues on environmental and natural resource management, and empowerment of women. Besides completing a number of research projects, he has published 7 books and 75 research articles in various reputed international and national journals.

**Sagar Dhara** is a male and belongs to an upper caste and class, and to the most rapacious predator species that ever stalked the Earth—humans, and to a net destructive discipline—engineering, that has to take more than a fair share of the responsibility for bringing Earth and human society to tipping points.

**Anantha Kumar Duraiappah** is with the Mahatma Gandhi Institute of Education for Peace and Sustainable Development (MGIEP), New Delhi. He has obtained his PhD in economics from the University of Texas in Austin, United States. He is an experienced environmental development economist with more than two decades of experience at the international level. His work focuses largely on the equity of access and use of ecosystem services. He has been the Executive Director of International Human Dimensions Programme (IHDP) hosted by the United Nations University, Bonn, Germany, and Chief of the Ecosystem Services and Economics Unit of the United Nations Environmental Programme (UNEP) in Nairobi, Kenya, apart from teaching at universities in Singapore, Italy, and the Netherlands.

**Marina Fischer-Kowalski** is professor of Social Ecology and Founder of the Institute of Social Ecology, Vienna, and is presently with Alpen Adria University and the University of Vienna. She has obtained her PhD in sociology from the University of Vienna. She is former President of the International Society for Ecological Economics, and co-editor of the *Anthropocene Review*. Her latest book is *Social Ecology: Society–Nature Relations Across Time and Space*.

**Nilanjan Ghosh** is a Senior Economic Advisor at the World Wide Fund for Nature (WWF), New Delhi, and Senior Fellow at the Observation Research Foundation (ORF), Kolkata. An ecological economist by training, he obtained his PhD from the Indian Institute of Management, Kolkata. His publications include six books and a host of research papers in journals such as *Water Policy, Conservation and Society, Journal of Industrial Ecology, Journal of Index Investing*, and *Economic and Political Weekly*, as well as book chapters.

**Santadas Ghosh** is with the Visva-Bharati, Santiniketan. He is a Fellow of SANDEE (Kathmandu) and a Senior Asian Fellow of Asian Centre for Development (Bangladesh). He worked extensively in remote islands in the Sundarbans delta in India, with his primary survey-based research work sponsored by the Ministry of Agriculture and Farmers Welfare (Government of India), NABARD, and ICSSR. His work contributed to several book chapters in edited volumes on environment and development published by Oxford University Press and Cambridge University Press.

**Haripriya Gundimeda** is with the Department of Humanities and Social Sciences at the Indian Institute of Technology Bombay and President of the International Urban Biodiversity Network. She had studied at the Indira Gandhi Institute of Development Research, Mumbai. Her research has been in diverse areas of environmental economics, energy economics, green accounting, and economics of ecosystems and biodiversity. She has written several monographs on incorporating natural resources and human capital into the national accounts, besides being the coordinating lead author for the chapter on Scenarios and Modelling of the Intergovernmental Panel on Climate Change and Biodiversity for the Asia Pacific Regional Assessments.

**Yamini Gupt** is presently with the Department of Business Economics in University of Delhi. Her recent research has been on climate change and the waste sector; degraded ecosystems and change in livelihood pattern; and the economics of the waste sector, having worked on both formal and informal sectors (including hazardous waste). She has to her credit several publications and completed international and Indian projects in these areas.

**Md Hafiz Iqbal** is a Bangladesh Civil Service Cadre Officer and is with Edward College. He received his BSS (economics) and MSS (economics) from the University of Rajshahi, Bangladesh. Later, he did MS (development economics) from Hiroshima University, Japan, and MSc (climate change and development) from Independent University, Bangladesh.

**Promita Mukherjee** is currently a PhD Scholar at the Department of Economics, the University of Calcutta. Her area of research deals with forest conservation and rural livelihood. She has also published a couple of research articles in some leading journals.

**Lekha Mukhopadhyay** has obtained her PhD from the University of Calcutta and is presently Associate Professor in the Economics department of Jogamaya Devi College, University of Calcutta. She has been a Fulbright Fellow in Environmental Leadership Program (2012–13) and World Bank Post-doctoral Fellow (2001–02). For a number of research works, she collaborated with various internationally reputed universities and research institutes, including Stockholm Environment Institute (SEI), United States and Asia, University of California Riverside, United States, and SANDEE. Her research interests encompass environmental planning and management, mining-environment-economy, common property resources, and participatory forest management.

**M.N. Murty** is a Professor of Economics (Retired), Institute of Economic Growth. He is currently Visiting Honorary Professor, TERI University, and Fellow, SANDEE. He specializes in public economics and environmental and resource economics. He has published 10 books including 6 books on environment and resource economics, and a large number of research papers in national and international journals of economics.

**Priya Parasuram** is presently with National Centre for Sustainable Coastal Management, Chennai. Her research interest includes social aspects of the coastal vulnerability and coastal management, traditional wisdom, regional- and national-level solutions for livelihood security, and concepts on improved community-level resilience against coastal hazards.

**Rajakumari S.** is presently with National Centre for Sustainable Coastal Management, Chennai. She has worked with several coastal/marine research studies, especially on pollution monitoring, delineation of sediment cells, assessment of tourism carrying capacity along the East coast of Tamil Nadu, multi-criteria analysis using remote sensing data, and coastal fishing space modelling.

**Biswajit Ray** is with the Department of Economics, University of Calcutta. His research focuses on issues relating to environmental economics, experimental economics, social economics, and gender and development. He has published several research papers from leading publishers and also served as a referee of several journals.

**Lok Mani Sapkota** has been working in the different aspects of participatory forest management in Asia and the Pacific. He has MSc in natural resources management from Asian Institute of Technology, Thailand, and is currently associated with RECOFTC—the Center for People and Forests, Thailand.

**Anke Schaffartzik** enjoys finding meaning through number crunching. As a researcher and lecturer at the Institute of Social Ecology Vienna, she has immersed in an interdisciplinary environment in which collaboration with ecological economists and political ecologists allows her to investigate linkages between resource use and socio-economic development, focusing on international resource use and trade.

**Stephen C. Smith** is with the Institute for International Economic Policy at George Washington University, Washington, DC. Smith received his PhD in economics from Cornell University, New York. He has been a Fulbright Research Scholar, a Jean Monnet Research Fellow, an IZA Research Fellow, a Visiting Fellow at the Brookings Institution, a Nonresident Senior Fellow at Brookings, a Fulbright Senior Specialist, a member of the Advisory Council of BRAC USA, and an Associate Editor of the *Journal of Economic Behavior and Organization*. Smith has co-authored (with Michael Todaro) *Economic Development*, authored *Ending Global Poverty: A Guide to What Works*, and co-edited (with Jennifer Brinkerhoff and Hildy Teegen) *NGOs and the Millennium Development Goals: Citizen Action to Reduce Poverty*. He has also authored or co-authored about 45 journal articles, numerous book chapters, and other publications.

**Amarnath Tripathi,** doctorate in economics from Banaras Hindu University, Varanasi, is with the Institute of Economic Growth. His research interests include agriculture, natural resource management, food security, food system, and climate change. He has published several articles in journals of high repute, such as *Environmental Management*, *Journal of Environmental Planning and Management*, and *Economic and Political Weekly*.

**P.K. Viswanathan** serves as Professor (Economics) at the Amrita School of Business, Amrita University, Kochi, India. Earlier he was with Gujarat Institute of Development Research, Ahmedabad. He has obtained his PhD in economics from the Institute for Social and Economic Change, Mysore University, Bengaluru. His research and teaching interests relate to economics of natural resources management; agrarian transformation and rural livelihoods; aspects of technology, institutions, policies, and governance; and Welfare Impacts of Trade Certifications in India's Plantation Sector.

# Index